D1259664

128.3 De Sousa, Ronald.
DES
      The rationality of
      emotion

$25.00   g /

DATE			
July 1, 2008			

WITHDRAWN

© THE BAKER & TAYLOR CO.

The Rationality of Emotion

The Rationality of Emotion

Ronald de Sousa

The MIT Press
Cambridge, Massachusetts
London, England

This book was set in Palatino by Graphic Composition Inc., 240 Hawthorne Ave, Athens, GA 30606 and printed and bound in the United States of America.

Library of Congress Cataloging-in-Publication Data

De Sousa, Ronald.
    The rationality of emotion.

    Bibliography: p.
    Includes index.   1. Emotions. 2. Rationalism. 3. Objectivity.
I. Title.
B815.D4   1987   128'.3   87-7761
ISBN 0-262-04092-1

To Manuel, my father, and to the memory of Lucile, my mother

Contents

Acknowledgments

I owe large debts to an embarrassingly large number of people.

The greatest thanks are due Kathryn Pauly Morgan, who helped over many years with a judicious mix of encouragement and skepticism. The differences between our paradigm scenarios have enormously enlarged the range of mine, and her extensive comments on several drafts, including the penultimate one, startled me each time into making improvements on nearly every page. Also very large is my debt to Amélie Rorty, whose influence on my ideas in the philosophy of emotions has been very great. I have also learned much from Robert Solomon, whose own work did much to open the contemporary philosophical debate on the emotions.

Other intellectual debts are acknowledged fairly copiously in the text and bibliography, but there are many people to whom I owe specific debts for particular ideas: Ellen Estabrook Taylor, for the epigraph to chapter 11, written when she was very young; Bernie Katz, for the reflection about popcorn and *The Exorcist;* and Birgit Langwisch, for the Python principle. Alison Gopnick encouraged me to think about developmental issues, and Neera Badhwar's own excellent work on friendship taught me a great deal.

The last two made extensive and astute comments on earlier versions, as did Jan Zwicky and Gordon Nagel. Robert Kraut and Helen Nissenbaum each brought me to see that our views had much in common; Nissenbaum also made many useful comments on a nearly final draft. Anne MacKenzie is to be thanked for teaching me much about intentionality, though I don't think she agrees with the use I make of her ideas. Joel Marks and Thomas Wren suggested many improvements to chapter 8. Ray Reiter patiently explained to me that philosophers like me don't understand the frame problem, and convinced me. Other friends and colleagues whose conversations have been helpful include Wayne Sumner, Hans Herzberger, Adam Morton, Israel Rosenfield, Lynd Forguson, Catherine Temerson, and especially Katherine Ashenburg, who sparked many enthusiasms and wisely tempered others.

Many other students and colleagues made valuable contributions to my ideas in seminars based on parts of the material of this book. I should especially mention Stan Clarke, Valerie Schweitzer, El Rand, Earl Winkler, Lisa Woudzia, and James Russell. I also enjoyed the stimulating hospitality of the Philosophy Department of the University of Saskatoon, to whom the ideas of chapters 5 and 6 were first broached in a week of seminars in the fall of 1982; two years later I got more help and more hospitality in the enviable surroundings of the Center for the Study of Language and Information at Stanford University.

In the last stages of revision Paula Caplan and Katherine Ashenburg offered many excellent suggestions for making the book accessible to nonphilosophers. Susan Brison also checked most of the manuscript and suggested many improvements.

Ihor Prociuk gave me invaluable help with the preparation of the figures with Apple Computer's magical MacDraft.

I must also thank some institutions. The Social Sciences and Humanities Research Council of Canada supported this project with several grants over many years. The University of British Columbia was my host in 1984, and in that year, thanks to their kindness and great generosity with efficient and humane computer services, I got more done on this project than in any other single year. I learned much from the University of Cincinnati's enormously stimulating colloquium on emotions in 1985, organized by Jenefer Robinson. And my own institution, the University of Toronto, has been flexible and generous in allowing me irregular leaves of absence.

Not least, I would like to thank Michael Jones, Ed Bickert, Doug and Jimmy Rainey, Georgia Kelly, and Miles Davis, who all soothed me at my desk, hour after hour.

And, finally, I must express my gratitude to my peerless, tireless, almost faultless secretary, ever on call: NOTA BENE from Steve Siebert and his friendly team at Dragonfly Software.

The frontispieces and jacket illustration are from Thomas E. Hill's *Manual of Business and Social Forms* (1885 ed.). I am grateful to Diablo Press of California for having rediscovered this work in their *Never Give a Lady a Restive Horse* (Diablo Press, 1967).

Some of the material in this book descends from articles published elsewhere. Some pages of chapters 4 and 9 appeared in *The Journal of Philosophy* in 1984 and 1980, respectively, and the latter has been reprinted in Rorty 1980. A draft of about half of chapter 8 was published in Marks 1986; and some paragraphs of chapters 6 and 7 remain more or less intact from the eponymous article published in *Dialogue* in 1980, as well as in Rorty 1980.

For permission to quote copyright materials, I am grateful to the following:

Faber and Faber, Ltd., and Random House, for the lines from "Heavy Date," from W. H. Auden's *Collected Poems;*

Faber and Faber, Ltd., for the lines from "Reference Back," from Philip Larkin's *Whitsun Weddings;*

Jarold Ramsey and the *Georgia Review* for the lines from "Volo ut Sis";

A. P. Watt and Macmillan Publishing Company for the quotations from "The Mask," "A Song," and "For Anne Gregory" by W. B. Yeats, copyright 1912, 1919, 1933 (renewed 1940) by Bertha Georgie Yeats;

McGraw-Hill, and John Wiley & Sons, for Figure 8.1., redrawn from a diagram in J. Dollard and N. Miller, *Personality and Psychotherapy,* (New York: McGraw Hill, 1950) adapted from N. E. Miller, "Experimental Studies of Conflict," in J. McV. Hunt, ed., *Personality and Behavioral Disorders* vol I (New York: Ronald Press, 1944), © John Wiley & Sons.

Introduction

My title promises an inquiry into the role of emotion in a rational life in the broadest possible sense. This inquiry has two aspects. One concerns the role that emotion does and should play in the exercise of the rational faculties as we traditionally conceive them: the acquisition of beliefs and desires, the transition between them, and their transmutation into actions and policies. The other aspect concerns emotions considered as a component of life and experience, and prompts us to inquire whether they may themselves be subject to rational assessment.

That second inquiry is as old as Plato, who first claimed that emotions and desires might be objectively true or false. In the *Euthyphro* Plato asked in effect whether we love something because it is lovable, or call it lovable because we love it. The first alternative I shall call the *objectivist* answer. It implies that the emotion in question apprehends something in the world that exists independently of our reaction to it. The second, *subjectivist*, alternative implies that the properties that appear to evoke our emotions are in fact nothing more than projections or shadows cast by those emotions themselves. In this book I shall argue for the coherence of an objectivist answer. Often our emotions constitute the apprehension of properties of a certain sort that I call *axiological*. This is not to deny that some things we call emotions—such as moods—are merely subjective, or that some of the right kind to be objective are, like beliefs, sometimes mistaken.

Despite a common prejudice, reason and emotion are not natural antagonists. On the contrary: I shall argue that when the calculi of reason have become sufficiently sophisticated, they would be powerless in their own terms, except for the contribution of emotion. For emotions are among the mechanisms that control the crucial factor of *salience* among what would otherwise be an unmanageable plethora of objects of attention, interpretations, and strategies of inference and conduct. What remains of the old opposition between reason and emotion is only this: emotions are not reducible to beliefs or to wants. Plato was right to think that if the soul has parts, it must have three, and not just two.

These central ideas about objectivity and rationality are developed in **chapters 6** and 7. The key idea is that our emotions are learned rather like a language and that they have an essentially dramatic structure. The names of emotions do not refer to some simple experience; rather, they get their meaning from their relation to a situation type, a kind of original drama that defines the roles, feelings, and reactions characteristic of that emotion. Such original defining dramas I call *paradigm scenarios.* Emotional objectivity is then measured in terms of the relation between the target situation and the paradigm scenario in terms of which it is perceived.

Earlier chapters lay the groundwork. **Chapter 1** offers a sampling of alluring problems, without the burdens of scholarly references or argumentative niceties. **Chapter 2** surveys a number of schemata for understanding persons, with their faculties and functions. In most of these schemata it transpires that emotions are either absorbed by other, better studied faculties or else somewhat uncomfortably lodged in the interstices between them. I shall here begin the argument, which will run through the whole book, that emotions need a place of their own in the theory of the person and are not reducible to more primitive faculties or functions.

Emotions are often thought of as the most biological, the most somatic of our mental functions. Indeed, in the most influential theory of emotions to come down to us from the nineteenth century—that of William James—emotions are viewed as nothing but the apprehension of bodily conditions. **Chapters 3** and 4 explore the emotions from a biological and "systems design" point of view. I shall make no effort to purvey a physiology of the emotions. But physiology does have something to contribute to our understanding of emotions, though that contribution can itself be sorted out only in terms of higher-level functions. Emotions are like Descartes's pineal gland: the function where mind and body most closely and mysteriously interact.

Actually, there are two separable questions about the biological nature of emotions. One concerns the right models for the physiological mechanisms involved. That is the topic of **chapter 3**. The other is more general: it concerns evolutionary origins. The questions are of course related. Paul MacLean (1960) has suggested that our emotions are mostly controlled by a part of the brain more ancient than the cortex but more recent than the brainstem. (The brainstem controls our most primitive instincts and most resembles the brains of reptiles.) This raises the question of what emotions evolved *for,* if indeed they can be said to have evolved as adaptations. Freud's speculations on these matters, and those of sociobiologists, are the topic of **chapter 4**. There I also begin to address the most intriguing lesson to be learned from taking a biological perspective on emotional objectivity. This is that intentionality or "aboutness"—frequently held out as the distinguishing mystery of mentality—admits of degrees. Simple goal-oriented devices such as tropisms represent the lowest level; and I shall argue that intentionality reaches its most developed form with the capacity to make reference to genuine particulars, as opposed to kinds or classes of qualitatively indistinguishable things. As we shall see, the attempt to make such references can never be guaranteed to succeed, and the belief that we are doing so must always remain something of a metaphysical leap of faith. Nevertheless, just such a leap of faith is involved in some of the most important of our emotions, namely, those involving an attachment to a particular person as opposed to a response to a situation type.

The discussion of intentionality will lead into the more detailed classification of objects of emotion, which is the main topic of **chapter 5**. That taxonomy, in turn, is presupposed in the discussion of the central problems of rationality in **chapters 6** and **7**.

Emotions are partly defined by their relation to time. Grief is not grief, which lasts only five seconds, nor can anything lasting for years count as surprise. The theme of the relation of emotion to time is also implicit in the claim that emotions originate in paradigm scenarios that go back to childhood experiences. It surfaces in **chapter 6**, where I raise some questions about the rationality of certain attitudes toward the future or the past. In **chapter 8** the focus on time becomes explicit, though from a somewhat restricted perspective. In that chapter I bolster my claims about the possibility of correct and mistaken emotion with a specific example concerning the temporal aspects under which something can be desired. I start from the common observation that one can sometimes get exactly what one desires and yet find no joy in it, and I explain this in terms of activities wrongly conceived by desire itself as they take place in time.

The last four chapters extend and apply the theory. In **chapter 9** I ask, When does feeling make it so? Sometimes, by a mechanism I shall call *bootstrapping*, our feelings do seem to create their own objects. But when is bootstrapping simply self-deception? This is an especially important question in the context of a view of emotions as conveying objective information about the real world. For the real world is partly the world we make, as the existentialist philosophers have taught us; yet that would be hollow glory indeed if there were no outside constraints on our powers of creation. For then there would be no distinction between being right and being wrong, no possible achievement either of creation or of knowledge.

Chapter 10 presents an interlude in the form of a dialogue, designed to illustrate the place of arguments in our lived emotions and to indicate how their origins in paradigm scenarios make such arguments virtually impossible to resolve. This also begins to give an idea of the importance of emotions to the ethical conduct of life in general.

The fact that an emotion can sometimes be wrong is not just an epistemic matter but a matter of ethics in a broad sense of that word. **Chapter 11** illustrates this in terms of the question, When is it wrong to laugh? As a friend to laughter, I used to think the answer might be *never*. But my own theory has corralled me into a more conservative position. It *is* sometimes wrong to laugh. That fact has something to teach us about the nature of humor, and it also confirms, from a novel angle, the thesis that emotions are irreducible to beliefs as well as to wants.

Chapter 12 addresses the broader question of the role of emotion in ethical life in general. I argue that the perspective presented in this book favors an expansion of the domain of the ethical, consequent on a more inclusive notion of what makes an emotion morally relevant. In this concluding chapter I focus especially on the ambivalence of our moral life. That ambivalence, I speculate, is deeply embedded in the nature of our emotions themselves. The ambiguity of bootstrapping provides one source of ambivalence. But another, deeper source lies in some ontologically fundamental features of our situation, which I call *basic tragedies of life*. The model for these tragedies is the fact of death. In all of them, a necessary condition of an ultimate good finds itself inevitably in conflict with the enjoyment or perpetuation of that very good. The ambivalence of our deepest emotions, I suggest, merely reflects the structure of those intrinsically conflicted aspects of the human condition.

The order of the chapters that follow is not arbitrary, but it may not be equally attuned to the interests and patience of every reader. The summary that precedes each chapter should make it easier to browse through the book in alternative ways. In particular, readers without philosophical background might begin with a streamlined pass through the book as follows: start with the two first chapters, read through the summaries of chapters 3 through 5, read the "core" chapters 6 and 7, skim through chapter 8, then finish with chapters 9 through 12. The omitted chapters may be more accessible in a second pass.

Readers may sense a certain lack of consistency in the level of detail at which different issues are treated. I view this as a regrettable aesthetic defect, which inevitably follows from the state of the subject. Nothing about the emotions is really *well* understood, in any strong sense of understanding. That is, we lack the ability to detail the mechanisms involved sufficiently well to construct, at least "in principle," an organism that works like us. So if I had waited to write this book until I were sure of thoroughly understanding even some parts of the topic, I would never have written it at all. But among matters poorly understood, some—such as questions concerning the objects of emotions—have been picked over quite a bit. On such topics I hope I have inched the subject forward. On other questions—such as the possible relevance of computational models to emotions—some of my speculations are indulged in from the vantage point of the proverbially disreputable armchair. But I daresay that on those topics no one yet knows any better. On a third class of questions, typified by those discussed in chapter 12, there is much wisdom that I have ignored. On those topics, my excuse for the sketchiness of my speculations is that they seemed to follow from the theory put forward in the rest of the book and are not much more outrageous, after all, than most of the views commonly accepted by the bona fide moral philosophers.

The Rationality of Emotion

Chapter 1

Getting Philosophically Involved with Emotion

The greatest goods come to us through madness.
Plato

Summary

Philosophical problems are often far removed from practical life. But those raised by emotion are different, not least because human emotions seem to promise us reasons to think that we are neither beasts nor machines.

Emotions form a kind of philosophical hub. They will lead us to problems of epistemology, ontology, logical form, philosophical psychology, and ethics. I give a sampling of these guiding problems here. Five have the shape of antinomies—tempting us with plausible arguments for opposite conclusions. A sixth concerns a pervasive feature of emotions that I call ambivalence.

1. The antinomy of rationality. Emotions are reputed to be arational or irrational; yet at the same time they bear complex relations to rationality. First, we speak, in various senses, of "reasonable" emotion. Second, whether themselves reasonable or not, emotions serve as explanations, excuses, or justifications for other acts and states. Third, they are also variously thought-dependent. Emotions in a strict sense are more thought-dependent than moods, but moods, too, are sometimes penetrable to thought. A very specific type of thought-dependency concerns the thought that a certain emotion is focused on some particular individual, rather than on a set of qualities instantiated by that individual. ("Love me, but don't love my twin.")

2. The antinomy of objectivity. The core idea in this antinomy derives from the plausibility of both alternative answers—the objectivist and the subjectivist—to the question posed in the Euthyphro: *Do we love because something is lovable, or do we call lovable whatever we love? On the one hand, emotions give us information about the world. But on the other hand, the qualities that our emotions find in the world are reputed to be merely subjective projections of our own will. And either way, in spite of a common prejudice in favor of the idea that we always know our own mind, we are often mistaken about our own emotions.*

3. The antinomy of activity and passivity. The word 'passion' suggests passivity; yet in many ways emotions seem to express our most active self. Sometimes, indeed, this activity comes close to creating something out of nothing: "Feeling so makes it so." This is the power of bootstrapping. But when is it legitimate?

4. The antinomy of integrity. Question 3 can be asked not only in relation to our conception of the outside world but also in relation to the role of temperament, spontaneity, or deliberation in human character. This is the problem of the "true self," which gives rise to the antinomy of integrity: which one, the spontaneous or the deliberate self, is the real self?

5. The antinomy of determinism: the classic argument according to which neither determinism nor indeterminism is compatible with free will. This antinomy has a specific form that relates to emotions. It is revealed by a thought experiment in which we ask, What would someone be like who had no faculty of emotion at all? The answer to this yields one of the book's central theses: that the faculty of emotion is actually required for the more conventional mechanisms of rationality to function.

6. The ambivalence of emotions has two aspects. One is that a single situation sometimes evokes several apparently incompatible emotions. The other is that many apparently positive emotions have a dark side. In some forms this ambivalence lies deeper than the mere fact that some things can seem good or bad depending on their context.

The fascination exerted by philosophers' pet problems is not necessarily proportional to their importance in practical life. If this is brought up as a fault, we philosophers should not attempt to deny it. "Quite," we should retort, "philosophy—the attempt to organize our understanding into an argued and coherent vision—is generally more interesting than practical life." Philosophy is intellectual neoteny: childhood reprieved, for those who are lucky enough to lack the gift or the need to be grown up, stretching indefinitely into adult life. The philosopher claims the child's disinterested curiosity, the privilege of asking questions in terms that do not presuppose the usual answers.

That is the ideal. In practice, the comings and passings of philosophical fashions make it all too plain that philosophers, no less than other mortals, are creatures of habit and convention. We keep thinking about the same old things. Nor do we always heed the non-philosopher's perfectly philosophical questions: "Why bother to think about that? And why think about it in just this way?" Too often the honest answer would be that most pernicious of nonreasons: "Because this is the way we've always done it."

Despite my best efforts, I am not sanguine about my chances of avoiding such unseemly conformism, or about the relevance to Real Life of what I have to say. The emotions, however, bear a rather peculiar relation to life and to philosophy. For emotions are themselves, in a sense which I hope to make clear, a kind of *parallel philosophy.* Like philosophy, they concern what gives meaning to life. They frame, transform, and make sense of our perceptions, thoughts, and activities. And yet, from the point of view of the uninvolved observer, they can seem nothing but an expense of spirit and a waste of time. On the other hand, those most preoccupied with their own emotions in practice tend to be most skeptical of reasoning about emotions. The emotions have often seemed to resist both understanding and rational control.

Curiosity about emotions is scarcely limited to philosophers. Most people have been puzzled about their own or others' emotions. And—another common concern—many people have worried about *how we are better than the beasts;* species-narcissism, a kind of childish quest for some special dignity about being human, is a trait widely shared both within and without the confines of professional philosophy. Much of the history of thought can be seen as the attempt to show why we are better than (other) beasts, or than machines —depending on where the competition currently seems most threatening.

In terms of that agenda, emotions have fared unevenly in the history of Western thought. Plato grudgingly allowed them—or perhaps just some of them—a role in controlling the beast in us, providing they acknowledged their subservience to a higher and purely rational element. He was the first of many dualists who found emotions something of an embarrassment. They fit awkwardly into simplistic models of the mind and body. They drag us from our dreams of pure reason, yet just as surely they are mental phenomena, irreducible to any merely physical principle.

Descartes taught that only humans have souls, on the ground that only we could reason, do mathematics, and talk. What we shared with the other animals were less exalted functions: "mere" perception, desire, and whatever else is needed to subsist, reproduce, and get around in the world without bumping into things. Clockwork automata, he thought, might do those things as well. Now that we have experience of more elaborate automata, we tend to draw the line on almost the opposite principle. Rather than face assimilation to mere machines, most of us prefer to be ranked with the animals. We have machines that calculate and analyze, performing at least some of the tasks traditionally assigned to reason. But the faculties most difficult for machines to emulate have turned out to be precisely those we share with the beasts. Among them emotions now seem particularly apt to feed our species-narcissism. For at least some emotions may well turn out to yield a safer refuge of uniqueness than any clearly definable attribute of rationality.

This is not a new thought. For a long time, poets, if not philosophers, have singled out some emotions—such as laughter and love—as characteristics belonging to the human essence. I shall argue later that although we would do well to give up our species-narcissism—for there is no interesting human essence—yet some solid bases can be found for a version of that traditional view.

For the moment, by way of beginning with an impressionistic prospectus, I want to single out six aspects of emotions that consign them to an intriguingly ambiguous position among three mythic paradigms: the *animal,* the *mechanical,* and what I shall call, borrowing from traditional imagery, the *angelic.*

The features in question include five antinomies embedded in the commonsense conception of emotion: the antinomies of rationality, objectivity, activity and passivity, integrity of the self, and determinism. A sixth feature is the ambivalence to which most emotions are subject. I now sketch these six problematic features of emotions. All will figure as themes of this book, though some will appear as leitmotifs rather than receive systematic treatment. Together they support the view that it is largely thanks to our emotions that we are neither angels, beasts, nor even machines, but something of all three.

Rationality

Are emotions rational? Prima facie, it seems both that they must and that they cannot be.

Ira brevis furor, said the Romans: anger is a brief bout of madness. A long tradition views all emotions as threats to rationality. The *crime passionnel* belongs to that tradition: in some jurisdictions it is a kind of "brief-insanity defense." We still say that "passion blinds us," and in common parlance to be philosophical about life's trials is to be decently unemotional about them. Many philosophers have espoused this view, exhorting Reason to conquer Passion. Furthermore, we think of many of our emotions as linking our nature with that of other animals, and that is part of the reason that we assume our emotions are not rational, that they belong to the "side" or "part" of us that is something less than human.

This is not to say that our "animal side" is the only source of our irrationality. At least one emotion that may reasonably be supposed to affect only humans—the fear of death—is notorious for the efforts philosophers have exerted to prove it irrational. The fear of death underscores some of the problems surrounding the rationality of emotions, for it does not appear to vary in relation to the certainty of death, which is constant. It depends on other factors, including its envisaged closeness in time. And what could that have to do with rationality?

The preceding remarks confound two different claims. One is that emotions are *arational*, the other that they are *irrational*. Only the former implies that they are like sensations, stomachaches, or involuntary twitches. For if they were, they would not be amenable to rational evaluation. In fact, three sorts of considerations link emotions directly or indirectly to rationality: our confidence in judgments of *reasonableness*, the use of emotions as *excuses and justifications*, and the *thought-dependency* of most emotions. These considerations spawn a number of puzzles to be addressed later. I sample them here to give an idea of their range and flavor.

Reasonable Emotion
We often speak of a particular emotion as "reasonable." What this means is not obvious. Sometimes it seems to mean nothing more than "I might feel this way too under similar circumstances." At other times it reflects broader but equally inarticulate conventional standards: "It's normal to feel this way." Sometimes it is equivalent to "appropriate." But at least sometimes a judgment of reasonableness invokes the possibility of argument and justification—notions central to rationality. Are emotions then assessed for rationality just like beliefs?

This raises many questions. Does the relevant notion of rationality differ from that which governs belief? One characteristic feature of rational belief is that it is normally arrived at by means of transitions from previous beliefs according to standard procedures. Desires are sometimes also arrived at from other desires on the basis of arguments, although there are interesting differences. Is there a corresponding process for emotions? Are the applicable criteria of rationality the same as those that apply to beliefs, or desires, or are they sui generis? And why it is that emotions have so often been thought to be outside the pale of rationality?

Emotion as Justification
If emotions can be reasonable, it is to be expected that they will sometimes figure in the justification or excusing of actions and other states. So far this says little. For any kind of fact might be so used.

But emotions do have a privileged status. This seems to be because we assume that they have intrinsic value (good or bad) and so are *motivators*. We say, "She killed him out of jealousy," "He did it for love." By specifying motivation, such statements explain, excuse, or justify.

The power of an emotion to motivate is independent of its own rationality. This suggests that one role of emotions is to ground assessments of rationality regardless of whether the emotions are themselves rational. And that brings us to more questions: Can emotions ground the rationality of anything besides actions? Desire is a plausible candidate; but what of belief? Can belief legitimately rest on emotion? Claims for religious faith spring to mind here. Religious beliefs might be thought to be legitimately grounded in emotion in two different ways: one, where the experience of a certain emotion, perhaps described as mystical, is held to justify a belief by inference to the best explanation. (Only God could make me feel like *that*.) The other is the Pascalian justification of faith in terms of the emotional comfort it brings. To assess these claims will again require some analysis of the different notions of rationality involved.

Thought-Dependency of Emotions and Moods

Emotions are variously responsive to changes in thoughts or beliefs. If I am grieved by bad news, my grief cannot survive the discovery that what grieves me did not, after all, take place. If I am angry at someone for cutting my best mustard, the anger cannot logically survive the discovery that no one has, in fact, cut my mustard.

This thought-dependency suggests that emotions can be rational, though derivatively so. Even when emotions involve physical manifestations, it is their mental causation that defines them as emotions and grounds our evaluation of them. Some years ago a preposterously nasty movie called *The Exorcist* built a vast success on the popular taste for Christian sadomasochism. Large crowds paid to be made nauseous; filmgoers were reputed to vomit in the aisles every night. But would they have demanded a refund, if it had got about that the physiological effect was actually caused by chemicals in the popcorn?

This thought-dependency of emotions is mitigated, in certain cases, by a certain characteristic *inertia*. When I discover that I cannot be angry or that my grief is unfounded, it is not uncommon for me to continue to feel vaguely upset and perhaps even to cast about for some substitute emotion. The feeling of the emotional upset can outlive the emotion, and in such cases it is understandable that one might look for a legitimate emotion so as to label this now nameless feeling. Sometimes an emotion finds a natural successor in a completely different one, often its opposite: grief gives way to relief; anxiety turns into anger ("Where were you, you *naughty* boy!")

Regardless of the effects of emotional inertia, thought-dependency is very variable. Grief, pity, compassion, and anger are among the emotions most clearly grounded in belief. But some others are much less so. Moods, in particular, have a rather special relation to belief. To feel cheerful is usually to "look on the bright side." Someone who is euphoric is likely to endorse various propositions, such as "life is good," which are beyond refutation by any simple fact or counter-example; they are so vague as to lack any content. One is not likely to be affected by the mere denial of such a proposition. On the other hand, one might well be put in a very different mood either by one single large disappointment or by an accumulation of harassing and annoying details ("I was in a great mood until I went down to the Motor Vehicles Office to get my license renewed!") Often cheerfulness is easily punctured, but it is not normally punctured by the denial of any of the propositions that would naturally be thought to express it.

Even this loose link between moods and beliefs is not impeccable, however. We all know a cheerful cynic who relishes the contemplation of the most dismal facts. An interesting variant of this species is the *philosophical manic-depressive*. This particular type cares passionately about seeing the world as it really is. Like Schopenhauer, she takes the view that only the most pessimistic outlook is compatible with realism. She therefore thinks she is seeing the world aright only when she is feeling especially gloomy. But the mere contemplation of the clarity of her own vision, which such a gloomy view must entail, touches her dearest ambition of lucidity. This cheers her up. In accordance with her principles, being now happy, she reasons that the world no longer looks to her as it really is. And that thought plunges her back into gloom. Which in turn restores her confidence in the clarity of her vision, causing elation once more. And so forth. Is all this rational? How are we to decide?

The special status of moods may suggest a simple explanation. Unlike most emotions proper, moods do not clearly have intentional objects. If I am sad (an emotion), my sadness must be directed *at* some loss which I view as its cause. If I feel listless (a mood), I can look for a cause, which might be low blood sugar; but I am not listless *at* low blood sugar or anything else. So moods can be only loosely connected to the propositions in terms of which they are expressed.

This explanation is plausible, but it fails to explain why something like the loose connection between thought and emotion applies also to some cases that are not moods at all and that clearly admit of at least one type of object.

Such is the case of love. In its relation to propositional beliefs, love behaves like a mood. It often expresses itself in terms of a proposition such as this: "This woman is the most perfect woman I have ever met or could possibly meet." This has three marks of what we might call an emotional *pseudoproposition:* it is difficult to pin down to falsifiable content; its truth is neither necessary nor sufficient for the persistence of the emotion; and it is not clearly related to those propositions that might, as a matter of fact, lead to a change of mind on the emotional level.

Yet love, unlike moods, seems tied a priori to an object. This is easily tested. Imagine someone saying, "I am passionately in love, but I don't yet know with whom. I shall have to conduct tests to discover who, of those around me (and why not of those I have never met?) has affected me so." This seems absurd. But here again matters are not so simple. For there are cases in life and literature where a similar declaration comes across as insight. In Gide's short novel *La symphonie pastorale,* a Protestant clergyman takes in, educates, and falls in love with a blind young woman. An operation restores her sight, and after having taken a good look at both the pastor and his son, she declares that it was the son that she was actually in love with. "He is the one," she explains to the pastor, "who has your face." And presumably that is a discovery that only sight could vouchsafe her.

Alcmene's Problem   The relation of love to its objects gives rise to another intriguing puzzle. I call it *Alcmene's problem,* in honor of the faithful wife of Amphitryon, whom Zeus was able to seduce only by taking the form of her husband.

We should assume that Zeus, being after all the king of the gods, put on an entirely convincing show. He took on—though only temporarily, of course, and in some strict sense remaining Zeus all the while—all the properties of Amphitryon. This is widely believed to be a mysterious trick, called 'incarnation', but not, for a god, an impossible one. Here is the logicomoral problem it raises: When Alcmene finds out, ought she to mind? The man she loved that night was, by hypothesis, qualitatively the same as her husband, though not the same numerically. But wasn't it for his qualities that she loved her husband? I don't mean to imply that his qualities must have been lovable ones. What she loved about him might have been quite unworthy. Nevertheless, there must have been something that she loved about him, and whatever it was, Zeus had that. This apparently implies that her desire to be faithful, under the circumstances (or her regret that she wasn't, if she finds out the truth later), is only compatible with a love that is literally completely irrational. For any reason she has for loving Amphitryon, however tenuous, must relate to some of his properties. And by hypothesis Zeus has them all.

These, then, are some of the subsidiary puzzles generated by the antinomy of rationality. One is that love, which takes an object, should in some respects resemble a mood, of which a defining property is to be objectless. More puzzling is the fact that the relation between love and its object could ever be as contingent as it is. Most disturbing is Alcmene's paradox: if her love is rational only if it relates to Amphitryon's qualities, then love must be either irrational or fickle.

These problems all admit of solution. But this will depend on our success in disentangling the different categories of objects. We shall need to sort out the variety of ways in which emotions are related to those objects, as well as the degree to which they can be specified in terms of propositions.

Objectivity

Closely connected to the antinomy of rationality is the *Euthyphro* question—whether the gods love piety because it is pious, or whether they merely call pious whatever they love. More simply, it is the question of whether emotions can be said to be *correct* or *incorrect*.

Emotions raise two very general epistemological questions. One concerns them as objects of knowledge: How can they be known? The other concerns their objects: Are emotions a way of knowing their objects? Do these objects exist independently, or merely as projections of the emotions? Both contraries can seem equally appealing.

Emotion as Information

The notion of adequation or fitting of thought and action to objective reality is an important aspect of the intuitive idea of rationality. Some emotions, though not all, seem to tell us something useful about the world. Fear, for example, is probably as useful as pain. Sometimes it seems counterproductive, but life without pain, though perhaps not so brutish, would in most cases undoubtedly be shorter. Similarly, one can easily think of useful functions for attachment emotions, for anger, for lust, and perhaps even for envy—or at least for the other side of its Janus face, "emulation." (For some other emotions such as despair, though, the task would call for special ingenuity.) And if emotions are ever useful, they must constitute differential responses to different states of the world, whether of ourselves or of our external environment. To this extent, emotions must be providing us with some information about the world, in some minimal sense implying no sophisticated grade of intentionality.

But what is the nature of this information? It cannot be straightforwardly knowledge, because just as the emotions are notorious for their supposed irrationality, so they are also generally held to be subjective, to tell us nothing of use that is really about the outside world. At best, the standard story goes, they are projections of our inner states, telling us more about the subject than about the object. Ethical and aesthetic judgments raise the same problem, and it is not surprising that both ethics and aesthetics have spawned "emotivist" theories, purporting to find in emotions the entire (and entirely subjective) basis of such judgments. Sorting out the question of objectivity for emotions, therefore, is unlikely to prove a simple matter. But we can console ourselves with the thought that once effected it may clarify important questions in the theory of value.

Emotions and Self-Knowledge

Like other mental states, emotions have sometimes been assumed to be immediately and incorrigibly knowable by the subject. But this assumption of the "transparency" of the mind, it must be said, has been more often made by philosophers than by those whose business it is to pay close attention to the emotions. Long before Freud, poets, playwrights, and novelists have emphasized the opacity of our emotions, the extent to which we are able to deceive ourselves about them. Emotions are both objects and causes of self-deception. We shall later look into the mechanisms involved in this double role of emotion in the fabrication of false selves.

All this, of course, compounds the previous epistemological problem. If we cannot even tell for sure what emotions we are experiencing, we can hardly use them as a reliable basis for inferences about the outside world.

Activity and Passivity

The very name of 'passions' classically used to speak of emotions implies that they are not under our control. In spite of this we commonly blame people for their passions. Once again, emotions fall somewhere in between clear cases of activity (intentional actions) and clear cases of passivity (involuntary physiological processes).

Emotions themselves, however, give us some reason to believe that we were too optimistic about the apparently clear cases. From one side, there is much reason to doubt that our intentional actions are always as active as their name implies. We mistake our own motivations, we rationalize our most automatic reactions, we deceive ourselves about what we desire and what we believe, as well as about what we feel. And on the other side, there is also evidence that much that is commonly thought to be involuntary can, through such techniques as biofeedback, be brought under our active control. Besides, much of our organic life may turn out to be already psychosomatic, that is, under the control of our mental life. But our mental life, according to some time-honored models, is the source of all truly free acts. So the canonical representatives of the passive and the active seem to have switched positions.

Expressions of emotion illustrate the point. They consist mostly in behavior under voluntary control: we can generally stop shouting, sighing, or crying whenever we decide to. But they also typically consist in symptoms, involuntary manifestations of the activity of the autonomous nervous systems, from which springs "behavior" only in the sense in which we are willing to apply the phrase to nonhuman animals.

The Power of Bootstrapping

A large literature of exhortation exists to exploit this ambiguity between the passive and the active aspects of emotion. Pascal—and Aristotle before him—recommends the cultivation of certain sorts of behavior, in order to bring about corresponding states of mind. On this view, earnest pretense is the royal road to sincere faith. These states of mind are not confined to emotions. They include beliefs, commonly thought to be paradigms of mental states *not* under voluntary control. Exhortation commonly urges contemplation of certain facts, images, or scenes. The goal is belief, or at least a more desirable attitude toward God, life, or death.

In the most interesting cases the exhortation is to a certain analysis of the nature of emotions themselves. The idea is that the acceptance of the analysis must logically entail certain attitudinal and emotional changes. One example of this method is the view argued by Sartre, and more recently by Solomon, that emotions are not passive but chosen.

This view is both liberating and oppressive. Liberating, in that it precludes feeling that one is a helpless victim of one's own emotions. To believe it is to be less likely to behave like such a victim and hence less likely to be one. But oppressive, too, in that it preempts a large and important class of excuses and therefore involves a significant enlargement of the sphere of one's own responsibility.

This analytical-hortatory genre is a special case of the Wittgensteinian concept of philosophy as therapy. And that, in turn, is an instance of the more general idea that power derives from insight. It is a particularly intriguing strategy in connection with emotions, because it is self-applicable. Like a placebo, its effectiveness is a function of belief, but the truth of the belief, in turn, is determined by the effectiveness of the strategy based on it. The strategy is a bootstrapping one.

If we think such methods will work, that will tell us a good deal about our conception of the emotions. Whether they do work, and when, will tell us something about what emotions actually are. And whether they are *rational* is yet another question.

The True Self; or, The Antinomy of Integrity

Closely related to the problem of activity and passivity is the antinomy of integrity.

Suppose you are a homosexual coming out to your best friend. Her reaction is spontaneous and violent. She expresses disgust, disappointment, and anger and finally walks away in shock, unwilling even to talk about it. The next evening she calls you up. She apologizes for her unreasonable, unkind, and prejudiced reaction. She realizes, she says, that sexual choice is a matter that needn't affect your friendship, and she expresses great regret at having behaved in such a way as to suggest otherwise.

You have, I submit, a dilemma. Your friend has offered two reactions. The first, spontaneous, was hostile. The other, considered, was friendly and sympathetic. Which was the more authentic? On which should you base your best judgment as to what kind of person she really is?

In favor of spontaneity, one can say that the first reaction was unreflective, uncensored, and therefore presumably genuine. From this perspective, her second reaction is suspect. In a very real sense, it may not be *her* reaction at all, but a phony one, calculated, perhaps, to save what might be lost by the destruction of your friendship.

On the other hand, might her prejudiced reaction not be a mere reflex, unrelated to her character? It stemmed, perhaps, from effects of a narrow-minded education that she has not yet had time to mend. So it is her considered reaction that should be accepted as authentic, not her thoughtless one. Or is thought, if it is second thought, of no account when we judge other people? Surely a capacity to improve upon impulsive judgment is just what differentiates mature persons from animals or children.

Again, there is much to be said for both lines of reasoning. Both spontaneous emotion and deliberate attitudes are intimately bound up with our conception of people's character and moral worth. Perhaps, indeed, what we call "character" is specifically the connection between deliberation and spontaneity: a function of the extent and consistency of the control exerted by deliberate attitudes over our spontaneous reactions.

Yet there may be a third view that undermines both sides. We might call it the *chemical view*. Coarsely expressed, the chemical view holds that the first reaction marks nothing more essential than the extent to which this or that hormone or neurotransmitter dominated the organism's chemical balance at that time. As for the second reaction, it is neither more nor less real but simply marks another stage in the friend's chemical history. Why should either have priority? To be sure, stability seems to count, and perhaps we assume that the second reaction, once arrived at, is there to stay. But even then, why should a fleeting reaction be less emotionally real, less an index of a person's character? To answer the original question, it seems we must be able to decide which chemical balance is more truly characteristic of our friend. Is this a genuine question, or is it just gibberish?

Whatever we think of the chemical theory, a balanced judgment in such cases does not promise to be easy. It must depend not only on getting a lot more detail about the facts of the case but also on having a sufficiently subtle theory about the complex relations among emotion, physiology, personality, rationality, and the self. Some of the questions that arise in this are are "existential"—involving such terms as 'authenticity', 'integrity', 'bad faith'. Others concern psychological issues merging into biology: Is there anything about our emotional makeup that is more or less permanent? And how malleable are our emotional dispositions? This last question can take several forms, in order of widening generality:

1. Is the "dictionary" of emotional states—the list of characteristics an individual might have intermittently—the same as the dictionary of relatively constant character traits that differentiate one person from another?

2. Is there a repertoire of emotions that defines, from an early age, the individual psychological characteristics, or individual temperaments, that make us permanently different from each other?

3. Are there genetic predispositions that generally differentiate members of different population groups or of different sexes?

4. Are there unchangeable instincts that define the range of behaviors and emotional reactions of which any member of the human species is capable? Or should we—as I propose to argue—countenance the possibility that standards of normality might sometimes apply only to the individual?

The Indeterminism of Reason and Nature

The "chemical view" has a flavor of determinism about it. But however much our bodily chemicals may influence our emotions, no simple determinism can be correct. Nor, however, is indeterminism any more plausible.

To sketch my reasons for this claim, I suggest a simple thought experiment: What would it be like for an agent to lack the capacity for emotion? This question is a useful first step to the identification of the role of emotion in human life. One approach to it, to be taken up later, is to ask what additional equipment computers will need before we can think of them as having emotions. But for the moment I want to ask, more abstractly, how lacking emotions might affect anything that we otherwise would call an agent. The answer will not tell us very much, since I have plunged into talk of emotion without attempting first to define it. But one plausible answer might go like this. Either an agent without emotion must be an *angel*, or it must be a *mechanism*, something, perhaps, like Descartes's animal-machine. So let us first ask, How does an angel know what to do?

One nice thing about theology, including Angel Theory, is that it allows a good latitude for speculation. There can be several views of what angels ought to be like. Milton's angels, for example, are not without emotions.* But on a more austere view, angels must be some sort of Kantian Rational Will, or perhaps like Spinoza's God, with goals that follow from the principles of reason itself and with a perfectly determinate system for fixing on means. By an angel, I shall henceforth mean a Kantian monster of this sort.

For an angel, nothing can be random, and nothing can be deter-

---

*When Adam inquires into the sex life of angels, Raphael explains:
Let it suffice thee that thou know'st
Us Happie, and without Love, no happiness.
Whatever pure thou in the body enjoy'st
(And pure thou wert created) we enjoy
In eminence, and obstacle find none
Of membrane, joint, or limb, exclusive bars. . . .
(Milton, *Paradise Lost* VII, 1257–1262)

mined merely by crass material contingency: nothing, in short, can be left undetermined by the principles of reason. But what if pure reason does not always yield unique solutions? Sometimes an angel might be faced with two options, equally loved of God. Is this a happy event? It is not. In fact, it marks the end of the angel's angelic nature. It is now stuck, more fatally than Buridan's ass, who died of exposure to two equidistant carrots. For the ass is easily saved by some nonrational contingency. The angel cannot be, without ceasing thereby to be an angel. Even free will cannot help the angel. Free will is a cute trick invented to evade the following inevitable dilemma:

Either (1) the free decision is determined by something, or (2) it is determined by absolutely nothing. In case (2) it is simply a form of irrationality. But in case (1) then either (a) it is determined by non-rational principles, which contravenes the assumption that we are dealing with a perfectly rational being, or (b) it is determined by rational principles, which contravenes the assumption that free will escapes the determination of reason.

The alternative supposition is simpler: that instead of an angel, an emotionless being would be like a machine. It is plausible to assume that in, say, an ant, everything that might be called a want is devoid of any emotional feeling: wants are really no more than tropisms. And anything we might be tempted to call a belief is either a releasing cue for some specific response or a standing condition fixing a range of possible responses.

Note now that the angel and the machine have something rather surprising in common: they are both completely deterministic. The difference lies entirely in the category of factors responsible for the determination. In the case of the angel only reason is relevant to the explanation of its behavior, whereas in the case of the machine we consider only mechanisms. But both models demand that the mode of explanation involved be completely exclusive. Neither can admit any explanatory contribution from the principle appropriate to the other. If I were to explain the behavior of the ant as partly conditioned by some teleological or rational principle, it would no longer be a purely mechanistic system. Conversely, an angel whose behavior was partly to be accounted for in terms of the contingencies of the mechanical properties of its matter would not, *ex hypothesi*, be the purely spiritual thing an angel is supposed to be.

The mechanistic model is traditionally reputed to be committed to determinism. Indeed, it is often contrasted on that basis with the model of rationality. In reality, if there is a contrast, it works exactly in reverse. The angel is more strictly deterministic than the machine.

Mechanism can tolerate randomness far more comfortably than the rationalistic model. Pure randomness is just nonexplanation; it does not really threaten the explanatory monopoly of mechanism. Rationalism, by contrast, requires not only that no other principle of explanation be introduced but also that it leave nothing unexplained. Brute resistance to explanation of any sort is therefore more of a threat to rationalism than to mechanism. Still, mechanism's tolerance of randomness is limited: for it does aim, after all, to explain later events in terms of causal laws working themselves out on the basis of earlier conditions.

As it turns out, I shall argue, both fail: neither mechanism nor rationalism (as so far sketched) can sustain the strict determinism to which they aspire. In any case it makes little sense to speak of determinism or indeterminism except relative to a specific level of explanation. But levels of explanation are not mutually impervious. So none can altogether escape contamination. The rational is constrained by matter, and the mechanical is undermined by both chance and teleology. Emotion, because of its ambiguous position, is often the vehicle of this contamination, introducing an element of physiological determinism into rational deliberation, or seeming to interfere with the unfolding of purely physiological mechanisms with something like rational causation. To put it more positively, emotion is often the level of explanation at which the mechanical and the rational can be integrated.

In particular, emotions will help to resolve the angelic dilemma. When faced with two competing arguments, between which neither reason nor determinism can relevantly decide, emotion can endow one set of supporting considerations with more salience than the other. We need emotion, I shall argue, to break a tie when reason is stuck.

This point of view will also yield a solution to the problem of actions done intentionally but "against one's better judgment"—the problem of *akrasia,* or "weak will." Akrasia has seemed paradoxical to many philosophers since Socrates. An akratic action is done for a reason: therefore, it is rational. But it is also irrational, for it flouts the best or "strongest" reason. But how can one follow reason, yet not follow the best reason?

The answer is of a piece with the resolution of angelic dilemmas: emotions affect the relative saliency of the two arguments, thus disconnecting the "stronger" from the train of action. One form taken by the ambiguous connection between emotions and rationality, then, could be summed up like this: The power to break the ties of reason, like other forms of power, can be abused.

Ambivalence

What I have called "antinomies" are so only in a rather loose sense. Yet all suggest that the questions raised by a philosophical look at emotions undermine a number of traditional dichotomies: between the rational and the irrational, the objective and the subjective, the active and the passive, the real self and the persona, and even determinism and indeterminism.

The analogue of an antinomy in the sphere of value is *ambivalence*. I have already alluded to the ambivalence of emotions by noting the "Janus face" of some emotions. Because this ambivalence forms a major theme of this book, I want to give an idea of what I mean by it here.

Christian lore defines about as many sins as virtues. There are three theological virtues (Faith, Hope, and Love or Charity) and four cardinal virtues (Prudence, Fortitude, Temperance, and Justice). The deadly sins are traditionally seven, usually listed as Pride, Avarice, Lust, Envy, Gluttony or Greed, Anger, and Sloth. Despair sometimes makes eight, but when stripped of theological connotations, it might be considered just another form of Sloth. It is striking that all the deadly sins except avarice and greed clearly bear the names of emotions—and one could argue about those two exceptions. And at least two of the theological virtues are also homonymous with emotions. This is clearly true of Hope. It seems to apply to Love as well, though perhaps not so obviously when it is called Charity. As for Faith, it seems at first to be an exception. But as we shall see, it may well be, after all, a paradigm case of emotion. Moreover, three of the four cardinal virtues (Prudence, Fortitude, and Temperance, though not Justice) are dispositions enabling us to resist the force of emotional temptations.

All this strongly suggests that most of what is morally interesting about human life is played out in the domain of the emotions. When we focus on their connection with sins, the capacity for emotion will be deplored. When we focus on the virtues, it will be celebrated.

More surprising is that individual emotions are ambivalent too. Sometimes the very same word is both the name of a vice and the name of a virtue, like Pride or even, in some contexts, Jealousy; more often there are two names for much the same emotion, but one is the name of a virtue and the other of a vice. So with Anger and Wrath, Pity and Contempt, Love and Lust—or, in a more modern vein, Love and Dependency.

Does ambivalence relate especially to emotion? Perhaps it has to do merely with the relativity of values to circumstances: it is a platitude that the same material object, the same physical act, the same food, the same words may seem and be either good or bad at different times. It all depends on subject, goals, or circumstance. But I shall argue that the ambivalence of emotions has a deeper source. It is among the causes, rather than merely another effect, of the relativities of our evaluations.

I shall explain this in due course. It is enough for the moment to point out that if ambivalent evaluations are grounded in emotion, there can be but three sources of their ambivalence: some ambiguity in whatever connects the emotion to the evaluation; an inconsistency among the several emotions that ground the evaluation; or an ambivalence inherent in particular emotions themselves. Each hypothesis must in time be given its due. For the moment I will urge only that the third not be dismissed unheard.

To make it more vivid, consider a diagnostic trick that sometimes surfaces among therapists at dinner parties, those psychological busmen's holidays. To discover a person's worst fault, goes the tip, ask her to tell you her greatest virtue. The obsessive-compulsive will say, "I'm neat." Sloth (and the slob) will say, "I'm easy going." "I have my dignity," says Pride, or "I am self-sufficient." "I know how to enjoy life," say Greed and Lust. "Say that I loved (not wisely, but) too well," says Jealousy. Sometimes a little indirectness will creep in: "I'm a good judge of people" may be as likely to stand for Envy as "I know my rights." But in the main the method is surprisingly revealing, as party tricks go. A slogan sums it up: *All virtue is vice (although not vice versa)*, and the nature of emotion lies at the core of that ambivalence.

Emotions as a Philosophical Hub

Emotion generates problems in all major areas of philosophy. A brief recapitulation, in terms of the disciplines into which philosophy is traditionally divided, will suffice.

There are problems of *ontology:* What are the real objects of emotion? and—a quite different problem—Are the objects of emotion real, that is, objective? Problems of *logical form:* How are statements of the form 'X loves Y because Z' to be construed? Problems of *ethics:* How are emotions related to value? How are they themselves to be evaluated? Problems of *philosophical psychology:* What is the role of emotions in the makeup of the person? What is their relation to the will? Depending in part on which of these problems you find most interesting, your theory of emotions will favor very divergent approaches. My own central preoccupation will be with the place of emotions in the theory of *rationality.* I shall be trying to articulate answers to questions like these: What contribution do emotions make to the rationality of thought, desire, and action? How does this role fit in with their reputation for irrationality? By what criteria, if any, can emotions themselves be assessed for rationality, and how do these criteria relate to those in use for the evaluation of other states or acts?

All this may seem altogether too rich a menu. Or it might be held that the whole enterprise is hopeless, like theology, on the ground that its subject matter does not exist. The word 'emotion', and a fortiori the family of related words that include 'passion', 'sentiment', 'attitude', denote no single natural class. Why assume that emotions constitute any single subject that might usefully be encompassed in a single discussion?

I concede that I am unable to give a definition of emotion. Instead, I can proceed by first outlining my subject matter negatively. The positive form with which emotions contrast is a triad of concepts: *perception*, *belief*, and *want*. Each member of that triad has been extensively studied and formalized, though there is no general agreement on a single theory for any of them.* All three play a central part in both the explanation of behavior and the theory of rationality. Indeed, their hegemony in psychological and rational explanation is so great that the question arises whether we need anything else. If we do not, then the entire field of human behavior and experience can be explained and described in terms of the categories of perception, wanting, and belief. They fill up the whole of that conceptual space, and what we call emotions will be merely complexes made up of those. If we do need something more, the additional concepts required may not be homogeneous; but they will have been sufficiently identified by their contrast with members of the better-studied triad. Most of that negative space, if any, is occupied by the emotions.

This book aims to bring that negative space into the foreground. To do this, my strategy will be to try as much as possible to understand emotions in terms of analogies with belief, want, and especially perception. Where the analogies fail, the special features of emotion

---

*Are perceptions just beliefs that are caused in a special way by sensory input? Or do they require a separate and irreducible account? Do beliefs admit of degrees? Or are they best represented as states that are either on or off? Are wants best represented as having individual states of affairs as their objects, or should we think of them as implicitly specifying complete world descriptions? Do wants and beliefs together determine behavior in the manner specified by the Aristotelian practical syllogism, or should we rather think of them as combining to produce decisions in accordance with the Bayesian calculus of expected desirability? These are a sample of the questions to which the theories of perception, belief, and desire seek answers.

will be more clearly visible. As a result, the impression of diversity among emotions will be confirmed in a fairly precise sense, particularly by contrast with belief and with want. I shall argue that beliefs and, more controversially, wants each form a definite species of mental state that can be characterized in terms of a specific criterion of success, which I shall refer to as their *formal object*. The formal object of belief—its criterion of success—is truth; the formal object of wanting is goodness. If emotions were merely compounded of beliefs and wants, they would have no criteria of success of their own. If they formed a congeneric species with belief and wanting, one would expect to discover a single criterion for success, corresponding to truth and goodness, for emotions as a class. I shall argue that there is no such single formal object of emotions: in that precise sense it is each emotion type that is congeneric with belief and wanting, not emotions as a class. What determines the "success" of fear—what justifies it, if you like—is that its target be fearsome; the criterion of success for love is that its target be lovable; for indignation, that its target be unjust; and so forth. If this is right, then the hunch that emotions do not form a natural class will have been confirmed.

But that is to get ahead of the story. It is time now for a more pedestrian beginning. If we are to become clear about the role of emotion in rationality, we should first ask, What is a rational agent? In the next chapter I offer a very brief sketch of some models of the person into which emotions have in the past been fitted or forced. This is followed by a thumbnail catalogue of theories of emotion, the disparate insights of which I shall attempt to integrate in the sequel.

Chapter 2
Models of Mind and Emotion

Yet all experience is an arch wherethro'
Gleams that untravell'd world whose margin fades
Forever and forever when I move.
Alfred, Lord Tennyson

Summary

When we think of breaking down the complexity of the person into simpler elements, there are two ways in which we might proceed. One is to look for parts or components, the other is to look for functions. A sketch of three classical models of the person—those of Plato, Aristotle, and Descartes—will illustrate these analytical strategies and sample some ways of dealing with the relation of emotions to other faculties.

Plato's parts of the soul—reason, desire, and emotion—exemplify the componential model. But although Plato's "homuncular" version of this approach promises an explanation of conflict, the arguments that support it are fallacious in several respects. Aristotle's functionalist hierarchy of the soul's faculties typifies the second strategy. Here there are no parts or agencies but rather a layered series of increasingly complex capacities, where the higher presuppose the lower: nutrition and growth, sensation, movement, desire, emotion, reason. Aristotle's account is more modern but does not explain conflict. Descartes's account, which is surprisingly free of simple-minded dualism, has both componential and functional aspects—which is the right idea.

Many variants of these strategies are possible, of which I attempt a classification relevant to more contemporary approaches. Primitive components might be thought of as items of physiology, or of behavior; and these might be combined with temporal categories on the scale either of evolution or of individual development. When this scheme is applied to emotions, different brands of componentialism result, depending on whether the primitives are themselves assumed to be simple emotions or simples of some other kind—such as other mental states or perhaps even physiological states.

The componential approach is often thought to raise a problem about emergence. If an emotion arises out of certain more primitive elements organized in a certain way, for example, does this mean that its felt quality must be deducible from the properties and organization of the elements? This problem dissolves as soon as we make the distinction between explaining something and deducing or defining it. In any case it is not a special problem for materialist theories of mind, because it arises at several levels in science, for instance, at the cusp between the physics of elements and the physics of compounds.

Functionalism too comes in a number of varieties, some hostile and some friendly to the idea of an identification of mental states (and specifically emotions) with underlying physiological states. Functionalism, I suggest, is less a theory than a research strategy applicable throughout science. It is the strategy of top-down analysis, which looks first at how some complex performs as it does and then seeks explanations in terms of the organization and capacities of its parts. Because the functionalist strategy is entirely general, it is unlikely to yield the differentiae of mental states in general or emotions in particular.

Several types of theories have been offered to define and understand emotions. Each has focused on some aspect or theoretical level at the expense of others. They have variously taken feeling, behavior, physiology, cognition, will, evolution, or social context to offer the privileged perspective or the defining element. The correct theory will have to avoid their partiality but will have learned from all of them.

There are more ways conceptually to slice a person than to skin a cat. And for each way there is likely an axe to be ground. Some models of the mind, for example, are designed to make it theoretically coherent to envisage the survival of the personality after death. Since no fact of science or logic requires life after death, this is an extratheoretical motivation. Among theoretical motivations, the most general (and most hoary) is the reductionist ambition implied by the ideal of a unified science. This ambition prompted the Greek and Lucretian atomistic models, as well as the various forms of modern brain-mind identity theories. Sometimes the motivation for a model of the person can be a mixture of the ideological and the theoretical. An example is functionalism, a modern (though very Aristotelian) alternative to atomism. On the ideological side, functionalism promises a theoretical substructure for the enterprise of creating artificial intelligence; but this promise is bolstered by the theoretical prospect of providing an escape from the sterile choice between dualism and mechanism.

In this chapter I propose to survey some of these models. I have two aims in mind. First, I want to illustrate the uneasy and sometimes procrustean way that emotions have been fitted into them. Second, I want to lay the groundwork for one of my central theses: that emotions are not reducible to any of the other things to which they have at some time or other been assimilated. That chiefly means beliefs and desires; but an exclusive grip on different features of emotions has produced other candidates: feeling, behavior, physiological change, cognition, will, instinct, and social convention.

First I shall look at some historical models of the person, in order to contrast homuncular or more generally componential theories with functionalist ones. Simple homuncular models, which picture emotions as one of a number of inner agencies in possible conflict, will be found unpromising; but other variants of componential approaches will be worth exploring in somewhat more detail. After that I shall paint in broad strokes the principal modern theories of emotions, in the irenic if unexciting hope that, although none will do, something can be learned from each.

Two warnings are in order. First, a complete taxonomy of the main models of the person is out of the question here. I shall be idiosyncratic, selective, and unhistorical. The models I discuss—those of Plato, Aristotle, and Descartes—are selected because they illustrate particularly well the issue of emotional conflict. They are intrinsically important and representative; but some of the ones I ignore—those of Spinoza, Hume, and Kant—are no less so.[1]

Second, the models I shall sketch do not necessarily reflect fully elaborated philosophical theories. Sometimes they are informal assumptions or pictures in terms of which we organize our perception, our understanding, and our talk of emotions and their role in our lives.[2] Such informal models can sometimes be stubbornly misleading. One example is the prevalence of the assumption that emotions or "feelings" cannot admit of any meaningful criticism. This view is undoubtedly grounded in a picture of emotions as "natural" bodily conditions or disturbances, as far beyond the reach of rational argument as an upset stomach. (The fact that upset stomachs can be psychosomatic, however, should prompt us to look twice at the picture.) Sometimes, by the bootstrapping phenomenon already alluded to, such views may actually influence the very phenomena they allegedly describe. In cultures where murderous jealousy is considered natural and inevitable, jealous husbands are surely less given to effective self-control.

I have one more reason for stressing the notion of informal models. I shall be arguing that emotions themselves act like models. Whatever their own susceptibility to rational criticism, they themselves give us frameworks in terms of which we perceive, desire, act, and explain. Their reputation for irrationality is partly due to their power to reinterpret the world. Because this power lies below the threshold of full critical awareness, it looms the more threateningly over simplistic notions of rational order.

What kinds of questions, then, will the sorts of "models" I have in mind answer about persons and their organization?

One question might concern what persons *consist in* at any given time. Another concerns how they *change*, whether on the scale of individual life, or of society, or of evolution. The latter question of course presupposes an answer to the former.

Straddling both questions, and obviously related to the problem of the difference between animal and human nature raised in chapter 1, is the question of what is *primitive*. If emotions are part of our animal nature, we might assume, they must be in some sense more primitive than other faculties. Primitiveness can be understood either in terms of constituents (what are the elementary parts of the person?) or in temporal terms (what are the evolutionary and developmental primitives out of which persons grow?). I set aside these temporal aspects for the moment, for they are not stressed in the classical models to which I now turn.

Parts and Functions

The notion of *part* of the person is subject to an ambiguity, which is apparent in the contrasting models proposed by Plato and Aristotle. Plato's main problem was to account for *inner conflict*. This led him to divide the person—or more exactly the soul—into parts, each of which was itself structured like a person.[3] The result was a variant of the componential model: a *homuncular* theory of how to parcel out the person.

Aristotle, by contrast, was interested in a *functional* account. His analysis of the person was intended, not to explain inner conflict, but to differentiate the basic functions or capacities of humans and other living things. He seems to have assumed that this was the only interesting problem: he criticized Plato's account for involving a redundancy of functions, as if it had been addressed to the same issue as his own account (*De Anima*, III.9). The misunderstanding is promoted by the fact that Plato's homunculi are identified in terms of their respective dominant functions: desire, reason, or emotion. But any homuncular model must involve functional redundancy. If the person is a committee the members of which can conflict as easily as work in harmony, then each member homunculus must be equipped with a complete set of at least the basic functions required to have preferences and to set about imposing them.

Either notion of *part* is subject to various interpretations. Let us look first at the homuncular.

Homuncular Parts

I have mentioned the problem of ambivalence: the propensity for simultaneous emotions to conflict and for single emotions to inspire conflicting evaluations. Plato made the first assault on this problem, though unfortunately his way of dealing with it will not work. Actually, he mistakes the problem for its solution: he thinks he can explain inner conflict by postulating parts of the soul, without noticing that some of the most puzzling of our inner conflicts pit the emotional "part" against itself.

Plato's homuncular theory is most easily understood in terms of the argument he gives to support it. That argument is based on the principle that it is not consistent to suppose that a single item either suffers or causes contrary effects, except by dint of some equivocation of sense, time, aspect, or respect. This principle anticipates Leibniz's law of the nonidentity of discernibles and on the face of it is irreproachable. If F and G are univocal contraries, and both x *is* F and x *is* G are true, then x must refer to two different things.

The trouble comes in the use Plato makes of this principle. He wants us to think of the impulse to do something and the impulse not to do it as contraries. But whereas it is undoubtedly true that the doing and the not doing are contraries, it does not follow that the corresponding impulses are also contraries. Plato's argument is fallacious in three ways. First, because the allegedly contrary terms are dispositional; second, because they are intentional; and third, because even if he were right in inferring inconsistency from conflict, he would need to demonstrate separately that the inconsistent sides represent stable homunculi rather than ad hoc combatants in a fleeting conflict.

Suppose, to simplify, that I have both an impulse to turn right and an impulse to turn left. We can acknowledge that the acts are incompatible: I could not perform both at the same time without some trickery—or equivocation. But it doesn't follow that I couldn't simultaneously have both the corresponding impulses. We tend to ask, "How could we possibly be experiencing these incompatible impulses?" But we might instead take the very fact that we can simultaneously experience them to show that they are not incompatible. The impulses are dispositions to incompatible actions and so cannot be actualized together. But that needn't entail that they can't exist together. It's reasonable to suppose that dispositions behave more like possibility than like truth. Possibilities can be consistent even when the corresponding actualities would not be: 'Possibly it will rain' and 'Possibly it won't rain' (at time t, at place p, etc.) are consistent, though of course it can't be true both that it will rain and that it will not.

The second fallacy springs from the fact that the impulses contain contraries only as intentional objects. Whether these intentional objects are themselves contraries is precisely the question at issue. From the incompatibility of p and q, it does not follow that Op and Oq are incompatible, where O stands for an intentional verb such as 'thinking', 'hoping', 'imagining', or 'desiring'. Again, more argument would be needed to show that a particular intentional verb works like truth rather than like possibility. The contrariety of impulses cannot be inferred from the contrariety of their content. So Plato has failed to show that such impulses must stem from separate, homuncular subjects.

Most "demonstrations" of the separateness of parts of the person make an intriguing but groundless assumption: that whatever is not shown to be divisible into separate parts must be a well-behaved continuing entity. The most famous case of this is Descartes's claim to have established his own existence on the basis of his doubt. As Lichtenberg remarked, this authorized at most the conclusion that "It is thinking," as we might say "It is raining," not the stronger claim that there exists a (continuing) thinker. This is also Plato's third fallacy. The argument from the experience of conflict could at best have established that different entities are involved in each such event. But how would we know that the participants remain the same from one occasion to the next? Why do there not arise fresh contestants, ephemeral Heraclitean entities, in each new case of conflict?

We might try the following answer on Plato's behalf. Let the entities involved in each individual conflict be different every time. Still, they can be sorted into *kinds*. And it turns out that they make up just three kinds: the desiderative, the rational, and the emotional. Let us then posit, as an inference to the best explanation, that these three kinds of impulse spring respectively from three enduring agencies that together make a person.

But this defense plays right into Aristotle's complaint of redundancy. If the homunculi in Plato's model of the soul are supposed to account for the different functions of the soul, they must fail. For each homunculus must to some extent reduplicate all functions (see Penner 1971). The desiderative needs some minimal quantum of rationality to satisfy even the simplest desires; the rational needs its own desires to have something to fight about; and the emotional needs both if it is to take sides with the rational, which is what Plato thinks the emotional part normally does.

Functional Division
Aristotle presents us not with a committee of subpersonal persons but with a hierarchy of functions, or types of capabilities. The sense in which they form a hierarchy is not that some dominate others but that some presuppose the existence of the others. The rational remains the highest, as with Plato, though in a different sense. But without the "lower" faculties—growth, locomotion, sensation, memory, imagination, emotion, and desire—there would be nothing to be rational about.

Nevertheless, the central problem addressed by Plato is left untouched by Aristotle's account. Plato's explanation of inner conflict may not be adequate, but Aristotle provides none. How conflict is possible, and what role the emotions play in it, are questions that a theory of emotions cannot evade: I shall have a good deal to say about it in this book.

Another more general question remains implicit in both stories: Is emotion reducible to a combination of some more fundamental categories? Aristotle's answer to this is unclear. Plato's answer is clear enough, but the reason for it is not. Why is emotion a *third* homunculus? Plato claims that it typically sides with the rational. But why then is it not identified with it? The argument from conflict could in theory be redeployed here, to show cases in which emotion was inconsistent with both the other homunculi. Instead, Plato performs a curious sort of two-step. He first cites the cases in which the emotional sides with the rational, to show that it cannot be reduced to the desiderative. And he then cites other arguments, based on the capacity for emotion in prerational children, intended to persuade us that emotion cannot be equated with the rational. This argument fails, because it does not establish that either is different from both at once.

Here, as often with the great philosophers, a bad argument can be no less significant than a good one. For it provokes us to inquire about Plato's extratheoretical motivation. Why was he so keen on believing that he needed three rather than just two parts of the soul? Why did this seem to him so obviously true that he overlooked the feebleness of his argument?

A scholarly reply would take note of Plato's motivation in political theory. His elaborate parallel between the soul and the state and their conditions of justice required something in the soul to correspond to the status of the guardians. But this seems arbitrary. One might just as well try to explain the need for a special class of soldier-guardians in terms of the division of the soul. The fact is that Plato seems to have noted something of the awkward ambiguity of emotion, especially in relation to what I called the antinomies of rationality-irrationality and voluntariness-passivity. That ambiguity undermines any attempted reduction of emotions to other categories.

Descartes's Compromise

Next, let us consider how the emotions fit into Descartes's model of the person. Given that Descartes is the other great dualist of the history of philosophy, one would expect him to cram emotions somehow into either body or soul. Instead, he is respectful enough of the facts to compromise his dualism. His account in the *Treatise on the Passions of the Soul* suggests that emotion is neither a separate homunculus nor a simple function of the soul or the body.

Descartes, even more explicitly than Plato, focuses on the ambiguous position of emotions in relation to the categories of activity versus passivity, thought-dependency and rationality, objectivity, and personal identity. They are located in the soul, which is by definition the seat of consciousness. They are called *passions* because the soul is passive in relation to them. But that does not differentiate them from ordinary sensations, which strictly speaking are passions too. In fact, for Descartes, emotions are a species of perception: they are "perceptions . . . of the soul which we relate specially to it, and which are caused, maintained, and fortified by some movement of the spirits" (Descartes 1649, art. 27). Perceptions are distinguished from each other by their *objects* (what they are "related to") and by their *causes*. We must further distinguish the immediate or *proximate* cause, which involves nervous activity or "movement of the spirits," from the "exciting" or *remote* cause. The difference between emotions and sensory perceptions involves both their objects and their "exciting" causes. Sensory perceptions have external objects: they are "related to the things which are without us, to wit to the objects of our senses." The passions, by contrast, are related to the soul. Moreover, sensory perceptions, but not passions, are standardly caused by their objects "at least when our opinion is not false . . ." (art. 23). Passions differ also from "hunger, thirst, and other natural appetites, to which we may unite pain, heat, and the other affections which we perceive as

Table 2.1
Causes and objects of Cartesian perception

Perception type	Locus of the object (what "related" to)	Immediate cause	"Exciting" cause
Sensory (hearing, sight)	Outside the body	Inside the body	Outside the body
Proprioceptive (pain, heat)	Inside the body	Inside the body	Inside the body
Active emotion of the soul (desire)	Inside the soul	Action of soul	In active soul(?)
Passion of the soul	Inside the soul	Inside the body	Outside the body

Note: The table distinguishes only four perception types. Insofar as the distinctions are made in terms of three two-fold distinctions, this is clearly fewer than would be yielded by a full enumeration of all the logical possibilities. The missing cases might be ones of misleading or nonveridical perceptions. Two examples: a perception referred to the external world, whose "exciting" cause is actually not external, would be a case of hallucination if its "exciting" cause is internal to the body. It would be a case of willful self-deception if its "exciting" cause is internal to the soul. These implicit extensions of Descartes's theory are taken up in chapter 5.

though they were in our members." These, call them *proprioceptions,* do not differ from the passions in the locus of their proximate cause (which is in the body) or of their exciting cause (which can be outside it). They differ instead in the locus of their objects, in that proprioceptions are "related" to the body, whereas the passions are related to the soul (art. 24, 29). Finally, they are distinguished from desires, "which may be called emotions of the soul related to the soul, but caused by the soul itself" (art. 29). (If Descartes believes in the complete freedom of the will, he would seem to be precluded from admitting that desire, in his sense, can have remote causes outside the soul.) These differentiae may be summarized in table 2.1.

The features of the external world to which the passions are referred are not simple qualities, as in the case of sensations, but states of affairs specifiable in propositions. This makes them susceptible to judgments of rationality, at least by reference to the thoughts on which they are dependent. Finally, though, they are useful precisely in the imperfection of that thought-dependency: their causation in the condition of the body gives them an inertia that lends agents a capacity for "following through" more consistently on their intentions. It gives our enterprises pith and moment, ensuring that they are not abandoned with the excessive flightiness of thought. Descartes shows his awareness of the ambivalence of emotions by making of their inertia both their virtue and their vice:

The utility of all the passions consists alone in their fortifying and perpetuating in the soul thoughts which it is good it should preserve, and which without that might easily be effaced from it. And again, all the harm which they can cause consists in the fact that they fortify and conserve these thoughts more than necessary, or that they fortify and conserve others on which it is not good to dwell. (Art. 74)

This brief sketch should suffice to show that Descartes is somewhere between Plato and Aristotle in the picture he draws of the soul. Rather than separate agencies in potential conflict, the passions are activities of the body that affect the soul. So in one sense they can be viewed as functions of the person as a whole, analyzed in terms of the relation between the mind and the body. In another sense, Descartes's analysis remains a componential one, though not of the homuncular variety. For in his view all emotions can be understood as compounded out of just six primitives: wonder, love, hatred, desire, joy, and sadness (art. 69).

Two General Strategies

To clarify the theoretical options sampled so far, I now digress to discuss the various ways in which talk of parts or of functions might apply to the emotions. Taking my cue from the models just discussed, I look at the two main theoretical strategies that are their inheritors in current philosophy of mind. These are *componentialism*, which looks for (not necessarily physical) primitives in terms of which to understand more complex states, and *functionalism*, which is more interested in organizational structure than in primitive atoms. A grasp of these strategies will pay off in the next chapter, when we examine attempts to understand emotion in biological and systems-theoretic terms.

Componentialism
The leading idea of componentialism is that complex things are to be understood in terms of *primitives*. The notion of primitives has an attractive ring. But this is mostly due, it will transpire, to the fact that it is suggestive in too many different ways. Simplicity is not self-predicative.

To begin with, we need to ask whether or not the primitives are in the same category as the complexes. If they are, then the search will be for simple emotions out of which others will be defined or constituted. Descartes's six simple passions are primitives of this kind. If the primitives are not themselves emotions, then they might be mental components such as judgment, evaluations, or desire, as in the theories of Sartre (1948), Robert Solomon (1976), Irving Thalberg (1977), or Joel Marks (1982). Or they might include physiological, anatomical, neurochemical, and behavioral components none of which is itself an emotion (see Lyons 1980 and Panksepp 1982).

All this is far from exhausting the possible meanings of 'primitive'. Indeed, if one had hoped for a univocal notion of the primitive—and thus for a key to the distinction between Beast and Human—their variety is not encouraging. Several other senses might be relevant to our attempt to understand emotions.

Temporal primitives could be defined in terms of *evolutionary* or *developmental* measures, about which I shall say more in chapters 4 and 7.

Physiological primitives are sometimes discussed as if they could be independently identified. The limbic system, for example, is often assumed to be "more primitive" than the neocortex. But this only makes sense if we have an independent criterion to fall back on. Mere localization in one or another part of the brain could not ground any intrinsic assessment of primitiveness, unless we already knew that the tasks handled in that location were simpler or that the structures in question were earlier in origin. About this, more in chapter 3.

Behavior has formed another basis for judgments of primitiveness that can then be used in the assessment of emotions. Behavior, in its turn, can be judged more or less primitive in terms of several criteria.

Many of our action-ascriptions imply complex changes in the world. These are usually accomplished by a chain of increasingly limited acts, linked by the "by-relation": I get privacy *by* closing the door *by* pushing it. Eventually the chain comes to an end at an action that I *just do,* such as moving my arm. There is nothing else by doing which I move my arm. Just moving my arm is, in Arthur Danto's (1965) useful term, a *basic action.*

But the basic units of behavior do not have to be acts. They might be *basic muscular movements* lying outside the chain of the by-relation (see chapter 4). The analyses of facial expression conducted by Paul Ekman and his collaborators, for example, decompose the expression of emotions into minute but not normally voluntary muscular elements (see Ekman and Friesen 1975).

Finally, behavior can be categorized in terms of *basic adaptive strategies.* Here too the lists differ from author to author; but the sort of items likely to be found in the lists are usually related to basic animal functions, such as those traditionally referred to as the *Four F's* ($F_{nourishment}$, F_{combat}, F_{escape}, and $F_{reproduction}$). Experience roughly bears out the expectation that complexity of forms grows with time; but we could scarcely infer that recent forms are necessarily more viable. For since the ultimate test of viability is longevity, it is invariably the most ancient forms that must win the contest of proven viability—by which test cockroaches must rank above primates. (Hence, perhaps, the common conviction that primitive structures or emotions tend to be the most stable.)

Emergence Suppose emotions are compounded either of simpler emotions or of other states. Does that mean that they are "nothing but" compounds of those more primitive states, or are they emergent? A property is *emergent* if it could not be deduced from the lower-level properties on the basis of which it may be explained. Consider, for example, the effect of drinking water after eating artichokes. If you are among the 60 percent or so of the population who have a certain kind of receptor in their tongue or palate, you will detect a characteristic sweet aftertaste. Now the question is this: could the quality of this aftertaste be deduced analytically from the nature of those receptors, supplemented with a chemical analysis of artichokes and water? If not, then that quality can be called *emergent*.

The question about compound emotions, then, is whether their properties—and especially their felt qualities or *qualia*—could have been predicted even from a thorough empirical knowledge of their constituents. My hunch is that they could not—but that this in itself is no objection to thinking of emotions as both explained by, and constituted of, primitive atoms of some sort. Let me explain.

What I have just said seems to presuppose that explanation is possible without deduction. For I have contrasted explaining a quality with deducing its nature. But has deducibility not been traditionally regarded as a necessary condition for scientific explanation? Actually, the question here is not whether deduction plays a role but whether the deduction can proceed directly from the properties and organization of the lower-level entities to the properties of the higher level. In the standard deductive-nomological model of scientific explanation, the laws figuring as premises of the deduction are themselves empirical laws: "Bodies attract each other," or "Smoking causes cancer."

As Robert Cummins has pointed out, however, not all explanation is causal. There is room for what he has called *analytical* explanations, either of a system in terms of its components or of a property in terms of the lower-level components and properties in which it is *instantiated*. Property instantiation, rather than identity, is the relation of lightning to electrical discharge, of temperature to mean molecular energy—in short, of just those "theoretical identifications" on which the so-called identity theory of mind was modeled. Property analysis is the proper domain of the question of emergence. In some cases of "property analysis" a purely deductive analysis is possible: "For example, 'Anything executing the bubble algorithm sorts numbers into order; S executes the bubble algorithm; hence S sorts numbers into order'" (Cummins 1983, 18). This explains, without recourse to anything empirical in the first premise, why S instantiates the property of sorting numbers into order. Here, clearly, there is no emergent property. In most cases of property analysis, however, the first premise of the deductive argument that explains why something instantiates a certain property must be established empirically. The first premise says that "anything having components $C_1 \ldots C_n$ organized in manner O . . . has property P" (p. 17). If that premise can only be known by empirical discovery, then P is emergent.

In that sense, emergence is to be expected at many levels of science. To see this, consider the following story. In the Beginning or shortly after, we are told, all was Helium Soup. Could E.U. (an Extra-Universal scientist) have predicted the future properties of gold on the basis of the properties of existing particles? I see no reason to think so—unless we are willing to endorse classical rationalism, in which case all truths could be deduced a priori.

But what if E.U. is allowed complete freedom to experiment with new compounds? She might take bits of helium off in her TUTU (Trans-Universe Transport Unit) into a universe where the conditions would allow for the constitution of gold. Then she can simply observe what the properties of gold turn out to be. In this way she will discover a new property of helium particles, namely, the property of being capable of being constituted into gold. The "deduction" of the properties of gold is now trivial. But that was cheating. If the properties of the helium atoms in isolation are related contingently to those of gold, as an empiricist must assume, no amount of observation of those properties in isolation can reliably ground an inference to the properties of gold.

Now that is exactly what is claimed for the emergence of the special qualia of emotions. No amount of knowledge of our chemical, physical, neurological, and even functional constituents could be sufficient to predict the wonderful qualities of our feelings. Yet surely the emergent character of gold in relation to helium, or of chemical properties in relation to those of their physical constituents, is not a problem for materialism: so there is no reason to think emergence is an obstacle to the explanation of mental qualities in materialist terms.

This account is intended to placate both the reductionist and the antireductionist. Reductionism is vindicated because the higher-level property is indeed explained by the lower-level one. On the other hand, the opposition is right in its claim that there is no conceptual sufficiency of the lower-level properties. Given the right empirical hypotheses, one can explain, but one cannot analyze or define, the higher in terms of the lower. Rightly understood, then, the nature of qualia poses no special problem for even a strong program of physiological explanation of emotions.

Functionalism

An important methodological question remains: whether it is better to start with instantiating primitives and work our way up, or to attempt to analyze the higher functions in terms of their component functions. These alternatives have become known as the *bottom-up* and the *top-down* research strategies. By and large (though not necessarily), componential approaches tend to follow the bottom-up strategy, since their aim is to explain the working of the whole system on the basis of its parts. As we shall see in the next chapter, something can be squeezed out of this approach; but one problem with it is that there is no obviously privileged level at which the "primitives" of emotion are to be found. The second strategy, that of *functionalism*, is for the most part unconcerned with primitives; it proceeds top-down. It seeks to take the complex capacities of a system apart into simpler ones. Sometimes the component capacities are capacities of components (see Cummins 1983, 29). But the functionalist strategy can go quite a long way by ignoring the nature of components and looking only at their organization—how they work together.

'Organization', however, is itself a relative term. A structured complex at one level of theory may constitute an atom from the point of view of some higher level. The constituents of the simpler structure may in turn be viewed as complex when the grain is further enlarged. Accordingly, the objects of study at each level may be understood in two ways. They may be considered in terms of the way they behave, without regard for their own constitution: the heart is that part of the body which pumps blood. But they may also be considered in terms of the behavior of the parts of which they are made: the heart is a striated muscle, controlled by the autonomic nervous system, and so on. The matter and mechanism of those parts may be just what we need to understand *why* the higher-level assemblies work as they do.

Such, in general, is the strategy of functionalism. But there are several specific theories sporting that name. This makes it tricky to assess how functionalism bears on the study of emotions.

In Hilary Putnam's (1960) version, functionalism amounted to an attack on the mind-brain identity theory, on the ground that there is no necessary correlation between physical structure and function, although of course the physical structure can place constraints on what is possible at the functional level. This point was already implicit, in essentials, in Aristotle's distinction between matter and form. For my purposes, the lesson in this type of functionalism lies in the relative irreducibility of various levels of theory. This will become important in chapter 4, where I shall argue that teleological and intentional language should both be given a certain amount of independence, without prejudice to the goal of a unified science.

A second version of functionalism, far from being incompatible with the identity theory, is in fact a form of it (see Lewis 1972). This starts from two assumptions: first, that our mental states can be viewed respectively as causes of our behavior and effects of the ambient stimuli; second, that only physical events can be causes or effects of other physical events. The marriage of functionalism and identity theory is then simply consummated by stipulating that if a mental state plays a given causal role—say, it makes me laugh—then it is to be identified with *whatever (physical) mechanisms actually play that role*. In sum, a form of the identity thesis turns out to be a corollary of functionalism.

The best-known implementation of this second version of functionalism as a theory of the mind specifies that the functional level relevant to mentality is the level of computational activity performed on mental representations somehow instantiated in the brain.[4] There is some dispute about exactly what that means. But that proposal can be useful to the present inquiry by suggesting this question: Is the relation of physiology to emotions more like that of the testes to the production of testosterone or more like that of the brain to the production of thought? Both are functional in a broad sense, but only the latter is likely to be computational. That, impressionistically, is one of the questions to be discussed in chapter 3.

Functionalism (apart from the particular form last mentioned) is not specifically about the psychological. Its basic insight can be applied throughout science. There is no reason that we should not take a functionalist view of the constituents of physical atoms, for example. In the sense of Putnam's version, this means that one might determine how the atoms behave at the molecular and atomic levels without reference to their further constituents (although the atoms might be constrained in turn by some functional features of protons, electrons, and so on). In the spirit of David Lewis's (1972) version, it means that we can speak of their constituents without needing to identify them otherwise than by their effects.*

In this perspective all is function, all the way down. But all is structure, too, all the way up. That just means that however high a level of assembly we choose, there might be some higher-level entity of which the items of the chosen level are mere components. To study the higher level, we would need to abstract from the lower. Functionalism in this general sense is not a theory but a research program: it commits us to explaining molar behavior at one level in terms of the organization of lower levels, but it does not commit us ahead of time to any specific list of ontologically basic or explanatory levels. This will become especially important in connection with the emotions. For as we shall see, an important feature of emotions is what I call their *level-ubiquity*. They manifest themselves as physiological phenomena, as psychological ones, as social ones—to name only a few of the relevant levels. And each level seems capable, under the right conditions, of affecting the others. A purely physiological need is apt to interrupt a flight of fancy; but at the opposite extreme a lively poetic meditation may make one entirely forget hunger, cold, or sex. This diversity of levels at which emotions can manifest themselves has given rise to an unusual variety of theories of emotion, each focusing, at the outset, on its own favorite level.

Some Typical Modern Theories

I turn now to a brief survey of some of these theories. Here again, my aim is not to try my hand at a review of the literature; good ones already exist.[5] In fact, although I mention a few names, I make no effort to pin the items on my list onto particular philosophers. My purpose is simply to illustrate how one might get started on the construction of theory by focusing on any one of several important facets of emotion. The theories I outline are not very much more elaborated than the "models" I have attributed to Plato, Aristotle, and Descartes. All are inadequate, as theories, because each is based on a partial view. My sketches do not pretend to do them justice; I aim only to suggest how each brings useful insights, even while remaining incomplete. I also suggest that as each one is refined, they have a tendency to converge. I would like to hint, of course, that what they converge on is the theory presented in this book.

---

*In fact, the essential device involved in Lewis's view is the *Ramsey sentence*, originally devised, in an operationalist climate, to allow physicists to talk with a clear conscience when they didn't know what they were talking about.

The views to be roughed in are the *feeling, behaviorist, physiological, cognitivist, conative, evolutionary,* and *contextualist* accounts. My sketch of each loosely follows a simple plan: I begin with a crude statement based either on a reconstruction of the intuitive basis on which it rests or on its earliest actual formulation. Next I sketch refinements that can be made to improve it in response to the standard objections to which the crude version is open. And I then state, rather baldly, the grounds for its remaining inadequacy.

The Feeling Theory
If one were to choose a theory of emotion to represent common sense, the *feeling theory* would probably be the best candidate. It is useful in showing a peculiarity of "folk theories," namely, that people think they believe them but do not in fact talk, perceive, or behave as if they did. On this view, emotions are simply assimilated to certain kinds of felt experience. Perhaps the view gets some plausibility from the parallel between such locutions as 'I felt cold' and 'I felt sad'. Emotions, or "feelings," are seen as another species of the genus that also contains sensations, itches, and proprioceptive or visceral perceptions, differing from those others chiefly in the objects toward which they are directed.

But what are those objects? Pure feelings typically have none; this perspective tends indeed to treat emotions as naked qualia, or qualities of awareness. An object, on this view, can be related to emotion only by contingent association. And that does not seem true to the important role of objects in the very identification of our emotions. That is the first of several standard objections to this view. Another is that pure feelings remain disconnected from behavior, motivation, belief, choice, and social and linguistic context, whereas emotions proper are normally tied to all these.

These objections, a defender of the feeling theory might reply, don't prove that emotions aren't feelings. Feelings are just the genus of which emotions are species, and the many functional connections that other feelings lack are just the specific differentiae of emotions. Something is a feeling if (1) it is conscious and (2) it results in some way from some bodily condition. Emotions meet condition (1), for as Freud remarked, strictly speaking 'unconscious affect' is a contradiction in terms (Freud 1915e, 78). And some have maintained, as we shall see, that they satisfy (2) as well because physiological change is a necessary condition for emotion. Moreover, the alleged fact that feelings do not have objects can look less plausible if we model feelings on perceptions rather than sensations. (I shall pursue this suggestion in chapter 6.)

That defense can certainly improve the prospects of the feeling theory. Nevertheless, it remains to some extent an evasion. For what we want to discover is precisely what differentiates emotions from other feelings. The feeling theory, at best, defines only a genus.

The main deficiency of the feeling theory, however, is that there are too many aspects of emotion about which it does not tell us enough. These point to several other perspectives. From the behaviorist and the conative theorist we can expect some light on the role of behavior and motivation; from the contextualist, on the role of social convention in defining what emotional state someone is in. We can expect physiological theories to tell us exactly what the acknowledged role of the body actually is; and look to evolutionary theory for some understanding of the original adaptive function of emotions. Finally, the cognitive and the conative theories should tell us more about the connections of emotion with belief and will.

Behaviorism

The *behaviorist* strategy stems from skeptical scruple. It dictates that what is not publicly observable, such as a conscious feeling, cannot be reliably known, unless it is explicitly definable in terms of its overt manifestations. Two notions once seemed promising for the implementation of this program. One is the notion of a *pattern* of behavior, the other is the notion of *disposition*.

On this view, some emotions are just complex patterns of behavior. No single overt act amounts to being sad. I may be crying merely to attract attention, or holding my head down just because I am shy, or listless because I am suffering from a vitamin deficiency, or dwelling on the subject of my long-lost lover only for lack of any more interesting topic. But if I do all or most of these things and others like them, then my behavior simply amounts to sadness. For a behaviorist, there is nothing more for sadness to be (see Ryle 1949).

Some other emotions, particularly those that are targeted on a person or object—love, resentment, anger, gratitude—call forth characteristic behavior only under certain favorable conditions. For some forms of expression, the target has to be around, for example. Although I can express my anger to someone other than its target, I will not do it in the same way, unless I have "displaced" it (see chapter 9). For these cases behaviorism appeals to the notion of a disposition, which is a property defined in terms of a conditional. The antecedent of the conditional specifies observable ("standing" or "occurrent") conditions sufficient for the expression of that emotion. (To be more exact, the conditions are sufficient subject to the usual incantation:

other things being equal.) Suppose I resent you. When your best friend sings your praises, or when you get the Nobel prize, or just when I see you, *then* the resentful behavior emerges: I make faces, say derogatory or sarcastic things, and so forth.

That, at any rate, is the basic idea. Behaviorism is not a fashionable view. Refutations of it abound, consisting of variants of the simple point that behavioral dispositions are in fact neither necessary nor sufficient for the presence of any given emotion.

One refinement might help. Helen Nissenbaum (1986) has pointed out that we must distinguish two different sorts of conditionals. In one sort the consequent is a piece of behavior: If I resent you, I shall sometimes slight you. In the other it is an occurrent emotion: If I resent you, I shall sometimes feel resentment. A behaviorist might modify the theory to take account of this distinction. But still the occurrent emotion would remain unanalyzed, leaving the feeling theory to prop it up.

Alternatively, the dispositional strategy can be reapplied. This is just what B. F. Skinner has done. His suggestion is that emotions are *second-order* dispositions, modifying the conditions of first-level learning: "Under different emotional conditions, different events serve as reinforcers, and different groups of operants increase in probability of emission" (Skinner and Holland 1961, 213). If I like someone, I may find her smoking tolerable, perhaps even sexy. But if I don't, I'll find it infuriating. Emotions, on this view, are *dispositional dispositions.*

This captures an important feature, which will figure prominently in the sequel: emotions control not merely behavior but also the ways that other mental events, states, and dispositions are organized. In this more subtle form, however, behaviorism has given up its crucial epistemological advantage. That advantage sprang from the rejection of unobservable explanatory mechanisms in favor of correlations between stimuli and responses. But second-order dispositions are just such unobservables, introduced to protect the behaviorist hypothesis against counterevidence. Any failure of corroboration for a concrete hypothesis about learning rates or the "probability of emission" of different "groups of operants" can simply be explained away by positing an emotional state. The account remains susceptible to objections to behaviorism, however, because its second-order measurements are still framed in terms of behavioral parameters alone. It thus fails to address the connections of emotions to other parameters, on which other theories or perspectives are focused, and which behaviorists have not shown us how to do without.

Physiological Theories
Emotions are of the body, more clearly than any other mental thing. That is the idea behind lie-detector tests: anyone, the (somewhat dubious) assumption goes, gets upset at telling a lie, and the physiological manifestations of this fact are beyond voluntary control.

Physiological theories come in different flavors. Most famously, that of William James (1884) attempts to take the mental component into account by making it out to be the *consciousness of the physiological processes themselves.* On this view, to be sad is essentially to be aware of one's tears, which are somehow directly caused by some perception or thought.

I shall look at physiological theories in some detail in the next chapter. But one elaboration of the role of physiology should be mentioned here. For William Lyons (1980), physiological changes constitute an essential part of an emotion by virtue of being caused by some *evaluation* (conscious or unconscious). That brings in an element of thought, which adulterates the purity of the physiological view but is crucial to the next perspective.

The Cognitive Theory
Cognitive theories focus on what I have called the *informational* content of emotions. This takes two forms. The more mundane emphasizes that the perception of the object of an emotion is an essential element of the emotion itself. In this sense, the objects and properties perceived are ordinary ones: to fear the lion that is coming at me, I must first detect it. But though perception in this ordinary sense can ground an emotion, it cannot *be* the emotion. The second informational element takes as its object not just the presence of the lion but its fearfulness. The emotion of fear could be the perception of that. The distinction between these two kinds of cognition will require a careful discussion of the different kinds of objects associated with emotions. I undertake this task in chapter 5.

In either form (and even if both ideas are included) the cognitive theory must meet the old objection that (in Aristotle's phrase) "understanding by itself moves nothing." Any piece of information, of course, may affect what I want and what I do as well as what I believe. But it need not. If emotions are cognitions, they must be just that subclass of cognitions that affect directly what we want and what we are likely to do. (They may, in accordance with Skinner's insight, affect the rate at which we change what we want and learn to do new things.) This is the point of the modified cognitive theories of Magda Arnold (1960) and Robert Solomon (1976): the "judgments" involved are not just any judgments, but *evaluative* ones, and at that only ones that are made with particular intensity.

Two points should be noted about the cognitive view. First, if the cognitions involved in—or, a fortiori, constitutive of—emotions are indeed evaluations, then they are open to some very old questions about their objective validity as cognitions. Emotions, as Solomon concedes, are peculiarly subjective judgments and therefore may not, after all, be cognitive in the full sense. As one cognitive psychologist has defined it, "cognition is the activity of knowing: the acquisition, organization, and use of knowledge" (Neisser 1976, 1). Surely, therefore, the term must be taken to imply the existence of some objective correlation between some representational state and some object in the real world. If emotion yielded information only about the person experiencing it, it would always include some cognitive element, but only *about*, not *for*, the subject. And that, surely, weakens the import of the cognitive theory beyond recognition. In this book I shall take the more sanguine position that emotions carry information about the world beyond the subject, although, as I shall show, they are not species of beliefs.

The second point is that the cognitive perspective must also remain incomplete until it can assimilate the lessons of the physiological theory. Any cognition, on any but purely immaterialist assumptions, must be instantiated by some physiological state of the knower.* But what is special about the physiological state involved in emotion? We need to know the difference between merely being cognizant of something and reacting emotionally to it. On the next theory, the crucial difference rests in the role of the Will.

The Conative Theory

A good way to get attention for a theory is to so present it as to shock common sense. Such is the theory of Sartre (1948). Emotions are commonly assumed to be states endured rather than things done; and three of the perspectives so far canvassed—those based on feeling, physiology, and cognition—support this assumption. That is precisely what Sartre challenges in his account of emotions as *intentional strategies*. According to him, emotions are meant to change the real world—admittedly not in realistic or rational ways, but magically. His account of fear, for example, presents a reversal somewhat remi-

---

*This is carefully phrased to remain neutral on the question of whether any cognition must be *supervenient* on physiological states of the knower. See chapter 9 for more discussion of the bearing on my topic of the sort of cases made popular by Hilary Putnam and Tyler Burge, to show that cognitions are "not all in the head."

niscent of James's. James says that we are afraid because we flee. For Sartre, fear is a voluntary strategy, a piece of intentional behavior, that consists in a magical but freely chosen attempt to remove the object. The trouble with magic is that it does not usually work (when it does, I call it successful bootstrapping). According to Sartre, it is only because the magical strategy fails that the frightened subject resorts to flight. So for him flight is neither the cause nor the effect of fear; nor is it a rational strategy in itself. Instead, it is just a *substitute* for fear (Sartre 1948, 63).

This intriguing idea cannot quite bear the weight of its own implausibility. It rejects, but does nothing to refute, the traditional consensus that passions are essentially passive. Nevertheless, it too incorporates some insights worth dragging with us in our collector's net, and, as Robert Solomon has tried to show, it can be strengthened with more arguments.

Solomon's suggestion is that although the cognitive account would seem to be among the Sartrean theory's most direct rivals, the two can be consolidated into one.[6]

The trick involves two moves. The first is to point out that the alleged passivity of cognition or belief rests on a false dichotomy. There is no rigidly exclusive contrast between activity and passivity. The second move has already been sketched: it consists in focusing on evaluative judgments that—to borrow the very terms under attack—spring as much from the Will as from the Understanding. We can acknowledge that emotions not infrequently serve a purpose. Solomon (1973) tells a story of a couple in which one partner picks a fight *in order* to avoid going to the movies as planned. In a case such as this the behavioral manifestations by themselves—pretending to pick a fight—would not serve. There is no satisfaction—or at least not of the right kind—in having consciously and deceptively manipulated someone. Much better to be overcome by a "passive" emotion that not only licenses a cathartic outburst but also happens to have the desired effect.

One remaining problem with this view, as illustrated by Solomon's story, is that deception appears to have been avoidable only at the price of self-deception. For the whole point of the emotional strategy is that it cannot avow itself to be a strategy. It rests on the very myth of passivity that it confutes. But surely not all emotions are intrinsically self-deceptive. Besides, there is undoubtedly something right after all about the traditional view of emotions as passive (see Peters 1962). From that core of truth even the ingenious maneuvers of Solomon's modified Sartrean theory cannot distract us.

As Robert Gordon has shown, to say that emotions are passive entails neither that they are states of the body that act upon our soul nor that they are altogether outside our control. This removes some of the motivation for wanting to classify them as actions or products of the will (Gordon 1986). In the kind of passivity they exemplify, they resemble perception more than they resemble disease. We may also remind ourselves that even if our emotions are not directly chosen, they may still constitute the deepest sources of our most active individual choices (see chapter 7).

The view of emotions as freely chosen is also undermined from two other directions. On one side, fashionable debates around sociobiology have revived interest in an evolutionary point of view. From another side, often in direct opposition to the sociobiologists, feminists have urged a contextualist view, stressing the ideological "load" in what we are disposed to think of as "natural." These perspectives are briefly sketched in the following sections. I return to the evolutionary in chapter 4 and to the contextualist in chapters 9 and 12.

The Evolutionary Perspective
The evolutionary perspective on emotions is not new. Its first propounder was Darwin himself (Darwin 1896). This perspective has at least three important ideas to contribute to the study of emotions.

First, given the potential in our emotional dispositions for both useful and disruptive consequences—already noted by Descartes— and given also that something of our emotional potential seems to be shared with other animals, it is likely that some of those dispositions are at least partly under genetic control. So it makes sense to assume that the theory of evolution will have some application to our subject.

Even so, not every characteristic can be expected to receive an adaptive explanation. Adaptation explains only when there have been two alleles in competition with each other. Adaptation only shapes evolution: what drives it is random change. That is the second point.

Third, it cannot be assumed that adaptation always works to fit behavior to preexisting morphological or physiological constraints. On the contrary, behavior can sometimes take the lead in shaping the morphology of a population—even unto death.

This last point is illustrated by the mechanism of sexual selection. Suppose there evolves an innate disposition for individuals to pick mates by some salient sign, such as color of plumage, or size of antlers, or even aggressiveness. This could easily happen, if the salient character happened to be correlated with some intrinsically advantageous characteristic. The sting is that the tendency to select a mate for the character in question can outlast its usefulness. At that point it might become irreversibly maladaptive. This will happen whenever the genetic material has come too far to be shaped back out of the once adaptive disposition. The population of Irish elks is thought to have become extinct for just this reason. At first, large antlers were correlated with useful strength and size; so the disposition to select large-antlered males was adaptive for females. But antlers grew "allotropically," that is, faster than body size. Past a certain size, large antlers came to be a handicap. But the females were stuck with an irreversible tendency to pick mates on the basis of the now harmful character (see Gould 1977).

In sum, it is implausible to suppose that emotions could have evolved to their present form, if they were more harmful in the main than some viable alternative. But it would be quite wrong to apply Pope's words, "Whatever is, is right," to matters evolutionary. It does not follow from the evolutionary perspective that selected traits are always advantageous in the long run.

Whatever the importance of evolutionary factors, it would be rash to assume that they could yield anything like a complete theory of the emotions. One reason is the existence of conventional and social factors that are at least prima facie irreducible to biological causation. I turn now to the perspective that is, at least by implication, the most alien from the biological in any form.

The Contextualist View

The view that I call *contextualist* draws its inspiration from Wittgenstein and has been advocated in various forms by Erroll Bedford (1957), Naomi Scheman (1983), and Robert Kraut (unpub.). The basic thesis can be put like this: *Psychological states are not all in the person* (or, alternatively, *Persons are not all in the skin*; for it might be insisted that persons are the sum of their states wherever these may be). It contrasts particularly with the feeling theory, but also with the others insofar as they cast emotions as states of individuals.

The most restrained version of the contextualist view is that only in a social context can feelings be named and talked about. Anything we talk about we have to learn to talk about. And learning requires public criteria of ascription. In this form, the contextualist view might be thought to have been anticipated by La Rochefoucauld's epigram, that hardly anyone would ever fall in love if they hadn't first read about it. In more pedestrian terms, our knowledge of our emotions is not independent of the social context in which we live. This undermines a common cliché linked to the passivity of emotions and their connection with our "animal nature": the myth of the *naturalness* of emotions. We seem closer here to the more cynical Sartrean view of the emotions as strategies and intentional choices.

According to more radical versions of contextualism, the very existence of emotions depends essentially, like the value of a dollar or the moves of a game, on facts about *conventional consent.* Extreme views have much to teach us, even when we yield to their enticement to reject them. This is certainly an extreme view. Emotions are not merely moves in a game. If they were, it would be hard to make sense of the emotions we comfortably ascribe to the animals: grief, revulsion, rage, boredom, fear. The view is somewhat more credibly applied to emotions highly dependent on convention for their occasions as well as their expression: anger and sympathy, and perhaps certain highly ritualized forms of love. But surely even those have closely related forms for which it is not plausible. We need only think of whatever animal antecedents we can find for anger, sympathy, or love. The main objection to contextualism as a theory of emotions, then, is that, like many antireductionist views, it offers us no avenue through which we might look for the links between more "primitive" and more "elaborate" forms. It turns its back on biology and in this way resuscitates, in a different guise, the errors of old-fashioned dualism.

To claim this, however, is to take seriously the idea that some emotions, or at least some mental states, are more primitive than others. My intuitions favor this idea; yet I will have to concede, in the light of my own discussion in these pages, that the idea of primitives is a very messy one. Moreover, there can be no doubt that every emotional state involves various levels of interpretation of the relevant situation and that these are determined by social context. As Erving Goffman has shown, a shift of "frame" can alter the entire character of a situation: "From an individual's particular point of view, while one thing may momentarily appear to be what is really going on, in fact what is actually happening is plainly a joke, or a dream, or an accident, or a mistake, or a misunderstanding, or a deception, or a theatrical performance . . ." (Goffman 1974, 10). Such shifts must inevitably affect emotion: "If this is 'Candid Camera,' then I feel altogether differently."

So there are insights to be conserved from the contextualist view. Indeed, my own view will turn out to be fairly strongly contextualist. I shall be arguing in later chapters that emotions are best regarded as a kind of perception, the objects of which are what I call *axiological properties.* Our original acquaintance with these properties goes back to our experience of *paradigm scenarios,* little dramas in which our natural capacities for emotional response were first enlisted.

To make this work, however, I shall need to integrate the insights of all the theories I have canvassed. From the feeling theory, we must retain the importance of felt quality. From behaviorism, we must remember that most emotions are intrinsically tied to the organization of our capacities for action, interaction, and reaction. But the evolutionary perspective suggests that those capacities have roots far older than our birth, even when they are most specific to particular individuals. We also need to explore further the fact that for most emotions to be worthy of the name, some physiological change must be involved. The cognitive theory draws our attention to the constitutive role of information. And we must take account of the fact that passion, in spite of its reputation for passivity, is sometimes the very embodiment of the will.

If all these levels are needed, where should we start? According to fashionable wisdom, Nature inclines us to the social. So if I were to follow my biological determinism, I should start with the conventional level. I choose, instead, to be conventional: and convention has it that the bottom level is the biological. So that is where I now turn.

Chapter 3

Emotion and Biology: Physiology and Function

What thou seest when thou dost wake
Do it for thy true love take.
Love and languish for his sake,
Be it ounce, or cat, or bear.
William Shakespeare

What more can we ever do
but hope the chemicals
keep coursing through?
Esmeralda Pernes

Summary

This is the first of two chapters about the biology of emotions. The next will take a broader evolutionary perspective. Here I first examine how thinking about emotions in terms of physiology and "systems design" might further understanding. For of all the aspects of what we call the "mind," emotions are the most deeply embodied. There is also a practical motive, which arises rather naturally in an age of engineering: if we can get to the mechanisms, we'll have better control.

This connection with the physiological is so obvious that some have wanted to define emotions in terms of physiology. For William James, the experience of an emotion was a sort of conscious ricochet of bodily disturbances caused by the apprehension of some object, involving no dedicated centers in the nervous system. (For others, physiological change is merely a necessary component of emotion.)

Objections against James fall into three classes: (1) There is no visceral perception, and it would not help if there were. (But James's claim involves more than the viscera.) (2) The physiological phenomena underlying emotions are just general arousal. Stanley Schachter and Jerome Singer's experiments are generally taken to back up this objection. (But they do not, if physiological changes are taken in a sufficiently fine-grained sense.) (3) There are emotional centers or circuits, located in the limbic system of the brain.

When properly interpreted, surprisingly much of James's theory can be salvaged. It gets a boost from the testimony of paraplegics, as well as from experiments involving facial muscle control. But neither James nor contemporary neuroscience can adequately account for the nature of emotional objects: this sets up a problem to be examined in chapter 5.

The most intriguing upshot of neurophysiological findings on emotions is the modularity of their mechanisms: in freakish cases, our feelings are amazingly independent of the beliefs or situations in which they seem conceptually rooted—rather as in the experience of those dreams in which we can feel terrified by a pencil or lyrical about a pool of blood. Yet we must also account for the fact that this modularity is seldom apparent.

Comparisons between the neurochemical systems underlying emotions and cognitions both support and qualify the surmise that emotions are a kind of perception. This too sets up problems for later: in chapter 6 I shall ask what this implies for the possibility of emotional objectivity; in chapter 7 I shall argue for a new hypothesis about the biological function of emotions in cognition and rationality.

The modularity of emotional mechanisms is mitigated by the fact that we cannot get far without a concept of normal function. (Sometimes, though, normality must be understood as applying strictly to an individual, based on temperamental differences rooted in different physiological thresholds.) The physiological level keeps kicking us upstairs: we cannot understand much about physiological mechanisms except in terms of their roles. This suggests the possibility of a systems or top-down approach.

There are two objections to this, the "top-up" and the "bottom-down" objections. The bottom-down objection is the claim that computers can at best simulate emotions but can no more produce one than they can produce a hurricane. The top-up objection is prompted, in one form, by the "level-ubiquity" of emotions: their peculiar way of interfering, and being susceptible to interference, at every level of thought and activity. In another form, the top-up objection is motivated by a form of the contextualist view, stressing the fact that physiology generates no theory of how emotions can have objects, or any kind of meaning. What is needed to make progress with that problem is a more comprehensive evolutionary perspective.

The Chemistry of Love: Emotion and Physiological Control

The love potion is an ancient fantasy: emotional control by direct chemical means. Often, in the fantasy, scientific verisimilitude is preserved in that the chemical merely lowers a threshold of susceptibility, while the object is supplied by experience. So it is with the potion that makes Titania love the "translated" Bottom. Modern ethologists might call it *chemically induced imprinting:* one is reminded of the famous photographs of goslings following Konrad Lorenz as their mother. (Now that Dorothy Tennov (1979) has renamed love *limerence,* the love potion is called phenylethylamine and has been found in chocolate—see Liebowitz 1983).

The hope of control seems the more urgent because emotions are traditionally blamed—or sought after—for the loss of "mastery" of mind over body. It is an old trope: emotion as madness, as the defeat of the Real Self by something alien to it—depression or ecstasy, manic delight or psychopathic rage. In an age of engineering it is natural to assume that if we can get to the mechanisms underlying our emotional states, we will thereby gain better control over our emotional lives. If the mechanisms are physiochemical, relief—or Brave New World—seems close at hand. And so we view with ambivalent awe the photographs of Jose Delgado (1969) literally stopping the charge of a bull by a remote-controlled electrode in its brain.

But is the hope of emotional control not mere therapy? Why should a philosopher be interested? Two hopes, or fears, depending on one's attitude, are associated with a physiological approach. The first accords with the componential strategy described in the last chapter. It is the prospect of learning from physiology what kinds of emotions there are, which ones are the primitive ones, and how these are compounded into the complex ones. The second is a reductive prospect: it is the idea that in the end emotions are "just chemistry." The reductive program will be strictly fulfilled only if the facts about physiology leave us nothing more to understand about emotions.

In the light of the discussion in chapter 2, complete reduction seems an implausible prospect. But we may still hope, more moderately, that biology might contribute to the *functional analysis* of emotions (in the sense of Cummins 1983) even if they are "emergent," by revealing something about the mechanisms that underlie them. Or so at least I shall be arguing.

Physiology and the Vocabulary of Emotional Description

Philosophers have generally kept aloof from the facts of biology. (Aristotle and Merleau-Ponty are two notable exceptions.) But this stance has been difficult to keep up with respect to emotions. One reason is that ordinary talk about emotions, from slang to poetry, is replete with physiological allusions. Consider, for example, the following common expressions, all of which are used to describe emotion: 'What a pisser', 'to shit a brick', 'to wet your pants' (PS effects);* 'My throat went dry', 'My heart was pounding', 'to break out in a cold sweat' (SS effects); 'to blush, or flush', 'to get hot around the collar', 'My blood ran cold', and innumerable expressions involving the heart (circulatory system); 'It took my breath away', 'I gasped' (respiratory system). 'Blowing hot and cold' is too distant a metaphor perhaps, but 'My love is as a fever' is sometimes a literal reference to temperature. Although it is rare actually to observe someone's "hair standing on end," pilomotor phenomena (hair movements) can be measured in the laboratory and generate well-worn metaphors; some things are literally "hair-raising," though feebly so (at most one gets "goose pimples," or one's "skin crawls"). Sometimes the correlation between organs and emotions is more literary than literal: "In my day, my dear, the organ of love used to be the heart." But consider the following description:

> When I see you, my voice fails
> my tongue is paralyzed,
> a fiery fever runs through my whole body
> my eyes are swimming,
> and can see nothing
> my ears are filled with a throbbing din
> I am shivering all over. . . .

Is this a protocol from a psychophysiological laboratory? No. It is a literal translation of some lines about lust by the poet Sappho, written some twenty-six centuries ago.

These explicit references to bodily manifestations in our common-sense talk of emotions must be explained, or explained away. Even a full-fledged mind-body dualism must meet this challenge. Descartes himself could not resist it: in his theory, the passions (like other forms of perception) temper mind-body dualism. They form, as it were, the systematic analogue of the anatomical pineal gland, connecting body and soul.

---

*The *central nervous system* (CNS) is divided into the *somatic* (SNS), which roughly handles conscious perception and voluntary actions, and the *autonomic* (ANS, sometimes also called "vegetative"), which handles the involuntary regulation of bodily functions. The ANS, in turn, is composed of two subsystems that in part are mutually inhibitory, the *sympathetic* (SS) and the *parasympathetic* (PS). SS uses norepinephrine (a relative of adrenaline) as its principal chemical "messenger" and very roughly has an exciting effect. SS effects include the inhibition of salivation and acceleration of the heart. PS's chemical messenger is acetylcholine, and PS responses include a tendency to contraction of the bladder and defecation. For more details, see Hubbard 1975.

One way to respond to the central role of physiological facts in emotion is to build them into the very definition of emotions. This is the route chosen in William James's famous theory.[1]

William James's Theory

William James's theory is surprisingly similar to that of Descartes (see table 2.1). The main explicit difference concerns the order of causation of the processes involved. James agrees that bodily processes can occur without reaching the threshold of consciousness. But for Descartes the conscious feeling and the bodily changes are caused simultaneously by the exciting object. For James, on the contrary, the feelings are caused *by* the bodily changes. His celebrated formulation has it that "we do not weep because we are sad, but rather we are sad because we weep." The external object (identified as the "exciting" cause in table 2.1) produces both SNS and ANS effects. These play a double role: they prepare the body for a behavioral response, and they are themselves perceived by something like proprioception (feedback from the position or situation of one's own bodily parts). This special proprioception constitutes the state of awareness that *is* the emotion (James 1892, 375).

As James stressed, this view has obvious consequences for the issue of control. If you want to change your emotional state, you might try changing either the ambient scene or your physiological state, whichever is more easily manipulated. (The consequences of this for self-deception are explained in chapter 9.)

So James's model, like that of Descartes, views emotion as a kind of perception. Unlike ordinary sensory perception, however, emotion is not regulated by specialized brain centers:

> If we suppose the cortex to contain centres for the perception of changes in each special sense-organ, in each portion of the skin, in each muscle, each joint, and each viscus, and to contain absolutely nothing else, we still have a scheme perfectly capable of representing the process of the emotions. . . . No new principles have to be invoked, nothing is postulated beyond the ordinary reflex circuit, and the topical centres admitted in one shape or another by all to exist. (James 1884, 140–141)

James's view comprises two theses. One is a claim about the nature of emotional consciousness: that it consists in a kind of perception of our own bodily states, which is sufficient to differentiate the several emotions. The other is about the brain: that it contains no special emotion centers. These two theses may seem independent, but there is a connection. If the brain has special centers for emotion, just as it has visual, auditory, and other perceptual tracts, then it would make little sense to speak of the activation of those centers as a kind of perception of their state. When I look at a candle, some specific parts of my cortex "light up"—as can be directly observed with the aid of some of the new brain-scanning techniques. But my perception of the candle is not a perception of the condition of my visual cortex.

Since James wrote, some fascinating pieces of experimental evidence have come to lend plausibility to the first part of his analysis, though the second has not fared so well.

One experiment is due to a researcher who is himself a paraplegic. George Hohmann (1966) interviewed twenty-five other adult males with spinal cord lesions at varying levels. The subjects reported that the intensity of their *feelings*—especially of anger, fear, and sexual excitement—was significantly diminished even when they were still capable of overt emotional behavior. On the other hand, they also reported "a significant increase in feelings of sentimentality," suggesting perhaps that some emotions are—not surprisingly—more visceral than others. (It is intriguing to speculate whether the results would have been the same with female subjects.) Hohmann concluded that disruption of the autonomic nervous system and its feedback mechanisms impairs emotional feelings and that the impairment is proportional to the extent of neurological damage.

Nevertheless, James's theory is often assumed to have been decisively refuted. It has been attacked from several directions. Some have claimed that we lack the appropriate capacity to perceive our own physiological states and that it wouldn't help if we did. Another line of attack is to claim that the physiological changes involved indicate merely general arousal and could ground no distinctions among different emotions. A third consists in showing that there are, after all, specific circuits that can be identified as "emotion centers."

First Objection: There Is No Visceral Perception,
and It Wouldn't Help Anyway

James Cannon adduced several arguments against James, based on experimental evidence. The first was that animals whose viscera had been disconnected from their brain "behaved with full emotional expression in all the organs still connected with the brain. . . . The absence of reverberation from the viscera did not alter in any respect the appropriate emotional display" (Cannon 1929, 145).

So far this does not refute James. James thought there was a direct path from the excitation of perception to the motor reaction in expressive behavior. So we should expect appropriate behavior whether or not the emotion is felt. Moreover, feedback from the muscular components of expression would remain unaffected by the splitting off of the viscera. On both grounds, cutting out the visceral paths would affect only the *felt* emotion, and only partly at that. But—as Cannon conceded (p. 145)—what his "reduced animals" *felt* they were unable to disclose.

Still, this defense makes an important concession. If ANS activity can be disconnected from behavioral (SNS) manifestations of emotion, then a question arises that James does not address: Which are the defining components of emotion? He cannot reply, "The conscious element alone," for then he would face a dilemma. He could declare that the visceral perception is infallible. But infallible perception is a contradiction in terms. Or he must admit the possible existence of illusory emotions, that is, cases in which the conscious state is as if the viscera were disturbed, but they are not. And this would entail that some other centers or circuits in the brain must be responsible for the illusion.

Second Objection: Emotions Just Involve General Arousal
There is little point in a theory that tells us nothing about the differences between various emotions. Theory demands typology, preferably one that introduces some simplicity. One way to secure this would be to take the atomistic route already canvassed: find a list of primitive emotions, and construct the others out of those. Descartes's choice of primitives (wonder, love, hatred, desire, joy, and sadness) is not implausible, but other classifications have distinguished four, eight, or ten primitive emotions. Most lists overlap in including fear and rage or anger, but no two are alike, and all are about equally plausible (see Plutchik 1980). In the light of such variety, any particular list comes to seem entirely arbitrary.

A fine-grained physiological analysis, however, might offer the promise of a nonarbitrary, biologically based taxonomy. This was indeed James's hope: "The various permutations of which these organic changes are susceptible," he surmised, "make it abstractly possible that no shade of emotion should be without a bodily reverberation as unique, when taken in its totality, as is the mental mood itself" (James 1892, 378). Here James seems to envisage looking to the physiological base for the criteria of identity, the very essence of the various emotions.

This too was attacked by Cannon, who pointed out that the visceral reactions characteristic of emotions differentiate them neither from other phenomena nor from each other. For with respect to visceral reactions, "we should expect not only that fear and rage would feel alike but that chilliness, hypoglycemia, asphyxia, and fever should feel like them" (Cannon 1929, 147). The same conclusion is usually drawn from the well-known experiment of Stanley Schachter and Jerome Singer (1962). Subjects injected with epinephrine (a stimulant of the sympathetic system) tended to interpret the SS arousal symptoms produced either as anger or as euphoria. Which they felt depended on whether they could consider either appropriate. That in turn depended in part on whether they had been informed (or misinformed) about the effects of the injection. If they had been told what to expect—palpitations, flushing, some tremor—the injections had little psychological effect. If not, their reactions varied according to their situation. Some were placed in a room where a stooge was acting angry; others in a room where a stooge was acting silly and euphoric. In both cases the subjects' mood tended to follow that manifested by the stooge. The physiological changes induced via the sympathetic system were not sufficient for the production of any specific emotional state. Further, depending on context, those changes apparently formed the physiological substrate of opposite emotions. The conclusion most frequently drawn is that, although some forms of general arousal are easily labeled in terms of some emotional state, there is no hope of finding in physiological states any principle of distinction between specific emotions. The differentiae of specific emotions are not physiological, but cognitive or something else.*

Nevertheless, such general arousal might be definitionally tied to the presence of emotion. This is the view of William Lyons:

> While there is no conceptual link between the notion of any particular physiological change or any pattern of physiological changes and the concept of any particular emotion, there is a causal connection between the cognitive-evaluative-appetitive part of an emotional state and the concomitant physiological changes. (Lyons 1980, 121)

---

*Actually, the factors that cause Schachter and Singer's subject to evince one emotion rather than another are not "cognitive" in any narrow sense. Schachter and Singer write that "cognitions arising from the immediate situation as interpreted by past experience provide the framework within which one understands and labels his feelings" (p. 174). But the most important factor in their subjects' situation seems to have been the presence of a stooge displaying a certain mood. So if the experiment supports one of the models discussed in chapter 2, it is not the cognitivist, as usually assumed, but the social or contextualist. Perhaps the social situation in which subjects were placed influenced their mood by a phenomenon of imitation. That seems plausible enough from a commonsense point of view. It's hard to remain gloomy in the company of a gay crowd, and at least initially embarrassing to be cheerful in a gloomy one.

What Counts as a Change? The Need for a Concept of Normality   But physiological changes take place all the time. How do we pick out the ones that count as "arousal" and make up an emotion? We need a concept of normal physiological condition, which strictly physiological criteria cannot provide. Two problems will bring this out. The first problem is that the range of physiological changes taken into account in Schachter and Singer's experiment is much too narrow to count seriously against James's view. The second is that the relevant physiological states have no naturally salient boundaries.

The first problem is obvious in the light of the following experimental evidence. Actors and scientists were trained to control specific facial muscles. They were then asked to use this skill to configure their faces purely mechanically rather than by any "method acting" exercise of imagination. This resulted in what looked like emotional expressions. Then certain standard measures were taken, such as finger temperature and heart rates. These measures, as well as their subjective experiences, were found to correspond to the emotions the subjects looked like they were expressing. Facial expressions typical of anger, fear, and sadness caused physiological conditions characteristically different from each other and especially from those of happiness, surprise, and disgust.[2]

To be sure, these effects are weak. And every good actor knows that the cool actor's performance can be totally convincing, whereas the "feeling" actor's emotional expression can be as inept as it is sincere (see Diderot 1981). Still, it seems clear that feedback from the muscles of the face can actually cause both feelings and visceral changes. So if we interpret physiological changes broadly enough, the claim that such changes cannot mark the differences between emotions must be wrong even for complex emotions. For those minute movements in the muscles of the face that Ekman and Friesen have so patiently mapped must obviously, like any other movements, be controlled by determinate neural activity. And so the physiological measures on the basis of which Schachter and Singer and Lyons base their claim about the nonspecificity of the associated physiological events must simply be the wrong measures. The rules of the game must be set out more clearly.

The problem can be put more generally. In one of the standard philosophical treatments of the subject, William Alston writes, "Physiological studies have revealed certain disturbances in normal bodily functioning as regular features of emotional states" (Alston 1967, 481). Alston does not say whether the existence of such disturbances is a sufficient condition of the presence of an emotion or merely a necessary one. But the implication, no less telling for being perhaps unintended, is that normally we have no emotions at all and are better off that way.

What counts as normal? The answer may be partly determined by considerations of efficiency: so again what is hidden in this phrasing is the common idea that emotions are irrational, that they interfere with the smooth unfolding of effective decision making. Sometimes this is no doubt true, if only because policies that were once effective may no longer work in changed circumstances. The hare's zigzag pattern of flight is not a promising strategy for evading a motorist who is trying not to hit it, and the automaticity of its response makes it impossible for the hare to apply its otherwise perfectly adequate capacity to avoid a moving object.

In some of our emotional life, we no doubt resemble the fleeing hare more than we care to admit. But the point I want to stress is this: the criterion of normality introduced by this example belongs not to the physiological level itself but to the level of functional behavior. Yet it is not our activities that Alston dubs abnormal but rather our physiology or "bodily functioning." But from the point of view of physiology, considerations of behavior are imported from a different explanatory level.

William Lyons has tried to avoid this problem by substituting the term 'unusual physiological change' for 'physiological disturbance' or 'bodily upset' (Lyons 1980, 118). He writes that "terms such as 'disturbance' or 'upset' . . . may lead one into the dual error of thinking that all physiological changes associated with emotion are of an alarming or disturbing nature and that all bodily changes associated with emotion are experienced by the subject of them" (p. 116). But this substitution, as Lyons realizes, creates a second problem. In the Heracleitean rivers of our bodily fluids, all is perpetual flux. What then counts as *significant* change? Lyons notes that "physiological changes such as a *decreased* pulse rate and *decreased* respiratory rate . . . also occur in emotional states, when, for example, a person is very happy and feeling unusually calm" (p. 116). True enough, but the observation again seems to betray a curiously limited viewpoint. Given the mechanisms of homeostasis, there is unlikely to be an increase in any chemical or electrical parameter that does not correspond to a decrease in some other. "The activation of the parasympathetic nervous system seems to be at the core of the physiological changes" associated with "relaxing emotions," as Lyons himself stresses in a footnote (p. 117). This is an obvious point: why then does Lyons think he needs to point out that there are decreases as well as increases in the physiological measures we are concerned with?

The answer cannot be that he is concerned merely with experienced physiological change. We have just seen him denounce this as an error. But he still insists that the relevant changes must be ones "of which the subject may or may not be aware depending on the circumstances" (pp. 117–118). Presumably the idea is that if I do become conscious of the changes in question, I will experience them as either increases or decreases of some value. But it needn't be one rather than the other. If I am rendered voiceless, like Sappho, there is a quantity whose measure is less; but is it not tied to another that is greater—constriction of the throat muscles, perhaps?

Lyons's scheme still falls short of taking the notion of physiological changes seriously on its own terms. To take it seriously, we might start by establishing *statistical norms* for the relevant physiological parameters. We would decide whether someone has an emotion much as we decide whether she has a fever: by taking measurements, as we might take a temperature.

Every biological parameter spreads its values over a normal distribution curve. Just as every individual has a slightly different normal temperature and heartbeat, so each person's emotional measurements would have to be calibrated individually to determine her "normal" unemotional state. Now suppose the level of some hormone in A is "normally" the same as the level of the same hormone in B when B is emotionally agitated. Are we to infer that A is perpetually in the condition that B is in only when upset? Or should we simply conclude that A and B have different temperaments? Or suppose A's measurements are consistently higher than B's, everywhere except in their sleep. Should we conclude that A's normal or unemotional level is lower (or higher) than B's?

The methodological requirement of calibration suggests one answer—something like *align all base lines*. But the hope of finding a basis for classifying people in terms of emotional tone or temperament—to describe one person as relaxed or "laid back" and another as anxious or "uptight"—argues for the contrary answer. So, too, does the practical utility of viewing some persons as permanently outside the normal range of some given measure, on the basis of complex inter- *and* intrapersonal norms. Uncontroversial examples of such a situation are any of those where a pathological condition, such as diabetes, phenylketonuria, or manic-depressive cycles, is corrected by maintenance doses of a drug intended to make good some biological deficiency.* A similar dilemma will arise with respect to the

---

*According to some neurologists, the so-called hyperactive child is actually in a condition of abnormally low arousal, similar to that of a "normal" subject in a very tired,

amount of change brought about in each individual by typical emotional stimuli. On a purely physiological measure, larger changes mean more intense emotions; but if we relativize such judgments to individuals, then interpersonal comparisons of emotional intensity will be meaningless.

These difficulties cannot be overcome if the physiological level is considered in isolation. For one more illustration, consider the case of pain.[3]

Among many puzzles about pain is the fact that in different people the same stimulus appears to cause different levels of pain. Is this because some people are more stoical than others? Do the same stimuli have different effects depending on circumstances? Or are some people less sensitive to pain?

According to Ronald Melzack, this last option is not available:

> It is often supposed that . . . people are . . . physiologically different from one another so that one person may have a low threshold (and feel pain after slight injury), while another has a high threshold (and feels pain only after intense injury). There is now evidence that all people, regardless of cultural background, have a uniform *sensation threshold*—that is, the lowest stimulus value at which sensation is first reported. (Melzack 1973, 24)

Yet Melzack describes astonishing cultural differences in reactions to physical stimuli. Celebrants of certain cults are able to hang from a hook planted in the muscles of their back and don't seem to mind much at all. Even within our own culture, war, sport, and childbirth commonly seem to call forth extraordinary responses to typically painful traumas. Such differences must be attributed to psychological factors affecting the neurophysiological mechanisms responsible for pain. The salient surface mechanisms—stimuli that most people would think sufficient to cause intense pain—may well be the only ones of which it is possible to be directly aware. But these may be far from the only determinants of the feeling of pain (see Dennett 1978b).

Very likely the lesson drawn here holds a fortiori for more complex emotions. The peripheral bodily changes have drawn our attention because they are noticeable from both inside and out. But the deep

---

bored, and fidgety condition. This hypothesis explains the "paradoxical" effect of Ritalin, a stimulant used to treat hyperactivity. Whereas in a normal subject Ritalin would cause an anxious or "overfocused" condition, in the hyperactive subject it merely brings the arousal level up to normal. See Dalby et al. 1977.

mechanisms are likely to be inaccessible to direct observation either by the subject or by others.

This has a paradoxical consequence for the issue of control. Even when we understand the minute details of the underlying physiology of emotions, our best prospects for their manipulation may not lie at that level. Instead, it may be at the psychological level after all—whether through biofeedback, psychoanalysis, or even old-fashioned exhortations to keep a stiff upper lip.

In sum, then, although the evidence is not all unequivocal, *the criteria of individuation of the relevant physiological states are not exclusively physiological. Instead, they are drawn at least in part from the functional vocabulary of needs, behavior, and judgments of normality.* We shall see how this continues to be valid when we turn to more serious attempts to find, pace James, emotional centers and circuits in the brain.

Third Objection: There Are Emotional Brain Centers
There has been much debate, over the past century or so of brain research, about the extent to which the functions of the mind can be localized. One standard method here is that of "cutting and snipping." The idea is to snip, cut, or cauterize some zone of the brain—or wait for some judicious accident to accomplish the same result—and observe the effects. The aim is to arrive at *localizations of functions.* These localizations, in turn, will help to classify mental phenomena.

The most telling blow to James's theory has emerged from the finding, in the brain research of the past sixty years or so, that there are indeed "centers" in the brain that specifically control at least the more obvious components of emotion states. These centers or modules comprise circuits of the *limbic system.* This is roughly the inner layer of the brain, below the cortical structures that control the processing of incoming information and the planning of voluntary behavior, and above the brainstem and cerebellum, which control balance, reflexes, and purely stereotypic instinctive behavior.[4] To give the flavor of this research, I now sketch some ideas of two representative neuroscientists, Paul MacLean and Jaak Panksepp.

MacLean's Triune Brain   In a series of fascinating papers Paul MacLean has argued that we have, in effect, three brains:

> In its evolution the primate forebrain expands along the lines of three basic patterns that may be characterized as reptilian, paleomammalian, and neomammalian. . . . There results a remarkable linkage of three cerebrotypes which are radically different in

chemistry and structure and which in an evolutionary sense are eons apart. There exists, so to speak, a hierarchy of three-brains-in-one, or what I call, for short, a *triune brain*. (MacLean 1975, 13–14)

This idea has an intriguing consequence in terms of the taxonomy of models of the mind presented in the last chapter. On MacLean's hypothesis, there is a literal basis to the idea of *inner conflict*. Plato and Freud were right: whatever divisions must be made within the brain are not confined to functional ones. Since the different "layers" of the brain are all connected with both the sensory and the motor areas of the cortex, they can conflict very much in the way envisaged by traditional divisions of the soul.

Once again, this casts light on the issue of emotional control with which I opened this chapter. MacLean puts the point more picturesquely: "We might imagine that when a psychiatrist bids the patient to lie on the couch, he is asking him to stretch out alongside a horse and a crocodile" (MacLean 1960, 300).

Another equally speculative consequence will acquire more weight as the argument of this book proceeds. If the limbic system is old mammalian equipment, this could mean that emotions evolved only with a relatively advanced and flexible degree of intelligence. A horse may need emotive circuits, but a crocodile has no use for them.

The possibility of conflict between the different "brains" must not be confused with their mutual isolation. The limbic brain, according to MacLean, plays a vital role in the regulation of the whole system and is extensively connected with the cortex or "neomammalian" brain. For more detail, I turn to Jaak Panksepp.

Panksepp's Control Circuits Like MacLean, Panksepp (1982) starts from the premise that the key neurophysiological changes underlying emotional states take place in certain hard-wired brain circuits of the limbic system, which humans have in common with other mammals. On this assumption, we can make sense of the notion of "primitive" emotions on the basis of a convergence of four distinct criteria, which work together to yield a taxonomy of basic emotions. In addition, Panksepp lists six characteristics definitive of emotions as a genus (labels are mine):

1.–2. *Innate adaptiveness* and *motivation*. The relevant circuits are set up to motivate appropriate behavior in "major life-challenging circumstances." Emotions, says Panksepp, "organize behavior by activating or inhibiting classes of related actions (and concurrent autonomic/hormonal changes) which have proved adaptive" (p. 411).

(It is not clear from this characterization whether the "concurrent" changes are side effects of the needs of behavioral organization or in some way functional in themselves.)

'Adaptiveness' is a term to be taken with caution. To call a trait adaptive does not mean it must do its bearer some recognizable good now (see chapter 4). Adaptation is a historical fact—or more likely a prehistorical one. It is therefore subject to speculative reconstruction. In the case of the basic emotive circuits, however, the benefits are likely to be sufficiently obvious to be safely inferred by relatively coarse methods.

3. *Sensory salience control.* Because of their links to the sensory and motor cortex and the existence of feedback, emotive circuits "change the sensitivities and responsivities of sensory systems" (compare chapter 2, on Skinner's second-order dispositions).

4. *Inertia.* "The activity in the underlying neural systems can outlast the precipitating circumstances . . ." (p. 411).

5. *Associative learning capacity.* We can learn to respond emotionally to stimuli that are new not only as particulars but also generically. The latitude allowed is presumably limited by the effect of the other innate circuits, as well as by any modifications of them already entrenched by previous learning.

Here a large rabbit gets into the hat. Like all the theories I have considered so far, Panksepp's account ignores the question of development. How do we come by our adult repertoire of emotions? What modes of learning are involved in acquiring responses that are "generically new"? And how new is that? (I shall discuss these issues in chapter 7.)

6. *Projection into consciousness.* "Activity in such circuits has access to and reciprocal interactions with brain mechanisms which elaborate consciousness" (p. 411).[5]

One consequence of this scheme is that a number of "primitive affective states" that have traditionally been regarded as emotions will not be so viewed, because they fail to meet some of these criteria. These include "surprise" and "disgust," which fail to "activate diverse classes of species-typical behaviors" (criterion 1) and lack "sustained regenerative feedback in the underlying brain system" (criterion 4); also pleasure and distress, because they are too "generalized" and appear to "cut across many distinct emotive states" (p. 411). Such exclusions should be welcome as indicating that the theory is not woolly toothless, although in my own usage in this book I shall sometimes be more lax.

What then of the taxonomy yielded by this method? Panksepp's primitive emotions are related to his four "behavioral control systems"—the "expectancy," "rage," "fear," and "panic" circuits (p. 414). And his claim to be offering more than just another list of primitives is that the verdicts of the four control systems are *convergent*. Anatomy, behavior, neurochemistry, and subjective experience all support the same classification.

Anatomically, though the systems in question are all located in MacLean's limbic system, they involve distinct neural pathways.

The *behavioral* patterns to which they give rise, Panksepp claims, each make sense as units. The four circuits respectively give rise to exploratory and appetitive behavior; attack, including biting; flight behavior; and vocal and other behavior characteristic of loss or grief.

The behavioral patterns identified correspond more or less to general needs or responses to important life-situations, but they are not specific (p. 413). They do not, for example, program precise sequences of sexual behavior. What they seem to do instead is facilitate the initiation of such activities, as well as sensitize the animal's appropriate receptors. Once again we are confronting the fact that emotions are second-order phenomena: they organize sequences of behavior in orderly ways, but they do not specifically program them.

If Panksepp's hypothesis is confirmed, one may expect that each circuit will have a characteristic *neurochemistry*. It is not clear whether this has yet been shown. Neurotransmitters vary in the specificity of their effects. Serotonin and norepinephrine, for example, appear to have complementary effects on general arousal. But dopamine and acetylcholine seem to be specifically associated, as mutual inhibitors, with the command circuits for expectancy and rage, respectively (p. 419).

As for the characteristic *experiences* to which they give rise, Panksepp suggests that they can provide the key to what's what in the emotional circuits. Introspection can even tell us something, by analogy, about other animals.

Perhaps Panksepp hoped to shock his hardheaded colleagues by the anthropomorphism of his references to introspection. Introspection is hard to check for either reliability (the correlation between different occasions of testing for the same thing) or validity (correspondence with some objective parameter). The phenomenology of emotions evokes names such as Proust or Freud, whose skepticism about emotional self-knowledge has been amply confirmed by experimental evidence.[6] In fact, however, the identification of Panksepp's "behavioral control systems" is rather less anthropomorphic than he thinks. Whereas the names of these circuits are suggestive of our commonsense emotional vocabulary, the principles of distinction among them owe more to general biological and ethological commonplaces about the nature and kinds of "life-challenging circumstances" faced by mammals (p. 421). Once again, our understanding of physiological mechanisms essentially relies on functional principles imported from other levels of analysis.

Still, if the criteria all fit, though they come from different theoretical levels, that makes for impressive corroboration. How good, we must ask, is the alleged convergence?

For a test case, consider the "panic" command system, which Panksepp describes as perhaps "the most controversial" of his systems. It is the system related to attachment, social loss, and grief (p. 411). Panksepp notes that there are "similarities . . . between the underlying neurochemical dynamics of opiate addiction and social dependence" (p. 417), which is suggestive. There is also a promising point of contact with the clinical and theoretical work of John Bowlby on attachment emotions. For example, Bowlby (1969) found that at least one stage of infantile reaction to loss is a hostility very reminiscent of the "explosive behaviors" of Panksepp's "panic circuit."

But what are we to make of the claim that the *desire* for social contact turns out to belong to a different basic command system than the fear of its loss? From the point of view of introspection, this seems arbitrary. But from the points of view of anatomy, neurochemistry, and evolutionary history, it may be convincing. So may the separation between the fear of loss and "fear" proper—which is another command circuit altogether. Why should anxiety be part of fear and not panic? How are the "explosive behaviors" of panic different from manifestations of rage? Answers to these questions based on introspective grounds seem to conflict with the neurological evidence.

If they conflict, which should we believe? Surely, it might be argued, here, if anywhere, phenomenology must prevail. Science can identify reasonably coherent patterns of brain activity (including the production of neurotransmitters) and behavioral responses, but only introspection can tell us what different emotions are.

The errors of this insistence on the primacy of introspection, however, are by now well known. The revelations of introspection may ultimately be explicable, but the taxonomies based on them may not turn out to be important. Such is the case with all things biological: many criteria must be juggled at once, and surface similarities and differences are just that—on the surface (see Nisbett and Wilson 1977).

The Story So Far

What then of James? I argued that if we take "bodily changes" broadly, his theory stands up well to Cannon's objections. Much of the experience of emotion may well be caused by feedback from peripheral muscles, especially those involved in emotional expression. I shall return to some implications of this idea for the concept of self-deception in chapter 9.

On the other hand, James was clearly wrong in claiming that emotions did not stem from special brain centers. Should we then infer (much as Russell once claimed that we only ever see our retina) that all we ever really feel is the condition of our limbic system? The answer to this is no; but the question turns out to be complicated, and I defer it until we come to the variety of objects of emotions (chapter 5) and consider the analogy between emotion and perception (chapter 6).

In the meantime we have seen that we need a comprehensive approach, fitting various perspectives together. For any given "life-challenging circumstance" and its characteristic associated response patterns, many factors need to be taken into account. Here is a list of some we have gathered so far:

1. The differential involvement in that situation of particular structures of the brain (MacLean's reptilian, limbic, and neomammalian brain structures).

2. The operation of characteristic neurotransmitters, if there are any.

3. The significance of diverse "temperaments" for various styles of arousal and behavior.

4. The unreliable character of introspective consciousness. Introspection is prone to constructing rationalizations or confabulations that have a powerful hold on our convictions but may ultimately have to be rejected.

5. Threshold levels and characteristic releasing stimuli, and how these might be modified.

6. Cybernetic factors (the type of information flow that might be characteristically involved in the different systems): how feedback loops enhance or inhibit some parts of the sensory system relatively to others, how cognitive factors influence the ANS and visceral response, and so on.

7. Finally, and largely as a corollary of the other factors listed, there will be differences in accessibility to various methods of emotional modification and control: differential responses to drugs, to biofeedback, to conscious learning, to standard behavior-modification techniques, and to psychotherapeutic insight.

Given sufficient complexity, practical and explanatory goals converge. A partial explanation of the mystery of temperament, for example, might be sought in differences of thresholds among the three brains. (Perhaps the crocodile, though more lethal, takes longer to rouse than the horse.) This, too, could have practical consequences, especially for the education and control of emotion. There might be physiological hard-wiring behind the Freudian idea that repression of the id is the riskier for trying to be total. Conversely, observed differences in emotional plasticity will reverberate back to increase our understanding of effects now little understood: differential responses to pain; the mechanisms of acupuncture, biofeedback, and placebos; individual differences in responses to alcohol and cannabis; correlations between emotional temperament and humor, "field dependency," expressiveness, aesthetic preferences, and even body types. Perhaps in the combination of all these factors we can hope to find a complexity to match the subtleties of Proust.

While waiting for other people to do all this interesting research, let me stress three aspects of the physiology of emotions that I find philosophically suggestive: its modularity, the importance of thresholds, and the links between emotions and cognition.

Moderate Modularity
The fierce battles that once raged over the issue of localization have died down (see Geschwind 1979; Rosenfield 1985). Most researchers now seem to agree on some basic facts of localization: the emotions would not exist if we had only a neocortex; they would not exist if we had no thalamus and hypothalamus. And although ablation of the frontal lobes is reputed to leave one somewhat listless, no amount of functional substitution in the neocortex can replace the limbic system. But beyond that, belief in Gall-type localization of brain "centers" has yielded to the notion of *functional modules* and to the search for intelligible *circuits* controlling them. Ever since Broca's studies of the neurological correlates of aphasia, it has been known that interfering with certain parts of such circuits, by either stimulation or ablation, can cause partial functional deficits (see Geschwind 1979; Crick 1979). Let us call these *microfunctions:* one example in the domain of cognitive functions is the ability to recognize written speech; another, the capacity to understand it. Both are part of "the speech function" in general, but experienced deficits prove them to be sepa-

rate microfunctions, consisting in their turn of more subtle microfunctions (see Crick 1979).

Similarly, emotional feelings, far from being definitive of emotions, turn out to be subsidiary microfunctions. MacLean reports that lesions or artificial stimulation in certain precise locations of the limbic system have produced "feelings of terror, fear, sadness, depression, foreboding, familiarity or strangeness, reality or unreality, wanting to be alone, paranoid feelings, and anger" (MacLean 1970, 341). These laboratory findings merely confirm experiences with which we are all familiar from our own dreams: sometimes we might be terrified by an egg, or enchanted by a saucer of mud. Feelings are microfunctions: they can be completely dissociated either from the accompanying behavior or from any normal eliciting situation; but as we shall see in chapter 4, this does not imply that all motivations, or all emotions, are equally intelligible.

Microfunctions can affect emotional expression as well as feeling, as one more story will illustrate. E. D. Ross (1984) tells of an otherwise normal schoolteacher who, as a result of injury in the right hemisphere (not the limbic system), became incapable of expressive intonation in speech. She despaired of keeping order in class, because she had completely lost the ability to sound angry. This made it impossible for the children to take her efforts to discipline them seriously. Such an incapacitation is picturesquely called *aprosodia*, by analogy with some of the aphasias that result from left-brain traumas. (Just as some forms of aphasia involve the inability to understand speech, and others to produce it, so there seem to be "sensory aprosodias" in which expressive intonation can be produced but not recognized.)

These phenomena and others already discussed suggest that, from a strictly neurophysiological point of view, the various constituents of what we usually call "emotions" can be pried apart. On the other hand, there is also evidence that when normal connections are not severed, the limbic system's command modules control coherent activity, not just disconnected bits. It seems that when aggression is elicited by direct stimulation of the hypothalamus, its targets are not random but instead fit previously established social dominance relations (Panksepp 1982, 416).

The separateness of the microfunctions indicates only that they are different parts of overall mechanisms that, when they function normally, are all of a piece. The modularity involved is limited by the fact that in the exercise of any particular function several mechanisms will work together, and also by the uncanny capacity of emotions to interfere and be interfered with by other functions at various other levels. This is the previously mentioned level-ubiquity of emotions.

Even limited modularity gives credibility to the idea of different temperaments. It supports the speculation that some people are more expressive than others without necessarily being more "emotional" in any broader sense, or, conversely, that some people may feel more than they express. And in turn, provided we are willing to accept a strong connection between the physiological pathways that Papez called the "feeling stream" and conscious feeling, we can speculate that some people's "feeling microfunctions" or "expressive microfunctions" are more active than those of others. This promises to give concrete meaning to the otherwise meaningless speculation that some people feel more than they show and others less.

The Importance of Thresholds
A growing number of chemicals are implicated in the circuitry of emotions. These include—to name a few—sex hormones such as testosterone, estradiol, and progesterone; the pituitary releasing-hormones that control them; neurotransmitters such as acetylcholine, serotonin, and dopamine; opiate-like endorphins (for a natural but still addictive high); and our fabled love potion, the amphetamine-related phenylethylamine. Some of those chemicals appear to be involved in general arousal. This might explain why a certain amount of fear or aggression seems sometimes to be an aphrodisiac. In one experiment, for example, heterosexual male subjects seemed more interested in sex after being interviewed on a fear-arousing suspension bridge by a female experimenter than when interviewed on a low bridge; when they were interviewed by a male experimenter, no difference was noted (Dutton and Aron 1974).

Apart from those cases, however, one might find it tempting to think of this chemical variety as correlated with the wide range of felt emotions. Could it be that every neurotransmitter is specifically responsible for a basic emotion? Panksepp was tempted by this speculation. But it is rendered implausible by findings such as the discovery of endorphins in the retina, where they appear to have nothing to do with the suppression of pain or the induction of euphoria. The functions of dopamine provide another example: too much is associated with schizophrenia; too little causes Parkinson's disease. That fact is no reason to think that schizophrenia and Parkinson's disease are in some obscure sense mutual antagonists. More likely the chemical has different functions in different locations: different circuits need to be kept separate and yet related. The variety of chemicals might be analogous to the use of several colored inks in a diagram. No ink—and no chemical—has a specific function; but all are used in different places to different effects, as the need arises for telling apart distinct but adjoining processes.

Nevertheless, the role of chemical agents is important for another reason. Chemicals exist in varying concentrations, and their effect depends on the existence of suitable receptors. This makes them intrinsically different from a purely mechanical or electrical signaling system. It strongly suggests that apart from their role in the transmission of signals the neurotransmitters and other chemicals involved act by affecting certain *thresholds of reactivity*. So the greater the role of chemicals in emotions, the more we should think of them as laying the groundwork for specific reactions and states of mind, rather than providing what we might think of as "finished" or complete perceptual states. This most literally fits the notion of a *mood*, which involves no specific object but only a certain class of dispositions toward various objects. But it may also apply more than we think to emotions that do have objects, as suggested by the intuitive plausibility of the conceit in this chapter's epigraph from Shakespeare.

This supports a general hypothesis anticipated by Descartes: emotions can be thought of as perceptual or cognitive. But they are not straightforward perceptions: rather, they are "second-order." They modify and condition perception, providing framework, not detail (see chapters 6 and 7).

Emotive-Cognitive Links

There is a twist worth noting to the idea of emotions as contributing to our cognitive equipment. Remember that neurotransmitters are involved in cognitions as well as emotion. They are responsible for the transmission of nervous impulses at every synapse. And we know from ordinary experience that cognition is susceptible to threshold effects too. (We take caffeine to keep alert.) Melvin Konner cites evidence that weak electrical stimulation of the amygdala in cats produces signs of alertness, whereas an increased current produces signs of fear—suggesting that alertness and fear are "mere points" on "a continuum of arousal."[7] And Rosenfield (1985) has suggested that the neurophysiological phenomena underlying depression might be an intensification of those produced by frustrated search.

Does this collapse the contrast between the cognitive and the emotive?

Not quite. The body's internal information-bearing systems are of two kinds: fast and slow. Roughly, the fast comprises the nervous system, and the slow comprises the chemical-hormonal. The distinction is not a strict one. Every cell in the nervous system communicates with others via chemical neurotransmitters. Some of these, the neuropeptides, are closely related in chemical structure to the hormones; all are analogous to hormones in the way they do their work. And the stimulation of the nervous system commonly results in modifications of the chemical balance in the hormonal system. Unlike electrical impulses, however, chemical messengers are not led to their destinations by following specific channels. Instead, they are diffused (though sometimes in highly circumscribed regions of the brain) and picked up by specific preadapted receptors.

These "slow" systems introduce a complication for the hypothesis that emotions are a kind of perception. Efficient perception is by definition *covariant with the environment*. A system involving slow-acting bodily modifications as information bearers must violate that condition. How much can remain, then, of the plausibility of the model of perception? This is the problem of *objectivity*, which will be taken up in detail in chapter 6. For the moment a hint will suffice: if emotion is dependent, not on some simple external stimulus or state of affairs alone, but on a complex that includes states of the organism as well as states of the outside world, then interpreting its deliveries as *information* may require that we assign any relevant properties to the complex as a whole, and not to any of its parts alone.

Apart from this qualification, the present section has softened, from the neurophysiological point of view, the usual contrast between the emotive and the cognitive. But we have also found evidence for potential conflict. For, if MacLean is right, much of the processing that constitutes emotion occurs in parallel, rather than in strict collaboration, with the activities of the cortex. That too, of course, finds notorious echoes in our experience. But here again the cognitive may turn out to be more like the emotional than we had assumed emotion could be like cognition. This is at least one possible explanation for the pervasive irrationality in our intuitive reasoning.

The Systems Approach: Top-Down Biology

In terms of the typology of methods outlined in chapter 2, I have been exploring a "bottom-up" approach to the emotions. But at every turn low-level taxonomies have had to be informed by higher-level functions. Emotions have been found to adjust thresholds, to organize responses to biologically important predicaments of life, to be moderately modular, and to be linked with cognition. Is this not enough to justify looking into a computational approach? Perhaps the correct strategy is to give up—for the moment—on physiology. Instead, taking a leaf from the book of artificial intelligence, we could just *make it all up,* starting from considerations about the causal roles that emotions play in the economy of our lives.

Top-Up and Bottom-Down

It is frequently assumed that such a strategy would lead us nowhere. In fact, emotions are often said to be the last and impassable frontier of computationalist theories of mind. The reasons for this stem from two diametrically opposed considerations. I call them the *top-up* and the *bottom-down* objections to computationalist accounts of emotions. The bottom-down objection is that emotions, of all our mental states, are the most likely to derive directly from our physiological constitution—that they have too much to do with our hormones and too little to do with anything that might be programmed. Georges Rey has put it like this:

> Having some semblance of [human emotional life] requires having as well some semblance of human physiology; in particular, having at least something like our system of hormones and neuroregulators . . . we so far have no reason whatever to believe that the actions and interactions of the hormonal with the cognitive system involve any rational relations among representations at all. The relations that do obtain appear to be merely causal ones. . . . (Rey 1980, 190–191)

If this objection is warranted, then we should persevere with a more physiological approach. Yet it is hard to keep the physiological level clean of intrusive functional categories, imported from other levels. The reasons for this bring me to the top-up objection.

The top-up objection arises from a contextualist perspective: emotions cannot be understood in terms of computational models, because they are *suprasemantic.* The involve our sense of self, our essential subjectivity, as well as our interpersonal relations; they are tied to history, to "forms of life."

So the program of approaching the emotions from a computational point of view falls under attack from both sides. In fact, these attacks are not as mutually antagonistic as they seem. A brief look at a classic distinction made in cognitive science will help to explain why.

It is one thing to implement a certain type of process, and another to implement a theory of it. The former produces the process, whereas the latter merely describes it. Unfortunately, the word 'simulation' has been used in both senses. Some critics of artificial intelligence (AI), such as John Searle (1980), insist that functionalist models of mind no more exemplify intelligent behavior than a computer model of the weather produces real hurricanes. Others, like Kenneth Sayre (1986), claim that because the basic processes postulated by functionalist models are of the same nature as those that take place in the computer—consisting in information processing—the contrast is inapplicable. So long as the actual information processing going on in the model is of the right kind, the postulated processes are "psychologically real." Processes of this sort, I shall say, *break the simulation barrier.*

To break the simulation barrier in this sense is not a sufficient condition for the production of an authentic mental state. The reason is that it does not imply that the relevant state might be produced in isolation. There are further constraints on psychological reality. The information processing in question must take place in the context of a certain kind of system; it must embody certain capacities; and it must have the right sort of causal history. Such conditions may be required by any answer to the question, How did the meaning get into the machine? For suppose we duplicated every detail of the functional organization of a system.* Suppose further that the duplicate actually functioned, at the microlevel as well as the level of input/output, exactly as do certain circuits in the brain, when someone has the thought that "water is transparent." Still, this would not amount to a thought that water is transparent, for roughly the sort of reason Aristotle had for denying that a severed hand is still a hand.[8] To give this difficulty a label, I shall refer to it as the *contextual barrier.*

In sum, there are two quite different questions about whether a certain system constitutes a genuine implementation or merely a simulation. One question is whether the artificial system implements the basic operations involved in the working of the natural one. No computer actually condenses moisture, produces air currents, or changes barometric pressure. Therefore, no computer breaks the simulation barrier for the weather. Yet conceivably the kind of thing that the computer does when it "simulates" the weather is sufficiently like the kind of things that go on in our brains when we *think* about the weather. But even if the basic operations are the ones that are being carried out by the computer, it is a separate requirement that they be carried out in a context in which they can be not merely symbolic operations but meaningful ones. To meet that second requirement is to break the contextual barrier.

---

*This might turn out to require type-identity of matter at some level, so as to avoid the charge that the two systems were not really functionally equivalent because at some level of decomposition their behavior could be told apart. For the present argument, it does not matter how stringently the equivalence is specified. One can even imagine doing it with actual organic cells artificially put together in a completely "realistic" way.

Armed with this distinction, we can reinterpret the bottom-down and top-up objections. The bottom-down objection says that no computational model can break the simulation barrier, because the processes that emotions consist in are not essentially computational. Emotions, as many have suspected on other grounds, are more like hurricanes than thoughts. The top-up objection says that no amount of programming can break the contextual barrier, because emotions are complete forms of life.

The Simulation Barrier   Some actual attempts at "computer simulation" of emotions will illustrate the bottom-down problem.

In the 1960s and 1970s a psychoanalyst-turned-computer-scientist, Kenneth Colby, programmed a simulation of a paranoid patient. This program, called "Parry," gained some notoriety for having fooled a number of psychiatrists into thinking they were talking to a human patient.[9] Here is Margaret Boden's summary description of Colby's (1973) model:

> Each belief . . . has a number, or "charge," associated with it that reflects the degree of emotional importance it has within the mind in question. These charges vary during the running of the program in a way corresponding to what, according to psychoanalytic theory, goes on in the person's mind. In addition, there are five numbers ("monitors") representing the emotional states of anxiety, excitation, pleasure, self-esteem, and well-being. These also fluctuate according to circumstances. The emotional monitors make a difference to the thinking that goes on, for they influence the fate of individual beliefs and help to select the particular defense mechanism employed when the system experiences psychological conflict. (Boden 1977, 24)

Another psychologist, Robert P. Abelson (1973), tried to model the effect of ideology on a belief system based on Barry Goldwater's. Abelson's programs make use of the notion of a *script*, in which events, actions, and transactions characteristic of a certain setting take place. The system consults the script (which might list the sort of things that standardly happen in a restaurant, for example) and uses it to interpret experience. A script, again in the words of Boden, is "potentially dynamic in that it can be used to show how the system's knowledge is deployed in constructing its subjective world and in interpreting new information consistently with its preexisting viewpoint" (Boden 1977, 72–73).

Later I shall expand on the notion of paradigm scenario, which bears some resemblance to the scripts of AI. For the moment I only note several points of contact between these ideas and the biological ones I have been discussing.

1. *Scripts* are programmed analogues to Panksepp's organized command modules. Both contribute motivation and organize response to some limited set of circumstances. And both in effect interpret the current situation and determine what sensorimotor resources to bring to bear.

2. Abelson's scripts and Colby's "charges" act on existing knowledge. This parallels the threshold control of the chemical systems.

3. The way that scripts work seems to mirror the limited access to cognition that emerged as a characteristic of emotion. Once engaged on a script, a computer may not deal appropriately with radically incompatible input. In this way scripts mirror the "inertial" effects of emotions.

Nevertheless, the Colby and the Abelson models surely fail to break the simulation barrier. The emotional factor in both of these programs is just "canned." It lacks a feature that seems most essential to real emotions: that the assigned values (or their dynamic interconnections) be a consequence of the sorts of material conditions of their implementation surveyed earlier in this chapter: the speed of hormonal diffusion, the physiological effects of SS stimulation, and so forth.

What would be needed to satisfy this condition? Let me offer one speculation.

Perhaps a machine that has emotions will have to "compute" only in the sense that a soap-bubble computer computes. If you want to find out the shortest path linking four points, you can work it out mathematically: that is computation in the ordinary sense. Or you can plant four nails in a board, top them with another board, and dip the whole construction into a soap solution. You will find that soap films settle into a position linking the points, instantiating just the desired solution. Yet the soap bubbles have not exactly *computed* a solution, although this sort of device is sometimes called an "analog computer" (see Dewdney 1985). The solution has arisen more directly from the physical setup itself. A number of models of the brain have recently been proposed that share this feature, that they all perform the equivalent of a sophisticated computation just by virtue of their "functional architecture" (see Pylyshyn 1984), that is, the causal powers inherent in their physical matter and structure.[10] Perhaps, then, the way that emotions emerge out of the complex interaction of biological factors somehow resembles the way that the soap bubble falls elegantly into place, virtually instantaneously, to solve, without computation, a difficult computational problem.

The Contextual Barrier   What of the top-up objection? As so far formulated it is rather vague, and anyway too large for this chapter. Yet in one sense it can be easily dismissed. The argument is simple and begins by granting the essential point: no human emotion, and perhaps no interesting semantics, can exist independently of relations between the members of something like our human community. So if a robot were to have emotions in the full sense, it too would have to belong to some community. (In subsequent chapters I shall begin to explore some of the conditions on the relevant relationships.) But that leaves untouched the question of whether there is a set of functional conditions that must be satisfied for an organism to have such relationships. And that returns us to the simulation barrier.

Two somewhat narrower concerns, however, help motivate the top-up objection: the *level-ubiquity* of emotions and the problem of *intentionality.*

The Level-Ubiquity of Emotions

A crucial feature of human life, deriving from its sheer complexity, is that almost any activity can be modified and interrupted, not only from the outside but also by some other internal "module." In the middle of reading, you may get hungry. Or if you are truly absorbed, you may forget to eat for many hours. In the midst of the transports of lust, you may remember an important telephone call. And so on. Much of this is organized by the structure of our appetites, emotions, and short- or long-term goals. But it may not be organized in any unique *hierarchy,* with a single controlling system at the center of it all. Instead, each of us may comprise a radical *heterarchy,* in which many partial systems work in parallel, of which any one can take over control according to need (see Hofstadter 1979). To the extent that this possibility undermines the top-down model, it seems to support something like the top-up objection to computationalism. Ordinary computers require a single master program that calls subroutines as required. In a heterarchic system there is no master program.

It is not clear that this is much of an objection to a more general conception of the computer modeling of emotions, rather than a reason to proceed with the exploration of heterarchic models. But it does serve to remind us of some important facts.

Given the biological complexity I have described, there seems to be no single principle governing mutual interrupts and adjustments. In my "instinctive" fear of a threatening bear, my reactions might range from idiotic and provoking flight to the trained tactics of an experienced camper. On the other hand, Freud has taught us to suspect that the most cerebral of activities may be driven by unconscious passions—that in the scholarly curiosity that has kept you reading this far, for example, you might be driven by infantile scotophilia. Moreover, entire emotional syndromes may themselves be objects of emotional appraisal. One may love love, hate jealousy, despise contempt, resent enthusiasm. And such second-order emotions may or may not be effective in controlling their first-order objects.

Aaron Sloman and Monica Croucher distinguish several possible measures of the power to modify and interrupt. The *intensity* of a motive is its power to attract attention, which is not necessarily the same as its *importance* or strength. Importance measures a motive's "power to be selected for action, and to override alternative motives." Both differ from *urgency,* which has to do with time: "Something not wanted very much can be urgent" (Sloman and Croucher 1981, 200). And I might be intensely preoccupied with something that is neither important nor urgent. Moreover, any further scrutiny of the dimension of "importance" would pulverize it into indefinitely many special dimensions.

In short, emotions operate at every level of the organization of the person. That is what I mean by saying that they are level-ubiquitous. But far from cutting off an AI approach, this level-ubiquity promises years of fun for researchers.

Meaning and Intentionality
The last set of problems inspired by the top-up objection returns us to some worries that were raised at the beginning of the chapter. These concern, in one way or another, the capacity of most emotions to be *object directed.*

One form of this problem is the problem of *composition,* which arises in connection with Panksepp's scheme for explaining complex emotions. Like that of James, this scheme founders on the question of how to analyze the relation of emotions to their objects. Recall that Panksepp's method of convergent criteria yields a taxonomy of basic emotions. He also offers an explanation of how complex ones arise, but his explanation—"blending"—is disappointing. Thus, "jealousy may arise from some admixture of panic, rage and expectancy" (Panksepp 1982, 419). But it is not clear how blending could ever add logical structure. And logical structure, not merely complications in behavioral dispositions, is what is needed to account for complex emotions. The structure of jealousy, for example, involves a number of different objects in different roles: the person one is jealous *of* plays an entirely different part in one's jealousy from that of the rival *because of whom* one is jealous.

But there is a prior form of the problem of complex objects. This is the question of how emotions, if they in some sense consist in neurochemical phenomena, can acquire objects at all, or indeed how they can have meaning of any sort.

A classic statement of this difficulty (which is not limited to the emotions) comes from John Searle (1980): A computational system, by definition, is one in which all operations are formal, that is, work on syntactically defined structures. But such a system can never acquire any meaning, unless it borrows it from some already accredited intentional system.

It is a mathematical fact that there are infinitely many isomorphs to any structure. So one must accept Searle's point that syntactic structure alone cannot yield semantics. Even if in fact syntactic constraints on our descriptions of the world could be detailed so thoroughly as to fit this particular universe uniquely, such uniqueness would be fortuitous. But what follows? In Searle's version the argument is intended to show that meaning can never autonomously get inside a machine. It proves rather too much, though. For it can easily be parodied to entail that for meaning to get into the brain is equally miraculous. A brain is just a cybernetic system formed by interconnected neural, endocrinological, and physiological subsystems. Clearly, its manipulations of organized brain states can never acquire any meaning.

How then do states of a person in general, and emotions in particular, acquire significance? In the next chapter I sketch an approach to this problem. The idea is that the primitive form of significance consists in what I shall call *natural teleology*—though it will turn out that some of the apparent implications of that term will dissolve under analysis. What we need are *causal links* from the world to the neurochemical, physiological, and cybernetic structures for which we postulate meaningfulness. On a biological approach, these will relate to the intrinsic needs of the machine considered as a total organism. Ultimately, connections to relevant kinds of things in the world must be established, perhaps with some such device as rigid designators (see Kripke 1980).

To flesh out this idea, we need to expand our biological perspective to include the lessons of evolutionary theory. This is the goal of chapter 4, in which I shall explore how the apparent teleology of adaptation relates to the individual teleology of motivation and action, in such a way as to make possible the full-fledged intentionality of human emotion.

Chapter 4
Evolution and Teleology: From Instinct to Intentionality

Biology teaches that . . . two views, seemingly equally well-founded, may be taken of the relation between the ego and sexuality. On one view, the individual is the principal thing, sexuality is one of its activities, and satisfaction one of its needs; while on the other view the individual is a temporary and transient appendage to the quasi-immortal germ plasm, which is entrusted to him by the process of generation.
Sigmund Freud

Summary

Emotions are mental phenomena. What does this mean? This chapter takes a detour to explore this question. I approach it in terms of the evolutionary transition from simple tropisms governing behavior to emotion-driven motivations presupposing intentional representation.

Evolutionary biology provides the "remote" level of explanation, as opposed to the "proximate," which consists in the sort of physiological factors discussed in chapter 3. Understanding evolutionary theory in the sense of the neo-Darwinian theory of natural selection places constraints on such explanations. In particular, this point of view can accommodate consciousness as an adaptation only if consciousness has behavioral consequences.

Corresponding to the proximate and the remote levels of explanation, there are two sorts of prima facie teleology: the adaptive and the intentional. The first is exemplified by the fact that organs and behavioral mechanisms fit the environment. The prototype of the other is deliberate action. But the capacity for motivation, which is presupposed by intentional action, is itself presumably a product of evolution.

This idea is at the heart of Freud's theory of instinct. To understand the relevant sense of human instinct, it is important to distinguish it from the more usual sense in which instinct implies fixed patterns of behavior. By contrast, human instinct determines emotional dispositions that motivate but do not determine. They need not be conscious, but they can still be mental.

The idea that something can be mental without being conscious is in part a theoretical and terminological decision. To justify this decision, we can use a now familiar analysis of teleology and function. 'The function of the heart is the circulation of the blood' means, roughly, that the heart is there because a consequence of its being there is that the blood circulates. This conception of teleology leads to two ideas that will help to situate the role of emotions.

First, teleology is not irreducible in the sense of being inaccessible to explanation in terms of lower levels. Still, it is "relatively irreducible," in that it is part of a cluster or family of explanatory terms that belong together. Similarly, the mental or representational level of description and explanation belongs to a cluster of related terms, of which some are "basic" at that level. A term is basic at some level of explanation if it cannot be explained by other terms of the same family. An example is the notion of "basic action": we perform some actions by doing something else, but a basic action is something we just do. Emotional terms may similarly be relatively irreducible.

Second, mentality or intentionality comes in different grades or degrees. "Quasi intentionality" is already present in elementary tropisms. An intermediate grade involves representations, bearing semantic and logical relations to a network of other representations. Emotions at that level may be conditioned by human instinct, but their objects are "fungible"—clusters of properties rather than individual targets. The highest level of mentality includes a capacity for singular reference. Insofar as this capacity need not be accessible to consciousness, this vindicates Freud's extension of mentality beyond the realm of consciousness. The highest level of intentionality, which is made possible by the resources of language and logic, provides for a uniquely human interpretation of attachment emotions.

I tried to show in chapter 3 that we cannot make sense of a neurophysiological account of emotions without relating it to higher-level explanations in terms of functions. In turn, however, we may feel the need for more general biological explanations of the fact that we have emotional capacities at all and that these are among our *mental* endowments. For this, we need to move to a different level of explanation. This is the task of the present chapter.

There are two major levels of causation within biology, sometimes known as the *remote* and the *proximate*. The neurophysiological phenomena discussed in the last chapter belong to the proximate—the level of the immediate mechanisms of emotions. Remote explanations have to do with how those mechanisms themselves arose; these must be sought in the theory of evolution by natural selection. Only natural selection promises an explanation for the almost irresistible semblance of teleology, or adaptedness to goals, pervading the morphology and behavior of organisms.

Until recently the "biology of emotions" has been mostly confined to the physiological, because it is the level most accessible to study. ("This is where we are looking, because this is where the light is.") Evolutionary explanations were limited to a few platitudes about survival or the good of the species. But recent controversies about sociobiology have revived interest in the ultimate, Darwinian level of explanation.

Can an evolutionary point of view help us to understand not only the physiological mechanisms of emotions but also how those mechanisms relate to our thought and behavior? In a nutshell, the answer is that to understand the biology of emotions at this more general level is to understand how *emotions motivate but do not determine.* From a bottom-up point of view, emotions arise only in creatures sufficiently complex to have a limbic system: we would probably not need them if our behavior were simpler. From a top-down perspective, the motivating role of emotions makes them part of our mental life. But what is "mental life"? And how does it emerge from the structures that support it? These questions belong to the vast puzzle of the nature of mind, into which, in this chapter, I want to fit a few small pieces.

Behavior, as well as the social structures that give it meaning and context, is subject to the pressures of natural selection. Insect societies provide the classic examples of species in which elaborate social structures are maintained by means of complex systems of releasing mechanisms, each of which gives rise to some very specific response. The consensus, however, is that we are not interestingly like insects. One crucial difference lies in our capacity to deliberate. Some have inferred from this that we cannot be biologically conditioned. That conclusion does not follow. What does follow is that the mechanism of this conditioning must differ from insect to human. In us, biological causality must be mediated by motivation and desire. Desire implies an object. At the most elementary level an object must be defined not in terms of a single behavioral response but in terms of a *satisfying situation.* But that criterion does not yet mark off (psychological) *wants* from (biological) *needs.* What does?

To answer this question, we must make an excursion. The excursion will take us through an examination of the different senses in which biological organisms and human purposes are both teleological, and of the way that one kind of teleology arises out of the other. I am not here referring to individual development, though that is an important question in its own right (see chapter 7). Here my discussion is limited to the logical conditions for the emergence of mentality. The answer I shall propose is that what makes emotions fully mental and specifically human relates to their capacity for certain sorts of *intentionality* and in particular, at the highest level, for *singular reference*.

But that lies at the end of my excursion. The tour begins with a look at evolutionary biology.

Evolutionary Explanations

I understand evolutionary explanations in the sense of the (neo-) Darwinian theory of evolution by natural selection. At the core of this theory there is a shift in perspective, bringing individual variants instead of types into the foreground of ontological priority. Instead of looking for explanations of deviations from true types, as in Aristotelian biology, Darwinian theory is committed to seeing individuals as primary and to seeking for explanations of the clusters of similarity we call "species."[1] This perspective constrains the allowable use of evolutionary concepts. Here are some rules of the game:

1. Evolution has no inherent direction or teleology. Since so many biological facts appear to embody teleological functions, this may still seem paradoxical. I shall return to it shortly. For the moment I simply put the point as a postulate: *All teleology in nature is an illusion fostered by the prestidigitation of natural selection.* The other principles are more or less corollaries of this one.

2. The prevalence of variation in nature is what makes the teleological illusion possible; but evolutionary change involves no progress, no inherent direction or "orthogenesis," no built-in drive to mentality or spirituality or group harmony or even complexity.[2]

3. Although it is rash to assume that every trait is adaptive, it is unlikely that an *important* and *pervasive* characteristic can be thoroughly maladaptive, if it is widely distributed in a *thriving* population. (Each of the stressed qualifications is necessary.)

4. On the other hand, evolution is, in François Jacob's (1977) nice term, a process of "tinkering." At any particular point, selection works with relatively small modifications to existing structures. As a result, some devices are more clumsy than they would be if they had been engineered from scratch.

5. In particular, since all selective advantage is relative to the capacities of individuals competing in a specific set of environmental conditions, or *niche*, whole genera can be left without some useful mechanism common in other groups. Deplorably, we have no wings. (And nothing is born with wheels.) This is because the implementa-

tion of the mechanism in question may be precluded by choices long since made. (Our arms, by now, are too long gone prehensile to grow feathers.) From a detached engineering standpoint, it will make perfect sense to say that things might have been done more efficiently.

Sexual reproduction makes a good example. From an evolutionary point of view, it is a major puzzle, because it seems risky and wasteful. Risky, because in each generation the luck of recombination may ruin a good thing, and wasteful because half of any successful genotype's genes are lost at meiosis (the division of the sexual cell). According to George Williams's hypothesis (one of several contenders in the field), the benefit of sex lies chiefly in its capacity to replenish the stock of variants at each generation, thereby increasing the chances that some variant will survive any given unexpected change in conditions. On this view, sex is beneficial mostly to those creatures that produce large numbers of offspring (Williams 1975). For humans, who are well adapted but produce few offspring, the benefit of sex (genetic variety) may well be outweighed by the costs (which include the destruction of good genotypes and the risk of inferior recombinations). Unless any individual could produce thousands of offspring, humans would be better off if they did away with males entirely and reproduced by parthenogenesis, like the inhabitants of Charlotte Perkins Gilman's utopian novel *Herland*. But it is too late now for that to occur by natural selection.

6. Selective pressure acts on phenotypes—actual living organisms with all their manifest characters. But what is selected, strictly speaking, is the genetic material that makes those manifest characters more probable. For selection to get a grip on a genotype, some of its genes must make, in the phenotype, a difference that is discriminable by selective pressures. This truism has dire consequences for certain theories of mind that attempt to break loose entirely from behaviorism. Suppose, for example, that someone asks what is the adaptive advantage of consciousness. In order for this question to have an answer, it must be possible to pin down some phenotypic distinction other than the subjective experience of awareness itself possessed by organisms endowed with consciousness. Otherwise, though consciousness might have been a by-product of evolution, it cannot itself have been adaptive. For selection could never have differentiated between those organisms that had consciousness and otherwise similar ones that did not.

7. The example of sex illustrates another principle that may seem too obvious to mention but is often forgotten—and is too important to omit. To say that a trait has been selected is not to say that it is useful in any particular case. Evolution is a rule-utilitarian process,

not an act-utilitarian one. The tiniest probabilistic advantage favoring one allele over another is sufficient to select that allele, but that is actually compatible with its being disadvantageous most of the time. (All that is needed is an average tipped by a few big gains, like some rich people outweighing many poor ones.) A corollary is that once circumstances have changed and the original alternatives are no longer available, some adaptations may become overwhelmingly noxious even on average.

Some consequences of these assumptions for emotions are these:

a. Although we all come with some basic equipment—brains, glands, and hormones—we cannot assume that our emotional dispositions are genetically identical. Even assuming that our emotions have been shaped by natural selection, the result may be, not uniformity serving a preordained purpose, but a mix of different dispositions distributed over the population.* (Compare (1) and (2).)

b. Nevertheless, the capacity to experience emotion seems to be remarkably universal, though whether the specific emotions experienced are also universal is far more dubious (see chapter 7). In spite of common talk of emotional "disruption" and "irrationality" in both psychology and literature, emotions are unlikely to be thoroughly maladaptive. (Compare (3).)

c. On the other hand, even if some emotional disposition is in general adaptive—or was in the niche in which it developed—it does not follow that it represents a best solution. (Compare (4).)

d. In fact, it follows neither that it must be beneficial in any particular case, nor even that it must still be beneficial at all, even on average. (Compare (5).)

e. If emotional capacities are to be more than epiphenomena, they must affect our behavior in such a way as to make some difference, however slight, to differential reproduction and survival. If consciousness as such is irrelevant, then, it must be possible for emotion to be mental without necessarily being conscious. This suggestion requires us to take seriously the idea of unconscious mentality, which I shall discuss in a moment. (Compare (6).)

f. Finally, if emotions are adaptive, either (A) they must be so in their own right, in which case we must look for their biological function; or (B) they must be side effects of other adaptations or constraints. (Compare (7).)

---

*Such a mix, when controlled by selective pressure, is called an *evolutionarily stable strategy* (ESS). The fact that there are about as many human males as females at peak reproductive age (though more males are conceived and females live longer) is an example of an ESS. The concept of ESS results from the application to selection theory of the theory of games and is due to John Maynard Smith (1976).

On assumption (B), it is not incoherent to claim that although emotions were shaped by evolution, we would be better off without them. (Someone might infer precisely this from MacLean's story about our three brains.) On this hypothesis, we need only assume that although they do weigh us down with a handicap, its weight is not such as to have wiped us out (yet).

Nonetheless, (A) is the richer avenue to pursue. The questions it suggests, moreover, can be taken to refer either to individual emotions ("What's the use of jealousy?") or to functional dyads ("What's the use of love and hate?") or even to emotional capacities in larger groupings that might be functional together ("What's the use of the social emotions?"). In the light of this last possibility, we may find some emotions that by themselves seem clearly maladaptive but are explained as adaptations nonetheless. Like some of the examples just given under the heading of sexual selection, they may be part of some adaptive "package" (see chapter 12). Two questions can be asked of such a "package":

First, what was its function in the "environment of evolutionary adaptedness"?[3] Every adaptation is relative to a specific environment or niche (see Lewontin 1978); but that niche may cease to exist. In that event, an emotion's ancestral function—even if we could discover it—will be no guide to its modern meaning. Nor will it allow us to justify the emotion as "natural."

Second, can we base a typology of primitive or basic emotions on some set of fundamental needs or functions? A great many researchers interested in the psychobiology of emotions—beginning with Descartes (1649)—have assumed as much.[4] In order to make sense of such a proposal, we should remember the constraint mentioned under (7), namely, that no emotional experience can be affected by selection unless it makes a difference to phenotypic behavior. If emotions are adaptive, it must be primarily because they affect behavior. From a biological point of view, the conscious quality of emotions as such cannot be directly adaptive. So we shall need to explore the possibility that emotions are essentially mental without being essentially conscious.

I propose to stalk the question of what is specifically mental about emotions by considering only their most obvious influence on behavior: their *motivational* force. To do this, I begin by asking how the more biological notion of *need* is related to the psychological notions of *motivation* and *want*.

There are at least two levels of (apparent) teleology, the *adaptive* and the *intentional*. At the adaptive level, the appearance of teleology in behavior stems from the fact that an instinct for the performance of certain types of behavior contributes to the fitness of those that have it. But instinct may not involve motivation. On the contrary: the standard conception of instinct, even when it leads to complex behavior such as nest building, implies predictable sequences of stereotyped responses to precise "releasing stimuli" (Tinbergen 1969). The case of the zigzagging hare mentioned in chapter 3 illustrated the fact that in typical situations such rigid instinctual patterns can be counterproductive. To avoid ambiguity, I shall refer to Tinbergen-type instincts as *T-instincts*.

Emotions, by contrast, determine motivation. And motivation, even where it concerns simple biological needs such as attachment or the "four F's," does not determine fixed patterns of behavior. Instead, it can produce quite different patterns of goal-oriented behavior in different circumstances. Such instincts, applicable to humans, I shall refer to as *H-instincts*.*

The two forms of teleology are sometimes confused, and the confusion is at the root of a familiar but misguided criticism of sociobiology. Sociobiology is a research program based on the application of the constraints of neo-Darwinian natural selection to behavior. The stock criticism I refer to is that it must be a mistake to apply (gene-) selectionist explanations to human behavior, because the intentionality of motivation has nothing to do with evolutionary or adaptive "ends" as such.[5] The criticism is misguided because it confounds two quite independent issues. One concerns the proximate causes of behavior. Clearly, human behavior is affected by individual mental factors, and depending on circumstances a single motive will produce different behaviors. Sociobiologists would not deny this. Their concern is (or should be) with a very different issue, which is whether the behavior *as brought about by the relevant motivation* may be *ultimately* explicable in terms of selection. The two questions are independent. Yet they are not unconnected: from an evolutionary point of view, we must take seriously the hypothesis that the capacity for individual teleology (motivation) was itself a product of adaptation.

---

*Note that although I speak here, as one often does, of the fitness of an individual, strictly speaking fitness is only a statistical and relative property of individuals—if it can be said to be a property of individuals at all. The fitness of an individual is roughly the statistical frequency of reproductive success in individuals of that genotype. But since, in point of fact, no two individuals (except identical twins) share a genotype, that must be relativized to a particular gene or set of genes. So we should really speak of the fitness of an individual with respect to some gene or gene cluster, as the statistical frequency of reproductive success of that gene or gene cluster. (For justification of this point of view on fitness and genes, see Dawkins 1982.)

Freudian Instinct: Determinism or Teleology?

This last idea is the basis of Freud's theory of H-instinct. I now pause to tell something of that story, which will shed some light on the relation between the two kinds of apparent teleology. It will also lead us back to the question of the conditions of mentality.

Freud once remarked that his studies had the flavor of short stories more than of scientific reports. Let us start, then, with a story. Recall that patron myth of psychoanalysis, the legend of Oedipus. It was prophesied for the infant Oedipus that he would kill his father and marry his mother. To avert this, he was ordered killed by exposure. But a shepherd rescued him, and the king and queen of Corinth adopted him and brought him up. When he grew up the prophecy was repeated: he would kill his father and marry his mother. Thinking that the prophecy referred to his Corinthian parents, he played it safe by leaving town. A few coincidences later he had fulfilled the prophecy.

Even if the content of this story were not so suggestive, something about its form would be significant: the predicted outcome is brought about through the very efforts made by the protagonists to avoid it. This is a pattern characteristic of symptoms, parapraxes (Freudian slips), and dreams: the repressed wish will come out, with poetic irony, in precisely the effort made to control it. Unconscious hatred "smothers with love" or "kills with kindness"; or one is so busy suppressing a sexual thought that it slips out unnoticed as an unconscious pun. In defense of this sort of account, Freud (1909) claimed that the method of psychoanalysis rested simply on an extension, from the physical to the mental realm, of the principle of determinism.

Not surprisingly, Freud was attacked for this idea with arguments very similar to those recently used against sociobiology. The complaint, in brief, is that Freud confuses determinism and meaningfulness.[6] But a glance at the Oedipus story suggests that the critics have missed the point. For the kind of determinism illustrated in that story would really better be called *fatalism*. Determinism and fatalism are often confused, perhaps because both seem to entail the impossibility of freedom. And on certain natural assumptions, they come to the same thing. Yet they are *logically* antithetical. The reason is this. The central idea of determinism is that every event depends on its antecedents. Fatalism, on the contrary, views some particular event (the one foretold by the oracle, or the expression of the repressed wish) as inevitable no matter what the antecedents turn out to be: "If it hadn't happened this way, the same thing would have happened in some other way." It makes no essential difference if we substitute 'likely' for 'inevitable'. Fatalism, like determinism, can admit of soft and hard variants. The point is that determinism is a causal notion, whereas fatalism is a teleological one. In the light of this, we might surmise that Freud is asserting, not that causal determination is at the root of all meaningfulness and intention, but on the contrary that the form of determinism applicable to human phenomena deals in meanings: that psychological determinism is to be understood teleologically.

Teleology and Natural Selection

Teleology has long had a bad press, although it has fared slightly better in recent years. A teleological explanation appears to involve reference to not-yet-existent events. "Not-yet-existent" does not imply "future," for a teleological explanation is not invalidated merely because the end state is never reached. So at all events teleology is not backward causation. Still, epistemological difficulties will arise for the claim that something can be explained in terms of an "end event" that never occurs—or occurs only by chance. So I shall speak of the end as a "probable outcome." How, then, can anything be explained in terms of a probable outcome?

The answer leads to a dilemma, which is the reason for the bad press. Either the probable outcome itself somehow determines the event (it is a "final cause"), or some representation of it is the determining factor. In the first case, how could a merely probable event bring about anything at all? A probable outcome no more exists than a future one. So we are even worse off than if we were positing backward causation. But in the second case, teleology seems to reduce to causation by representational states. And since psychology is likely to need the notion of causally effective representational states anyway, we can dispense altogether, for theoretical purposes, with the extra category of teleology.

As will appear, I think this traditional line is at least partly right. But it is much too short. Our excursion demands a longer route.

When does it become tempting to explain anything teleologically? Only when the event is otherwise improbable. This is clearly illustrated by the *argument from design*. The charm of that argument stemmed from its power as an inference to the best explanation[7] of apparent improbability. If no single causal law can explain the convergence to adaptation of very different organs and functions, then the hypothesis of a planner with adaptation as her goal is inevitably attractive. Thus, in spite of Hume's (1779) ingenuity in refuting the argument from design to the existence of God, this argument did not become completely unreasonable until Darwin. Evolutionary theory removes the intrinsic improbability of complex adaptation, because the stepwise course of selection multiplies exponentially the number of logical possibilities canvassed by the random processes of mutation.

This point can be illustrated in terms of the following model: Imagine that the ecological space available at any one time is limited to ten experimental types and that exactly one type per generation survives to reproduce. In such a model, in just six generations the surviving types will represent one possibility in a million. (If every possibility were realized in some possible world, the number of possible worlds needed to represent all the possible outcomes would be multiplied by ten in each generation, totaling 10^6.) The crucial trick here is the preservation of the characteristics of the "winner" in each generation. Contrast this with what we might call "Empedoclean" evolution, after the Greek philosopher who first suggested the idea of evolution by selection of chance combinations. In Empedoclean evolution, acting on the same conditions, each generation throws up a fresh batch of ten "hopeful monsters." There is no preservation of the characteristics of the previous winner. It can be calculated that in order to reach a better than even chance of coming up with a "one in a million" specimen, one would need some 700,000 generations. Empedoclean evolution, then, is a process that does nothing to make the existence of adapted organisms any less of a miracle. Darwinian selection represents the taming of the improbability of life.

Evolution by selection mimics the goal-directedness of teleological process, dispelling the illusion of either "basic" or intentional teleology. Adaptedness is related to survival not teleologically but tautologically: it should not be surprising that the organisms that have actually survived are "adapted" to survival, for if they weren't, they wouldn't be here. What looks like an end state is merely the end of the story so far.*

The general process of adaptation, then, cannot strictly be called teleological. For we can identify no single end—except the completely trivial one of survival—on which different strategies of nature converge. We cannot, for example, claim even metaphorically that Nature aims to produce organs of locomotion of one kind or another:

---

*Occasionally this is claimed to show that the theory of natural selection is trivial. That is silly. For it is a fully contingent fact that some characters rather than none were able to survive at all, and it is an enormously difficult empirical question what characters presented a reproductive advantage at any particular point of choice, and why.

there is no objective sense in which organisms lacking such organs are less successful than those that have them.

Any given species, on the other hand, is capable of certain ranges of behavior that converge on identifiable end states. The process of evolution, though not itself teleological, has resulted in mechanisms that are: homing instincts, tropisms of all kinds—and emotions.

We need a conception of teleology that fits both adaptive and intentional types, accounts for its distinctive "fatalistic" flavor, and does not rest on the attribution of conceptual capacities to lower animals. Ignoring some refinements, the following notion fits that bill:[8] *Teleological laws are a special case of causal laws, containing in the antecedent an allusion to a consequence of the explanandum.* The rest of the present section explains this in more detail.

Take (1) to represent the general form of a law of nature,[9]

(1) $(x) (Ax \rightarrow Bx)$

where the arrow is a suitably interpreted connective.* This says that "All cases of A result in cases of B." The differentia of teleological or functional laws is given by specifying that the antecedent, Ax, can be expanded as in (2):

(2) $(x)(Bx \rightarrow (\text{probably})\ Gx)$

This says that "B generally has the consequence that G." The resulting schema is (3),

(3) $(x) ((Bx \rightarrow Gx) \rightarrow Bx)$

which expresses the full idea that B happens *because it tends to promote* G. Alternatively, if (3) is true, then we can say that a *function* of B is to promote G. Informally, B has that function if its *existence* can be explained in terms of its tendency to bring about G.

The chief virtue of this account is that it provides a genuine analysis of the notion of goal. (G in (3) is a "goal" not by stipulation but in virtue of its place in the schema.) The schema applies equally to all the different things for which we are inclined to give teleological or functional explanations: artifacts, instinctual behavior, and intentional acts. The differences between those classes lie in the types of explanation that must be given of the fact that the teleological law holds in each case.

---

*The connective is not the material conditional of elementary logic, which is notoriously inadequate to specify a causal law, but something like *causally implies* or *implies as a consequence of natural laws*. I need not apologize for the unanalyzed (and therefore potentially question-begging) character of such a connective, for all that is claimed for it here is that it is potentially whatever is needed to express *nonteleological* causal laws.

To show this, I begin by noting a defect of the formulation just given. Any causal law $(A \rightarrow B)$ can be trivially given teleological form (4):

(4) $(x) ((Bx \rightarrow \text{Inst } (A \rightarrow B)) \rightarrow Bx)$

("Bx happens whenever it results in the instantiation of the law $(A \rightarrow B)$.")[10] We need to add the qualification that ordinary causality is the default assumption: the label 'teleological' applies only to what cannot be reformulated in nonteleological form. The additional structure in (2) must be ineliminable. But when is this the case?

Ernest Nagel has suggested that reduction of a teleological law can be effected by finding a categorical condition materially equivalent to the conditional forming the antecedent (see Nagel 1961, chap. 12). Thus, in an animal tropism, the condition 'is in a state in which turning right is generally conducive to increased reception of light energy' might be replaced by 'is caused by light gradients affecting its sensors to orient itself to the right'. The trick is to find such a mechanism. Charles Taylor speculated that in some cases, as a matter of empirical fact, none would be found:

> It is commonly assumed . . . that such a translation-out-of existence can always be effected. . . . But we have no right to make this assumption. Of course, any given antecedent condition of B which fulfilled the conditions for the description (in terms of the instrumental predicate) would also fulfill some other "intrinsic" description, E. But this is not to say that B's occurring is a function of E's occurring, i.e., that B depends on E. (Taylor 1964, 13)

Taylor's thesis here is that some instances of teleological laws may be *basic:* this means they will neither be reducible to, nor explicable on the basis of, nonteleological laws and facts. Since any causal law can trivially be put into teleological form, a law will not be held to be teleological unless it cannot be translated into nonteleological form. Causality, we might say, is dominant, teleology recessive. Taylor's original contribution was the claim that there might be teleological laws in this strong, irreducible sense and that whether there are or not is an empirical question. But what, then, is the answer to this empirical question?

Jonathan Bennett has argued that there are no basic laws of form (3):

> Given any purported law of that form, we can always contrive a situation where an R animal [one that is suitably positioned, or "Ready"] so situated that [B would lead to G] nevertheless fails

to do [B] because—to put it roughly—the facts which make it [true that B would lead to G] are not epistemically available to it. (Bennett 1976, 46)

This leads Bennett to introduce a concept of *registration,* which covers belief, perception, preprogrammed plans—in short, any representational state. The amended law schema says that x does B whenever x apprehends or "registers" that B would promote G:

(5) (x) (t) $((Rx \text{ at } t \ \& \ x \text{ registers that } (Bx \rightarrow Gx) \text{ at } t) \rightarrow Bx \text{ at } t+d)$
(Bennett 1976, 49)

But now it seems Bennett has given up precisely the point that made Taylor's account distinctive. For when the instrumental predicate is within the scope of an intentional operator ('registers'), then— on standard views of intentionality and reference—the ascription no longer implies real reference to the probable outcome. (See Chapter 2 on Plato's second fallacy.) Purposive behavior can be described in terms of *causation by intentional states.* This formulation is not without problems, but we have those anyway, for they concern the nature of representational or "registration" states and their objects. There is nothing left over, in the real world, for the pure teleological form of explanation.

Are there any cases of pure or basic teleology in Taylor's sense? Only if there are miracles, in this precise sense: we can't prove that there aren't any such cases, but it would never be rational to accept anything as a bona fide instance. For the most we could know at any particular time is that we haven't yet discovered the underlying mechanism. In the light of past progress in finding mechanisms to explain apparently "insightful" or teleological behavior, what could justify giving up the search? Brute teleology would represent a cul-de-sac of science.

Still, Nagel's strategy may not always be practical. The categorical mechanism that it postulates may be epistemically inaccessible. In such cases we might be able to establish the *truth* of the teleological formula beyond reasonable doubt, while its *mechanisms* remain a matter for speculation. More important, finding the mechanism may not give us the explanation we seek. A teleological mechanism goes into action just when it is likely to have a certain result. That is what the teleological law *asserts,* but it does not really *explain* it. What does?

Possible explanations are of the two sorts already discussed: in terms of *natural selection* or of *representation and planning.* These are associated, respectively, with the two types of prima facie teleology:

the adaptive and the intentional. How are these two sorts of explanation related?

Relative Irreducibility

Within a certain type of explanation, we may have a number of hierarchically related principles and laws, some of which explain others, and some of which are just brute facts at that level of theoretical analysis. This does not mean that no explanation is possible for these facts, rather, it means that their explanation must move to a new level. They are only *relatively* brute or autonomous.

It may be useful to illustrate this notion first in terms of an example that has nothing to do with the mental. Consider the autoimmune response. Edwin Levy and Mohan Matthen have argued that we can speak of the immune system, when it is triggered not by a foreign substance but by "misrecognition of self," as literally making *errors* (Levy and Matthen 1984). Even if we can always give a merely chemical account of the response and its causes, to do so may result in the loss of an epistemologically indispensable level of description and explanation. For it is only if we think of the response as springing from a device whose *function* is the protection of a particular organism—a notion that has no place in chemical and physical description as such—that we can identify some of these reactions as "normal" and others as "errors." In this way, various useful concepts—"individual," "response," "teleological law"—are tied together into a relatively autonomous or irreducible level of explanation. This is not, however, a "basic" or absolutely irreducible level in Taylor's sense, for the methodological reason stated a moment ago, namely, that we can never establish that no underlying causal mechanism exists.

Some familiar facts about the philosophy of action provide a more directly relevant example. Many of our action ascriptions imply complex changes in the world. These can be regarded as tasks accomplished. When we ask how these tasks are accomplished, we get an answer in terms of a chain of more limited acts, linked by the *by-relation*. Eventually the chain comes to an end, at an action that I *just do*. I frighten the prowler by turning on the light by flipping the switch by moving my finger. But there is nothing else by doing which I move my finger. It is, in the useful term introduced by Arthur Danto (1965), a *basic action*.

This does not mean, of course, that there is no explanation of my moving my finger: on the contrary, there is a long story, which is only partially known but which at least involves, at a number of levels, muscles, levers, nerves, synapses, neurotransmitters, the movement of potassium ions through cell membranes, and so forth. But these are mere events, not actions or things I do, though some of them are things I can learn to do, *by* undergoing biofeedback training, for example. Thus, although basic actions do not constitute a fixed repertoire, they are the terminus for chains of explanation in terms of the by-relation. They illustrate what I mean by relative irreducibility.

Another chain of explanations runs in the opposite direction (figure 4.1).[11] This one is governed by the *why-relation*. This is easily fitted to the teleological structure of (5): I moved my finger because I "registered" that it was instrumental to flipping the switch, and registered that flipping the switch was instrumental to turning the light on, to finding the peanut butter, to eating the peanut butter, to satisfying hunger. Now if I'm asked what I want the last for, I'm at a loss. At most I can take one more gasping and dubious step in the same direction and say, "For pleasure." Again we are at a terminus of explanation at a given level, but again this does not imply that motivation is radically inexplicable. What then lies beyond this level?

The Unconscious Mind

What lies beyond, I suggest, is the adaptive type of quasi teleology; it is what Freud calls the "frontier" of "Instinct" (see Freud 1915c, 118). This is avowedly hardly more than a placeholder for a lacuna: but to see clearly where there is a lacuna and what sorts of explanations should fill it is already progress.

Recall that the selective pressures that ultimately determine whether a genotype will perish or survive are applied to phenotypes with their particular behavior. Though each of two analogous outcomes may be brought about by entirely different mechanisms—by T-instinct or by H-instinct—both may be due to a selective pressure for that outcome. An organism may be programmed phylogenetically to give a precise response to some specific range of stimuli; or it can be programmed to acquire such a response.

Donald Symons cites a nice case where both alternatives are implemented in a single species. The mallard duck, like other animals, is able to recognize conspecifics as potential mates. But this capacity is hard-wired in the female and learned in the male. Presumably this is because the male's plumage is highly distinctive and therefore can be picked out by means of a relatively coarse schema, whereas recognizing the female requires much finer discrimination (Symons 1979, 16).

Some organisms are programmed to have certain built-in representations of outcomes, fitting in with a capacity to make inferences of

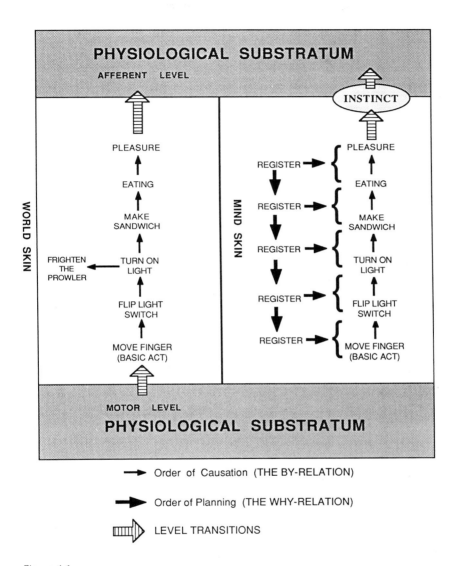

Figure 4.1
The by-relation and the why-relation

the type schematized above in terms of the why-relation. Such a system can obviously be rudimentary or complex. In sophisticated form, the registrations or representations involved cannot readily be replaced with any descriptions of the physical states that underlie them, because their correlation with those underlying states is not one to one. In other words, the representations are emergent, in the sense that I argued is innocuous because it is not unique to the relation of mentality to its underlying structures.[12] At the lowest limit, though, the mental space represented as lying between the afferent and motor levels of physiological substratum can shrink to nothing. One will then have nonmental or quasi intentionality: stimuli are translated into responses without the need for any level of relatively irreducible representation. In such a simple system there is no difference between biological need and psychological want, no gap between the determination of *what can be wanted* and the determination of the repertoire of possible responses, *what can be done.* Instinct at that level is T-instinct, determining a repertoire of automatic responses.

For Freud, by contrast, instinct determines now responses but *internal stimuli* (Freud 1915c, 119). This matches the present conception of H-instinct, determining not desired responses but desired outcomes.

The notion of H-instinct raises the question, What ultimately can be wanted? Suppose for a moment that psychoanalysis were able to answer this question. It would seek the explanation of some of our wants in our unconscious motivation, while accepting others as simply basic at the mental level of explanation. Further explanation would require a move to another level. It might show that a person couldn't really be believed if she claimed that she *just wanted a saucer of mud*—not *for* anything, but just in itself (see Anscombe 1957).

The notion of H-instinct faces a major problem, however. The tip-off is a disanalogy between the two streams of explanation and their stopping points that can be read off figure 4.1. When we anatomize how an action is performed, there is no alternative, at the stopping point, to a transition out of the psychological level to the neuro-chemical-physiological "motor" centers. But instinct, although not necessarily conscious, is still supposed to be a psychological concept. As we saw in chapter 3, even the classification of types of physiological processes involved can proceed only on the basis of higher-level, psychological categories. What justifies this discrepancy? Why do we not go, here too, straight to the physiological level? This is the problem of the justification for the concept of *unconscious mind.* Granted that the explanation of our conscious intentions must go beyond the level of consciousness, why do we want to insert here a level that is still mental though not conscious?

Freud was well aware of this line of questioning. In response he notes that whether we adopt this terminology is ultimately a matter of convention. But he gives six arguments in support of the view that "the equation of what is conscious with what is mental . . . [is] totally inexpedient" (Freud 1915e, 167ff.). The arguments are these:

1. Our conscious life has "gaps"; the connection of our acts and states is "unintelligible" unless we "interpolate . . . unconscious acts."

2. Such interpolation affords us "an effective influence over the course of conscious processes"—by which he means, of course, psychoanalysis.

3. Latent (but recoverable) memories, like unseen objects, are most simply and naturally assumed to go on existing unobserved.

4. "All the categories which we employ to describe conscious mental acts, such as ideas, purposes, resolutions, and so on, can be applied" to these interpolated mental acts.

5. Posthypnotic suggestion has "tangibly demonstrated the existence and mode of operation of the mental unconscious."

6. We attribute consciousness to others on the basis of their behavior, without perforce being directly aware of it ourselves. "Psychoanalysis demands nothing more than that we should apply this process of inference to ourselves also." But it would be bizarre to attribute to ourselves another "unconscious consciousness" (for that matter, we might need more than one: for some unconscious contents are insulated from each other). So it is convenient to take the analogy only part way and postulate an unconscious mind.

None of these arguments is very strong as it stands. Gaps in intelligibility (1) are only disturbing if one assumes that the mental must be intelligible in isolation. But we have seen that we are always bound to find somewhere a break in intelligibility requiring a transition to another theoretical level. Why not, then, stipulate that the break always comes where consciousness is lost?

Freud himself considers this alternative possibility in connection with latent recollections (3); perhaps they simply "correspond to residues of somatic processes from which what is psychical can once more arise." But he claims that it begs the question. Actually, it would be more accurate to say that it shifts the burden of proof: why shouldn't we deem that the mental coincides with the conscious?

The same applies to the argument from posthypnotic suggestion (5). We can interpret the facts as Freud does, but we could also stipulate that posthypnotic suggestion works by setting up physiological conditions that under the right conditions give rise to appropriate but emergent mental states.

As for the effectiveness of the analytic procedure (2), it requires the interpolation of unconscious mental contents only if other interpretations are excluded. Perhaps, when beliefs or wants seem to "come into consciousness," they are in fact coming into *existence*. It would then be these newly generated beliefs and wants that are the effective agents in modifying "the course of conscious processes." This alternative hypothesis is supported by the notorious fact that therapists of different schools have roughly equal rates of cure (see Shapiro and Shapiro 1982). Since different therapists hold entirely different theories about the contents of the unconscious, the simplest hypothesis is that the unconscious has no content at all. So far, then, the issue remains moot.

Arguments (4) and (6) are more promising.[13] Argument (6) automatically lends force to some of the others by undermining the commonsense primacy of consciousness. In defending it, however, Freud somewhat undermines argument (4). For one of his reasons for not postulating an "unconscious consciousness" is that "some of these latent processes (have) characteristics . . . which run directly counter to the attributes of consciousness with which we are familiar." Here he is alluding to the indifference of "primary process"—the characteristic working of the unconscious—to logical, spatial, or temporal order. Primary process is essentially nonverbal and governed by laws of its own (see Freud 1911b). This ill comports with the contention (4) that conscious and unconscious contents belong to the same categories.

Freud's arguments need reinforcement. To justify classifying both conscious and unconscious as mental, we need to show that in this theoretical context what they have in common is more important than their differences. We can make some progress by taking a second look at sequences of T-instinctual behavior in the light of the account of teleology sketched above. The point of this exercise is to see whether we can catch T-instinct *in flagrante metamorphosi,* turning into H-instinct by the addition of some crucial factor.

Quasi Intentionality

T-instinctual behavior typically involves different phases, each of which can begin only when the previous one has been completed. There is no point in making the motions necessary for weaving the nest together unless some twigs have been successfully collected (Tinbergen 1969). Such sequences therefore involve *feedback.* The mechanism involved in the testing or evaluation of feedback must already have some characteristics in common with representation. It must make discriminations in accordance with which activity continues, is modified, or stops.

This is sufficient to give the structure of the act its teleological form. It also involves two features that have been traditionally associated with intentionality:[14]

1. *Intentional inexistence.* The condition "represented" in the testing mechanism may never actually occur. This is the functional analogue of *failure of reference* in belief and of *failure of satisfaction* in desire.

2. *Generality.* This has two senses, distinguished by their respective contrasts:

a. The first contrast is with *specificity.* Animals can be fooled by relatively coarse decoys. There are two reasons to expect this as a result of natural selection. First, it is costly to refine perception: guarding against unlikely mistakes is not worth the cost. Second, a fine standard of discrimination may exclude too much in the face of the broad variability of nature. Selection finds an equilibrium at a degree of specificity adequate for practical purposes. (This goes for learning as well as evolution.)

In the first sense, then, generality is a matter of degree and results from adaptive cost-accounting. But the second sense is purely logical:

b. The second contrast is with *particularity.* However finely or coarsely it is specified, the "object" represented will always remain a general type, never a particular. A specification can be as fine as we like without narrowing down what fits it to a particular individual. This contrasts with the typical function of a name, which is to refer to a unique individual regardless of whether that individual can successfully be told apart from others exactly like it.

Intentional inexistence and generality define what I shall call *quasi intentionality* (Ann MacKenzie (unpub.) aptly calls it *nonmental intentionality*). What more is needed to make the higher, mental grade of intentionality—intentionality *tout court?*

The Importance of Singular Reference

Quasi intentionality cannot but display generality in both senses. However refined the testing mechanism in the feedback loop, any particular that fits the "representation" involved will have some properties that make no difference. An ordinary mental act, by contrast, can be general, but it is also capable of intending singular reference. This capacity for genuine singular reference, I suggest, represents the crucial additional step in the direction of full-fledged mentality. And the test of it, in turn, is the capacity for what I shall call *nonfungible identification.*

In law, an object is said to be fungible if it belongs to an equivalence class any member of which can substitute for any other in the fulfillment of a contract. Money is the paradigm fungible: individual dollar bills are not material to a debt. On the other hand, if you lend me a vase and I return another, I have not returned what I borrowed, though I have perhaps offered an adequate substitute. Analogously, I shall speak of mental acts requiring only general reference as *fungible* and of those that involve singular reference are *nonfungible.*

The conceptual apparatus required to understand this distinction requires certain essentially logical or language-like resources. This is not something I can prove, but I cannot imagine how, without such resources, I could tell the difference between referring to that actual dog *Fido* and merely referring to *whatever has that bundle of Fidoid properties.*

This might be contested. Doesn't Fido himself, speechless though he be, have the ability to recognize a particular individual? Well, once again, we could say that, but if we needn't, we shouldn't. (It is singular reference, now, that appears as recessive, where general reference is dominant.) And we needn't, because there is an obvious alternative explanation: Fido has picked out a number of characteristic qualities, including voice tone, smell, perhaps a certain rhythm in my walk, and so on, and these properties are quite sufficient to account for my fond pet-loving illusion that Fido loves me, as a particular, *de re.*

But what if we couldn't fool the dog? Well, that would be magical. But it would also be irrelevant. In principle, as Zeus showed with Alcmene, we can fool even someone equipped with the logicolinguistic tools required to make singular references. The point concerns what the dog intends, not what it knows.

But couldn't we at least offer evidence that a dog is attached to a particular as opposed to a mere bundle of qualities? Here is an ingenious proposal to that effect (made in conversation by John Perry). Suppose we first ascertain, by suitable experimentation, that Fido is perfectly indifferent between two dishes, A and B. But as soon as we have fed him out of A, he becomes attached to it in preference to B. This is not due to any intrinsic property of A: we have good reason to believe that the only description relevant to Fido's attachment is just "the first dish from which he is fed." Had that been B, his attachment would have been for B. Is this not the sort of historical-causal story that we would tell in trying to explain a person's attachment to a particular person or thing?

A parallel with the psychoanalytic notion of a "transitional object" (the "security blankets" to which toddlers cling when they need reassurance) lends plausibility to this suggestion. The term 'transitional object' (Winnicott 1971) alludes to three sorts of transitions: (1) between the merging and the differentiating of self and mother; (2) between a part of the self and an independently existing thing; and (3), most importantly in the present context, between the prelinguistic and the linguistic stages of development.

In both the case of Fido and that of the child, we assume some similar causal story: we come to care about some particular thing for historical reasons, normally because of some association that lends new importance to previously irrelevant distinctions. A child's attachment to her "Blankie" is clearly of this historical nature. And the favored dish in the example of Fido shares another important feature with the human case: namely, that there is no requirement that the target remain qualitatively identical. The dog's dish was full and is now empty; no matter, because it was the one that was first full. If Blankie mustn't be washed, it's not because washing would change its properties in general—for after all it used to be clean—but because washing would change those special properties (smell? feel?), slowly accumulated over time, that seem to guarantee that it is still the identical object.

But in spite of these points of resemblance, it remains impossible to establish that Fido's attachments involve genuine singular reference, rather than merely a certain bundle of properties. To bring out more clearly the implied contrast between dogs and people, let me tell another story.

In *Solaris*, a story by Stanislaw Lem (1970), Kris, the narrator, is one of a crew of researchers vainly attempting to establish communication with Solaris, a sentient but uncommunicative planet. The disillusioned rump of researchers remaining on the Solaris research station find themselves plagued by a spooky phenomenon. Doppelgängers of persons from their past materialize in the research station. It is assumed that each doppelgänger is manufactured by the sentient planet according to the information stored in the victim's own brain. Kris is confronted with a doppelgänger of Rheya, a lover from his past who is long since dead. Embroidering slightly on Lem, let us assume that the information used to manufacture the pseudo-Rheya is as complete as possible, matching not only explicit beliefs but also inferences, both logical and informal, that Kris might conceivably be in a position to make. The doppelgänger is even true to the fact that Kris doesn't know everything about Rheya. (If she couldn't surprise him, she wouldn't be convincing. Any real person you know will afford some surprises.) In short, we can ensure that in qualitative terms Kris cannot possibly discover that the doppelgänger is not the original. And yet—here is the important point—he knows that this cannot possibly be the real Rheya, because the real Rheya is long dead. And that is why the doppelgänger arouses horror rather than joy. The distinction presupposed by Kris's distress is a purely numerical one, because none of the properties that might be assumed to be relevant to his affection can be lacking. Yet he is so horrified by the appearance of the doppelgänger that—until he forms a *new* relationship with her—he tries to get rid of her by any means possible. Why? Why not instead welcome someone exactly like your long-lost lover or friend? The reason must be that Kris cares about the particular identity of that singular person, Rheya, more than he cares about her properties. The reason, in short, stems from Kris's capacity for singular reference, or nonfungible identification. Kris, unlike Fido, can intend a logical distinction even between qualitatively indiscriminable individuals.

If this interpretation of Lem's story is plausible, it shows that we *care* about individuals and that we assume we can refer to them even though we can never guarantee that our references succeed. This grasp of the possibility of singular reference, I suggest, is a necessary condition of full-fledged (mental) intentionality. I shall argue in chapter 8 that this capacity is related to one source of the richness of our emotional repertoire, rooted in the possibility of *time-indexed* desires. These focus on particular moments or stretches of time, making possible more complex forms of both rationality and irrationality. And we shall see in chapter 5 how this capacity constrains the nature of some emotional objects.

A Decision Tree for the Ascription of Mentality
A minimal condition required by the capacity for singular reference is that the organism in question have a *biography.* For no expression can genuinely refer to a particular, if there has been no moment at which that reference was fixed for some particular user. (For this reason, no innate idea could ever actually refer, except in the Pickwickian sense in which a chiromancer's client might exclaim, "A tall dark man! That must be George!") But as we have seen, having a causal history is not sufficient: Fido has one too. I can provide no full account of the additional conditions that make genuine singular reference possible. There is one suggestive clue, however, which I shall pursue in chapter 7: that reference can be inherited secondhand from other members of a community of users. So it commonly presup-

poses the kind of social matrix that many have, on independent grounds, thought crucial to the human difference.

These features, I submit, make singular reference a promising criterion of the passage from quasi intentionality to full-fledged mentality. Their relevance to emotions should be plain: some emotions are essentially directed toward singular objects, whereas others are better described as aroused by certain qualities. It seems a plausible speculation that this marks one of the differences between some of the more "primitive" emotions, which are of the latter kind, and some of those that depend essentially on specifically human capacities.

None of this commits me to any view of the mental as radically irreducible to the biological. On the contrary: given the notion of relative irreducibility, the question of what should count as mental can be answered pragmatically without worrying about the ultimate likelihood of interlevel explanation. When it is sufficiently useful to speak of mentality? The discussion so far suggests the following criterion:

When a putative "registration," although apparently teleological in function, is due to phylogenetic programming, there is no call for introducing the language of mentality. But when (1) it has been at least partly conditioned ontogenetically, and (2) it involves a level of relatively irreducible representations, and (3) it involves a capacity for singular reference as well as a general capacity for differential response, then it makes sense to speak of unconscious mentality.

Figure 4.2 summarizes the sequence of decisions that the proposed criterion involves. If we find that the behavior of an organism apparently conforms to a teleological pattern but cannot be attributed to any conscious intention, we have two live options. (The hypothesis that we have stumbled across a genuine case of absolutely irreducible nonmental teleology in Taylor's sense is presumably not a live one.) We can look for an explanation of the phenomenon in purely causal terms—classing it with what Jonathan Bennett (1976, sec. 22) calls "fraudulently teleological," which is roughly what Ernst Mayr (1975b) calls "teleomatic":

> Teleomatic processes simply follow natural laws, that is, lead to a result consequential to concomitant physical forces, and the reaching of their end state is not controlled by a built-in program. The law of gravity and the second law of Thermodynamics are among the natural laws that most frequently govern teleomatic processes. (Mayr 1975b, 389)

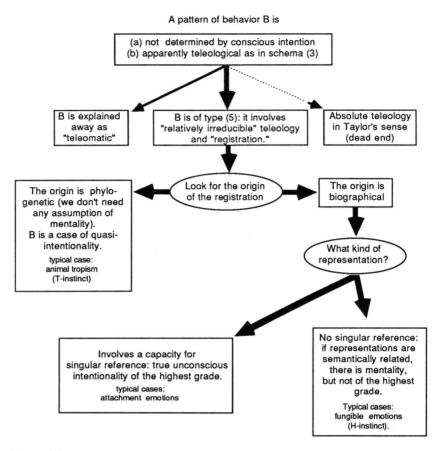

Figure 4.2
Decision tree for the attribution of unconscious mentality

Or we can accept it as teleological in the relatively irreducible sense. In this case we will treat it as conforming to a law of the form articulated by Bennett as (5). The next question is whether the origin of the state of "registration" is phylogenetic (that is, lies in a built-in adaptive program) or whether it belongs to an individual's biography. The two are not mutually exclusive. But for methodological purposes let us suppose there are pure cases. According to the preceding argument, the case in which the origin is biographical is the only one in which the use of mentalistic language seems compelling; but even the fact that the apparent motivation was conditioned by the causal history of the particular organism is not sufficient. The final decision, then, is whether it is plausible to ascribe to the organism the representational apparatus required for singular reference. If so, we have reached the highest level of intentionality. If not, the required representations may still be relatively irreducible, in which case we have an intermediate level of genuine intentionality, giving rise, for example, to Fido's specific but fungible emotions, the objects of which are logically general.

Emotions and the "Biologically Natural"

However deeply emotions are rooted in biology, I have argued that they are mental phenomena. This piece of taxonomy need not be taken too seriously, since we have no very clear idea either of what that means or of what role the concept of mentality will play in future science.[15] But one common assumption is that mentality is essentially connected with consciousness. That assumption has been the topic of the present discussion. Insofar as there are good reasons for talking about the mental as opposed to the neurophysiological, Freud was right in thinking that those reasons extend to the unconscious mind. His arguments, however, are not sufficient to establish that processes that do not conform to the logical and semantical rules of conscious representation should also be included. That limitation means that dreams and fantasies, and other instances of what Freud called "primary processes," are also properly speaking mental.*

To countenance unconscious mentality, however, is to face a further problem. Any ascription of teleology must be able to distinguish gen-

---

*The present criterion fits in with a puzzling remark of Freud's: "Even in the Unconscious," he says, "an instinct cannot be represented otherwise than by an idea . . ." (Freud 1915c, 22). In other words, instinct itself is not mental: it only has mental consequences. For instinct itself is by definition phylogenetically conditioned; the "ideas" that represent it, on the other hand, must in part be the products of individual learning. What Freud strictly calls instinct, which involves "primary process thinking" un-

uine goal states from mere causal correlates of its end state. (When I set out to meet Cicero, I may end up with Tully without even trying.) This is not really a problem for conscious intentions, since their criteria of identity are stronger than extensional equivalence. (I can want to meet Cicero without wanting to meet Tully, even though the extensional equivalence of their names means I can't meet one without meeting the other.) But where there is no conscious registration, we must perforce make our ascriptions on the basis of behavior, supplemented by any other available evidence. So is there any way of telling what the real goal or object of some nonconscious state might be?

One possible aid would be a theory of where it is possible for chains of motivation to stop, or more generally what our *natural repertoire* of emotions might be. Here we need an explanation that is not determined by the individual's history alone but appeals to what is phylogenetically wired in. In fact, this consideration applies even where there is avowal of conscious intention. For if we take the unconscious seriously, as I have argued we should, we cannot simply go by what people say they want. We need to check their claim against a theory of what, at the most basic level, can be wanted. Could you make sense of someone who said, "I just want a saucer of mud"?

One possible answer is this: someone might think she just wants a saucer of mud, but the claim is unbelievable unless one can guess at how evolution can have programmed such a want, or at any rate laid down the basis for its acquisition. And evolution can have so programmed us only if such a want (or its basis) had an adaptive advantage at some stage. This could happen either because of some need for mud or because we needed something else that wanting mud would make us more likely to get. But though one cannot *just* want a saucer of mud, one can *want* it. Depending on the explanation for the want, we may find such a want "perverse." To understand perverse wants and emotions is to be able to link them up, through facts about an individual biography, with some want that was preprogrammed, that is to say, with some instinct in the Freudian sense.

With two important reservations, this line of reasoning is sound. The first reservation stems from the considerations adduced at the beginning of this chapter: there are grounds for skepticism about adaptationist assumptions implicit in the account just sketched. It per-

---

confined by logical, temporal, or semantic rules, is really altogether submental. But the "ideas" generated by instinct behave like mental representations, and they are mental even if not conscious.

fectly accords with biology that some things may just happen. The second reservation follows from the first: even innate standards of normality may be strictly individual, reflecting a unique nature. This will make it very difficult to tell for certain whether someone is acting "normally" or not.

Besides, normal wants and emotions must be explained using the same general strategy as perverse ones—a strategy of tracing them to their origins. So the trick of differentiating the normal from the perverse will prove a delicate one.[16] I shall make a beginning of sorts on this question in this book, based on the assumption that the only meaning we can give that distinction is in terms of an extended notion of *rationality* as applied to emotions. On this view, both the biological root of an emotion and the route that has led to its present form will contribute to the basis for judgments of emotional rationality.

In this way the theory of H-instinct will link the explanation of individual patterns of teleological behavior to specific biological constraints. It will also help to explicate the crucial difference between T-instinct, as it is relevant, say, to the behavior of insects, and some notion of H-instinct that might be helpful to the explanation of human behavior. A hard and fine line between the two is not to be expected, and this partly accounts for the feeling that the so-called higher animals are obviously closer to humans in this regard than are the insects.

Three Morals

To conclude this chapter, I single out three morals suggested by our bio/logical excursion.

First, some notion of instinct may still have application to the human case, despite the protestations of those who press the case for the uniqueness of human beings. But H-instinct and T-instinct must be clearly distinguished. Where motivation and emotion are involved, we are dealing with H-instinct, and we have no reason to expect fixed or predictable patterns of behavior. But the viability of the concept of H-instinct does give us some reason to look for forms of emotion and motivation that are natural. Remembering the primacy of individual variation over types in modern evolutionary theory, however, we should not infer that natural instincts, wants, or emotions will be universal ones. Instead, we should assume that we might make sense of the notion of *individual natures.*

The second moral is that there are different grades of intentionality. Part of the differences between the different grades has to do with the ways in which their apparent teleology can be explained. Two explanations are available. One is in terms of selection; it can apply both to adaptation and to certain patterns of learning. The other is in terms of representation. Only genuine representations require that we posit a mental level of explanation and description. So emotions will fall firmly on the side of the mental, so long as they involve representations.

Finally, the type of representation involved will differ in terms of its capacity for different types of reference. Only singular reference requires the highest form of intentionality; though I have found no reason to insist that it must always involve consciousness. We can therefore expect that the type and extent of object-directedness in emotions will be a guide both to their classification and to the discovery of those that we can fairly regard as most characteristically human. So it is to questions about the objects of emotions that I now turn.

Chapter 5

Emotions and Their Objects

Love requires an Object,
But this varies so much,
Almost, I imagine,
 Anything will do:
When I was a child I
Loved a pumping engine,
Thought it every bit as
 Beautiful as you.
W. H. Auden

Summary

To prepare the way for an inquiry into whether, and how, emotions can be objective, we need to ask first how they relate to their objects. The question is so complex that some people have despaired of usefully treating it as a single question at all. But the unity of the topic is sustained by the thought that, in various ways, emotions provide us with information about ourselves and the world. Objects represent the variety of types of such information and their different relations to behavior and thought.

Again I begin with some puzzles, intended to set the stage for the next two chapters as well as this one. One puzzle casts doubt on the idea that emotions have objects in the world at all (what I hope may never come to pass). Another raises the Euthyphro *question: even if emotions do relate to real objects, are the properties that arouse our emotions really in those objects, or are they mere shadows of the emotions themselves? A third concerns whether we can incorrigibly know the objects of our own emotions (can I love, but not know whom I love?) A fourth is whether objects of emotions are identical with their causes (drunkenness may cause irritation but is not its object). A fifth is whether we can sometimes get rid of an emotion merely by redefining its objects ("We have nothing to fear but fear itself"). And the last is the problem of "fungibility": might the object of an emotion be replaceable provided the replacement duplicates the qualities of the original? Or, on the contrary, is love "not love which alters when it alteration finds"? All these puzzles exploit our conflicting intuitions about whether emotions are "objective" or "subjective."*

The method followed in addressing these puzzles is to analyze some cases, in order to motivate a comprehensive typology of objects of emotion. Seven categories of object are distinguished. A "target" is an actual particular to which an emotion relates. Targets must be distinguished from "focal properties," which are, under certain conditions, "motivating aspects"—what it is about the target that actually explains the emotion. To qualify as a motivating aspect, a focal property must figure in the causal explanation of the emotion and provide for it a minimal but intelligible justification. Emotions also have "causes," "aims," and "propositional objects." Most importantly, the character and conditions of appropriateness of any emotion type are defined by its "formal object"—roughly, what the focal property must be like for the emotion to be fitting.

How best to represent the relations between these various objects? Two alternative logical forms suggest themselves: a relational schema and a conjunctive one. In the relational schema, emotions are relations; the different types of objects are represented by variables of different categories. The conjunctive schema is built on the model of Donald Davidson's treatment of the ontology of events and construes emotions as generic "commotions" qualified in an arbitrary number of ways. I argue that the relational schema is more useful (though it does not explain everything) mainly because it does a better job with the puzzles of fungibility. The solution to those puzzles involves a crucial distinction between causes and explanations: the target, a particular, must figure in the causal history of a nonfungible emotion, whereas its motivating aspect, being a property and not a particular, belongs in their explanation. It was Amphitryon who figured crucially in the cause of Alcmene's love, but his qualities are needed to explain why. So although Zeus takes on all of Amphitryon's qualities, he is not the target of Alcmene's love.

The present typology of objects will equip us to tackle the central problem of this book: what the prospects are for emotional objectivity and rationality.

In this and the two following chapters I shall argue that emotions can at least sometimes be assessed, in their own way, for both objectivity and rationality. In this chapter I tackle the preliminary task of sorting out the variety of "object-directedness" in emotions. In chapter 6 I give reasons to think that emotions have something to tell us about the world, and I explore a "perceptual-epistemic" model according to which they can be ascribed an analogue of truth or correctness. That will prepare the way for the conception of emotional rationality that will be developed in chapter 7.

What Are Objects? Six Problems

I would like to begin by saying what I am talking about. But though I assume that we understand roughly what objects of emotion are, I cannot produce a definition. They are whatever an emotion is *of, at, with, because of*, or *that*. But as we shall see, the looseness of this characterization can hardly be overstressed. We need a taxonomy motivated by what we should like to say about the kinds of things emotions relate to, and the nature of those relations. In philosophy the best motivation lies in *aporia*. I shall begin, therefore, with six problems deliberately intended to promote strangeness.

The First Problem of Realism: Pseudorelations?
Most emotions, such as anger, fear, or love, appear to relate the emoter to something else, referred to by name or definite description. Sometimes (in fear or love) the something else need not be as the subject believes it to be. In some emotions (fear, but not so clearly love or anger) it need not even exist. But how can there be a real relation with a nonexistent thing?

A similar puzzle relates to propositional objects. Some third-person ascriptions of emotion require the truth of some contained proposition: 'He is indignant that the motion passed', for example, would be misleading if the motion had not passed.* Others come with no such requirement: to fear, to hope, to be eager, and, paradigmatically, to desire that p, do not imply the belief that p. On the contrary, they suggest (without quite implying) that p is false. So is there anything here to which the emotion is related? Or do we have only a pseudorelation generated by a grammatical illusion?

The Second Problem of Realism: The Euthyphro Question
In a second sense, the question about the reality of objects concerns whether there is any objective matter about which our emotions can

---

*A propositional attitude is called a *factive*, if it is properly ascribed only if its propositional content is true. The prototype of a factive is knowledge: *He knows that p* implies that p is true. The presumption of truth, however, is more easily defeasible in the case of, say, embarrassment than in the case of knowledge: *She knows that p—but p is false* is odd; *She is embarrassed that—as she thinks—p, but p is false* is not odd. At any rate, factive emotions (embarrassment or anger) definitely require that there be some proposition *believed* that evokes the emotion. Opinions differ concerning how many emotions are "factive." See Gordon 1969, and below, on "propositional objects."

be right or wrong. On this common sense is divided. We dispute about the appropriateness of our emotions: and dispute carries a presumption of objectivity. But on the other hand emotions are notoriously supposed to be subjective. Some are more so than others: we exact more detailed justification for indignation than we do for love; but that too requires explanation.

Such is the question Plato posed in the *Euthyphro*. It amounts to this: Are my emotions "all in the mind," or do they have real correlates in the outside world? Unfortunately, in this stark form the question is almost impossible to discuss. I shall be content with a more manageable question: whether, and how, the objects of emotion are less objective than those of other modes, such as ordinary sensory perception, the objectivity of which is generally taken for granted. "Taken for granted" does not mean "known to be true." As the history of philosophy demonstrates, no category of objects is immune to skepticism: individuals, universals, solid objects, theoretical entities, mind, or body. But here a comparative answer will suffice.

Privileged Access
Elizabeth Anscombe once toured America with the following story. A man went to sleep while leisurely making love. He dreamed he was shoveling coal and taking great pleasure in that activity. Then he woke up and discovered what he was really doing. "Good heavens," said the man, "I was mistaken in the object of my pleasure." If this story is intelligible, then it shows, at least prima facie, that it is possible to be mistaken about some objects of emotion. This contradicts the ancient prejudice that we have "privileged access" to our own mind and its objects. But for some emotions that prejudice is exceedingly plausible. How, for example, could I be in love and not know whom I loved?

Object and Cause
Many analyses of the relation between emotions and their objects view the object as *constitutive* of the emotion (see Sartre 1948; Kenny 1963; Solomon 1973). This means that the nature and identity of the object partly determine the identity of the emotion. Often—especially in the case of aesthetic emotions—it is natural to assume that if the emotion didn't have *this* object, it wouldn't be *this* emotion. (Only that recording of the Archduke Trio can make me feel *just so*.)

On the other hand, for O to be an object of an emotion E is commonly for O to be taken by the subject to be the cause of E. If I am distressed because you stole my teddy bear, I naturally believe that my distress was caused by your theft. Now unless I can blame you twice over—first for theft and second for distress—this gives rise to a dilemma. Is it the fact of your theft that caused my distress, or my belief in the theft? It cannot be the fact, it seems, because I would still be distressed if I were mistaken in thinking you had stolen my teddy bear, and there were no such fact. But it cannot be my belief, either. More exactly, if the cause *is* my belief, then this is an unknowable truth: one of those things that cannot be both true and believed. For if I believed that the true cause of my distress was my belief, surely I couldn't continue to be distressed at you.

These sophisms owe what power they have to the same source as the last three problems. All exploit our conflicting intuitions about the *Euthyphro* question—whether emotions genuinely connect us to the outside world or merely color our vision of it. In different ways, the next two puzzles also exploit this tension between the subjective and the objective.

The Magical Therapy of Solvent Analysis

"I'm feeling something, but I don't know what I'm feeling, and I feel that if I knew what I was feeling I wouldn't feel it any more," says a character in Alan Rudolph's film *Choose Me*. This might serve as the motto for a certain kind of philosophical therapy—or, as we shall see in chapter 9, as a formula for self-deception.

More instructive in the context of my present interest in objects, there is a curious disappearing act with objects that seems to follow from William James's famous slogan: "Our feeling of . . . bodily changes as they occur *is* the emotion." But suppose I am terrified *of* an approaching elephant. There is one 'of' too many here. See how it works: I recall James's analysis and think to myself, "Ah, this state which seems to be the consciousness *of* an approaching elephant—it is in fact merely an awareness *of* certain bodily changes! Those changes are no doubt caused by an awareness of an approaching elephant, but they themselves aren't dangerous: only the elephant is, and it isn't what I am aware *of*. So the *true* object of my fear is my body, which is literally *nothing to be afraid of*."

That too is a sophism, of course. But it serves to draw our attention to the fact that the "awareness of . . ." that emotions involve stands in need of more scrutiny.

Fungibility

Philosophers of perception sometimes debate whether what we really perceive are *things* or *qualities*. In connection with emotion this question has a special urgency. We have already encountered it as

"Alcmene's problem" and in connection with the plight of the denizens of Solaris. It can also be seen in the rather brutal treatment of love that we find in Plato. The ideal of love apparently advocated in the *Lysis* and *Symposium* involves a conversion from the loved one to his lovable qualities in themselves: we are urged, as it were, to commit adultery with our beloved's own good qualities.* (Should I be jealous of my own virtues, if you left me for them?) But this is only the last stage of love's saintly madness. At earlier stages, what rationality requires of us is merely holy promiscuity. Having realized that what we love in a young boy is his beauty—first physical, then intellectual—the rational thing to do is to love every other boy equally if he exemplifies the same qualities. This is Plato's dilemma: either endorse high-minded promiscuity, loving whomever you have reason to love, or admit that your love is literally groundless.

This is the problem of fungibility again. Actually, this problem splits into two distinguishable puzzles. To give them handles, I shall call the first one *Plato's love triangle*. It is strictly a problem about the ontology of the objects of emotion: when I love you, is it really you I love, or is it just your qualities? The second, which I shall continue to refer to as *Alcmene's problem*, is a corollary of the first: if there *is* an ontological difference between particulars and the sum of their properties, why should this matter?

Someone might answer, "It matters because it leads to incoherence. If the object of love is a bundle of qualities, you might find yourself in love with someone you had never met—your lover's twin, perhaps. And that's absurd." But this answer begs the question, for the situation is absurd only if the objects of love are, for some logical or metaphysical reason, necessarily unique. In chapter 4 I tried to clarify what it means for an emotion to be directed at a particular. But why should love be of this kind, and not rather, as Plato thought, directed at properties? When Zeus visits Alcmene in the guise of Amphitryon, he hasn't merely dressed up. He's taken on all of his qualities. (Indeed, he may be more like Amphitryon last month than Amphitryon will be when he returns.) So when Alcmene finds out, why (logically or morally) should she mind?

In the rest of this chapter I shall offer an analysis and typology of objects intended to resolve these puzzles. Before I do so, however, I should consider a proposal to sidestep the problem altogether.

---

*For example: "Once you have seen the vision of the very soul of beauty you will never again be seduced by the charms . . . of comely boys, or lads just ripening to manhood; you will care nothing for the beauties that used to take your breath away and kindle such a longing in you . . ." (Plato, *Symposium*, 211d).

A Skeptical View

In an incisive discussion of some staples of the recent literature, Helen Nissenbuam has concluded that the question of the "object-directedness" of emotions is a pseudoquestion, whose incoherence guarantees its insolubility. She distinguishes two senses of "object-directedness" or "intentionality." In one sense, these phrases merely mark the fact that emotions have a content, specifiable in terms of propositions and/or denoting expressions. In this sense, the intentionality or object-directedness of emotions is merely a grammatical matter without ontological implications. In another sense, the phrase implies genuine relation to some existing object. Moreover, she notes, two additional requirements have sometimes been placed on "objects" of emotion: one is that they be classifiable in terms of certain linguistic markers; the other is that they help to explain the existence of the emotion (Nissenbaum 1986, 6ff.). She suggests that many of the more bizarre doctrines propounded by Anthony Kenny (1963) and others on the "noncontingency" of the relation of emotions to their objects may be traced to the incoherence of those various requirements on "objects." Once those requirements are kept apart, she contends, puzzles such as those I have labeled "pseudo-relations" will vanish.

Nissenbaum also points out that each account of the intentionality of emotions is tailored to fit only a subclass of cases. So each theory's favored cases automatically furnish a stock of counterexamples to all the other theories (p. 65). If this is so, then there is no single legitimate problem about the "objects of emotions." Instead, we should study the various "aspects" of *emotional episodes.* These include the individual or state of affairs on which the emotion is "focused," as well as various explanatory properties (p. 72).[1]

This skeptical dismembering of the enterprise has its attraction. Indeed, my own strategy will have much in common with it, as I begin, in the next two sections, by trying to arrive at a taxonomy of the different factors that are commonly lumped together under the name of "objects."

Nevertheless, I shall continue to speak of those various factors as objects and to think of my inquiry into their ways as part of a single enterprise. The perspective of the last two chapters should help to explain why. I view emotions as emerging, like our other mental capacities, out of biological roots that connect us to the world, including our own past and future. The mode of this connection has gradually shifted from the simple causality of reflexes to increasingly sophisticated modes of representation, with the emergence, first, of quasi intentionality, second, of relatively irreducible motivation, and finally, of the full capacity for singular reference. The unifying idea behind all kinds of object-directedness is the idea of *meaningful representation of information*. The information I have in mind is not confined to the world outside the subject: if I am angry at you, my anger tells me not merely that you have done some wrong but also that I am in a position to assess and react to it. The many kinds of information implicated make for a rich mess, but one mess, after all, can still make one topic.

Where there is information, misinformation lurks. The present perspective on objects therefore leads naturally to my central preoccupation in this book: the possibility, extent, and nature of the *objectivity* of emotions—and hence, as I shall explain in chapter 6, of their rationality. It is this unifying concern that moves me to continue thinking of the multifarious factors gathered under the general rubric of "objects" as properly part of a single inquiry. To meet Nissenbaum's objections, however, we need to base our typology on something more solid than superficial grammar.

The Typology of Objects

To make a start on such a typology, I shall proceed on the assumption defended in the last two chapters: that it makes sense to think of emotions as having biological functions. The first hypothesis to be explored is that emotions can profitably be compared to perception. In pursuing this hypothesis, I shall be guided by an important methodological principle advocated by Ruth Millikan. This principle, which I shall call the *priority of success,* Millikan explains as follows:

> If . . . mental intentional states (believing that, intending to, hoping that) are members of proper function or "biological" categories, then they are . . . intentional states not by virtue of their powers but by virtue of what they are supposed to do yet perhaps cannot do. . . . [I]f . . . we push the analogy with biological categories, only *true* beliefs are capable of performing the defining functions of beliefs. We will then be free to look for the defining attributes of beliefs among relations between *true* beliefs and the *actual* world outside. False beliefs will then appear merely as things that were "supposed to" have had such and such relations to the outside world. (Millikan 1984, 17–18)

Similarly, when emotions purport to have objects that do not actually exist, I shall assume that the normal case is the purported case, and that the normal case is the one we should analyze first. (Once again, the concept of normality seems indispensable.)

Let us return to the first of our introductory problems: the problem of "pseudorelations." A straightforward way to bring out the features of normal cases is to compare them with various ways in which things can go wrong. So my procedure will be this: I shall sketch some skeleton cases in which something has gone wrong and collect the lessons they suggest into a series of theses about types of objects and their relation to emotions and their causes. (For more convenient reference, these and other labeled propositions are collected in the Appendix.)[2]

Targets
Many emotion ascriptions make an apparent reference to an actual particular. Sometimes the purported reference fails.

Suppose Calvin says, "I am angry at the person who stole my bicycle." But he is wrong in thinking that his bicycle has been stolen at all. This can be read in two ways.

In one class of cases Calvin has no suspect in mind. The sign that something has gone wrong here is that although Calvin's ascription of anger to himself is sincerely based on the existence of certain feelings, those feelings would not survive Calvin's discovery of the relevant facts.

Another variant differs only in that Calvin believes of a specific person S that S stole his bicycle. Here again, the ascription would be modified by Calvin's discovery either that someone else stole it or that no one did. The difference between the two variants can be expressed in terms of the grades of intentionality discussed in chapter 4. Both variants credit the world with containing a real bicycle thief. But in the first the thief is specified only generally, whereas in the second she is referred to as a singular individual.

In another class of cases, like hope or fear, the nonexistence of the particular purportedly referred to does not always extinguish the emotion, even when it is known by the subject of ascription. Usually the discovery that the object of fear (a lion loose in the city, say) does not exist is enough to dispel fear. But sometimes—in cases of "irrational fear" (or "theological hope")—such knowledge would have no effect.*

---

*Cases where disbelieving in ghosts, say, fails to dispel the fear of ghosts encourage the thought that emotions form a sort of parallel epistemic world. So perhaps does the related case of emotions experienced in the context of fiction; on these, see Walton 1978.

This first group of cases suggests the first two theses, which also embody terminological proposals:

(I) *Target.* The *target* of an emotion is a real object, typically an actual particular, to which that emotion relates. The target is that real object, if any, *at* which the emotion is directed.[3]

(II) *Proper target.* A target of an emotion is also its *proper target*, if and only if it would remain unchanged by the subject's possession of full relevant knowledge.

An important point to note here is that although there are some apparent exceptions, emotions have targets *in their own right*. The apparent exceptions occur when there is a specific reference within the propositional content of the emotion. In such cases the referential conditions are fixed not by the nature of the emotion but by that of the proposition. Thus, if I aspire to find my old bicycle, where I falsely believe that I had one, there does seem to be something wrong in virtue of the failure of reference, and the failure is traceable to the presupposed belief, not to the emotion. But targets cannot in general simply be assimilated to particulars referred to in some belief in which the emotion is grounded. In at least some cases no belief is either necessary or sufficient for the existence of the emotion. A typical example is love, which is notoriously compatible with the most inauspicious beliefs about its target. Nor can reducibility of the target to a component of a proposition be salvaged by substituting propositional objects of desire for those of beliefs. For as Jerome Shaffer (1978) has shown, the irreducibility of targets is a feature of desire itself. (This is no accident if, as I shall argue in chapter 6, desire usually has an emotional component.) Though sexual desire is typically satisfied by sexual contact, 'Kathy desires Marian' neither entails nor follows from any variant of 'Kathy desires to have sexual contact with Marian'. I shall return to our capacity for emotion de re (see "Fungibility Revisited").

Focus and Motivating Aspect
Where there is a target, the emotion—again in normal cases—will be *motivated* by some attribute of the target, which will be a *focus* of the subject's attention. Here again, there are a variety of ways in which an emotion can somehow go wrong with respect to the motivating attribute. The third thesis also fixes some terminology:

(III) *Focus, focal property, and motivating aspect.* Emotions having targets typically involve a *focus* of attention, which is the apprehension of some (real or illusory) *focal property* of the target. Under certain conditions, which define the standard case, the focal property is also the *motivating aspect* of these emotions.

Cause

To explore the conditions in question, let us look at a case involving *contempt*. Contempt is an emotion with a target that may or may not be a proper target and a focus that may or may not settle on a motivating aspect.

Case 1. Wendy despises Bernie, she thinks, for his vulgar musical taste. But really his musical taste has nothing to do with her feelings. The truth is that Bernie's voice, though she has never actually noticed it, reminds her of her hated grandmother, and that is what arouses her feelings of contempt.

Implicit in the description of this case is a distinction between motivating aspect and cause. Bernie's voice, not his musical taste, is the cause of Wendy's feeling of contempt. So although Bernie's musical tastes are the focus of her contempt, they are disqualified from being a motivating aspect.

This gives us thesis (IV), which is also illustrated by Anscombe's case about mistaking the objects of pleasure.

(IV) *First causal condition.* A causal connection between the focal property and the occurrence of the emotion is a *necessary condition* for the former to be a motivating aspect.

The first causal condition has an important corollary. Since Wendy is wrong, as anyone might be, about the causes of her feelings, thesis (IV) entails that there is no privileged access to motivating aspects. Call this thesis (V):

(V) *Corrigibility.* There is no privilege of incorrigibility in the subject's access to motivating aspects.

Only two things *can*—for different reasons—be known without empirical investigation by the subject of belief or emotion: the focus of conscious attention involved, and the fact that the grounds would, if true, be relevant or adequate. The former is known without observation in virtue of mere linguistic convenience: we need some word for whatever the subject thinks is a motivating aspect, and the phrase 'focus of conscious attention' will do. The latter is known without observation because relevance is a logical and not a causal matter; but it is not incorrigible, since we can all make mistakes in logic.

Is the causal condition also sufficient? Could it be that Bernie's voice is the real motivating aspect responsible for Wendy's contempt in case 1? It seems obvious that it could not. Buy why?

One specious answer is that the motivating aspect has to be a focus of *conscious* attention. Wendy has not actually noticed Bernie's voice, let alone become aware of the peculiarly provocative association that links it to her detested grandmother. If she had, would it then be the motivating aspect for her contempt? No. For reasons discussed in chapter 4, an unconscious focus is just as surely relevant as a conscious one. Two more cases will help to make this clear.

Case 2. Wendy despises Bernie, ostensibly because of his taste, but the real cause of her contempt (though she is quite unaware of it) is that he is a Jew.

In case 2 Wendy's antisemitism does clearly constitute the motivating aspect even though it is unconscious. But that diagnosis will not work for case 1, because the voice-association in case 1 does not play the same role as the antisemitism in case 2. A third case will bring out the difference:

Case 3. Wendy thinks she despises Bernie for his musical tastes. But she is really the subject of an experiment on the chemical control of the emotions, and the real cause of what she takes to be her attitude is some direct physiological intervention in her brain.

In case 3 it is clear that the intervention in Wendy's brain could not possibly constitute a motivating aspect. The difference with case 2 is that antisemitism, but not chemical influence, might in some context be used to justify the emotion as correct or legitimate. Though that is a bad reason, chemistry is no reason at all. I shall say more later about this demand of intelligibility. For the moment I merely make it explicit as thesis (VI):

> (VI) *Intelligibility condition.* Motivating aspects must be *rationally related* to the emotion they cause, in the sense that they must constitute *intelligible rationalizations* for the emotion.

Motivation, in the relevant sense, belongs to the sphere of rational discourse. It must therefore aspire to conformity with rational norms.

Beliefs illustrate a similar constraint. Grounds of belief need not be conscious, since not all legitimate inference is explicit. But a cause of belief does not count as a ground unless it could figure as the premise of an intelligible inference. Though association often causes belief, in itself it is a nonrational connection.

Thesis (VI) makes a similar claim for emotion. The focus, whether conscious or unconscious, not only must be causally effective but also must be of a kind that, *if* it became a content of consciousness, would make the emotion intelligible. This is not the same as to say that it would legitimize it, or even that the subject, once aware of it, would not repudiate it altogether. But the difference between the disreputable motive of antisemitism and the cases of mere association or of chemical intervention is that in those cases the rationalizing connection is not even intelligible.

In case 1 I described the association as causing Wendy's *feelings* of contempt. This was due neither to imprecision nor to coyness. The explanation follows from what I have just said: we cannot say that the association arouses Wendy's contempt *tout court*, because the discovery of the real cause of her feelings must almost certainly render the word 'contempt' inapplicable.

Illusory Focus
So far the troubles with focus have been due to the failure either of (IV), the first causal condition, or of (VI), the intelligibility condition. One more possible trouble with focal property remains to be considered: the case where it fulfills all the conditions so far listed for being the motivating aspect but where it is based on a false belief:

Case 4. Bernie admires Wendy. The focus of his admiration is that when she was six years old she played solo violin with the Toronto Symphony Orchestra. But Bernie is mistaken. The story on which his belief rests is a stubborn legend, which has persisted in their circle in spite of Wendy's denials.

This case (call it *illusory focus*) requires that we refine our conception of the role of causation. For it puts us squarely before both of the problems about realism: pseudorelations and the *Euthyphro* question.

So far I have established that some causal relation between focus and emotion was necessary, but not sufficient, for the corresponding focal property to qualify as motivating aspect. Now in case 4 the focus of Bernie's admiration clearly satisfies (IV), the first causal condition for being a motivating aspect. But what exactly does the causal relation hold between? Since the focus is illusory, the focal property is not available to be the relatum of any causal connection. Is the relatum in such cases then the focus itself—an epistemic state (conscious or unconscious)? If it is, the first problem of realism is solved. For there is some real thing that is the relatum sought: namely, the relevant epistemic state.

But this solution won't do. The proposal to treat some mental state as the desired relatum projects us into a particularly bizarre form of the problem of realism. If it were correct, then you would always be wrong about the cause of your emotion regardless of your beliefs about it. For the content of your belief is that the relevant focal property is the cause of the emotion. But on the present proposal that cannot be true, for the cause of an emotion is always the belief itself. Nor can that belief figure as its own content, because that would make it viciously self-referential. It would become the belief that the emotion was caused by the belief that the emotion was caused by the belief. . . .

The solution to this tangle may be found in the parallel with inferential knowledge. In inferential knowledge the structure of causality and justification involves two levels. On one level the belief must have been caused, and not merely justified, by the other beliefs that constitute its grounds. This necessary condition says nothing about the truth of the premises. But in addition the belief in the premises must have been caused by the fact itself (or, if facts cannot be causes, by some event bearing a suitable relation to the facts).

Similarly with emotions. The grounds of the emotion correspond to the premises of an inferential belief: they must cause the emotion, or else they are nonstarters.

This gives rise to a second claim about causality, thesis (VII):

> (VII) *Second causal condition.* For a focal property to be a motivating aspect, it must be an actual property of the target.

The first causal condition requires merely that the right causal connections exist inside the subject. The second allows the world to be relevant to emotion. It provides the element of genuine relation guessed at by our preanalytic intuition.

Aim

The connection of the emotions with the world is not all one way. In chapter 4, in fact, we looked mostly at the other direction of causation: the effect of emotions, through motivation, on the world. This may remind us that the word 'object' has yet another meaning. Emotions also have objects in the sense of goals or *aims.* And although aims do not relate directly to the perceptual model, I shall, for completeness, include an emotion's aims in our classification of objects.

As we saw in chapter 4, aims are most commonly arranged hierarchically. Aims, like causes, can be remote or proximate. Robert Solomon has argued that all emotions share a higher-level aim: "Self-esteem is the goal of every passion" (Solomon 1976, 97). The aims I have in mind here are the more proximate, consisting rather in immediate expressive behavior.

From an evolutionary point of view, the *behavioral* effects of emotions must have been essential to making them just what they are. In simple cases this means that an emotion will have a characteristic immediate aim—something that it would *make us do*. In the case of "violent" emotions these might be governed by Panksepp's behavioral subsystems. In other cases the aim is vestigial—only some form of expression, perhaps even only an inclination to some utterance.

A few thought experiments are enough to show that aims can differentiate emotions: could we jump for depression? slouch from joy? smile with envy? rave with benevolence? snicker out of pride? The answer to all these questions is, Well, yes, but not *really*. We could snicker out of pride, given a suitably convoluted chain of motivation. But in some intuitive sense we couldn't do those things as natural expressions of the emotions in question—though what counts as a natural expression is hard to say.*

One more qualification is needed. The natural aim of an emotion is not to be confused with the aim that someone might have in expressing or even in feeling one. Striving to evince a sense of humor in order to impress someone with one's wit could be a certain kind of "aim," but that aim, far from contributing to the nature of wit, obviously undermines the claim to have any. The "naturally" expressive aims with which I am concerned here are not in this way self-defeating. On the contrary, they partly define the character of the emotions they express.

I record the contribution of aims to the identity criteria of any particular emotion as thesis (VIII):

> (VIII) *Aim.* The motivational role of emotions defines their characteristic *aims* and acts as a constraint on the character of each specific emotion.

It will be useful to have this sense in place when in chapter 6 I come to consider the analogy between emotion and perception. For one of the objections to that analogy will be the claim that the only appropriateness of which emotions are capable stems from their practical utility.

Formal Objects
Cutting across the categories already discussed are two ways in which an emotion can fail to be appropriate. C. D. Broad made a start on describing these:

---

*Compare the problem of determining under what conditions desire and belief cause an action "in the right way" to make the action an intentional one. Donald Davidson has described the case of a climber so unnerved by his own desire to let go of the rope holding another climber that he lets go in fact; "yet it might be the case that he never *chose* to loosen his hold, nor did he do it intentionally" (Davidson 1973, 79).

Some kinds of emotional quality are *fitting* and others are *unfitting* to a given kind of epistemological object. It is appropriate to cognize what one takes to be a *threatening* object with some degree of *fear*. It is inappropriate to cognize what one takes to be a fellow man *in undeserved pain or distress* with *satisfaction* or with *amusement*. Then again, an emotion which is fitting in *kind* to its epistemological object, may be unfitting in *degree,* i.e. inordinate. . . . (Broad 1971, 293)

As Broad concedes, much more needs to be said about this notion of appropriateness. To begin with, there is a contrast that Broad did not draw sharply enough. Both his criteria—of kind and of degree—can in some measure claim to lay down some conditions of rationality for emotions. But, as he explains it, the difference between kind and degree seems itself to be merely a difference in degree: the inappropriateness of amusement to pain seems to be no more than a particularly nasty example of a disproportionate reaction. But surely it is more than that. We need to delimit the very *conditions of intelligibility* for a given emotion in terms of the properties it implicitly ascribes to the target. The idea we are looking for is that of the *formal object,* which I define in thesis (IX):

(IX) *Formal object.* For each emotion, there is a second-order property that must be implicitly ascribed to the motivating aspect if the emotion is to be intelligible. This essential element in the structure of each emotion is its *formal object.*[4]

The formal object is a second-order property in the sense that it is supervenient on some other property or properties: something is frightening by virtue of being dangerous, for example. But I shall sometimes speak more loosely—and more naturally—as if the formal property were simply a property of the target. In this looser sense, an emotion is *appropriate,* in part, if the target actually has a focal property in virtue of which the formal object fits the target. Other necessary criteria of appropriateness, including intensity and fittingness on ethical or aesthetic grounds, are quite properly matters of degree and are highly sensitive to context.

The notion of formal object applies to any state having a content assessable for correctness: it is then, by definition, the *standard of correctness* for that state. Thus, *truth* is the formal object of *belief,* and goodness or *desirability* is the formal object of *want.*[5] The specific formal object associated with a given emotion is essential to the definition of that particular emotion.

"Emotion," as Richard Wollheim (1984, 35) has put it, "is a formal word." Suppose I say, "I've just had a thought." You ask, "What thought?" If I now give you the object of my thought—its target and/or propositional content—I have specified my thought. But merely to provide the target of an emotion, or even its motivating aspect, does not yet specify what emotion we are dealing with. For that, we need to pin down the formal object.

There are as many formal objects as there are different emotion types. As we shall see, the resulting multiplicity of formal objects has important consequences. It explains why the evaluation of the emotions tends to be an even messier business than the evaluation of truth or goodness (see chapter 7), and why the contribution of emotion to ethical life is especially complex (see chapter 12).

Two Approaches to Canonical Emotion Ascriptions

I have collected seven types of factors having some claim to be called "objects" of emotions (plus some glosses and variants): target (ostensible or proper), focus and focal property, motivating aspect, cause, aim, proposition, and formal object. Is there some way to regiment this information into a compendious general formula, so as to parlay our typology of objects into a typology of emotions themselves?

Logical Form

It is sometimes a fruitful strategy in philosophical analysis to replace common or garden grammatical forms and categories with a model in terms of which the sentences of ordinary language can be construed.[6] This is the method of *logical form*. The point of it is to find "canonical" models for ordinary sentence types that exhibit interesting semantical categories and inferential relations in their visible structure. (Hence, they are commonly, though not necessarily, provided by the representation systems of symbolic logic.)

There are three expected benefits of this exercise. First, many sentences are structurally ambiguous: they can simultaneously admit opposite truth values on different interpretations. Since a canonical representation is committed to a single interpretation, such representations can serve to disambiguate English sentences. Second, logical form is supposed to expose deep structural differences and similarities beneath the grammatical surface. Those deeper structural relations—assuming that they have some psychological reality—explain some of our intuitions about meaning and inference. Third, if we are to have any hope of modeling emotions in information-processing systems—even without aiming, for the moment, at breaking the simulation barrier—we shall need some theory about the deep structure of the sentences that ascribe them.

One classic example of the method of logical form is Russell's treatment of definite descriptions, which I shall use to illustrate disambiguation.

According to Russell (1905), a sentence containing a definite description, such as 'The cat is on the mat', bears only a superficial resemblance to one containing a genuine proper name. (A genuine proper name is one whose meaning consists entirely in the fact that it refers to some actual particular.) Instead, it is best represented by a model in which no single item corresponds to the definite description. A predicate F attributed to the bearer of a true proper name a is of the form Fa, or 'a is F'. But the English grammatical form (1)

(1) The A is F

is represented as having the very different canonical form (2),

(2) $(\exists x)(y)((Ay$ iff $(x=y))$ & $Fx)$

which says that *exactly one thing is A and that thing is F.*

In the classic use of it for disambiguation, Russell's model distinguishes two interpretations of 'King George IV wished to know whether Scott was the author of *Waverley*'. One is (3),

(3) George IV wished to know whether (2), that is, whether
$(\exists x)(y)((Sy$ iff $(x=y))$ & $Wx))$

which Russell paraphrased back into English as 'George IV wished to know whether one and only one man is Scott and that man wrote *Waverley*'. The other interpretation is (4),

(4) $(\exists x)(y)((Sy$ iff $x=y)$ and George IV wished to know whether $(Wx))$

which translates back as 'One and only one man is Scott and George IV wished to know whether that man wrote *Waverly*'.

A similar distinction of "scope" can be made for other mental states, including emotions. Thus, George IV might have been interested in, enthusiastic about, or resentful of the fact that Scott was the author of *Waverley*, in either of the senses corresponding to (3) and (4)—depending on whether Scott is being identified as the target of the emotion within or without the content of the emotion. This was the distinction involved earlier, between the two interpretations of Calvin's anger at the bicycle thief.

To illustrate the second use of logical form—to shed light on intuitive patterns of inference—I turn to Donald Davidson's treatment of event and action sentences.

Following Anthony Kenny (1963), Davidson (1967a) notes our capacity for inferring the occurrence of an event characterized by fewer adverbs from the occurrence of an event more elaborately qualified: from 'Caesar was murdered by Brutus at the Capitol on the Ides of March with a dagger', we readily infer that Caesar was murdered. This causes no problem for common sense, but it does pose a problem for any theory that views events as having the logical form of a relation between constituents represented by the adverbial phrases. For the first description is then apparently of a five-term relation, having the canonical form $R(stuxy)$, whereas the bare fact that Caesar was murdered is a one-term relation, $R(x)$. The point is that standard logical theory, to which these representations belong, contains no *syntactically driven* pattern of inference that can explain the obviousness of this informal one. To solve this problem, Davidson (1967a) has suggested that quantification should be over events rather than over the objects involved. Adverbial qualifications—'by Brutus', 'at the Capitol'—become predicates of events in the model. The inference in question then simply involves deriving one or more conjuncts from a conjunction. Our intuitions are explained by the obvious validity of going from (5) to (6):

(5) x is a murder-event and x is F and x is G and x is H. . . .
(6) x is a murder-event.

From these examples it is easy to guess at the promise of a logical form approach to emotions and their objects. First, we can hope to effect a regimentation into a definite number of basic patterns of the variety of constructions used in emotion ascriptions. Second, we may hope to place these constructions into a context where the theory correctly predicts our intuitions about what inferences to make, as in the case of Calvin's bicycle. Both these advantages would be indispensable in any attempt to set up a computer model of emotions and the rules for their attribution.

To see how much of this promise can be made good, I consider two possible models of sentences about emotions. On the *relational* schema, emotions are relations between the subject and the various kinds of objects I have listed. On the *conjunctive* schema, they are construed on the model of Davidson's events.

The Relational Schema
One simple way to begin is to collect as many features as seem relevant to the characterization of some typical emotion, and to think of

an occurrence of that emotion as a *relation* between them. The structure of anger, for example, would seem to include an implicit reference to all the factors listed above. So anger would fit the *relational schema*,

(RS) *Relational schema*. $R(Stfacmp)$

where R stands for an emotion type, S is the subject, t the target, f the focal property, a the motivating aspect (which in the standard case is identical with f), c the cause, m the aim, and p the proposition specifying the ground of anger.

An important point hangs on the fact that I have not included a symbol for the formal object. My reason is that I regard the formal object as implicit in the specification of the species of emotion involved. We might, alternatively, have read R in schema (RS) as a constant ("experiences some emotion") rather than as a relational variable standing for an emotion type. In that case the formal object would belong within the parentheses, as a specification of the kind of emotion R is. But it is more perspicuous to pack the formal object into R because this draws attention to the fact that emotions do not form a species congeneric with beliefs and wants. Rather, *each emotion type is a unique species defined by its formal object.* This is not to imply that once the formal object has been fixed, anything goes for the other parameters. Clearly, as shown by our tiny thought experiments about jumping for depression and other ill-matched aims, other parameters constrain the range of emotions they fit in with. But formal objects do not merely constrain the emotion, they define it.

According to (RS), a case of anger would be canonically represented by specifying all the variables in the schema. Who is angry? At what target? Focusing on what about the target? Motivated by what about the target? To what behavior? Because of what event? And angry exactly that what proposition is true?

Not all emotions have the same number of relevant constituent factors, or *polyadicity.* Depression is typically targetless, hope at least sometimes so. Love typically lacks a propositional object; it is, as we say with unconscious precision, typically thoughtless. Jealousy and perhaps pride have two targets instead of one.* And so on. (But does any emotion altogether lack an aim?) Hence, different classes of emo-

---

*On Hume's analysis, pride always involves the self, as well as the thing of which I am proud (my house, say) and the motivating aspect (my house's beauty). The self and the thing can be thought of as an ordered pair of targets; though being simply proud of myself for some quality would seem to be a slightly different case of pride, since the second target is superfluous. See Hume 1739, pt. 2; also, for a discussion, Davidson 1976.

tions might be at least partly differentiated by the logical form of the sentences in which we ascribe them, whereas emotions of the same kind would differ from each other in terms of the values of a given set of parameters. But beyond that the formula leaves out a good deal of the detail that has emerged already. It also raises further difficulties that, as we shall see, are not fatal but look serious enough.

First, the terms in this relation are alarmingly heteroclite. The term appearing in the place of S is a referentially transparent singular term. The target, t, is normally also a singular term, but it could be interpreted on the model of either Russell's (3) or his (4). If Zeno is dismayed that someone stole the finish post, then either there is someone with whom Zeno is dismayed, or Zeno is dismayed with whomever it was, and so on. Moreover, it is not entirely clear how to categorize a and f. They are apparently both properties, but a case could be made for the claim that they are really *instantiations of properties*, something like *dependent particulars* in Aristotle's sense, like *the particular whiteness in some man*. In which case they would, after all, have the logical status of particulars.

Second, what is perceived as the cause cannot always be tied to a particular at all. The closest we might come to a characterization of the cause may be the whole sentence itself. In the case of Zeno's dismay, we might insist that there is a putative target—the thief—but we might also think of t as an event or situation rather than a conventional particular: c, a, and the unspecified thief who takes the place of t then all collapse into p, for the content of p is precisely *that (some) t is a*. And on Zeno's own account p might be just what caused his anger. I return to the problem of propositional objects in the final section of this chapter.

Third, the terms in the relation, although seeming too diverse in one way, are also not diverse enough. For uniformity, the virtue of regimentation, is also its vice. It precludes the exploration of subtleties that might be involved in the idiomatic differences that it is precisely the point of the logical form approach to ignore. Many emotion verbs or verbal phrases do not have direct grammatical objects, even when they have objects that can intuitively be thought of as targets. 'Love', 'hate', 'resent', 'fear', 'despise', 'regret', 'envy' are some that do; 'hope' does not; nor do any of these common verbal phrases: one is 'in love or angry with', 'resentful, envious, or jealous of', 'embarrassed by', 'grateful to', and so on.

Many ordinary idioms could use some regimentation. Jealousy's two targets, for example, are not clearly distinguished. When you say 'Ellen is jealous of Sarah,' is the latter Ellen's lover or her rival? And although there is probably a difference between the case where I am annoyed *with* you and the case where I am annoyed *at* you, what precisely is the nuance, if any, conveyed by the fact that I can be *annoyed with* you but not *jealous with* anyone? Perhaps ordinary language is haphazard here. But we should not allow the logical form approach to force us to that conclusion a priori.

The Conjunctive Schema
The inference from 'Zeno is dismayed that someone stole the post' to 'Zeno is dismayed' is obviously valid in virtue of some structural feature. But (RS) exhibits no features capable of explaining such inferences across different polyadicities.

This sounds very much like Davidson's problem with the varying polyadicity of events: events of higher polyadicities (the murder of Caesar by Brutus at the Capitol on the Ides of March with a knife in the back in the morning before the people . . .) should formally entail ones of lower polyadicities (the murder of Caesar), but on the relational view of events no available principles of inference explain this (see Davidson 1967a).

Moreover, it would be nice to think of emotions as *species* of a *genus*. Adapting Davidson's strategy here might seem to make this easy. Every (occurrent) emotion could be viewed, with Descartes and Lyons, as a feeling in the soul linked to bodily changes. Let us call this a generic *commotion*. Then the species can be characterized in terms of the predicates of that commotion. The distinction among emotions will be marked by the number and nature of the parameters fixed in each one. Occurrent emotions are, of course, events, so this is a direct application of Davidson's ontological proposal. Any ascription of emotion would refer to an event, x, which is an emotional commotion, characterized by a number of conjunctive properties. This is the *conjunctive schema*,

(CS) *Conjunctive schema.* $(\exists x)$ ([Commotion]x & Sx & Tx & Ax . . .)

where $S, T, A,$ and so forth, stand for such properties as *is felt by S, has target t, has motivating aspect a,* and so forth. A refinement of this approach might borrow from the physiologist the idea that there are different fundamental types of commotions—linked to Panksepp's four basic circuits, perhaps, with many emotions being mixtures. Will this give (CS) the advantage over (RS)?

(CS) was derived from a theory invented to allow for the treatment of events as particulars, referred to by singular terms. This is useful for the theory of targets in two ways. First, targets are sometimes events, and since by definition targets must be particulars, the logical form we ascribe to their assignment should not preclude this. A second reason for taking some targets to be events is that only events are causes, and targets are often intuitively identified with an emotion's cause. (I return to this point presently.)

These are advantages of (CS). But they are not decisive. We need to test both models against a single problem. Let us apply them to the first problem of fungibility, Plato's love triangle. (CS) yields something like this as the logical form of 'S loves t for (being) a':

$(\exists x)$ ([Commotion]x & [had-by-S]x & [at-target-t]x & [for-aspect-a]x)

One problem here is that the predicates in the formula (like Davidson's predicates of events) are unstructured as far as this representation goes. Nothing, in the representation as such, explains why the target's position is in any categorial way different from the motivating aspect's. It leaves the problem of Plato's triangle untouched. In the words of Yeats, "How can we know the dancer from the dance?"

On the relational schema, by contrast, we can distinguish between the categories of the terms in different positions. It is a quasi-grammatical point that targets are particulars: one may well love someone *for* her qualities, but one loves *someone* (or, to be at least initially broad-minded, *something*): and it is t in (RS) that names the target, not whatever follows the 'for' or 'because'. The focal property, by contrast, is a property (or at least a "dependent particular"). Schema (RS) dictates that p, t, a, and c belong to different logical categories in virtue of their position in the relation. So to abandon "the dancer for the dance"—or to fail to tell them apart—is to make, pace Yeats and Plato, a simple category mistake.

Besides, (RS) does not really saddle us with the problem of variable polyadicity that motivated Davidson's ontology of events. There is a solution to that problem that will work for emotions, though not for events.

The problem with events was that there is no *determinate* number of properties an event can have. So learning all the possible inferences we might make would be indefinitely exhausting work. That is a powerful argument for Davidson's proposal. But with emotions we can simply assume that any given type has a unique polyadicity, so that it is fully specified by some determinate number of core parameters. It is not *jealousy* unless there are two targets, which moreover must be related in prescribed ways both to each other and to the subject; but the propositional object can be left hazy. Conversely, *regret* requires at least a propositional object, although it is unclear whether a target is implied as well. On a given occasion not all might be specified, but the ascription would then be treated as elliptical. 'She loves' means she loves *someone*. On another occasion we might add further details, but these would not be needed to identify the emotion.

The balance tips in favor of the relational model. (RS) seems immune to the problems that led to the invention of (CS) and seems to give us more insight into the logical form of Plato's triangle.

Still, one would like a deeper explanation of what really makes the difference between categories of objects: this is not transparently exhibited by (RS). We are given room to make category distinctions between particulars in different positions, but the theory of logical form expressed in (RS) has nothing to say about the significance of those distinctions. In terms of the hope of finding a representation of emotion ascriptions usable in the context of computer simulations, (RS) is a start, but it is clear that we shall need to fill in a great many more structural details.

Moreover, there were two puzzles of fungibility, and only one receives even the formal solution just mentioned. The other, Alcmene's problem, cannot be explained in quite the same way, because there is no difference of category between Amphitryon and Zeus: they are both targets. If the motivating aspect resides in the target's possession of some relevant property, then the distinction between target and aspect does not solve Alcmene's problem. So let us pursue that problem a bit further.

Fungibility Revisited

Must Alcmene love Zeus? Most people would deny it. Perhaps the reason is merely a distracting irrelevance, namely, the curious but common belief that one can only love one person at a time. In some forms of love, especially the sort of sexual love that Dorothy Tennov (1979) has baptized *limerence*, the uniqueness of the limerent object is a definitional requirement, answering to something many people experience. But not all loves, let alone other emotions, are of that kind, and the problem arises as well for other forms of love. Suppose I love tall skinny men in general. Still, the extension of my affection to a fresh candidate meeting this requirement is not just a matter of logic: even the best of reasons do not compel.

In the last section I claimed to find a partial solution to Plato's love triangle in the category difference between target and focal property. But this might yet be challenged. Grant that the target and the motivating aspect belong to different logical categories: we can still go on to ask, "What explains that just this characteristic is a motivating aspect? Why is it, in other words, that this color, shape, or virtue confers desirability on the object that has it?" Any answer must appeal to some second-order property of the character in question: its power to confer desirability. The desirability-conferring feature of some characteristic, in turn, either is self-evident or requires a further explanation in terms of some third-order power. That also must either be self-evident or . . . , and so on.

This threatening regress reveals a deeper motivation for Plato's problem: we need to explain why some explanations are explanatory and others not. Why is it sometimes obvious that a given emotion is or is not appropriate?

We accept an explanation either when we are led to say (1), "Now I see why S must be feeling E" or when we are led to say (2), "Now I see why S is justified in feeling E." Option (1) is the end of a chain of causal explanation, (2) the end of a process of rational explanation. They are easily confounded, because when an emotional reaction strikes us as normal, the two go together: S is feeling E just for the reason that one would expect. But how exactly are these two levels of explanation related?

Explanation and Cause

In a well-known paper Donald Davidson (1967b) has drawn attention to a crucial distinction between singular causal statements and causal explanations. I shall argue that this distinction can solve both puzzles of fungibility even if we opt for the relational schema.

Singular causal statements are extensional: 'C caused E' implies the existence of both C and E, and its truth value is the same regardless of the descriptions under which C and E are picked out.

By contrast, a full-dress causal explanation is general and intentional: it brings the events in question under the scope of a general statement linking the kinds of events that they are. I speak of a "full-dress" explanation because informally a singular causal statement— 'The fire was caused by a burning cigarette'—counts as giving an explanation. The evidential backing for a singular causal statement typically includes a full-dress explanation. (Or more precisely, as Davidson showed, the singular statement implies that there is a full explanation, even though we might not know what it is.) Consequently, the precise way that the events are picked out is material to explanations but not to singular causal statements.

Here is how this applies to the present problem. Targets, referred to by singular terms, are particulars that must have been involved in the event that caused the emotion. The motivating aspects, on the other hand, are properties in virtue of which the target played its role: they form the putative basis of an explanation for the emotion. They must therefore be capable of appearing in an explanatory statement.*

As I have argued, the category difference suffices to explain the fallacy in the regress generated from Plato's love triangle—the problem of whether the real objects of love are particular or general. For by establishing a category difference between target and motivating aspect, it makes it prima facie impossible that the one should be taken for or substituted for the other. The boy's qualities explain his attraction, but his presence is what caused it. But now, thanks to the further difference between cause and explanation, Alcmene can also be relieved of her dilemma. Although she could not tell Zeus from Amphitryon, still it was Amphitryon and not Zeus who was involved in the cause, and so is the target, of her love.

The present approach, embodied in schema (RS), sharply separates the categories of target and motivating aspect, and singular causal statements from general explanation statements. This does not require us to give up Davidson's view of events, on which causes are most naturally viewed as particulars. But it means renouncing the representation of emotion states themselves as events with only conjunctive structure.

This solution does give rise to a problem, however, which is the converse of the previous one. Naïvely put, the earlier problem was to differentiate target from aspect. The present problem is rather, If target and aspect are so very different, what have they got to do with one another?

Love is directed at a target, and although dependent particulars (the dimple in his cheek, her kindness) may function as targets, there is a difference between loving his dimple and loving him *for* his dimple. Moreover, it is at least possible to love without having any idea why. On the other hand, although you may not know precisely why you love, it does not follow that you love "for nothing," as Plato put it—that there is no quality *for which* you love. Some qualities are deemed more worthy than others of supporting love: beauty, for example, is commonly disparaged in that role, though solemn research confirms the imputations of light-hearted cynicism,

---

*I don't say: an explanatory *law.* Whether there are laws in this domain is a moot point: this is the debate on "anomalous monism" (see Davidson 1970b and the large literature spawned by that paper). But for my purposes it doesn't matter: a good generalization can be an explanation too.

That only God, my dear,
Could love you for yourself alone
And not your yellow hair.[7]

Moreover, there are few people for whom some changes of qualities would not be deemed to justify love's change (if he became a vegetable, I might well pity him, perhaps even feel an obligation to look after him, but could I love him?).[8] For most people the change can be brought about, like the onset of love, by trivial alterations, or by nothing objective at all except a change in their own attitudes. The view that "Love is not love / Which alters when it alteration finds" is only the premise of a proof that love is indeed not love: love's bondage is poetic license. So why not accept Platonic fungibility?

A partial answer lies in the logical path just traced: a cause is not the same as an explanation. That a particular has played a causal role in the production of an emotion, however, is not sufficient to qualify it as the target. Many particulars might have played such a role without being in any sense targets. (Though Dido's asking Aeneas to recount his sorrows was the cause of their renewal, she was not their target.) A further requirement is that the target have been apprehended as having the relevant motivating aspect. That aspect in turn must instantiate the formal object. If I am indignant at David, my condition must have been caused by some event involving David, which caused me to apprehend him as doing me harm, for example. That is thesis (X):

(X) *Relation of target to formal object.* The target of an emotion, where it exists, is a particular that has played a crucial role in the causation of the emotion in virtue of being apprehended as instantiating some motivating aspect. The motivating aspect in turn instantiates the formal object that defines that particular emotion.

A number of problems remain. For example: although thesis (X) implies that we might change or redistribute our love in virtue of changes in relevant properties of the target, it is not always clear what the original target is. The situation is complicated by the phenomenon of Freudian transference. How do we acquire the capacity to change objects under certain conditions—to transfer love from Mother to Other? And how, under other conditions, do we acquire the capacity *not* to transfer our love to other objects presenting the right motivating aspects? (See chapter 9.) These psychological problems are salient mainly because of their connection with certain moral problems: when is it right, and what makes it right, to transfer love from one object to another in the first instance and then to become, according to the ideology of monogamous love, immunized against further such transfers?

The case of Alcmene poses the question, If it was Zeus in her bed in the guise of Amphitryon, why should she mind? In summary, the discussion of fungibility has led us to a partial answer in terms of logical form: she should mind, because not to would be a category mistake. But underlying this grammatical consideration are some natural metaphysical and psychological ones. The metaphysical answer harks back to chapter 4: our attachments are to particulars, and if there are no particulars, or if we have the wrong one, then something has gone wrong with the ontological correlate of our emotion. The psychological answer, in brief, is that we are so wired as to acquire attachments in the course of our causal interaction with such individuals as are posited in our metaphysics. The fabric of our social and emotional life depends on our ability to transcend the original fungibility of all reactivity and transform it into nonfungible emotions. Much of the rest of this book will be spent amplifying the implications of both of these answers.

Before I close this chapter, however, two unfinished matters need to be taken up again: the problem of nonexistent objects and the role of propositional objects. The first, I shall argue, reduces to the second.

Nonexistent Objects Again

So far I have ignored cases where the target does not exist. It is time now to turn to the problems they pose.

Lacking a target is only sometimes an indication that something has gone wrong: I might fall in love with a fictional character, say, or—a rather different case—be enraged against somebody who doesn't exist or about something that didn't happen. Some emotions, such as certain fears or hopes, normally lack targets even though they have grammatical objects. (Yet emotions of either sort can be surprisingly similar. The main difference between the aesthetic and the religious emotions, for example, is that the latter involve delusion about the existence of their target.)

Both sorts of case can be dealt with, if not solved, by classifying them with problems we have anyway. Then at least we seem to have one less problem than before. The strategy is to assimilate these cases to those where we have only a propositional object.

The notion that all the objects of an emotion can sometimes be packed into its propositional object applies fairly straightforwardly when there is no actual individual involved though the language of ascription makes it look as if there were. No particular plays the right causal role to be the target of hoping for a promotion or for life after death. Although one might phrase hope in terms of a direct object ("hoping for a break"), the break is not a proper target in the sense defined. In terms of the canonical notation of (RS), the simplest way to represent hope is as having no target: the only object that is mandatory for hope is propositional.

Other interpretations are admittedly possible. We could think of hope on the model of Hume's theory of pride, as always having the self as its target. Or, as I shall explain presently, the proposition itself might be construed as the name of a complex individual, an event or situation type—but it will turn out that this *is* to take the object of hope as purely propositional, lacking a target in the ordinary sense. However they are represented, one feature to keep in mind about these cases is that the absence of an actual target can in no way be construed as a defect. In this they contrast with some other cases of missing targets to which I come in a moment.

Sometimes, of course, the propositional object includes some referring expression. Whether there is any temptation to regard that as designating a target depends on the case. Consider a child who hopes *that her parents will take her to a movie,* where the child has a particular movie in mind. Both the parents and the movie enter *de re* into the propositional object. The child hopes that just these persons will take her to just this movie, which—whether the child knows it or not—stars Robert Redford. My own intuition is that in this case only the movie counts as a target. But nothing of moment hangs on this. On the other hand, if the child's hope is merely to be taken to some movie or other—if the reference to the movie is not *de re*—then there is no target at all. Instead, we have a case similar to those that MacKenzie called "general desire" (see chapter 4). These cases of "nonexistent objects" therefore require no analysis of their own: they will be solved as soon as we understand propositional objects. (Which may not be very soon.)

Cases in which a target is expected and mistakenly thought to exist will yield to the same treatment, even where its nonexistence somehow invalidates the emotion. If there is a putative target, then there must exist the belief that some particular has played a characteristically crucial role in the genesis of the emotion. When Eugenio is awed that the Virgin Mary has appeared to him, his feeling has the Virgin Mary as its putative target. Here the emotion must therefore be taken as having only a propositional object, which involves an irreducibly mental representation. But such an emotion is, in a clear sense, defective in the manner of a false belief. (See Millikan 1984, esp. p. 139.)

If we are to sweep the problems of missing targets under the rug of propositional objects, it is important to establish that there are cases of *pure* propositional objects. This can be done in terms of a case described by Irving Thalberg:

> The leader of a big-game expedition declares: "I'm frightened of cannibals because, after all, they do eat human flesh." There is an analytic connection between the phrase used to describe the objects of his fear (cannibals) and his reason for fearing them. Therefore no distinction is possible. (Thalberg 1964, 208)

Not so. The claim trades on an ambiguity in the quoted sentence. On one reading, the leader may not think he has any chance of being eaten. He may fear some other contingency associated with the diet of cannibals—the temptation to adopt it, perhaps. On another reading, however, the sentence merely expresses a fear *that he will be eaten.* This is what I mean by a *purely propositional object.* Such objects exhibit quasi intentionality, as characterized in chapter 4: they are possibly nonexistent, they are general, and they are indeterminate, that is, have no reference to any particular.

The two readings are not incompatible, of course. Indeed, in the standard case one would fear the cannibals because they eat people and also fear being eaten for the very same reason.

There is one more complication. One can fear *being eaten,* meaning that the idea of being eaten is indeed a fearful thing, whether or not there is any chance of such a fate. In such cases (typically marked by a gerundive construction instead of a 'that'-clause) the objects might be construed as propositions posing as targets, or "hybrid propositional objects." They are what John Perry and Jon Barwise have called *situation types* (see Barwise and Perry 1983). Situation types are general: 'the virgin's appearing to Eugenio'; 'a cat's being on a mat'. When instantiated by particulars playing their stipulated roles, they make *facts:* if Rum Tum Tugger is on Tom's best mat, that makes it a fact that a cat is on a mat. A situation type can be more or less specific: 'a cat's being on a mat' and 'Rum Rum Tugger's being on Tom's mat' are both situation types.

In the remainder of this chapter I shall look at propositional objects both "pure" and hybrid. I shall ask especially how the identity of our emotions is affected by the thoughts that such propositions express. This will yield the last thesis in this chapter's series; after that we shall at last be ready to consider the claims of emotion to some form of objectivity.

Propositional Objects and Thought-Dependency

Of the emotions that involve characteristic thoughts, some emotions appear to be founded entirely on belief. To change them, all one need do is change the relevant belief. Others appear almost totally impervious to such changes. The members of yet a third class can fall into either of the first two, depending on the context.[9]

Embarrassment, shame, being pleased at, and grief are of the first sort. For my embarrassment to vanish, it is sufficient that I should find out either that no one was watching my faux-pas or that I did not in fact commit one. Grief can be stopped with a word—though depending on the word it might turn into some other emotion: joyful relief ("She recovered") or anger ("April fool! She's not dead!") But that is another matter.

Worry and hope are at the opposite end of the spectrum. No belief is either necessary or sufficient to induce emotions in this class, and to this extent they are apparently not belief-dependent at all. Note that they are still necessarily thought-dependent in the weaker sense of having propositional objects. In this they contrast with love or desire.

Anxiety, contentment, resentment, joy, and guilt are examples of the third kind. Some forms of anxiety are quite resistant to reason; others can be dispelled by the appropriate piece of news. And similarly with the other examples.

Even at the least thought-dependent end of the spectrum, some beliefs may be sufficient to remove an emotion or even a mere appetite. If I become persuaded that what I thought was chocolate mousse is in fact dung, my hunger may not die down but my desire to eat probably will. And we can all imagine some discovery, however implausible, that might suddenly end love or sexual desire.

Two questions arise about propositional objects and thought-dependency. First, what accounts for the variation in the extent of thought-dependency along the spectrum I have described? Second, what is the nature of the connection between emotions and their propositional objects?

On the first, I have nothing to offer but a couple of hunches. The specificity of the characteristic propositional objects varies along the spectrum: the more thought-dependent an emotion, the more specific its object. The objects of grief, for example, are more specific than those of anxiety. In addition, there are degrees of sophistication: some emotions are more linguistically tied than others and so, perhaps, less primitive; though what counts as primitive, as we have seen, is by no means simple to say.

On the second question, I offer a puzzle, which supports the contention that we need hybrid propositional objects or situation types. (I see little theoretical difference between thinking in terms of situation types and thinking in terms of propositions, as the problems of identifying one or the other will most likely be equally intractable.)[10]

The puzzle is about worry. When I worry that p, what (I worry) could possibly be the actual object of my worry? Consider again a pair of cases offered by Irving Thalberg, who points out that the kind of thought-dependency that goes with embarrassment, delight (that), or resentment is different from the kind that goes with worry, hope, or suspicion. The difference is that in the former class but not in the latter the corresponding proposition is entailed by the emotion ascription. Thus, he points out, 'John is embarrassed that he is late for dinner, but he doubts that he is (late for dinner)' is "patently ridiculous" in a way that does not apply to 'John is worried that he is late for dinner, but he doubts that he is' (Thalberg 1964, 201–202).*

What then is the object of John's worry? It cannot be *the fact that he is late for dinner,* since he may not be. Nor can it be *the belief that he is.* For if he believed that he was, he might deplore it, but it would be too late to worry about it. Is it then *the high probability that he is late?* Surely not: for one can easily worry about the improbable as well as the probable—and there is no particular threshold of probability at which any (unpleasant) prospect becomes worrisome. Perhaps then it might be *the expected desirability* of a prospect: the product of its desirability and its probability, in the sense of Bayesian decision theory. But some very improbable though very undesirable things may not be "worth worrying about," and some not very hateful but rather probable prospects may worry me—though both have the same expected desirability measure.

The moral is, I think, that there are emotions that relate normally neither to a target, either particular or general, nor to any fact or

---

*Robert Gordon (1969) makes the intriguing claim that all emotions taking 'that'-clauses as objects are either *knowledge-requiring* or *knowledge-precluding.* Actually, this seems to be an artifact of the use of 'that'-clauses in emotion ascriptions rather than a feature of emotions as such. For note that worry (one of the items on Gordon's list of knowledge-precluding emotions) can be directed to something that one either knows about or does not. But in that case it is introduced by 'about', not by 'that'. Perhaps, Gordon might retort, the word 'about' indicates that the object of the worry is not the fact anymore, but some further uncertainty that the fact generates: in other words, I can never worry about anything I know but only about possible consequences, which I cannot actually know. But consider another case. Guy can be interested *in* James's coming, whether or not he knows whether it will take place, but he can be interested *that* James came only if he does know. Since the knowledge implication is present only in the second case, it cannot be an intrinsic feature of interest as such.

truth. Instead, they seem to relate to propositions as such—or perhaps to situation types. In either case my hunch is that the most promising direction in which to look for an analysis is a functional one, attending to the role of the emotion in the mental economy of the subject and designed according to Millikan's principle of the priority of success. This will mean synthesizing the semantics of such cases from components each of which is solidly tied to a real situation. The first component will arise from looking at the network of behavioral and other dispositions associated with cases where the situation type is actually realized (that is, where the proposition is true). The second will arise from looking at the network of dispositions associated with the relevant formal object. The formal object will still define the actual nature of the emotion and define its conditions of appropriateness, in terms of whether the proposition or situation type has a property that instantiates the formal object. My attitude to being late for dinner is appropriately one of *worry* only if being late for dinner is rude or inconvenient or imprudent, or in short has any property on which supervenes the higher-order property of being *worrisome.* This is my last thesis:

> (XI) *Propositional object.* If an emotion has a purely propositional object, it consists in an attitude appropriate to some fact, proposition, event, or situation type that has a property instantiating the formal object of that emotion.

Thesis (XI) implies that, for any mental state that can be assessed for rationality, there must be some description of its object, however trivial, under which the state is appropriate or rational. This extension of the principle of intelligibility will be taken up in chapter 7. For the moment, the foregoing should suffice to guide us around the topic of objectivity, which is the next order of business.

Chapter 6
The Rational and the Objective

I want you to be . . .
be year by year however whatever yourself
be merely that, and my want
will turn to flower gladly in your changing light.
Jarold Ramsey

Summary

The title of this book strikes many people as a joke: it is commonly assumed that emotions are subjective and irrational, or at best arational. This chapter begins with an exploration of the concepts of rationality and objectivity and goes on to the task of explaining how both could apply to emotions.

The topic can be entered from any one of a triad of concepts: truth, objectivity, and rationality. In the first few sections of this chapter the focus is on objectivity. But objectivity gets part of its meaning from its contrast with subjectivity, which is not one concept but several.

Four possibly relevant meanings of subjectivity must be disentangled: phenomenology ("what it's like" to have my experiences); projection (the illusion that the shadows of my own attitudes are real properties of the world); relativity (the fact that some properties come into being only as a result of an interaction between a subject and the world); and perspective (the "I-ness of I"; the elusive fact that every experience and every choice is necessarily made from a certain point of view, or point of agency). Neither phenomenology nor relativity is incompatible with viewing emotions as importantly analogous to perceptions, in a way that supports at least a graduated claim to objectivity. Projection is the only form of subjectivity clearly incompatible with objectivity, since it roughly amounts to finding something in the world just because we want it to be there. Perspective also undermines objectivity, but not in such a way as to preclude the analogy of perception. Furthermore, it casts an interesting light on the special nature of emotional attitudes. It turns out to be a surprising consequence of the multiplicity of formal objects of emotion that there is no such thing as hypothetically emoting—no simple analogue of entertaining a proposition without believing it.

The latter part of the chapter flips over to a consideration of rationality as the master concept, possibly subsuming objectivity. I explain several principles that define rationality as I understand it, in any domain. If emotions are to be shown to be rational, this must be done in accordance with these principles:

First, any concept of rationality must be founded on a criterion of success. Success, in this sense, is defined as the attainment of the formal object of the state in question; for example, truth is the success of belief, good of want. Second, a state is judged irrational, as opposed to arational, in terms of some set of goals. But then it must admit of some description under which it is rational in terms of more immediate goals. This is the principle of minimal rationality: given any irrational state, some actual context can be circumscribed in which that state is rational. This is closely related to the third principle, which is that any states assessed for rationality must be mental or intentional though not necessarily conscious. Fourth, we normally have no direct access to success (for example, truth or goodness, or the outcome of actions); therefore, the rationality of a state is typically assessed in terms of its origins. Fifth, the demands of rationality are generally not positive requirements but constraints. Thus, logic typically says not, "Believe this," but, "You can believe this or that, but not both."

Finally, all the previous principles apply to either of two broad categories of rational assessment: the cognitive (typically applicable to beliefs) and the strategic (typically applicable to actions and desires). Does either of the two apply to emotions? Here I offer more arguments against the reduction of emotions either to beliefs or to desires. One argument, inspired by Derek Parfit, is intended to establish that in ordinary desires there is an irreducible emotional element, which cannot plausibly be assessed merely in terms of its consequences. Each emotion has its own kind of "rightness" or criterion of success (its formal object); but the class of emotional formal objects forms a genus that I group together under the label of 'axiology'.

By and large, common sense holds that emotions are typically both subjective and irrational. This belief has tended to have either of two opposite but equally deplorable effects. Among those who prize knowledge and rationality, it promotes the idea that emotions are essentially unimportant, or important only as distractions from the serious business of life. On the other hand, given the irrationalist premises that pervade much of current culture, it fosters the automatic justification of any behavior on the grounds that one must "go with one's feelings": since feelings are "purely subjective," no sensible debate or rationalization of them is possible.

Some support for this subjectivist view is provided by traditional philosophical models of the mind. A glance at table 2.1 reminds us that for Descartes, for example, whereas perceptions are experienced as localized inside or outside the body, passions are experienced as localized in the soul. This makes it look as though the subject of emotion, the *soul*, also plays a role analogous to that of the *object* in perception. Yet one is likely to experience passion as being evoked by something in the outside world. If passion is devoid of any objective ground outside the soul, as so much philosophy and religion have claimed, that experience must be mere illusion. On Descartes's view, both the subject and the object of the passions are, quite literally, "all in the mind"; only their mechanism of teeming animal spirits inhabits the body. It is no comfort that the remote cause of emotion is outside the self: in terms of the analogy of perception, that remote cause is analogous not to an object seen but to the light of the sun.

Nevertheless, there is also a presumption of objectivity lurking in the very consideration most frequently adduced against it: the existence of disagreements about emotional response. Subjectivists find comfort in lack of agreement; but the very possibility of disagreement presupposes common standards and common meanings. In that sense, *disagreement presupposes objectivity.* This is not, of course, to say that disagreement shows the presumption of objectivity to be correct. (The history of theology does not prove the existence of God.) But it demands that the issue be raised.

Truth, Objectivity, and Rationality

Chapter 5 turned up three features favoring the presumption of objectivity. The first was that the ascription of at least some emotions is tied to a causal condition (the second causal condition, thesis (VII)) that links the emotion to objective facts about the outside world. The second, encapsulated in theses (VI) and (XI), was that not any emotion can be intelligibly ascribed in relation to just any object. A focus of attention may provide appropriate motivating aspects for some emotions but not others. This is a matter of degree: it is bizarre to experience intense amusement at the perfectly familiar taste of potatoes; it is morally sinister to feel euphoria at the intense suffering of an innocent person; and it is altogether unintelligible—in the absence of some clever story—to be told that someone experienced excruciating remorse at the thought of having once smiled at a child. Third, we found a minimal condition for an ascription to reach the ground level of intelligibility. This has to do with the existence of a formal object corresponding to each specific emotion (theses (IX) and (X)).

I shall expand on all three points. But first I want to clarify the relations among a crucial triad of concepts: *objectivity, truth,* and *rationality.*

Paper, Scissors, Stone
In the familiar children's game, paper is cut by scissors, scissors are broken by stone, but stone, in turn, can be wrapped into submission by paper. If one asks which of the three related concepts of truth, rationality, and objectivity is the most fundamental, one can find oneself running in circles in a way rather reminiscent of that game.

Intuitively, *truth* has to do with a correspondence between language or thought and the real world, conceived of as existing independently of our conscious states. *Objectivity* seems more fundamental, because we might make sense of states other than thoughts or propositions that correspond to something in the real world. The perception of a certain quality, for example, can be objective, though we would not normally think of it as true. Truth, then, seems to be merely a species of objectivity. But objectivity must get part of its meaning from its contrast with *subjectivity,* which, as we shall see, is not one thing but several.

As for *rationality,* it has to do with strategies for the attainment of truth or objectivity. So from one point of view it is a subordinate concept, the point of which derives from the other two.

From another point of view, however, rationality is more basic than objectivity. It embraces actions and policies of all sorts, including policies about what to believe. Moreover, it seems conceivable to envisage a notion of *rationality without objectivity.* Just this position is scouted in the *Theaetetus,* where Plato has Protagoras profess that all truth is relative: whatever anyone believes is true-to-that-person. Nevertheless, Protagoras claims that it is rational to pay a high fee for his teaching, because it can make his client feel better. Socrates points out that this is reasonable only if it is true that the sophist's client will feel better for his ministrations. Only true-to-the-client, insists Protagoras. In the end, Socrates pounces on Protagoras with the observation that Protagoras must agree with his own critics, and so refutes himself. With this ploy, Socrates wins by losing, by an instructive twist that Plato has left the reader to work out. Technically, Protagoras wins that last round. Having replaced the notion of truth with one of *truth-to-each-believer,* he does not have to concede that he is contradicted by anyone who says, "Protagoras is wrong," for that means only, "Protagoras is wrong-for-me." But this is exactly how

Socrates wins: for if no contradiction is possible, then there is no possibility of language. Imagine a parent's efforts at teaching language in a Protagorean world. "Chair," says the child. "Chair-to-you," says the parent, "but grapefruit-to-me." Such lessons will remain amicable, but forever fruitless.

The Socratic victory over complete relativism seems to imply that truth, after all, is more fundamental than rationality. So as we shift our point of view, it looks in turn as if truth dominates rationality, which dominates objectivity, which dominates truth: paper, scissors, stone.

It will not help to protest that this last argument against Protagoras merely establishes the need for *intersubjectivity* rather than for any objectivity in a transcendent sense. Admittedly, the argument can have no bearing on the issue of whether the realism presupposed by truth and objectivity is a metaphysical one—whether the world exists absolutely independently of our knowledge of it.[1] This is not the place to fight the battle of realism. Suffice it to say that common sense will not be dislodged from the assumption that intersubjective agreement is valued as evidence of truth. If truth were not at issue, intersubjective convergence might admittedly be valued in its own right. Bernard Williams (1985) has argued that ethical convergence may be quite unlike the scientific in being only practical. But in this picture, unlike the Protagorean, practical convergence rests on a basis of ordinary truth (if we all walk in the same direction, that is a merely practical matter; but *that* we are doing so is a matter of fact).

In what follows I shall make no further attempt to rank the concepts of truth, objectivity, and rationality. I shall focus mainly on the last two, taking first objectivity and then rationality as central. My purpose is to discover to what extent, if we take for granted the possibility of rationality and objectivity in the most favorable cases, emotions can be said to share those features.

Let us begin, then, with objectivity, and specifically with a closer look at the contrasting term that gives objectivity part of its meaning: subjectivity. Curiously, the two notions are not quite symmetrical: subjectivity is a more complicated concept.

Four or Five Kinds of Subjectivity
At least four and perhaps five distinct meanings have been attached to the notion of subjectivity. To give them labels, I propose to call them *phenomenology, projection, relativity,* and *perspective.* The possible fifth is *agency,* which may or may not be reducible to some of the others.

Phenomenology is what I have already referred to as the problem of "qualia." As I explained in chapter 2, this is really a problem about emergence, and emergence, rightly understood, is not a problem.

Projection embodies the subjectivist answer to the *Euthyphro* question. It is the view that the properties attributed to the object are merely shadows of our choices.* On the existentialist view, all values are projective in the sense that we bring them into the world as images of our will. In Sartre's slogan, "Nothing foreign has decided what we feel, what we live, or what we are" (Sartre 1956, 554). The implication is not, as common sense might have it, that those things are determined by factors outside the sphere of *anybody's* decisions, but that *we* have decided them for ourselves, in an exercise of pure criterionless choice.

Relativity is the view that the properties attributed to the objects are really produced by relations between the object and the observer. Its prototype is again to be found in Plato's *Theaetetus* (152ff.), as the "secret doctrine" of perception attributed to Protagoras. According to this doctrine, the perceptual qualities of objects come into existence as a result of the interaction of subject and object. A less uncompromising form of this view is defended by Patrick Nowell-Smith (1954, 84ff.). in his discussion of what he calls "aptness words." These are words like 'beautiful', which have the surface form of ordinary adjectives but are standardly used to express a reaction or attitude normally caused by a certain range of objective properties in the target. They contrast both with descriptive adjectives, like 'green' or 'helicoidal', and with "gerundive" adjectives such as 'obligatory' or 'incumbent on you', which carry a definite exhortation to specific behavior. One form of relativity is perspectival relativity: the fact that things look different from different angles and distances. Perspectival relativity will become important in chapter 8, where the question is raised whether it is rational to discount desires and emotions when their objects are removed in time or space. What must be stressed about perspectival relativity is that it is in no way incompatible with objectivity (see Wiggins 1976, 349ff.). It is therefore not to be confused with the next form of subjectivity, which is (pure) perspective.

Perspective is the most elusive form of subjectivity. Its name misleadingly suggests perspectival relativity, but it is the only pronounceable name I can find for something different. One form of it is

* 'Projection' has a special meaning in psychoanalysis, where it refers to the unwitting attribution to someone else of my own characteristics—usually ones I profess to despise. The sense in which I use the word is broader. (Think of the projection of a movie onto a screen.) But I want to retain the flavor of the psychoanalytic sense: it is essential to projection in my sense that the content of what I project comes entirely from myself and that I am utterly convinced that it is an objective part of the world I perceive.

the problem of the "I-ness of I." Anything we know or perceive is known or perceived *from a given point of view*. We can never attain "the view from nowhere," in Thomas Nagel's memorable phrase (Nagel 1986), however much we aspire to it. Only God's omniscience could be free of perspective, but even that leads directly to a paradox. For God's objectivity precludes God's omniscience: if there are perspectival truths, then each of us knows something that even God cannot know. In my case the piece of esotery which thus disproves the existence of an omniscient God is that *I am Ronnie*.

This paradox of omniscience should help us to see that the problem of perspective is not so much a problem about the self as such, as is often assumed, as a problem about what is to count as real information. The point may become clearer if I try to convey it in terms of a slightly different problem that does not overtly involve the self at all.

This is a problem concerning *time*. It arises from John McTaggart's (1934) characterization of two time series, or ways of thinking about time. The subjective series (which he called the "A-series") is organized in terms of *past, present,* and *future*. The objective (the "B-series") is organized in terms of *before, simultaneous with,* and *after*. The problem is that there does not seem to be any specifiable information that can be given in the subjective series that is not captured by some objective series formulation. For example, the information content of 'Yesterday I had bratwurst' is merely made explicit, but not essentially changed, when it is rephrased as 'On the day before that contemporaneous with the writing of the sentence token 'Yesterday . . . ' by Ronnie, Ronnie had bratwurst.' Something crucial seems to be missing in the reformulation, namely, that this writing is going on *now*. Yet the challenge to say what is missing can never be met, since to say it I would either have to give a synonymous "A-series" or subjective formula, which would beg the question, or I would have to phrase it in terms of an "eternal sentence" (see Quine 1960) containing only objective time parameters.* This seems to be precisely the same difficulty as that of explaining what is the additional informational content of the fact that *I am Ronnie*, over and above the em-

---

*An ancient sophism illustrates the necessity for our ordinary logic of assuming that all propositions in an argument are eternal (or formulated in B-series terms, with fixed and consistent interpretations for all the implicit parameters). The sophism offers a valid argument, of the form 'A = B; B is C; therefore A is C', with true premises and a false conclusion:

1. The present writer is Ronnie;

2. Ronnie is sitting;

(therefore)————[here Ronnie gets up]

3. The present writer is sitting.

pirical fact that Ronnie is the writer of these words and the trivial fact that Ronnie is Ronnie.

Insofar as it is not exhausted by projection, the subjectivity of *pure choice* may also come under the heading of perspective. A choice must always be somebody's, like a point of view, and no one can ever literally make anyone else's choice for her. But because it involves the equally mysterious element of agency, perhaps we should think of choice as a fifth brand of subjectivity.

Notice that these different senses of subjectivity relate differently to the triad of concepts introduced above—truth, objectivity, and rationality. Truth and objectivity are both clearly incompatible with projection. But they are not *clearly* incompatible with phenomenology, and they are clearly *not* incompatible with relativity. 'Objectivity' is often used, as by Nagel, to mean a transcending of any particular perspective; but Nagel seems to think that truth is compatible with perspective.[2] (That is why it is too simple to assume that truth is simply a species of objectivity.)

Equipped with these various senses of 'subjectivity', I can better tackle the claim that emotions are subjective, and frame my counterclaim.

Subjectivism about Emotions

Robert Solomon has defended what he calls a "subjective theory of the passions." According to him, emotions constitute our "subjective world," molding it into our "surreality" (Solomon 1976, 66ff.). The contrast implied is with *the* world, or Reality. Solomon speaks of the subjective world of emotions as involving a "standpoint" or "perspective," whereas "objective reality is all here now, all at once" (p. 69).

So far, this is perspective-subjectivity. That construal is reinforced by his comment that subjectivity makes a "selection," or edits some things out of objective reality. Clearly, from wherever I stand, some things will not be visible. (Thomas Nagel (1986, 126) describes the "blind spot" that follows our every effort at an increasingly englobing perspective.) But there are other elements. The element of choice already cited is partly perspectival, as I suggested, but it is also part projection and perhaps partly irreducible. Moreover, Solomon assumes that truth is a species of objectivity. From the subjective point of view, he writes, the question of truth "need not (and sometimes cannot) arise" (p. 56). But the only kind of subjectivity that is *clearly* incompatible with truth claims is projection. More precisely, there is a range of subjective preferences and desires that, if projected onto the world, foment illusion. (See chapter 7, on "Subjective and Objective Desires.") But merely having such subjective desires need not involve projection: if I prefer chocolate to vanilla, I need be under no illusion unless I claim, on no better grounds, that vanilla is inferior.

Solomon argues that my "surreality" consists not only of an edited version of reality but of additional elements of *evaluation*. Presumably those additional elements are projective, or possibly phenomenological. But only the missing elements, those we edit out by looking at the world from a particular point of view, are strictly speaking due to perspective.

Another possibility is that the additional elements are *relative*, in the manner of the emergent relative qualities brought into being by the interaction of subject and object in Protagoras's secret doctrine. It is important to avoid confusing projection and relativity. My taste in vanilla—whether chosen or otherwise determined—is an innocent and objective relational fact about me and vanilla, unless I project it onto the world as a claim to have detected an objective quality fitting a formal object. Even if I do project my taste in this way, however, the question of whether I am mistaken is not just open and shut—or so I shall argue (see chapter 7).

I have proposed that the "subjectivity" of emotional reactions or desires can be factored into different claims, corresponding to different varieties of subjectivity. Emotions are on the frontier of the subjective and the objective, as they are on the frontier of the mental and the physiological, of the active and the passive, of the instinctual and the intentional. None of these frontiers is sharp: the problem is to map them. So let me now consider the claim to objectivity of (some) emotions in the light of each type of subjectivity. The guiding question here will be, How far can we push the idea that emotions are a kind of perception?

The Analogy of Perception

The thesis I am driving at is this. The ways in which emotions are subjective do not sufficiently undermine the analogy of perception to exclude a significant claim to objectivity. Emotions can indeed be viewed as providing genuine information. But the analogy is not so close as to warrant the assimilation of emotions to perception, any more than to beliefs or desires.

Phenomenology

Usually there is something it is like to have a certain emotion—so much so that some philosophers have claimed emotions could be identified by their felt qualities. But emotions do not have to be conscious: they merely have to be mental. Having a phenomenological quality is a sufficient condition for being a conscious state. So we cannot assume that every token of an emotion is subjective in this sense.

In any case the phenomenology of emotion would not undermine the analogy of perception, since ordinary sensory perceptions also (usually) have a phenomenal quality. That is their subjective side. But obviously perception is also standardly objective. And that, according to Ruth Millikan's principle of the priority of success, suggests that the successful or objectively valid phenomenal experiences may be the *normal* ones in terms of which the *function* of phenomenal experiences should be understood. On some views, in fact, the phenomenal quality simply *is* how the objective property conveyed *appears from that perspective,* whether we know it or not. So the quale factors out into two aspects, one of which is subjective in the sense of perspectival relativity (which is no obstacle to truth but only to completeness), and the other of which is simply objective information conveyed by the sensory "transducers" whose function it is to convert physical quantities into representations. This is the line taken by Paul Churchland about sensory perception in general. Our eyes, for example, are "flawless spectrometers" that provide us with indications of "the reflective, absorptive, and radiative properties of the molecular aggregates" from which comes electromagnetic radiation in a certain range—even when we don't know that this is what they are doing (Churchland 1979, 27).

Now it seems pretty clear that emotions do not have organs or transducers (see Kenny 1963, 56). We shall inquire presently to what extent this undermines the perceptual analogy. First, however, let us assess the analogy of perception against the other modes of subjectivity.

Projection
In the analogy of perception, full-blown projection corresponds to hallucination; partial projection corresponds to illusion. In terms of the categories introduced in chapter 5, the difference between hallucinations and illusions is usually that in the former case there is no target, and in the latter only the focus is illusory whereas the target is real. ("Usually," because there are exceptions. Many religious beliefs are directed at nonexistent targets, yet they are classed with illusions.) In the case of emotions, projection is normally at issue only with respect to focus: Don Quixote's mistake about Dulcinea concerned her virtues, not her existence. One could quibble about this: an alternative interpretation is that Dulcinea does not exist at all,

though Don Quixote wrongly takes Aldonza to be she. If a target is made up of whole cloth, though, then there is certainly something wrong with the emotion regardless of the cause of the mistake. Emotions, like perceptions, can have illusory focus or hallucinatory targets. But not all focal properties are projections; and the possibility of marking the distinction is all that is required by the analogy of perception.

Relativity

I claimed a moment ago that although relativity is frequently intended as a sense of subjectivity, it does not actually preclude objectivity. But I still owe an argument.

One time-honored line of approach to the question of objectivity lies in the distinction between primary and secondary qualities. According to Locke, primary qualities (such as motion, shape, size, solidity, and number) intrinsically resemble their representative ideas, whereas secondary qualities (such as color, felt warmth, fragrance, and texture) owe their qualia to the "powers" to produce them that reside in the primary qualities. These claims define a sense in which secondary qualities are subjective in the sense of being relative to the interaction between the (objective) primary qualities and the observer's sensory equipment. It is sometimes claimed that this thesis was conclusively refuted by Berkeley, who is said to have showed that the relativity to observers and conditions of observation characteristic of secondary qualities contaminate the primary ones.[3] But in fact the refutation ascribed to Berkeley confuses phenomenology, relativity, and projection. It assumes that if the appearances of things are relative to the sensory and conceptual apparatus of the perceiver, this means that their attribution to the outside world is mere projection, with no objective correlates beyond themselves. This is a tempting move, because if some quality attributed by an observer to a target depends totally on the perceiver and not at all on the target, then relativity collapses into projection. But no lesser degree of relativity can effect this collapse. At most, Berkeley's arguments show that the conflation of these different senses of subjectivity leads to idealism— which, incidentally, seems good reason for keeping them apart.

We need a criterion that will tell us when relativity shades into projection. What would such a criterion tell us about emotional objectivity?

Consider the case of aesthetic, or what are sometimes called *tertiary*, properties. Examples are *beauty*, *grace*, and all those that are known by metaphorical adjectives alone: *light, airy, spacious, dark, brittle*, and so on. They also include correlates of nonaesthetic emotions: *pitiable, sad, depressing, fearsome, hateful, lovable.* (Many, like *warm,* fit comfortably in both lists.) Are these correlates "real" or not? Even as we survey this short list of examples, our intuitive answer is likely to waver. What is clear is that it is not clear: there is no dichotomy here. Perhaps, like many a simplistic dualism, this one can be reconstructed into a useful gradient, or complex of gradients.

The question we need to ask is this: To what degree is the perceptual state of which the tertiary quality is the focus *covariant* with the subject, and to what extent is it covariant with the object? Unfortunately, given the discussion of objects in chapter 5, that question immediately splinters into smaller ones: Is it covariant with the proper target? Is it covariant with the motivating aspect? With the cause? What is the role of the formal object? Does the presence of the property definitive of the formal object admit of measurable criteria?

Generally, when we look at the operation of a sensory channel, we find a range of causes underlying the covariance of transduced representation with the relevant range of properties in the object. In the case of sight, for example, one must first circumscribe the formal object of sight. According to our standard definition, the formal object must be a property implicitly ascribed to the object (or strictly speaking to some relevant quality of the object) for the representational state to be one of seeing as opposed to one of hearing or tasting—or for that matter of grieving or eating. The proper object of sight is to be a *visible quality.* It is a "sight," in the sense in which we trivially *see* (but not taste or hear) *sights* (but not sounds or flavors). Variations in your sensations of sight may result from (1) variations in (some subset of) the intrinsic or primary properties of the object, but also from (2) environmental factors (conditions of light, temperature, and so forth), (3) your physiological apparatus and its condition, (4) your experiential history and current beliefs and desires, and even (5) social and ideological factors.

Insofar as your sensory apparatus works properly, it will be decreasingly sensitive to factors (2)–(5) in roughly that order. According to Jerry Fodor and Zenon Pylyshyn, this makes for an essential distinction between perception and general cognition: by and large, our beliefs are modifiable in the light of factors of type (4) and (5), but our perceptions are not. Pylyshyn (1984) describes sensory transducers as largely "cognitively impenetrable" (see esp. pp. 134–135); their workings are determined by their "functional architecture." This last phrase refers to computational *mechanisms* whose own workings can be explained entirely at the physical level, without reference to the relatively irreducible levels of semantic representation.

I shall follow Fodor in speaking of this feature of perception as the informational *encapsulation* of perceptual *modules* (Fodor 1983, 64ff.). Actually, Fodor's modules are not senses like sight and hearing but rather such things as "motion detectors" or phonetic perception devices. But for simplicity, since my purposes here are merely illustrative, I shall speak of "sensory channels" as if they referred to eyes, ears, and so forth. When our eyes function normally, we see what is before us, which is to say our representational states are determined by factors of type (1) with some contribution (especially with respect to secondary qualities) by factors of type (2). When we see ghosts or pink rats, the interference of factors of type (3), and possibly (4) and (5), indicates a breakdown in the normal encapsulation of perception, undermining its objectivity.

The consequence of our having no organs of emotion can now be seen more clearly: emotions are typically susceptible to the whole gamut of factors ranging from (1) to (5). At first sight, all this would certainly seem to make the case for emotional subjectivity in the sense of relativity.

And there is worse. Not only will emotions be more subjective than perceptions. They will also apparently be more subjective than other unencapsulated states—namely, beliefs. The reason goes back to some facts about physiology that were surveyed in chapter 3.

As we saw there, it is arguably a defining characteristic of emotion that it involves a more conspicuous participation of the body than do other mental states. Moreover, the bodily states involved tend to be part of the "slow" rather than the "fast" systems of internal information processing: those involving the relatively sedate messaging of hormones rather than nervous fibers. The latter fact acts as a kind of drag on the covariance with properties of type (1) that we demand of a perceptual system. As Descartes first pointed out, the body's inertia means that once begun, an emotional reaction is difficult to stop, even when the grounds are removed. One consequence of this feature is a certain fluidity in the definitions of the various cases discussed in chapter 5. Remember Bernie, in case 4, who raves in admiration for Wendy because of something that never actually happened. And suppose he discovers his mistake. Given the inertia of emotions, his body may preserve some emotional momentum in the absence of continuing grounds, and it may well be that some merely associative link between his feelings of admiration and some irrelevant idiosyncrasy of her manner will become established. His case will then have turned into something more like case 1, in which Wendy thought her attitude was based on a judgment when in fact it was based on an association. The structure of Bernie's emotion will have fallen apart—one cannot strictly admire, or resent, or despise, or be angry, if there is no legitimizing belief to support the emotion. But one can continue to fume, or rave, without exactly remembering why. In such circumstances one may well be tempted to make up a rationale. In this way, as we shall see in more detail in chapter 9, the position of emotions as the "frontier" between the biological and the mental can lead us into self-deception.

Now with purely cognitive beliefs too there can be a kind of inertia. It can take several forms. First, beliefs near the center of a "web of belief" are more hardy than those at the periphery in case of conflict (see Quine 1957). Second, we tend to continue to believe conse-quences of beliefs that themselves have been given up.[4] Suppose I seem to see Jo-Ann walking in the direction of the office and infer, since I am driving and barely on time for a meeting, that she will be late. I then look again and find it was not Jo-Ann. Still, I will likely unthinkingly continue to assume that Jo-Ann will be late for the meeting and be surprised to see her there before me. Third, even scientists commonly tend to look for reasons for beliefs they already hold. If one argument won't do, we look for another for the same conclusion. And finally, we sometimes simply continue to believe things in the face of good arguments and evidence, simply because we want to. All this is true, and yet there is lacking a crucial analogy with emotions: for there is nothing (except in the last two cases, which are compounded of emotions anyway) like the continued emo-tional arousal that prompts us to cast about for some emotion or other to replace the one that has been undermined. The reason for this is traceable to the peculiarly strong role of the body that formed the basis of the (exaggerated) theory of emotion as general arousal dis-cussed in chapter 3.

All these grounds of difference between emotions and beliefs seem like a heavy burden for the perceptual analogy to bear. Nevertheless, all is not lost. There are three kinds of mitigating factors.

First, the case of Bernie self-deceptively confabulating grounds for an existing emotion—which, as I have just noted, has its parallel in belief—actually indicates that as a matter of fact we take some mea-sure of objectivity for granted: otherwise, we could not speak of self-deception. I merely note this here, reserving fuller discussion for chapter 9.

Second, I have already pointed out that the encapsulation of per-ception is a matter of degree. The tertiary properties are definitely not encapsulated, but the secondary are so only up to a point. There is a continuum. The position of representational states on that con-tinuum depends on the complex variety of their causes. In practice, we often have no trouble making the distinction between responses evoked by intrinsic qualities (including tertiary qualities) of a target and those that are merely relative to individual idiosyncrasies.

An example will convey this intuition. Lynne and Leon are both passionately moved by the Kreutzer Sonata. But in Lynne's case her emotion is one whose object is the music itself: its melodies and harmonies, its movement and modulations. Leon, on the other hand, is generally tone deaf. This sonata is the only piece of music he ever enjoys. He enjoys it because it reminds him of his mother, who used to put it on the phonograph when she read him bedtime stories.

In this story Lynne's focus is on genuine motivating aspects of the music. Leon, on the other hand, is responding to a purely idiosyncratic association. He is not reacting to any intrinsic quality of the music at all. There are two signs of this in terms of the suggested criterion of covariance. One is that Leon's response lacks any systematic correlation with the specific qualities of this particular piece: any other music, if it had just that personal association, would arouse the same feelings. Also, his reactions to different pieces of music are not systematically related to each other. There is a quality-space within which this music resembles and contrasts with other music; and whereas Lynne's responses to different sorts of music are systematically related to that quality-space, Leon's are not. The extremity of their two cases does not conceal the fact that the difference between Lynne and Leon is a matter of degree; but that is all I claim.

Furthermore—and this will bring us to the third factor mitigating the disanalogies between emotion and perception—even a clearly modular perceptual device need not be conveying information about any *simple* qualities. A good example is phonetic perception, which, though highly modular, turns out not to be explicable as perfectly covariant with any purely acoustical properties of speech. Instead, what is perceived is the actual *intended production* of the phonetic units in question, as articulated by the organs of speech (see Liberman and Mattingly 1985). Our phonetic perception is crucially conditioned by our own capacity to produce speech, though the process involves neither inference, nor argument from analogy, nor imaginative effort—in fact, no conscious or intentional activity of any sort.

This unexpected complexity in a simple perceptual module opens up the possibility that we should expand the range of properties that we are willing to think of as being perceived. This is my third and most important consideration: *The objects of emotion may be of such complexity that the interference of factors beyond covariants of primary properties classed in type (1), far from undermining objectivity, actually enriches the objective range of emotion.*

In reviewing the physiology of emotions, I urged that we cannot make sense of the role of emotions in human life unless we recognize their level-ubiquity. In the individual's repertoire of emotional responses lies a complex reflection of ideological factors, which in turn interact with other levels of determination. To stipulate that emotions cannot be perceptual unless they are encapsulated would beg the question of how much is encompassed in the level of reality that they apprehend. If their objects are actually complex situations involving factors at various levels, then the equivalent of perceptual appropriateness will precisely reside in the penetrability of emotions by factors at those various levels. As we shall see in chapter 7, emotions do mimic the encapsulation of perception in certain specific ways that will prove crucial to one of their central functions. But they are still not encapsulated modules in the same way as perception.

Perspective

I have been looking at some facts that make emotions look more like beliefs or desires than like perceptions, and at other facts that point to the opposite conclusion. I now want to argue that emotions belong to a broader class of *attitudes*, which share with beliefs a lack of specific organs and consequent encapsulation but share with perception the feature that they must be in some sense essentially perspectival. Like a perception, but unlike a belief, an attitude is something one cannot hypothetically adopt. Attitudes and emotions are like the gag that falls flat when we try to recount it: you have to be there. In this sense, all attitudes are essentially perspectival.

Think about being subjected to the complaints of a very angry man with whose cause you cannot sympathize. Perhaps a businessman is telling you how mortifying it is to work for a female boss. You can easily accept various factual premises "for the sake of his story," even if you doubt their truth. But you could only share his indignation if you actually shared the attitudes on which it is founded. Still, you intuitively know that sharing these attitudes is what *would* enable you to feel the indignation. This is a crucial point. For without the possibility of this sort of second-order knowledge about the relation of attitudes to the emotions that derive from them, there could be no criticism of another person's emotion. When we ask, "How can you get so indignant about *that?*" we usually know the answer only too well: you can and I can't, because you have some attitudes that I don't share.

The same holds for other emotions. To find a story sad, or exciting, or frightening, it is not enough to be told that something is sad or exciting or frightening. I must already be disposed to find certain things sad, and so forth. This is not to deny that I can be made to care for the most unlikely objects: a good writer of fairy tales can generate emotional involvement with the inner life of a frog, a cockroach, or even an inanimate object. But the point is that although my attitudes can be modified and manipulated by a competent artist or writer, the manipulator must have a raw material of attitudes and emotional dispositions to work with in the first place.

This is related to a point made by Bernard Williams: Expressions of emotion, like expletives, are "not logically manoeuvrable enough to provide a model for . . . value judgements." The insertion of an expletive within the antecedent of a conditional does not defeat its expressive power: "If he has broken his blasted tricycle again, he'll go without his pocket money" carries a note of irritation that is not canceled by conditionalization.[5] This points to an essentially perspectival element in emotion itself, not merely in its expression. Just as only I can express my emotion, so only I can have it, and just as either I express it or I don't, so either I have it or I don't. There is no such thing as hypothetically experiencing it, any more than hypothetically expressing it.

One way to see this is to bring to mind the importance of role-playing in psychotherapy. The function of role-playing is to induce emotions that the unaided imagination cannot summon; it may be necessary for understanding the emotional and practical consequences of those emotions. But the essential contrast with belief is right here: to believe $p \rightarrow q$, we don't have to role-play believing that p.

But wait, you might be thinking. Belief too is an attitude; although I can hypothetically entertain a proposition, it is only loosely speaking that I can hypothetically entertain a belief. So there is no disanalogy between emotions and beliefs after all.

In a sense, this is true. The disanalogy comes when we ask what we are doing when we *entertain* a possible belief. The answer is that we are *all but endorsing* some *proposition*. To endorse it is simply for me to view it as true: belief too is perspectival in this sense. But now what would it be to entertain—without endorsing—a possible emotion? Not, surely, to do all but endorse it. For endorsement is just another attitude. To endorse a proposition is simply to *believe* it—not to *emote* it, whatever that would mean. The kind of "endorsement" that would be meant where an emotion is in question depends essentially on what emotion it is. And that is determined by its formal object, if any. (A belief is belief because its formal object is always truth, but every emotion has its own formal object.)

This strengthens the perception analogy. With perceptions too, although it is possible to imagine seeing something without actually seeing it, that cannot be described as "all but endorsing the perception." There is no clear analogue, either for perception or for emotion, of the pure proposition that gets entertained in hypothetical belief.

To summarize: I have tried to make a case for the possibility of emotional objectivity, based on an analogy with perception. Some subjective aspects of emotions—phenomenology and relativity—favor the perceptual analogy without undermining the prospect of a degree of objectivity. With projection and perspective the case is less clear. But because they are also associated with choice, those features encourage us to think of emotions in terms of the point of emotion for a subject. To do so is to flip from viewing the questions of truth and objectivity as primary to the alternative leading idea of rationality.

Six Principles of Rationality

In the next few pages I set out some principles applicable to assessments of rationality of every possible kind. The last of these principles, by distinguishing cognitive from strategic rationality, will illustrate the fact that even the pursuit of objectivity can be viewed as a species of rationality. If you find any of these principles contentious, you can take them simply as circumscribing the notion of rationality that I am presupposing. If that notion turns out to be helpful, let that stand as my argument in its favor.

Success
The reason each emotion has its own formal object is that each emotion implicitly ascribes a property to a target—or more precisely to a focal property or motivating aspect of a target. But in what sense do these formal objects *exist*? Needless to say, formal objects do not exist as separate and rival targets. That much should be clear from Plato's most famous mistake: the Theory of Forms collapsed target, motivating aspect, and formal object into a single Supertarget, which therefore had to be—impossibly—both general and particular. Rather, to say that there is a formal object amounts to the presumption that, when disagreements occur, *there is something to disagree about.* Could this presumption be correct?

To answer this question, I must introduce the concept of *success* for an intentional state. (To avoid unnecessary complications, I explain this in terms of propositional attitudes.) I define success as the attainment by an intentional state of its formal object. Recall that a formal object gives the *point* of a certain emotion, state, or activity. In this sense, the point of believing is to believe what is true. (Hence Moore's paradox: "I believe it, though it isn't true.") Similarly, the point of wanting is to want what is good. Good is the success of want, and truth is the success of belief. Note that if we define *satisfaction* of a propositional attitude, in accordance with standard practice, as the truth of the propositional object, success coincides with satisfaction in the case of truth. But this is not so for wants: because not every good is realized, not every successful want is satisfied (see de Sousa 1974b).

There is a further complication in the case of Good that makes "I want it, though it's bad" less intuitively paradoxical than Moore's sentence.* The complication is that wants, unlike beliefs, are intrinsically comparative; they can be "prima-facie" or they can be "all-things-considered." But a few qualifying phrases will restore the analogue of Moore's paradox for wants. "I want X more than anything else, all things considered, though there is nothing at all about any aspect of X that is good or desirable for me or anyone"—is undoubtedly odd. Good therefore remains criterial for the success of wanting.

This special notion of success allows us to bring the notion of formal object explicitly under the aegis of rationality. This is the import of my first principle of rationality. (The principles set out in this chapter are collected in the Appendix, following the labeled sentences discussed in chapter 5.)

> (R1) *Success.* The formal object of a representational state defines that state's criterion of success, in terms of which the rationality of that state is assessed.

Minimal Rationality
Paradoxes like Moore's and its analogues suggest a generalization of the intelligibility condition (thesis (VI)). The force of the *principle of minimal rationality* is that any intentional state amenable to rational criticism must fit some true description that represents the state as rational.

This is most easily explained by reference to actions. No event is an action unless it has a teleological structure. Actions are determined by wants and beliefs. The wants determine the goal of the act

---

*I ignore yet another complication because it affects beliefs and desires alike: both can be assessed for intensity or degree. Degrees of belief are usually identified with subjective probabilities, though Isaac Levi (1967) has introduced a separate notion of degree of confidence, orthogonal to subjective probability assessments. Degrees of desirability work with subjective probabilities in Bayesian theory to yield a theory of rational action, as well as a (now rather discredited) theory of actual behavior.

(even if the act is done "for its own sake"). The beliefs pertain to the circumstances and to ways of attaining the goal. And if the description of the act is sufficiently circumscribed, no distinction can be made between the act's teleological structure and its rationality. It is only when we enlarge the context to include other beliefs and wants, as well as the arguments that have served to bring them into existence, that the charge of irrationality can be made to stick.

This applies to the craziest act, providing that it is still an act. One winter day, Percival walks into a lake. He is crazy: in the light of his projects and his plans, his action makes no sense. But it was not somnambulism, nor was he pushed. He just wanted to walk into the lake. That's a crazy want, but in the light of just that isolated want his *action* is perfectly rational. And so, in the light of some narrow context of wants, is every irrational action.

It is frequently pointed out that when Aristotle declares that "Man is a rational animal," the word must be taken in a *categorial* sense, meaning the kind of animal that can be either rational or irrational. In the categorial sense, 'rational' contrasts with 'nonrational' and is entailed by 'irrational'. Taken in the *evaluative* sense (contrasting with 'irrational'), on the other hand, the Aristotelian dictum is clearly false. The evaluative sense presupposes the categorial sense: to be either rational or irrational (evaluatively) is to be rational (categorially). In terms of this familiar distinction, the principle of minimal rationality is this:

> (R2) *Minimal rationality.* It is a necessary condition of an intentional state or event's being describable as *categorially* rational, that under some true description it can properly (though perhaps vacuously) be said to be *evaluatively* rational.

Here are two well-known illustrations of the principle of minimal rationality. One is Quine's principle of charity in radical translation: Why should I not allow myself to translate a native belief as something of the form 'p & not-p'? Because an explicit contradiction could not intelligibly be posited as true (Quine 1960, 58). Such a proposition lacks the condition of minimal rationality and therefore cannot be the content of any belief. Another illustration is provided by Freud's analysis of parapraxes. Why are Freudian "slips" not merely accidents? Because they *can* be seen as having the structure of minimally rational acts: if enough abstraction is allowed from the realistic circumstances in which the parapraxis occurs, and if certain assumptions can be made about the existence of a certain context of beliefs and wants, the event can be fitted into that context and ascribed the minimally rational structure that is definitive of an *act*. That was the main justification for taking seriously the concept of *unconscious mentality* in chapter 4. It does not matter that in a broader context the act is irrational.

But the principle can also be abused. One example of abuse is the "Socratic paradox," the doctrine that no one desires the bad. The claim that desire is always *sub specie boni* depends on abstracting from precisely what determines whether or not a want is for something actually good. There is a grain of truth here: for a state to count as a want, it must posit that some proposition instantiates the proper object of wanting—that is, is good. In that minimal context all wants are for the good. The restriction of context insulates them from the broader context in which they can be seen to be irrational. They are therefore (evaluatively) rational under those minimal descriptions. But the minimal context is seldom adequate to any interesting evaluation of the act or state.

Intentionality
Appropriateness in terms of a goal or criterion of success is not a sufficient condition of rationality. As we have seen, there are two different types of teleology: the adaptive and the intentional. If God existed, it would have been rational of God to endow mammals with lungs and livers if God intended they should thrive. But that does not make the functioning of lungs and livers rational, nor does it make it rational of those organisms to have those organs. It is primarily individuals who are assessed for rationality, with respect to states that display at least the intermediate or "mental" level of intentionality. For this reason, inconsistency cannot ever be literally ascribed to a creature without language: the inconsistency will necessarily stick to the ascriber. (See de Sousa 1971; also chapter 8.) This is the third feature of rationality:

(R3) *Intentionality.* The teleology implicit in rationality applies only to intentional acts or states.

This principle limits the use we can make of biologically determined "goals" in assessments of rationality. (Remember, however, that we have reason to countenance unconscious intentionality.)

Origins
Rationality is neither necessary nor sufficient—alas—for the attainment of success. A rational belief can be false, and a true one irrational. A rational action can fail, and an irrational one succeed. This

partial independence of rationality from success gives rise to the next principle:

> (R4) *Origins.* The assessment of rationality of any act or belief looks both forward to consequences, logical and causal, and backward to origins.

The forward look assesses consequences in terms of some characteristic standard of success. For an action, this standard will be an actual goal—something as specific as someone's death, if you are planning a murder. For a belief, it will be truth; for a want, goodness. (Belief and want illustrate the need to include logical as well as causal consequences: if I believe what is true, it logically but not causally follows that my belief fits or matches the world.) For any emotion, the criterion of success will be specified by that emotion's particular formal object.

A god would have no use for rational methods. Omnipotence, omniscience, and omnibenevolence would guarantee success every time.*

But for us it is generally impossible to look directly at consequences, either because they are metaphysically inaccessible (like truth or goodness) or more simply just because they are future. That is why we are unavoidably interested in origins. Origins are, in a sense, second best. Sometimes we have as good access to the truth value of a belief as the commonsense brand of realism I am presupposing can demand: "Yes, there are carrots in the fridge." But then we do not need rationality. More often, though, origins are all we are able to look into. We typically scrutinize them in order to assess whether a state or action is *likely* to meet its characteristic standard of success.

Constraints

If you can establish that your total state of mind is inconsistent, then by definition what you have established is that it is certain at least partially to fail. That is why inconsistency is irrational. But if you find an inconsistency, you know only that something is wrong, not what it is. Once more you are thrown back to scrutinizing the path that led you to each of your inconsistent beliefs.

The same holds for rational action: at best we can predict success

---

*Would a god have a use for emotions? The answer to that would be a short metaphor for the long story I am telling in this book. We might see the Christian myth of incarnation as expressing a dim awareness of the fact urged above, that even if the formal objects of emotions are real, they can only be apprehended by perspectival beings.

and then wait for the outcome. But we can more directly inspect the coherence or our deliberations.

In short, rationality tells us what to avoid, not what to do or believe. Rationality forbids inconsistency and arbitrary distinctions: it imposes constraints, defined by criteria of consistency and nonarbitrariness. The idea of constraint can be encapsulated in this formula:

(R5) *Constraints.* Rationality never prescribes, but only constrains, by proscribing inconsistency and distinctions without a difference.

The Cognitive and the Strategic

As I have characterized it, rationality is always a teleological concept. Its *telos,* according to (R1), is specified by its criterion of success. An *act* is irrational if it tends to frustrate the agent's ostensible or ultimate goal. A *want* is irrational in the light of other wants claiming precedence in a hierarchy of wants and ends specifying what is good. A *belief* is irrational if, given the way it was arrived at, it is unlikely to be true.

This formula about belief presupposes that we can make sense of something like *epistemic utility,* in terms of which we assess the rationality of judgments as if they were acts. This is a well-explored and useful point of view;[6] but it is not incompatible with a measure of autonomy for "epistemic ends." Evolution is a rule-utilitarian process: the value of curiosity—epistemic utility—is no doubt in general subordinate to less abstract biological ends; but we should expect curiosity to have its own momentum even when it is not otherwise useful. I propose to mark this relative autonomy of curiosity by distinguishing two sorts of rationality: the *cognitive,* applicable directly to judgments and beliefs, and the *strategic,* applicable primarily to actions or wants.

Both standards of rationality can be defined in strategic terms. This explains the attractiveness of pragmatism. Truth, on this view, is just the goal or standard of success of the enterprise of belief. But we should not infer that the pragmatic is the more fundamental concept, because the tables can be turned. We could as easily think of successful action in terms of the fundamental idea of the epistemic goal, the concept of *matching.* (That is why the attempt to find the most fundamental concept of the trio truth, objectivity, rationality is like the paper, scissors, stone game.) The difference between strategic and epistemic rationality could be viewed as just a matter of the direction of fit: the cognitive aims to fit mind to world, whereas the strategic aims to fit world to mind. (See Searle 1983, 7ff.)

These two types of rationality can come apart. Sometimes believing something would be strategically rational but epistemically irrational. This is the basis of Pascal's notorious bet. Pascal urged us to believe in God even if the probability of his existence is arbitrarily low (provided it is finite). For if God exists, and we go to heaven, the expected gain remains infinite even when multiplied by that tiny probability. Conversely, if God exists and we disbelieve, the expected loss is infinite, since we get sent to hell for having bet against God. In either case the trivial gains and losses of a finite life are submerged, even when multiplied by the overwhelming odds that God does not exist. If Pascal's options were exhaustive, the reasoning would be strategically sound, though still cognitively irrational. (See Jeffrey 1965.)

Is there a criterion, in cases like Pascal's bet, for what is rational *absolutely?* I see no prospect of finding one. The question can always be rephrased in each of two ways, predetermining opposite answers. I can ask, "What should I do: believe it, or not?"—which calls for the answer, "If it's useful to do so, then believe it." Or I can ask, "What should I take it to be: true or false?"—which demands the answer, "If it's highly improbable, then don't believe it."

(R6) sums up the difference between the two paradigms of rationality:

> (R6) *Cognitive and strategic rationality.* A representational state can be assessed in terms of the value of its probable *effects* (in the causal sense): this evaluates its *strategic* rationality, or utility. By contrast, a state is *cognitively* rational if it is arrived at in such a way as to be probably adequate to some actual state of the world that it purports to represent.

The somewhat redundant parenthesis is intended as a flag to forestall confusion between the effects referred to in (R6), which are practical, and the "consequences" alluded to in the characterization of success as opposed to origins in (R4), which can be purely logical.

Principles (R1)–(R6) are not intended as a complete characterization of rationality. But they suffice to frame my central question: *What is the nature of the rationality involved in the assessment of emotional rationality?*

Note that (R1)–(R5) are plausible for both strategic and cognitive rationality. But the distinction between them embodied in (R6) allows for three possible answers to the main question about the rationality of emotion. It might be strategic, or cognitive, or sui generis. In the third case it seems sensible to assume (subject to revision) that (R1)–(R5) define a genus of rationality. They would then also be true of emotional rationality. But is there any reason to believe that the emotions, if they are subject to the present criteria at all, will present anything more than a composite of the two main types?

The Irreducibility of Emotion

If emotions are just combinations of beliefs and desires (see Marks 1982), then the principles governing their rationality would presumably be fully accounted for by cognitive and strategic rationality. I have already given two related arguments against this reductionist view: the problem of hypothetical attitudes precludes emotions from being simply beliefs; the variety of formal objects of emotions stops them from being identified with either beliefs or desires. I now offer two more arguments specifically directed against the assimilation of emotion to desire.

The first is that emotions and desires are differently affected by changes in relevant beliefs. I have already noted the familiar fact that some emotions crucially depend on beliefs, so that a judicious change in beliefs will eradicate an emotion. Nothing is easier to cure than grief, if only we can change the sufferer's belief that she has lost some loved one. Desire, by contrast, seems in general to be organized hierarchically, so that changes of desire consequent on changes of belief usually leave in place a residue consisting in some more general desire.

Suppose Stuart desires to see a certain movie, until he discovers that it was made by the director of *Close Encounters of the Third Kind*. Inferring that this new one is likely to be informed by the same meretricious vulgarity of mind, his desire ceases. Still, although his new information may have destroyed his specific desire, it may leave intact a more general one of which the former was merely an instance: the desire, perhaps, to see some good movie. There is nothing irrational about the endurance of that general desire. By contrast, if getting rid of a specific emotion leaves any rational residue at all, that residue will not consist in a more general emotion looking for a suitable target. If I learn that you did not steal my bicycle, I may look around, self-deceptively, for something else to blame you for. But that is clearly irrational.

Here we might adduce, as a counterexample, the "philosophical manic-depressive" of chapter 1. She was the one who insisted on looking on the depressing side of things in order to see them more clearly. In looking for the dark side of each happy circumstance, she seems to be retreating to a generic "residue" of gloom. Yet she is not obviously irrational. But if not, the reason is instructive, but of no comfort to the claim that the philosophical manic-depressive is a counterexample. That reason, I venture, is this: her clear-sighted gloom is so general that it functions as a foundation or framework for her assessments of rationality and is not open to any clear standards of its own. So it is not exactly that her residual gloom is rational, but rather that it is beyond the pale of rationality. I shall discuss the role of emotions as frameworks for rationality, rather than candidates for rational assessment, in chapter 7; and in chapter 9 I shall advert to the risks in the process of bootstrapping involved.

The present argument about "rational residues" is designed to establish that the evaluation of emotion calls for different criteria than the evaluation of desire. But it is not wholly general and therefore not quite convincing. If some emotion leaves no rational residue, this could mean that its constitutive desires are not hierarchically organized in the way I presumed. Someone might come up with an example of an emotion in which a hierarchical component of desire does result in a rational residual emotion.

The next argument is intended to bypass this objection. It shows that desire itself, in addition to its connection with action, sometimes has a phenomenological or emotional component. So we shall need some criterion of rationality for that additional component of "emotional desire." The demonstration of the existence of emotional desire will have another advantage: it will enable me to simplify some of the arguments in the sequel by using desire itself as a paradigm of emotion.

Can Desires Be Intrinsically Irrational?

Hume thought no desire could be intrinsically rational or irrational. (He would have conceded that a desire might inherit irrationality from a belief on which it is based. But that case is not of interest here.) Against this view, Derek Parfit has recently argued that besides any indirect ways in which desires might be irrational, "there is . . . a different and simpler way in which a desire may be irrational. It may be a desire that does not provide a reason for acting" (Parfit 1984, 120). Parfit adds two riders. First, he points out, even the most irrational desires can give us indirect reasons for acting (for example, to relieve the discomfort caused by an irrational phobia). Second, even where the desire does directly provide a reason for acting, "the reason is seldom the desire." Rather, it is "the respect in which my aim is *desirable*" (p. 121).

I see two problems about this way of defining intrinsic irrationality of desire. The first is that it has things backward. To see this, imagine adapting Parfit's principle to belief:

(PB) A belief is irrational if it fails to provide a reason for believing (or desiring or acting).

Let us also add riders analogous to those quoted from Parfit for desire. The first rider would be that irrational beliefs indirectly provide reasons. When I catch myself out in yet another superstition, for example, it gives me a reason to be suspicious of my self-image as a perfectly rational man. The second rider would be that even when a belief is rational, it is seldom the *belief* that is a reason for anything. Rather, it is the *likely truth* of its object. Would (PB) be an acceptable account of what we mean by (ir)rational belief?

Surely not. That a belief is irrational explains why it does not provide a reason. But that is not what it means for it to be irrational. On the contrary: it is irrational because there fails to be a reason for *it*, not because it fails to provide a reason for something *else*. Such is the force of the preoccupation of rationality with origins, as expressed in (R4).

The second problem is this. Let us agree that there are rational and irrational acts. It does not follow that there are any intrinsically irrational desires. The reason is that it does not even entail that there must be *any desires at all*.

Functional Want versus Emotional Desire What is needed for rational action is not desire but something weaker. Call it *functional wanting*, which needs to satisfy only the conditions of quasi intentionality. If a computer is programmed to pursue certain goals and to find means to those goals, it is thereby given functional wants. But functional wants are not full-fledged desires.

To see this, consider another intuition of Parfit's. What if someone says, "This attitude is irrational, because it's bad for you"? Parfit comments, "The fact that an attitude is bad for us does not show this attitude to be irrational. It can at most show that we should try to change this attitude. . . . Grief is not irrational simply because it brings unhappiness . . ." (Parfit 1984, 169). If you share this intuition, as I do, then what is in question here is more than functional wanting. The use of grief to illustrate something about desire shows that what Parfit is concerned with is *the kind of desire that is appropriately assimilated to an emotion*. If it is ever plausible to speak of an emotion as reasonable or unreasonable, then we can do so regardless of its consequences or those of any acts to which it might lead. The fact that something is bad for us is definitely a reason (ceteris paribus) to avoid it. It is sufficient to brand as irrational any action designed to procure it. But if, as Parfit says, it is not enough to make the actual desiring of it irrational, then the rationality of action is not a sufficient determinant of the rationality of desire.

The opposite point of view has been forcefully presented by Arnold Isenberg (1949b), who argued that even when it is natural to feel shame or regret, it does no good and therefore is irrational. But if we want to know whether to judge emotions in strategic or cognitive terms (or something else altogether), this simply begs the question. For whether the emotion does any good is only relevant if we are already committed to the strategic criterion. The same assumption is made by Laurence Thomas (1983), who argues that the negative emotions do serve a useful purpose. The question of the utility of negative emotions will be addressed in chapter 12. My aim here is only to point out that we can make sense of a notion of rationality and of a notion of desire to which utility is irrelevant.

For additional support to the claim that we need a concept of *phenomenological* or *emotional* desire, consider two other arguments, also inspired by Parfit. The first begins with the question of whether we can have desires about the past. Parfit thinks we can, while conceding that this "changes the concept" and that it "would be more natural to call this a *wish*" (p. 171). Now personally I do think that only what is envisaged as future can logically be desired. Wish, in my idiolect, carries something like the phenomenological component of desire without the action-oriented aspect: it is *desire minus functional want* (conversely, functional want is desire minus phenomenological desire). But Parfit's intuition supports my claim anyway. For desires about the past make sense only if we allow that their connection with action is indirect. In terms of the distinction introduced earlier, such cases will be only indirectly reason-providing, like an irrational phobia demanding to be humored.

One more argument might be gleaned from some remarks of Parfit's about the limits of possible desires. But this one is more dubious. Parfit argues that we should not confine desire to cases where some action is (practically or logically) possible. In particular, we should not assume that it is always irrational to desire something in the past:

> We can admit one way in which desires are tied to acts. If people could not act they could not have desires. But we can have a *particular* desire without being able to act upon it. . . . The Pythagoreans wanted the square root of two to be a rational number. . . . This removes the ground for denying that we can have desires about the past." (Parfit 1984, 172)

We must distinguish two questions: first, whether it is irrational to desire the impossible; second, if it is, whether it is so irrational that the ascription of such a desire is beyond the pale of minimal rationality—and therefore itself irrational. My own intuition is that it is irrational to desire what one knows, or believes, to be impossible.* Bearing in mind the distinction between success and satisfaction, however, it is important to remember that the attainable and the worthy are not, alas, extensionally equivalent. For states, as opposed to acts, success and rationality pertain to formal objects, not to the satisfaction of practical aims. The rationality of desires, like that of beliefs, must be granted some autonomy from the rationality of actions.

Let me repeat: I am interested, not in criteria of rationality for functional wanting, but in those that would apply to emotional or phenomenological desire, based on the nature of their formal objects. And my argument has been that the relevant criteria are reducible neither to cognitive nor to strategic rationality, though there are important parallels with both. What, then, are these criteria?

The Axiological Level

That question will occupy me in chapter 7. Before I turn to it, however, it will prove useful to revive some near-defunct terminology. In old textbooks on ethics, students were instructed to distinguish between two different levels of ethical discourse: the *axiological* and the *deontological*. Axiology was the theory of what was worthy or valuable; deontology told you what you ought to do. Obviously, the former is relevant to the latter, but the two can be kept logically distinct. We might make some progress if instead of thinking of the rationality of desire in deontological terms (as in Parfit's suggestion that it must be tied to practical reason), we consider the problem as one for axiology.

This is not easy to work out. A purely axiological approach cannot be made to yield an adequate theory of (full) desire, because a general connection between desire and action is obviously essential, as Parfit points out in the passage just quoted. Intuitively, desire looks in two directions: at pure value on the left, as it were, and at appropriate action on the right. The hypothesis I have been exploring is that just as the criteria of rationality for action look partly toward desire, so

---

*Parfit rightly does not say that what the Pythagoreans wanted to be true was something that *we know now* to be impossible, though they did not: they were the ones who found out. How long did their desire endure after they discovered the proof? Not long, I would surmise. In any case, on the usage I endorse, their discovery turned their desire into a mere wish, which in my scheme is an emotion, not a want.

the criteria of rationality for desire look at least partly to value. That is the emotional face of desire.

Not all the things that we prize or value are things we desire to do anything about. Consider once again the model of the aesthetic. Of course, we could attempt to order all possible aesthetic objects, dictating, other things being equal, the order in which we should contemplate them. But this seems forced. And in many cases the sort of action involved would not really amount to anything at all, except thinking about it. Parfit gives a lovely example of a valuable whim, borrowed from Nagel: "One might for no reason at all conceive a desire that there should be parsley on the moon, and do what one could to smuggle some into the next available rocket; one might simply like the idea" (p. 123). Parfit comments, "It is an excellent whim. (That there be parsley in the sea is, in contrast, a poor whim.)" Now clearly the excellence of the whim is assessed quite independently of any efforts actually to smuggle parsley onto a rocket. For me, at any rate, the thought is enough: this is a piece of conceptual art. Clearly, there is something there that it is not irrational to value. But what, over and above the aesthetic experience of thinking about it, are we to do about it?

You may be thinking that for present purposes, directing your attention to something must be counted as an action. But although this is true, the claim that something is aesthetically valuable does not need to be taken to imply that one *ought* to turn one's attention to it, even ceteris paribus, under any circumstances. It does entail that if you did contemplate it, you would, if you are normal, find it worthy. I take this to be one more argument in favor of setting apart an independent level of axiological rationality, which it is the purpose of chapter 7 to explore.

Chapter 7

The Rationality of Emotion

Le coeur a ses raisons, que la raison ne connaît pas.
Blaise Pascal

[In] rare moments of experience . . . we feel the truth of a commonplace, which is as different from what we call knowing it as the vision of waters upon the earth is different from the delirious vision of the water which cannot be had to cool the burning tongue.
George Eliot

Summary

How are we to understand emotional or "axiological" rationality? I pursue analogies with both the cognitive and the strategic models, testing them against intuitions about emotional desire. Both models are instructive, though each breaks down.

A concept of autonomy due to Jon Elster has affinities with the strategic model and seems to promise to make sense of rational desire in terms of its causal history: a desire is autonomous if it is not shaped by irrelevant causal factors. But a look at a sampling of cases undermines this promise and suggests that we should distinguish two different classes of desires. Subjective ones are potentially projective in the sense of chapter 5, whereas the objective, like cognitions, purport to correspond to the real world.

One might attempt to characterize the difference purely in strategic terms: subjective desires would be those one can envisage changing without loss. But this idea is shown to be unworkable by the existence of a third category, "self-related" desires. These may be vital to one's integrity and self-concept (and for that reason one wants them not to change), and yet they make no claim to objectivity. So we still need the cognitivist metaphor of "matching."

Applying this idea of matching to axiology, I propose that emotions have a semantics that derives from "paradigm scenarios," in terms of which our emotional repertoire is learned and the formal objects of our emotions fixed.

This fits in well with emerging facts about how our emotional capacities develop, and it can also be squared with the general principles of rationality, particularly minimal rationality.

One problem with this point of view is that it seems inevitably conservative in relation to emotional change. But this objection can be met: an emotion can be minimally rational without being rational. A principle of "emotional continence" guides the criticism of emotions by adjudicating the claims of different scenarios on a given situation. This principle enjoins us to construe the situation in terms of the broadest possible set of scenarios. Its practical application is difficult, however, because emotions seldom clash directly. The reason is that the variety of their formal objects places them in different dimensions of evaluation.

In the second part of the chapter I return to the perspective of rationality. I ask how emotions contribute to the rationality of beliefs, desires, and behavior. The leading idea is that in organisms sufficiently complex to exhibit intentionality, pure reason—cognitive or strategic—will need supplementation. An especially virulent problem is the "philosophers' frame problem": we need to know when not to retrieve some irrelevant information from the vast store of which we are possessed. But how do we know it is irrelevant unless we have already retrieved it? I proffer a very general biological hypothesis: Emotions spare us the paralysis potentially induced by this predicament by controlling the salience of features of perception and reasoning; they temporarily mimic the informational encapsulation of perception and so circumscribe our practical and cognitive options. In several ways, this idea confirms the irreducibility of the axiological level. Most notably, emotions play a role in acrasia that could be played by neither belief nor desire: they tip the balance between conflicting motivational structures, but they do so neither in a merely mechanical way nor merely by adding more reasons.

How is the determination of criteria of emotional "success" by paradigm scenarios compatible with their roles as determinants of salience? These two functions suggest opposite answers to the Euthyphro *question. This problem dissolves, however, if we remember that there are several types of subjectivity. Patterns of salience can be subjective in some senses, without being viciously projective. But we need a concept of individual normality, in terms of which the rationality of an emotion might be judged. Correct axiological assessment is then control of salience by a normal scenario.*

In chapter 6 I sketched the somewhat intricate relations among objectivity, truth, and rationality. That was not easy to do, because all three concepts are so fundamental that they can scarcely be defined. We are bound to resort to metaphors, which may themselves presuppose the basic concepts they are intended to illuminate. Another cause of difficulty is that each of the three concepts seems to claim priority over the others; though if we allow certain lines to blur a little, we can reduce the triad to a pair. From one perspective, objectivity and truth, understood in terms of the core metaphor of *matching*, are necessary to make sense of rationality. But from the opposite perspective, rationality, with its core metaphor of *success*, englobes truth and objectivity as merely special cases defined by their own brand of cognitive success.

In the face of these complexities my strategy has been to proceed alternately on both fronts. In terms of the metaphor of matching, I have argued that emotions may at least sometimes be meaningfully assessed for objectivity, somewhat on the model of perception. But I have resisted the assimilation of emotional objectivity to truth: emotions are not beliefs. Switching to the metaphor of success, I have urged that each emotion has its own formal object, congeneric with truth, but representing a specific standard of success, as different from truth or goodness as these are from each other. We can think of the different formal objects as independent *dimensions of evaluation*, which I call *axiological*.

In this and the next two chapters I persist in this dual-front approach. I first explore the nature of axiological rationality, by comparing it to both the strategic and the cognitive models. For greater clarity I conduct this part of the discussion in terms of desire, meaning, of course, neither "full-fledged" nor "functional" desire but emotional desire.

In the opening paragraph of this book I distinguished two major questions: one about the role of emotions in overall human rationality and the other about the rational assessment of individual emotions. So far I have mostly addressed the second. The latter part of this chapter will bring the first question into focus and offer a further hypothesis about the biological role of emotions in our rational life.

In chapter 8 I shall return to the perspective of objectivity; I shall give an argument to show how we might make literal sense, in a very specific respect, of the idea that some desires are objectively mistaken. And in chapter 9 I shall widen the field to discuss cases where the "bootstrapping" of emotions shades into emotional irrationality.

Rational Desire

Some people think assessments of emotional rationality can only be strategic. Like Protagoras, the partisans of that view hold that the measure of an emotion lies in whether it makes you feel good, promotes your goals, and perhaps disposes you to behave in commendable ways.

On this view, one might concede that our emotions provide information, but only about the likelihood of future behavior, satisfaction, or practical success: they would not be subject to cognitive rationality. They would be only *natural signs*. A natural sign can be interpreted as providing information in the light of natural regularities; but that it is so interpreted is not its function in the sense explicated in chapter 4 (see Millikan 1984, 120). If emotions are natural signs, they can provide information without being truly representing states on the model of perceptual or cognitive ones.

Among the partisans of such a pragmatic or strategic view of the role of emotions were many philosophers in the eighteenth-century tradition. They saw some emotions, the "moral sentiments," as forming the basis of social and moral life (see Rorty 1982). But however important that role might be, it ascribes only instrumental value to emotions. And that raises a dilemma: if you make the value of an emotion depend on its consequences, you need criteria of assessment for those consequences themselves. Some of them are likely to be further emotional states, if only of felt happiness or misery. If you know how to evaluate emotional states, you didn't need to inquire into these remote ones. But if you don't, they are of no help anyway. It seems therefore that we still need a criterion of *intrinsic* rationality for emotions and desires. Could such a criterion still be of the strategic kind?

Autonomy
One proposal that might help here is due to Jon Elster. Elster endorses the idea (consonant with our principle (R4) about origins) that a belief or desire is irrational if it has been "shaped by irrelevant causal factors." In the case of beliefs the capacity for appropriate shaping amounts to *judgment*, "defined as the capacity to synthesize vast and diffuse information that more or less clearly bears on the problem at hand" (Elster 1983, 16). In the case of desire the analogous notion is *autonomy*: any inappropriate external influence on my desires will make them irrational, just as an epistemically irrelevant cause of belief would make my belief irrational. (Note that Elster's concept differs from the more usual notion of autonomy, which precludes any external cause. See Morgan, unpub.) Obviously, these characterizations beg for a more substantive criterion of appropriateness and relevance. Like the concept of judgment, that of autonomy has little content. Both should be taken as something like regulative

concepts. But for our purposes that is not important. At this stage I will be content with the general shape of the right view.

The conception of rational desire implied by this proposal seems to be that of individual, self-generated will. This agrees in flavor with Parfit's suggestion that a rational desire provides reasons to act, without making the objectionable claim that this fact is criterial. If my desire is not really my own (if, like Titania's love, it has been induced by some chemical means, for example), then it is not autonomous and hence not rational. Elster's concept of autonomy also stresses the contrast between a criterion for "mind-world" matching, which suits judgment, and one aimed at some kind of coherence within the agent. It may seem, for this reason, more akin to the strategic than the cognitive model. But let us see how this squares with some examples of desires assessed for rationality.

Parfit (1984, chap. 8) describes three types of cases, illustrating respectively (1) clear cases of desires that are intrinsically irrational, (2) clear cases of desires that cannot be irrational, and (3) interesting controversial cases.

Clearly irrational desires include wanting to suffer great pain at some time in the present or future, without any other goal to which this might be a means; a desire to jump off a high place (without either a parachute or a death wish); and desires involving certain second-order preferences based on completely arbitrary lines, such as *future-Tuesday indifference*, which means not caring about anything that happens on a future Tuesday however painful or pleasant it might be (Parfit 1984, 124).

Desires that cannot be irrational, as Parfit describes them,

> are the desires that are involved in purely physical pains or pleasures. I love cold showers. Others hate them. Neither desire is irrational. If I want to eat something because I like the way it tastes, this desire cannot be irrational . . . even if what I like disgusts everyone else. (Parfit 1984, 123)

Controversial cases include various kinds of *temporal bias:* caring more about the present than about the future, or on the contrary discounting the future, or transferring from the past or from the future the motivating force of desires that are not presently felt. Those particular controversial cases will be dealt with in chapter 8. Now let us see what lessons may be gathered from the (supposedly) clear cases.

Clearly Irrational Desires   The three cases under this heading are quite heterogeneous.

What is irrational about merely desiring pain? It violates no *logical* constraints. Parfit does not speculate about how the desire originated. But it is hard to imagine any normal origins, compatible with autonomy, for the desire for gratuitous pain. Pain is the paradigm of what is intrinsically undesirable. This has nothing to do with either its causes or its consequences: rather, it seems to be just a fact. So far, if either model fits, it is the cognitive. But rather than saying it is irrational gratuitously to desire pain, perhaps we should say that it is just a misdescription. The case is *impossible:* a violation of minimal rationality.

The impulse to jump, by contrast, is clearly possible. And its intuitive irrationality seems to have everything to do with strategic considerations. The impulse to jump is irrational, because it might incline you to jump, and jumping would be bad for you. This does not preclude an explanation in terms of autonomy, but to give such an explanation we would again need to rely on some substantive notions of what is or is not normal.

Whatever is wrong with future-Tuesday indifference is not based on any standard specific to desire. It violates one of the constraints mentioned in (R5): the requirement that cases not be differently treated arbitrarily. But this requirement of reason is not one that necessarily sits well with the ideal of autonomy. Existentialists might claim that it is of the essence of autonomous desire that it eludes any requirement of nonarbitrariness. If my desires are arbitrary, that makes them all the more my own. So the evident irrationality of future-Tuesday indifference again seems to demand an explanation in terms of the cognitive rather than the strategic model.

Can we categorize, in terms of Parfit's intuitions, the case of the person who says she *just* wants a saucer of mud? Remember that as the case was described, she wants it not under the false impression that it is nutritious, nor, like Nagel's case of parsley on the moon, as an aesthetic whim, nor because it is pleasant to look at or muck about in. She just wants it.

What should we say of this case? It is not painful, like the first clear case. Is it irrational because it is like drawing an arbitrary line (she doesn't want other things that are like mud *even a tiny little bit*)? Is it irrational because it is a case of desiring "something that is in no respect worth desiring" (Parfit 1984, 123)? Or is it of the sort that cannot be irrational because, like a bodily sensation, it is irreducible and undiscussable? My intuition is that none of these explanations is very plausible. We need instead a *history* that will connect the desire both with particular events in which it had its origins and with the general facts about human instincts that made it possible for those particular events to result in just this desire.

Desires That Cannot Be Irrational The need for a history supplemented by biology can be further illustrated in terms of the cases that Parfit says cannot be judged either rational or irrational. The claim that his examples are of this sort is unconvincing. Recall that a desire induced by direct chemical intervention would typically be nonautonomous: clearly it is not *my* desire, even though I am the one to experience and perhaps act on it. "Purely physical" desires, therefore, can also be alienated. And if by direct intervention, why not by psychological means? An orthodox psychoanalyst might claim that the causal story that it is necessary to tell in order to explain certain desires (coprophilia, for example, or certain other forms of masochism) is altogether incompatible with the development of a fully autonomous self. Now this might be hard to establish, but it seems to me that the conceptual apparatus that it presupposes makes sense. What is lurking here, once again, is the difficult concept of *normality:* a desire is not autonomous if it did not originate in some normal way. Since origins are relevant to both strategic and cognitive models, however, this will not help us to decide between them.

The cases I have looked at have alternately seemed to favor the strategic and the cognitive model, without fitting either very neatly. In cases of the second type, where the criterion of autonomy held sway, the strategic model seemed plausible; but some desires of the first type—where intelligible at all—drew us to the cognitive model. One possible explanation is that we are dealing with two different sorts of desires or emotions. Let us explore this possibility.

Subjective and Objective Desires

The Devil's Bargain: A Moral Tale

Once upon a time there was a man who aspired to emulate Faustus, though he was not as clever. In the usual manner he summoned the Devil, and slyly he offered his soul in exchange for the granting of a single wish. The Devil smiled, but the man didn't worry. "My soul," he offered, "for the promise that I shall have what I desire forever." The Devil's smile grew wider. But what could go wrong?

Had the man been a little smarter, he would have remembered Bertrand Russell and specified the scope of the quantifiers. What he meant was this:

At any future time t, let me have at t what I desire to have at t.

But what the Devil agreed to was this:

At any future time t, let me have at t what I now desire to have.

So the man lived forever, in what soon turned out to be Hell, and never even got to meet Faustus.

At first the moral of this story seems trivial. Of course we change, and to have always what I desire just now would indeed be hell. (Sometimes Dante's damned are punished in the surfeit of what they sinfully desired.) So the simple moral is, When you are making plans, allow for changes of heart.

But things are not so simple. When we desire food, drink, sex, or sleep, it is usually obvious to us that the desire will last only as long as it is not gratified. We expect our moods and our whims to be similarly transient. But other desires and emotions—admiration, love, the sense of beauty, and perhaps, sometimes, even regret or revenge—seem to come with a secondary desire for their own continuation: it is painful, while one is in their grip, to think of them as ephemeral. The latter kind feel this way because they seem to correspond to some *objective value*. Grief typifies a third category in which one is pulled both ways at once: in grief one wants the pain to go away, but if the grief is caused by the loss of a loved one, the very thought that grief will subside can itself be a source of renewed grief. People who divorce sometimes long to be released from the pain of missing a presence they no longer enjoyed, while saying they will regret forever (and never want to cease regretting) a certain kind of failure—the breakup of a family, the failure of understanding—that the divorce entails.

Perhaps our pseudo-Faustus would have foiled the Devil, if only he had desired, at the time of his wish, only objectively valuable things. For what could go wrong then?

The idea of objectively valuable objects of desire brings us back to one of my central motivating problems, the question asked of Euthyphro. Do we desire something because it is desirable, or is it desirable because we desire it?

One modern answer is that it depends on the desire. One kind, *subjective* desires, comprise roughly what Parfit calls "mere preferences," providing *agent-relative* reasons. The other class are *objective* desires, which in the *Euthyphro's* terms are desired because they are desirable. They are roughly Parfit's *agent-neutral* desires, corresponding also to what Stephen Schiffer has called *reason-providing* desires, as opposed to *reason-following* desires.[1] I stick with "subjective" and "objective," because I will shortly introduce a third category of "self-related" desires, and because although subjective desires are not subjective in all of the four (or five) senses distinguished in chapter 6, they are both relative and potentially projective.

This distinction between the two kinds of desire naturally evokes the cognitive model with its core metaphor of matching. Nevertheless, one might seek to account for it entirely from the strategic point of view. Here is how a proposal on these lines might go.

Think of subjective desires as those that we do not mind thinking of as changing. By contrast, it will be painful to envisage the loss of those desires that appear to be for something objectively good:

> Nay, if I wax but cold in my desire,
> Think heaven hath motion lost, and the world, fire.
> (John Donne, Elegy XII: "His Parting from Her")

The presumption of objectivity in the latter desires does not commit us to a Platonic view: it does not imply that nothing is objectively valuable except what is eternal. It implies only that the *value* of what is valuable is timeless, not that what is valuable must exist forever. (Compare: the truth of what is true is timeless, though the things and events of which it is true need not be.) To take an extreme case, one of the things we might prize as having objective and timeless value may be *fleeting pleasure*: "Death is the mother of beauty," said Wallace Stevens in "Sunday Morning." By definition, fleeting pleasures would lose their identity, and therefore their value, if they were to persist forever.

Armed with these distinctions, let us return to our pseudo-Faustus: from the strategic point of view, it seems he might have foiled the Devil even without any knowledge of true value. Perhaps he need only have included among his present desires a second-order desire that his desires remain constant. Would this idea have saved him?

Some desires come with positive second-order desires. Others come with a negative second-order desire: a desire that they not continue. Second-order desires are easy to confound with judgments of objective value, because in most cases they are the foundations for such judgments (see Frankfurt 1971). But this is not a necessary feature of such desires. One can imagine wanting a certain desire never to stop (thus having the positive second-order desire) but knowing, at the same time, that this second-order desire is merely incontinently caused by the first-order desire. Perhaps this was the case with Augustine when he uttered his prayer: "Give me chastity, but not yet."

Now the fact that second-order desires can be either positive or negative, regardless of whether they are thought to represent objective value, might seem to undermine the project of distinguishing subjective from objective desires in terms of attitudes to their future alteration. But we might save it by appealing to a third-order level of desire. Even when my first-order desire D1 (a simply physical desire, let us say) generates a second-order desire D2 that D1 continue, the test of a sincerely negative evaluation of D1 is that there be a desire D3 for D1 (and perhaps also D2) to disappear. In this way, then, we might still make the distinction between objective and subjective desires in terms of attitudes to the future.

Nevertheless, this attempt to deal with the difference between subjective and objective desires solely in terms of the strategic point of view will not work. The reason is that there is a third category of desires, which are clearly not objective and yet meet the strategic criterion for being so.

Self-Related Desires

People change, and so do their emotions and desires. Our pseudo-Faustus might have tried to protest that changes in his own desires were not part of the bargain, but the Devil would not have been impressed. We all have emotions and desires the loss of which we would deplore, because we would feel our own self-concept undermined. They do not have to be virtues: I love my stamp collection; I am a woman who needs to feel glamorous; I live only for the moment's passion; I am a man given to indignant rages. Yet we are not so mad as to think that any of these idiosyncrasies reflects objective value. If I projected the formal object of my emotion, taking it for a real feature of the world, I would be clearly self-deceived. But I need not do so. And yet emotions in this category can be vital to my individual well-being. The emotional quality of intense passions and simple appetites of youth are an example. One might quite intelligibly celebrate their loss in old age, as Cephalos does in the opening pages of Plato's *Republic*, but it is more usual to mourn them, as does Yeats:

> I have not lost desire
> But the heart that I had;
> I thought 'twould burn my body
> Laid on the death-bed,

For who could have foretold
That the heart grows old?
(W. B. Yeats, "A Song")

Such desires seem to be the proper domain of Elster's category of autonomy. They are the ones that spring from our own being, and their value is undiminished by the fact that they are liable to change in ways we can neither predict nor control. Sometimes, indeed, one might claim that a certain degree of mutability in such desires is itself valuable. We would then have a second-order desire—the desire for mutability—that could be considered an objective desire defining a timeless value.

The deceptively simple parable of the Devil's Bargain has led me to distinguish three kinds of desires: those that we regard as intrinsically subjective, those in which we cherish constancy because they have moral or aesthetically objective import, and finally those that are morally significant not simply because of the value of their object but because of what our *having* such desires means for our self-concept, our energy, or our integrity. The existence of the self-related desires in this third class, however, is incompatible with the purely strategic perspective on the contrast between subjective and objective desires.

It is time, therefore, to return from the perspective of strategic rationality, rooted in the idea of practical success, to the alternative perspective rooted in the idea of matching. Taking the hint from the cases considered a few pages back, in which the rationality of emotional desires seemed to hang on their history, I shall now explore the conditions of rationality of emotions in terms of their origins. What follows can be viewed as first steps in search of a *semantics* of emotions.

Paradigm Scenarios

We have already seen how classical writers on the emotions, from Descartes on, are fond of making lists of primitive emotions, then going on to show how the more complex are built out of those. The diversity in the resulting lists is warning enough that this is an unpromising method. And yet it cannot be denied that there are, in other animals as in human babies, modes of behavior that we take to express something like human emotions. I think we can understand, in principle, how our repertoire of emotions gets built up, without positing a set of "primary emotions" that get combined like basic blocks or even mixed like primary colors. We do need a repertoire of primitive instinctual responses, but emotions are not mere responses.

My hypothesis is this: We are made familiar with the vocabulary of emotion by association with *paradigm scenarios*. These are drawn first from our daily life as small children and later reinforced by the stories, art, and culture to which we are exposed. Later still, in literate cultures, they are supplemented and refined by literature. Paradigm scenarios involve two aspects: first, a situation type providing the characteristic *objects* of the specific emotion-type (where objects can be of the various sorts identified in chapter 5), and second, a set of characteristic or "normal" *responses* to the situation, where normality is first a biological matter and then very quickly becomes a cultural one. It is in large part in virtue of the response component of the scenarios that emotions are commonly held to *motivate*. But this is, in a way, back-to-front: for the emotion often takes its name from the response disposition and is only afterward assumed to cause it.

Recent work on the development and function of smiling in infants provides a striking illustration of this last point. According to Daniel Stern, babies are born with an innate capacity to smile. At the very earliest stage, smiling seems to be a purely biological function, which elicits adult responses without involving any intentional communication. Between six weeks and three months, the baby begins to use the smile "instrumentally," that is, "in order to get a response from someone" (Stern 1977, 45). This does not affect the way the smile looks: in some way it is the same response. But what has changed is how it originates (p. 44).

From this stage on, the behavior needs to be reinforced visually if it is to persist: blind children seem to lose expressiveness in their smiles. The necessary reinforcement comes, of course, from feedback provided in interaction with caretakers. But we should not assume, as both psychoanalysis and behaviorist psychology might incline us to do, that the child is merely a passive recipient of shaping by parental and other external influences. For there is evidence that the feedback received in turn depends on the innate character of the infant's smile. How an infant is treated determines the paradigm scenarios that define its emotional repertoire; but its treatment, in turn, partly depends on its own innate facial characteristics and behaviors. To that extent, physiognomy is destiny.

Those original facial characteristics and behaviors of the infant are spontaneous and purely physiological: at that stage they *mean* nothing at all (Stern 1977, 43–44). Yet we might read these facts as telling us that, in a way, the ultimate initiative in determining the infant's emotional constitution belongs largely to the infant itself. This may be, in the end, what the notion of emotional temperament amounts to. If so, believing in temperament does not require us to believe in primitive emotions: the primitives out of which emotions emerge are not emotions.

A child is genetically programmed to respond in specific ways to the situational components of some paradigm scenarios. But what situational components can be identified depends on the child's stage of development. An essential part of education consists in identifying these responses, giving the child a name for them in the context of the scenario, and thus teaching it that it is experiencing a particular emotion. That is, in part, what is involved in learning to feel the right emotions, which, as Aristotle knew, is a central part of moral education (*Nicomachean Ethics*, II.2).

The process whereby emotions are constructed out of dispositions to respond can be observed from the first few months of life.[2] Mere feedback loops give way to complex interactions that it is plausible to think of as scenarios. First, between six and nine months one can generally make a baby smile by smiling, and cry or frown by frowning. There is "vicarious resonance," but no intentionality. At the next stage the caretaker's expressions have become signs to the infant of what it can expect her to do and feel. After nine months this includes looking to her for guidance as to what to look at and how to feel about it. The infant will follow the caretaker's gaze and, more important, look to her to learn how to react. Late in the second year of life toddlers seem already to have the sense of the existence of other subjects. They become aware that different participants in the same scene will, by virtue of their different roles, feel differently from each other. As we should expect if paradigm scenarios indeed define the very character of our emotions, we acquire the capacity to talk about emotions in terms of the stories that give rise to them sooner than we can talk about the origins of other mental states such as perception. Before the age of three, toddlers can understand that one person's action may lead to another's distress and that certain types of events typically cause certain emotions. They also know that by taking a sequence from an emotional scenario out of context, one can play-act or "pretend" emotions that are not actually being felt. And by the time toddlers are four or five years old, they have a very good sense of what kinds of stories lead to what simple emotions. Learning these scenarios continues indefinitely, however, as the emotional repertoire becomes more complicated. (Sentiments of guilt and responsibility are not generally understood by six-year-olds well enough for them to infer who is feeling what in stories where such sentiments would be appropriate.)* Indeed, perhaps we enlarge our repertoire, much as we increase our mastery of language, well into adult life, though with increasing resistance.

This fits in with the fact that some emotions are more thought-dependent than others. It depends on the paradigm scenarios to which they are related. If the paradigm scenario cannot be apprehended without complex linguistic skills, for example, we shall not expect to find in someone who lacks those skills an emotion specifically tuned to that scenario. That is why, as Iris Murdoch has put it, "The most essential and fundamental aspect of culture is the study of literature, since this is an education in how to picture and understand human situations."[3]

On the other hand, prelinguistic responses such as flight or attack can subsist to define so-called primitive emotions of fear and rage. Thanks, perhaps, to their dependence on relatively separate parts of the brain, they retain their power even over individuals whose repertoire includes the most "refined" emotions. We observe this most easily in other people.

The Principles of Rationality Applied

In sum, the role of paradigm scenarios in relation to emotions is analogous to the ostensive definition of a common noun.[4] Their role can be sharpened by relating it to the principles of rationality elaborated in chapter 6.

According to (R1), formal objects define a state's criterion of success. Where the state is an emotion, its formal object is fixed by a paradigm scenario, which defines an axiological quality. The emotion is objective, self-related, or subjective, depending on whether the qualities in question are legitimately attributed to the real world or are merely projected onto it. The essentially dramatic structure of the formal object helps to set the axiological level apart from the cognitive and strategic levels of appraisal on which it is partly modeled. But it does not stop axiological properties from having a phenomenological aspect: every scenario has its own feel.

---

*Inge Bretherton also gives a telling example of a six-year-old's fully developed sense of the difference it makes which role one is playing in a scene:

Mother: "It's hard to hear the baby crying like that."

Child: "Yes it is. But it's not as hard for me as it is for you."

Mother: "Why not?"

Child: "Well, you like Johnny better than I do! I like him a little, and you like him a lot, so I think it's harder for you to hear him cry." (Bretherton et al. 1986, 541)

The dramatic structure of the formal objects of emotions has another important consequence. In a sense, we might characterize an emotion's formal object as its *mode of appropriateness*. But that carries a misleading suggestion that emotions as a class have a single specific formal object, which is to all emotions as truth is to beliefs and desirability to wants. In view of the diversity in logical structure of different emotions as it emerged in chapter 5, it would be better, though messier, to concede a sense in which emotions do not form a kind in the same way as do wants or beliefs (see Rorty 1980). There is no general criterion for a set of things to constitute a "natural kind" (see de Sousa 1984). But the view of formal objects I have been expounding suggests a strict criterion for the limited category of representational states: A group of such states form a natural class, if and only if they have the same formal object. Appropriateness is the genus of the formal object in question. But that genus includes truth and goodness too. It tells us nothing about the differentiae of success conditions for emotions. I have argued that axiology has some features in common with the cognitive, and some with the strategic forms of rationality. But in the end even axiological success is only a genus. Even emotion must find, in the peculiar character of its paradigm scenario (enraging, engaging, sinister, shameful, and so on), its own specific formal object. This explains, as I shall argue more fully in chapter 12, why there are, in the words of Bernard Williams, "few, if any, *highly general* connections between emotions and moral language" (Williams 1973a, 208).

In relation to paradigm scenarios the principle of minimal rationality (R2) works like this. Since emotions are learned in terms of paradigm scenarios, they cannot, at least within a given social context, be criticized for inappropriateness if they occur in response to a relevantly similar situation. Here we must carefully distinguish the emotion itself from the behavioral response that the scenario might involve: it does not follow from the rationality of the emotion evoked that the stock response will continue to be seen as rational. Where the response is an action or strategy, it needs to be assessed in its own terms. It may be that a further narrowing of the context is needed before the minimal rationality of the behavior is guaranteed. Surprising one's lover in bed with someone else, one may react with jealousy and rage. In our culture this situation maps onto some primal sense, first rehearsed in infancy, of being robbed by another of vital physical attention. It has become the paradigm scenario for jealousy and so the emotion aroused by it must be counted appropriate. (In other cultures where polygamy is the rule, infantile jealousy may come to be represented by rather different situations.) But even if the original scenario, as learned, involves the response of murderous aggression, this will not necessarily make murder rational. That act will have its own minimal rationality as an extreme act of revenge, but the mere existence of the scenario will not determine whether extreme revenge is ever rational.

The intentionality principle (R3) stipulated that (categorial) rationality applies only to intentional states. Accordingly, as I stressed in my brief discussion of the role of development in the setting up of paradigm scenarios, there are responses before there are intentional states, but there are no scenarios, and therefore no emotions, until those responses can be integrated into an intentional structure, enabling the child to understand the meaning of different possible roles.

The bearing of the fourth and fifth principles is best understood by considering them together. Constraints, in the sense of principle (R4), are most easily understood as applying to *transitions* between states and to the *coexistence* of states. We do not usually judge a belief in isolation, for example, except on those rare occasions when we can directly assess its truth. Hence the emphasis on origins prescribed by principle (R5). For two reasons, the importance of origins in the assessment of rationality carries over with especial force to the axiological sphere. The first reason is that judgments of transition and coherence tend to be uncertain in the domain of emotions. (One example, which I shall consider at length in chapter 11, is the question of whether the same thing can be both comic and tragic at the same time.) The second is that for beliefs, origins are merely a clue to the likely attainment of the formal object; but here—in the form of paradigm scenarios—they constitute the formal object's very definition.

Some Objections

One problem raised by the present account is this. It appears to suggest that the rationality of an emotion is fixed irretrievably by its origins in socialization and that nothing can affect the appropriateness of an emotion provided the evoking situation fits the paradigm. What then of the changes in emotional dispositions that we call "maturing emotionally"? And what of the possibility of striving for greater emotional rationality? Can we not, for example, repudiate certain scenarios altogether in an effort to be rid of sexist or racist emotions?

This objection parallels the charge, justly laid against a certain kind of "Oxford philosophy" a couple of decades ago, of misusing the notion of paradigm. The smiling bride, according to a once popular argument, is the paradigm of a free agent: "If you want to know whether we ever act freely, look at the smiling bride. That's what it is, by (ostensive) definition, to act freely. So, as you can see, there are free acts." But that a concept is learned in a given context does not mean that the concept cannot be revised and refined, that our understanding of it cannot be deepened to the point where we are able to ask without contradiction whether it is appropriate to the paradigm itself. A smiling bride, we say, is *a picture of happiness.* But what a picture *shows,* it does not typically *instantiate.*

A paradigm can always be challenged in the light of a wider range of considerations than are available when the case is viewed in isolation. It can be revised in the light of competing paradigms that are also applicable to the situation at hand. However, the emotion will retain its basic intelligibility (its minimal rationality) provided it can be seen in the light of its own, narrowest, proper scenario. Further, a scenario can become completely inert, obsolete: this will take place if every situation that fitted the original scenario comes to be seen, from a more comprehensive perspective, as fitting another (set of) scenario(s). In some North American subcultures, for example, the sentiments and scenarios once associated with such notions as "chastity" or "satisfaction in affairs of honor" have altogether lost their power to move either to feeling or to action. Situations that would once have evoked those sentiments are now simply felt in terms of quite different scenarios.

This suggests the following principle:[5]

> (PEC) *Principle of emotional continence.* Let your emotions be appropriate to the widest possible range of available scenarios.

Here is a somewhat politically charged example. How do you feel about prostitution? The answer will depend on the model to which—emotionally—you assimilate it: Is it wage labor? (Or is wage labor just prostitution?) (See Jaggar 1980.) Is it free-enterprise independent business? Oppression of women? Oppression of men? Therapy? Or theater? A mature emotional reaction to prostitution, according to (PEC), is one that is tested against all these potentially applicable scenarios.

The complications of working out what (PEC) would mean in practice are enormous, because—as I shall explain—the emotional level of rationality is the deepest and most inclusive. But the attempt to restructure one's emotions by "consciousness raising" is based on something like the principle of emotional continence. Beyond a certain point, moral progress is often a matter of rising above principle—by getting a more adequate feel for a certain situation in all its ramifications, by viewing it as a complex scenario. Almost by definition, a moral principle is bound to construe any situation to which it is applied simplistically.[6]

Mark Twain's Huckleberry Finn provides a savory example of emotion successfully rising above principle. Although tortured by his moral conscience, Huck gives in to what he assumes must be emotional and moral weakness. When he refrains from turning in Jim, the fugitive slave, he does what he "knows" is wrong according to every principle of honesty and gratitude known to him (see Bennett 1974).

Nevertheless, an objector might ask, in what sense can we maintain that the process of one paradigm being supplanted by another is rational? And to what extent can it be maintained that there is any objectivity involved here? Am I not saying that attitudes, dispositions, and habits may change unaccountably, since what leads to change—what one might barbarously call "emotional regestalting"—is simply beyond the pale of rationality? Do emotions not remain as subjective after as before such changes?

My brief answer is no: not all changes of mind are equally subjective or irrational. The tendency to think otherwise springs from an unrealistic picture of the rationality of belief changes and from unwarranted standards for "objectivity." I said that an emotion is appropriate (or minimally so) in a given situation if and only if that situation is relevantly similar to (can accurately be "gestalted" as) a suitable paradigm scenario. To be sure, what can be seen as similar to a given scenario admits of a certain amount of leeway. Can the complicated friendships of sophisticated Bloomsburyites adequately be seen as instantiating "the Eternal Triangle," for example, or would that scenario be truly stifled, in those circles, by a metascenario in which it appears as vulgar? We can hardly expect mathematically precise answers to such questions. But not just anything goes, either, as some have learned to their cost, like Pentheus in Euripides' Bacchae, who have attempted to "rationalize" their lives in terms of invented scenarios insufficiently rooted in human nature and the facts of life. True irrationality of emotion involves the perception of a situation in terms of a scenario that it does not objectively resemble. I shall discuss an important class of such cases in chapter 8. Change of mind rests on unconscious links and transformation rules that have turned one situation into another. Emotional irrationality is a matter of muddled scenarios: a loss of reality, intensified in neurosis and extreme in psychosis. The minimal rationality of those emotions must be sought in terms of the scenario unconsciously evoked. Psychotherapy typically looks for clues to the transformation in free association, and it is a sound principle of therapy not to rest in the search for the original scenario until the emotion inappropriately evoked is accounted for as minimally rational.

Two further complications block any easy answers to questions about rationality in practice. (This is lucky for my theory, since if easy answers to complex problems could be deduced from it, they would constitute a quick reductio.) The first complication stems from the fact just noted, that a given situation and response may evoke several clashing scenarios. Emotions are not necessarily compatible, even when they are all equally adequate. (The perception analogy will help again to see how this is possible: when you are looking at a Necker cube ▢ or a duck-rabbit picture ⟨⟩ you cannot see both cubes or both animals at once; yet what you are interpreting as one or the other is in some sense just one thing.) In some cases emotions mix, in varying proportions; in other cases one emotion, like a perceptual gestalt, crowds out another. The rules governing these phenomena are among the "constraints" of axiological rationality demanded by (R5). Unfortunately, I don't know what they are.[7]

The second obstacle to finding clear-cut examples of those constraints at work is the variety of formal objects. Rational coexistence is a matter of consistency, not compatibility. The latter concerns simultaneous satisfaction, whereas the former concerns simultaneous success. The two are easily confused, since they coincide for the case of beliefs. But they do not coincide for goodness, or for the different species of axiological appropriateness. Wants are consistent, not if their objects can all be *true* together, but if they can all be *good* together. Similarly, the condition of consistency for emotions is not whether their targets, motivating aspects, or propositional objects are compatible but whether their formal objects are logically consistent. And if each emotion has its own formal object, then the constraints of consistency will only relatively rarely have occasion to apply.

Let me repeat an important consequence of this last point: the objectivity of axiology does not imply that there must be uniqueness of axiological "correctness." This fact, amounting to the *multidimensionality of value,* will prove crucial when we come (in chapter 12) to look at the contributions of emotions to ethical life.

In effect, I have been arguing that paradigm scenarios, in setting up our emotional repertoire, quite literally provide the meaning of our emotions. There will be more to say in later chapters about the axiological level of reality that they pick out. For the rest of this chapter I want to switch back to the strategic model, guided by the metaphor of success, and return, though at a more abstract level, to the question of the biological function of emotions considered in chapters

3 and 4. In the next sections I offer a new speculation about what that biological point might be. This will fulfil my promise to say something about the role of emotion in rationality as a whole, and it will also tell us something more about the nature of emotional appropriateness.

What Are Emotions For? A New Biological Hypothesis

As we saw in chapter 3, there are many speculative theories in the field about the biological usefulness of emotions. Most of them relate to the survival value of such basic behavior patterns as the traditional "four F's." But the relevance of those speculations to my present purposes is limited. The reason is that I am specifically interested in emotions as such. (Even where for simplicity I speak of desire, I am interested chiefly in what I have called 'emotional desire'.) And those basic survival functions have no need for emotions at all. It is logically possible that evolution might have set us up simply to want the right things and to have true beliefs or perceive the relevant aspects of our environment. This fact is reflected in traditional theories of rational decision-making, in which emotions have acquired their bad reputation. For in those theories there is neither need nor room for emotions, except as disrupters of the orderly course of rational deliberation.[8] Since I have insisted all along that emotions are not reducible to desires and beliefs, it is time to say more positively what, in relation to rational behavior and belief, the role of emotions might be.

The suggestion I want to make is best approached by elaborating on a thought experiment broached in chapter 1. Let us try to imagine what it would be like for us to be without emotions. This must not be confused with the speculation that we might be without "functional wants," or even without a certain class of wants, of the sort attributed to "emotional" people. The confusion is common in science fiction attempts to describe emotionless beings, who generally turn out merely to lack concern for other people, or else are inhumanly single-minded and constant over time. In fact, the problem is deeper and more abstract than is imagined in such stories.

I see two forms that such beings could take. A truly emotionless being would be either some kind of Kantian monster with a computer brain and a pure rational will, or else a Cartesian animal-machine, an ant, perhaps, in which every "want" is preprogrammed and every "belief" simply a releasing cue for a specific response. My hunch here is that it is because we are neither one nor the other, "neither beast nor angel," that we have emotions as well as beliefs and desires. But let me try to do a little better than a hunch.

What is it that animal-machine and Kantian angel have in common? I submit that it is *complete determinacy:* in the first by mechanism, in the second by reason. In fact, of course, the two monsters are equally mythical. The fact of biological variability precludes any animal-machine of the sort just described. Two individual ants, even two individual viruses, will not do exactly the same thing under every condition. But they come close enough: close enough in particular so that individual ants have no need of special clues to tell them how, from a repertoire of equally probable alternatives, other ants are likely to react. Ants, unlike primates, have no need for communicativeness of emotional expression. But among animals like us, to read the emotional configuration of another's body or face is to have a guide to what she is likely to believe, attend to, and therefore want and do. Such dispositions tend to be given different names depending in part on their duration: a short one is an emotion, a longer one a sentiment, and a permanent one a character trait. Ants need no character, and if they emoted, they would not need to know it of one another.

What about angels? There, I suggest, full predictability would also elude us: not because of angelic variability, but because there is no such thing as fully determinate rationality. This is true of both the cognitive and the strategic varieties.

Consider the cognitive level. On many issues, logic gives no unique prescription. Logic suggests that in consistency we should avoid false beliefs and pursue true ones: "Don't believe an inconsistent set," but "Believe the consequences of your beliefs." Plausible as they are, these principles are not always compatible in their application, nor do they prescribe their own ordering. Even at the lowest level we require informal policies to supplement hard logic. More important areas of indeterminacy have to do with what subjects to investigate and what inductive rules to adopt. No logic determines *salience:* what to notice, what to attend to, what to inquire about. And no inductive logic can make strictly rational choices between the extremes of "soft-headedness" and "hard-headedness." (The terms are borrowed from the *Theaetetus* (191c), where Plato describes two sorts of "tablets" in the mind. Soft ones easily take impressions but just as easily lose them; hard ones are difficult to scratch but once imprinted are less easily erased.) Plato's problem was what statisticians now call the problem of the choice of *significance level:* how probable must it be that your hypothesis is true on the evidence, and how improbable must it be that it should be false on the evidence, before it is rational to accept it? Inductive logic does not tell us, and statistics offers only sophisticated rules of thumb.

But there is an even worse problem, not reducible to those of either logic or induction. It is not just that we know too little and are not powerful enough logicians to make the best even of that. We also know too much.

Knowledge Access and the Philosophers' Frame Problem
The recognition of a class of problems generated by the fact that we know too much is a major contribution of artificial intelligence to philosophy.

Because a machine starts out knowing nothing, the task of getting it to act intelligently reveals how much we know—but didn't know we knew. One class of such knowledge is constituted by what we might call "Piaget-processes"—pieces of knowledge that we acquire very early, by some mixture of maturation and learning, and that have to do in some way with "the way the world works." (I am not speaking here of procedural knowledge, or "knowing how." We need to learn to do things too, of course; but here I am concerned only with factual knowledge.) I know, for example, that when I've poured the beer into the glass, it's not in the bottle any more. This kind of knowledge is constantly required to interpret the simplest of instructions, as well as to disambiguate simple sentences.* The extent of such knowledge is vast: it is not merely semantic but encyclopaedic: one does not acquire it by simply having a good grammar and knowing the meanings of the words involved.[9] Think, for example, of the general knowledge required to know that snow-shoes, alligator-shoes, and horse-shoes are not respectively made of snow, worn by alligators, or used to walk on horses.

Even an encyclopaedia may not be enough. John Haugeland has called this the "No Topic" problem:

> "I left my raincoat in the bathtub, because it was still wet." Does 'it' refer to the bathtub or the raincoat? To the raincoat, obviously, because 1. a raincoat's being wet is an intelligible (if mildly eccentric) reason to leave it in a bathtub, whereas 2. a bathtub's being wet would be no sensible reason at all for leaving a raincoat in it. But where are these reasons to be "filed"? They hardly seem constitutive of the general, commonsense concepts of either rain-

---

*I once heard Paul Ziff offer a charming example: "I saw her duck . . . when they were throwing rotten eggs . . . and then I saw it swim out to the middle of the lake." Note, here, how our cognitive system somehow automatically retrieves the information needed for our flip-flops of interpretation.

coats or bathtubs (let alone wetness); nor are they part of some other concept, for which there just doesn't happen to be a word in the given sentence. (Haugeland 1985, 202)

Assume encyclopaedic knowledge, supplemented by an appendix entitled "No Filable Topics." The worst problem still remains: how will the system have access to this knowledge, and how will it ignore what is not relevant?

Both aspects concern, not the acquisition of knowledge, but the use we make of the stupendous quantity of knowledge we already have. When we plan some action, we can assume that the vast majority of the world's facts will remain unaffected by it (see Hayes 1987). Yet some will not: we can never do just one thing at a time, and some of the side effects of what we do may turn out to be important. When we act, we need to track relevant change and "bear in mind" what does not change for possible future reference. But the number of facts that change, and the number of facts that stay the same, are both unmanageably large. Assume all the powers already listed—logic, induction, and more-than-encyclopaedic knowledge: the *philosophers' frame problem*, roughly, is how to make use of just what we need from this vast store, and how not to retrieve what we don't need.* Daniel Dennett has given the problem a vivid illustration. He imagines a robot being informed that a bomb is about to go off in its hangar. The robot duly decides to leave the hangar, but, alas, the bomb is on the robot's own wagon: though it knew this and many other things about its environment, it had not "thought" to draw the inference. So its designers instruct it, in future, to draw the consequences of what it knows. Unfortunately, when the experiment is repeated, the robot sits, lost in computation, long past the time for action; at the time the explosion occurs it has "just finished deducing that pulling the wagon out of the room would not change the price of tea in China." In the newest version the designers try again, instructing it, this time, to ignore irrelevant implications:

[T]heir next model [was] the robot-relevant-deducer . . . R2D1. When they subjected R2D1 to the test . . . , they were surprised to see it sitting, Hamlet-like, outside the room containing the ticking bomb. . . . "Do something!" they yelled at it. "I am," it retorted, "I'm busily ignoring some thousands of implications I

---

*I call the problem I am concerned with the *philosophers' frame problem*, mostly to avoid being accused of misunderstanding the *real* frame problem. According to members of the AI community, this is their problem and all philosophers misunderstand it. See, for example, McDermott 1987 and Hayes 1987; but see also Dennett 1987 and Fodor 1987 in the same volume.

have determined to be irrelevant. . . ." but the bomb went off. (Dennet 1987, 42)

The philosophers' frame problem is not reducible to the problem of induction. The problem of induction is about what inferences are warranted. What gives rise to the philosophers' frame problem is that we need to know whether a consequence will turn out to be relevant *before drawing it*. If it is relevant and we have not retrieved it, we may act irrationally. But if it is irrelevant and we have already drawn it, we have already wasted time. This is the problem at its most virulent: How do we know without finding out what not to find out if we know?

The Strategic Insufficiency of Reason
The deficiencies of pure reason apply not only to cognitive problems but also to choices of strategies in the light of existing desires. Where action is concerned, all our uncontroversial principles of rationality are captured by Bayesian decision theory, which is based on the idea that life consists in gambles. Its maxim is "Maximize expected gain." Expected gain is the sum of gains and losses afforded by each possible outcome, weighted by its probability. (Pascal's bet, described in chapter 6, is an application of Bayesian theory.) But Bayesian theory is not enough to yield unequivocal outcomes to practical problems. For suppose you are considering whether to take a fair bet. By definition, from the Bayesian point of view, a fair bet is equivalent to no bet at all: its expected desirability is zero. Whether we make a bet, therefore, requires additional principles. Yet there is clearly a significant option between the choice to minimize the greatest possible losses ("maximin") and the choice to maximize the greatest possible gains ("maximax"). One can make up a principle here, of course, as one can for consistency or for induction. But no principle can claim to be dictated by rationality alone.

A little paranoia would help in these various cases, both with knowing too little and with knowing too much, as well as with the insufficiency of strategic reason. The point of the bathtub scene, for example, will be more immediately obvious to anyone who has a fetish about getting things wet. An entire scenario will flash before such a person, and the question of "how to file" the information will be answered in terms of the importance of that kind of scenario and its typical features. And the choice between maximin and maximax strategies is obviously associated with such emotional and character traits as boldness or timidity. In all these cases we may surmise that emotions are one source of the necessary supplemental principles.

To see how this might work, think of some conditions in which the philosophers' frame problem will not arise. I argued that it must arise for angels, which are logically perfect but finite in knowledge and in power. (God, as I pointed out, needs no principles of rationality of any kind.) But it will not arise for ants: a completely mechanistic system will need no devices for solving the frame problem. The motor system of ants, I surmise, is controlled by information confined to a limited range to which their sensors are attuned.* Similarly, as Jerry Fodor and Zenon Pylyshyn have argued, we ourselves get around in the world with the help of sensors, or perceptual modules, which in themselves do not work significantly differently from those of the ants: they are informationally encapsulated. The frame problem arises only when we consider what to do with information interpreted and stored in an intentional system. The role of emotion is to supply the insufficiency of reason by imitating the encapsulation of perceptual modes. For a variable but always limited time, an emotion limits the range of information that the organism will take into account, the inferences actually drawn from a potential infinity, and the set of live options among which it will choose. This, then, is my biological hypothesis:

(BH1) *New Biological Hypothesis 1.* The function of emotions is to fill gaps left by (mere wanting plus) "pure reason" in the determination of action and belief, by mimicking the encapsulation of perception: it is one of Nature's ways of dealing with the philosophers' frame problem.

Consider how Iago proceeds to make Othello jealous. His task is essentially to direct Othello's attention, to suggest questions to ask: "Did Michael Cassio, when you woo'd my lady / Know of your love?" and then to insinuate that there are inferences to be drawn without specifying them himself, so that Othello exclaims (III, iii, 106–108):

By heaven, he echoes me
As if there were some monster in his thought
Too hideous to be shown.

---

*Compare the fascinating thought experiments of Valentino Braitenberg (1984). Because his vehicles are *constructed*, with the aid of gradual complications in the application of simple principles of afferent-efferent connections, it is easy to see the kind of behavior of which such constructions would be capable. But if we look at their behavior itself, its sheer phenomenological complexity is baffling, and we can hardly resist the temptation to honor them with the intentional labels—fear, aggression, love, anxiety, and so forth—with which Braitenberg graces, with tongue somewhat in cheek, the various stages of his vehicles' increasingly sophisticated meanderings. But his vehicles do not yet suffer from the philosophers' frame problem.

Then more directly Iago advises, "Look to your wife." Once attention is thus directed, inferences which on the same evidence would before not even have been thought of are experienced as compelling: "farewell, the tranquil mind. . . ."

In this example the emotion is changed via the manipulation of what Othello thinks about, notices, and infers. But such manipulation is not always possible. It can be blocked by the grip of a pre-existing emotion. Even where an emotion is already regnant, the order of causal accessibility of emotion and attention is not fixed. As commonsense "psychologists" we learn to "play on" people's emotions—sometimes the more abusively for being more shrewd. Iago is a master psychologist in that sense: a con man, which is to say, a sophist of the emotions. The con artist and the sophist differ in the emphasis they place on different methods, but in each there is some of the other. A sophist needs to divert attention from her most slippery arguments, and one way to do it is by manipulating emotion or else overtly inducing it by the use of rhetoric. This is the art of the political orator, as well as the wooing lover. But a con artist must also be, like Iago, adept at "passing" bad arguments by making them look plausible. In the light of this example, the present hypothesis can be restated as follows:

> (BH2) *New Biological Hypothesis 2.* Emotions are species of determinate patterns of salience among objects of attention, lines of inquiry, and inferential strategies.

Some Consequences

To get a better feel for this hypothesis, let us see how it bears on some of the questions addressed in this book.

Emotions Set the Problems
First, we can now see why, though emotions are neither judgments nor desires, it has been tempting to assimilate them to one or to the other. On my view, emotions set the agenda for beliefs and desires: we might say they ask the questions that judgment answers with beliefs and evaluate the prospects to which desire may or may not respond. As every committee chairman knows, questions have much to do with the determination of answers: the rest can be done with innocuous facts. In this way emotions can be said to be judgments, in the sense that they are what we see the world "in terms of." But they need not consist in articulated propositions. Much the same reasons motivate their assimilation to desire, of which one kind or com-

ponent, as I have argued, can itself be classed as an emotion. Logic leaves gaps. So as long as we presuppose some basic or preexisting desires, the directive power of "motivation" belongs to what controls attention, salience, and inference strategies preferred.

For this reason emotions are often described as guiding the processes of reasoning—or distorting them, depending on the describer's assessment of their appropriateness. Indeed, this is in great part what all good novels are about. In extreme cases we think of reasoning as being distorted into self-deception: but there is seldom a sharp mistake in logic of which the self-deceiver can be accused. As I shall argue in chapter 9, self-deception is not different in kind or mechanism from normal cases of reasoning about matters of concern. The difference may largely rest in the relation of a piece of reasoning to what is expected in the circumstances.

Consider for example the way that we are wont to discount experience for distance in space, time, or affection: we care less about pain if it is far enough in the past or the future, and we are relatively indifferent to distant disasters. This seems reasonable, within vague bounds: but are there no rules of rationality that prescribe the rate of discount? The thought of our own death is subject to this discount. We are usually curiously indifferent to it, but as Tolstoy vividly shows in *The Death of Ivan Ilyich,* the prospect of death might provoke such a shift in a man's patterns of salience that an entire life is seen aright for the first time: Ivan Ilyich's emotions are axiologically adequate only when he faces death.

The Irrationality of Emotions

Although emotions are manipulators of reasoning, the experience of emotion tends to be an "intuitive" one: it is not easy to formulate reasons for one's shifts of attention. To be sure, there are great differences between types of emotion on this point: it does not clearly apply to indignation, surprise, or embarrassment. But many emotions do not come fully equipped with reasons on which they are based. This applies not just to the most diffuse or least "thought-dependent," such as joy or depression, but also to those, like love or mistrust, that are specific in their targets and sometimes even loquacious about their propositional objects. Even these are often not given to much pretense of having been brought about by reasons: "I can't explain: he just gives me the creeps." An explanation sometimes offered for this is that emotions are somatic phenomena; that they consist largely in autonomic reactions, of which the phenomenological component consists in dim awareness. We found some support for this view in the modularity of some of our mental mechanisms. But from the point of view of the theory of rationality a preferable explanation can be given in terms of the model I have sketched: paying attention to certain things is a *source* of reasons, but it comes *before* reasons. Like scientific paradigms, in the sense of Thomas Kuhn (1969), emotions are better at stimulating research in certain directions than at finding compelling and fair reasons for their own adoption. They are too "deep" for that, too unlike specific beliefs.

Not only are emotions not assimilable to beliefs: often they are experienced as "gut feelings" in direct opposition to overt belief. Consider for example the fear of flying.[10] Those who suffer from fear of flying are likely to remain unaffected by sound statistical knowledge about the relative safety of air travel. They can be distracted from it, but mere argument is unlikely to dispel the fear. This need not be, as so often thought, because the emotions are not cognitive at all but merely bodily phenomena. Instead, it can be due to the fact that the body contributes to the phenomena at hand a different pattern of emphasis that merely cognitive considerations cannot overcome. The beliefs themselves may be common to both the state of calm and the state of fear. (In chapter 9 I shall go further into the question of the peculiarly unconvincing character of what, by synecdoche, I shall call *lovers' arguments*.)

Emotional Transitions

I have argued that there is bound to be a good deal of biological atavism, and considerable variation in the levels of antiquity, in the determinants of our emotions. And this means that they will be variously well adapted to the circumstances in which they are now likely to arise. On the present account, this is to be expected. For to be inclined to look to certain things may have a very different utility in different circumstances. Here, as elsewhere, the overall usefulness of some device of nature is quite compatible with its noxiousness in particular cases, as Descartes noticed when he explicitly linked the variable utility of emotions with what one might call their inertia (see chapter 3; also Rorty 1978). But inertia is not, as on Descartes's view it should be, the general case. What we find instead are variable patterns of continuity and transformation between emotions. Here are some examples:

In some cases the discovery that an emotion was premised on a false belief, instead of simply canceling the emotion, will transmute it into another. Indignation can turn into remorse upon finding that it was unjust; and we have all seen a parent punish a lost child when, on finding it, anxiety turned to anger. In such cases the focus of attention is not changed by the mere change of belief: so there is a kind of inertia of attention. But since the facts are now different, new features of the situation naturally become salient to the same attentive set, in turn provoking shifts in the dominant patterns of concern.

In other cases the emotion's habit of looking for certain sorts of facts and facilitating certain sorts of inference will simply look for more. There is a good example in George Eliot's *Middlemarch*. When Mrs. Farebrother learns that Lydgate is not the natural son of Bulstrode, she does not take this to be sufficient grounds for ceasing to think ill of Bulstrode: "The report may be true of some other son." Here the emotion can be clearly seen as a disposition to persist in asking certain questions.

Conversely, there are cases where something comes to change that disposition without any change in the object or in any directly relevant belief. A friend of mind felt intimidated by a man she met, apparently because of his character. Later she discovered that the man had been her student. "I'm not afraid of him any more," she said, although not claiming to perceive any difference in his character, "because I have this maxim that you can't be afraid of students." From the point of view of a teacher, signs of intellectual threat are not salient, nor are they easily inferred. The story is a good illustration of the fact that although we usually think of emotions as grounded in beliefs, they operate by evoking whole scenarios, at a metalevel in relation to beliefs.

Arbitrators of Weakness of Will
These facts about emotional change are related to a more general point about the voluntariness of emotions. In spite of the "irrationality of emotions" tradition, we commonly hold people responsible for their emotions. This seems to presuppose that emotions are at least to some extent in our power. The hypothesis I have offered suggests an explanation for the limited extent to which this is true: namely, the limited extent to which attention is itself in our power. This sometimes leads to paradox, as we shall see in chapter 9. It is also related to the fact that emotions are widely reputed to play an important part in the genesis of *akrasia,* or weakness of the will, defined as *doing something intentionally that one has overriding reasons not to do.* The problem of akrasia has been one of philosophy's most notorious conundrums ever since Socrates tried to prove the concept self-contradictory. The best modern account of the phenomenon is that of Donald Davidson (1970a).[11] His solution is inspired by a familiar fact about statistical inference. Statistical premises support their conclusions only if they take account of the whole of the relevant available evidence. Otherwise, it could be true both that there is a high prob-

ability of rain tomorrow (say, on the basis of the cloud pattern) and that there is a very low probability of rain (say, on the basis of wind or temperature). Similarly, reasons for action provide only undetached conclusions of the form 'On the basis of R_1, I should do A', which is compatible with 'On the basis of R_2, I should refrain from doing A'. In order to detach a categorical practical conclusion, there must be an additional factor. Davidson argues that whatever the causal status of that additional factor, it must satisfy a certain rationality condition, which he calls the *principle of continence*. This principle, on which (PEC) was modeled, enjoins that one should act on the most comprehensive set of available reasons.

Akratic actions fail this condition. This means that there must have been some causal condition, other than whatever it is that results in the implementation of the principle of continence, that somehow plugs the output of some partial argument into the motor system.

The best candidate for the agency that plugs one argument over another into the motor system is emotion. The reason is this. It cannot be a merely physiological factor that is in itself arational, that is, beyond the reach of assessment for evaluative rationality. Otherwise, Elster's principle of autonomy is violated, and it becomes unclear whether the action is an intentional act of the subject's at all. On the other hand, the causal factor in question can be neither a desire nor a belief. The reason for this was expressed with characteristic pith (and uncharacteristic wit) by Aristotle himself: "When water chokes, what will you wash it down with?" (*Nicomachean Ethics*, VII.3). By hypothesis all the reasons, both cognitive and desiderative, are already in. So whatever tips the balance cannot be another reason. It must be something that, in some sense, acts on reasons.

So the additional factor required to turn the argument into an action (to "detach" the practical conclusion) can be neither a purely nonrational factor, nor a belief, nor a desire. Only emotions are left. Since they can, as I have argued, be assessed for rationality, they are not excluded by the first constraint. And if, as claimed in my central hypothesis, their essential role lies in establishing specific patterns of salience relevant to inferences, then they are perfectly tailored for the role of arbitrators among reasons.*

This is interesting not only for what it tells us about akrasia and for the neatness with which it fits the central hypothesis. It also adds a powerful argument to those I have already offered against the reduc-

---

*Note that since emotions also sometimes conflict, other tools of rationality may be brought in to determine the issue in those sorts of conflict. There is no inconsistency here, if the person is, as I suggested in chapter 3, a heterarchic system.

tive view of emotions as just complexes of beliefs plus desires. For since emotions play a role in akrasia that is available neither to belief nor to desire, they cannot consist in either.

Salience and Paradigm Scenarios: The Euthyphro *Once More*

I have been expanding and illustrating the idea that our emotions underlie our rational processes. This claim—this model of emotions and what at the most general level they are for—was introduced to make it plausible that there is some objectivity, related to biological significance, to the proper objects of emotions. But it is time to address a problem.

In the last chapter and the first part of this one I offered a defense of a cognitive-perceptual analogy to axiological properties. On this view, paradigm scenarios determine characteristic feelings, and an emotion can be assessed for its intrinsic rationality—a kind of correctness or incorrectness—in terms of the resemblance between a presenting situation and a paradigm scenario. This suggests an objectivist answer to the *Euthyphro* question: emotions—at least objective ones—are not mere projections but apprehensions of real properties in the world.

In the second part of this chapter my thesis has been that emotion deals with the insufficiencies of reason by controlling salience. And the answer to the *Euthyphro* question suggested by that, it might seem, is a subjectivist one. For salience would seem to be a matter of rearranging things that are already there, rather than discovering new ones.

How can these two theses harmonize, if they amount to opposite answers to the *Euthyphro* question?

The answer lies in attending to the distinctions made in chapter 6 between different kinds of subjectivity: phenomenology, relativity, projection, and perspective. *Phenomenology* does not preclude correspondence to a real property. Indeed, it usually indicates such correspondence. I argued that a measure of *relativity* is just what we would expect from taking seriously the analogy of perception. If the world is real, it will look different as we move around. When a paradigm scenario suggests itself as an interpretation of a current situation, it arranges or rearranges our perceptual, cognitive, and inferential dispositions in terms of some real configuration of human experience. *Perspective* is just the mysterious fact that whatever we are aware of must be apprehended from some point of awareness: it is irrelevant to whether what we are taking in is really there or not.

That leaves *projection*, which is the only sense of subjectivity in question in the *Euthyphro*. We need to ask, therefore, whether the control of salience effected by emotions amounts to projection.

The answer in outline is simple: projection interferes with objectivity when it is illegitimate and does not when it is appropriate. But that sounds too easy to be helpful. The point will acquire substance if we think back to the psychoanalytic context for the notion of projection.

A psychoanalyst typically works by making inferences about the patient's condition. But such inferences can be made in two ways. One consists in fitting the situation of the patient into a plausible scenario ("an Oedipal problem," for instance) and making inferences "by the book" about how the patient feels in the real predicaments of life. The other involves the therapist's own feelings as an additional source of inferences. The latter method, called "working with the countertransference," is a valuable tool to a good analyst. But obviously it involves the risk that, if the therapist has not been "successfully analyzed," her feelings will be mere projection in precisely the sense that precludes objectivity. In one case the feelings evoked in the analyst will enable her to lock into the patient's actual scenario, in terms of which she can then "read off" other features that might have taken a long time to uncover by a more analytic route. Here we have legitimate "projection." In the contrary case the scenario is not really the patient's but one springing from the analyst alone. It can therefore tell her nothing useful about the patient.

Outside the therapeutic environment the situation is much the same. By controlling salience, the paradigm scenario mimics the encapsulation of perception. This inhibits certain perceptions and inferences and fosters others. But if the resulting pattern is appropriate to the situation, it does not constitute illegitimate projection.

But how are we to interpret the notion of appropriateness involved here? There are two possible routes. One is to look for some insight into what the normal scenarios dictated by human nature may be. On this view, emotions will be objectively correct if and only if they correspond to scenarios stemming normally from human nature. This is more or less Aristotle's route. But it is not one that is appealing in practice, simply because of the difficulty of giving substance to the idea of a human nature. But there is no reason to feel thus confined. The standards of normality involved may be social as well as biological. Further, there is also room, I believe, for a notion of *individual normality*.

To those who assume that normality must ultimately always point to some statistical facts, this may sound self-contradictory. But two sorts of considerations support it. One goes back to some of the facts

of biology surveyed in chapter 4. We saw there that individual variation is a basic fact of biology. Earlier in this chapter I also cited some
facts about emotional development suggesting that the very social
genesis of the paradigm scenarios that will define an infant's emotional repertoire may be at least partly controlled by individual temperament. For these reasons, if it makes sense to speak of normality
for a social group, it also makes sense to speak of the normality of a
single individual, as something only partly shaped by the former. In
chapter 9 I shall develop some of the consequences of this idea.

The argument begun in chapter 6 offered what I take to be plausible
theses about the conditions for ascription of rationality. In this chapter I have tried to show how these can be applied to emotions. The
main conclusion for which I have argued is that axiological rationality
is distinct from both the cognitive and the strategic kinds, though it
bears instructive analogies to both. Despite familiar claims about the
subjectivity of emotions, I have argued that an objectivist answer to
the *Euthyphro* question can sometimes be supported: emotions tell us
things about the real world. To be sure, their mode of objectivity is
relative to the characteristic inclinations and responses of human and
individual nature. The biological function that makes them indispensable to complex intentional organisms—ones unlike either ants
or angels in that they are not subject to simple determinisms—is to
deal with the philosophers' frame problem: to take up the slack in
the rational determination of judgment and desire, by adjusting salience among objects of attention, lines of inquiry, and preferred inference patterns. In this way emotions remain sui generis: the canons
of rationality that govern them are not to be identified with those that
govern judgment, or perception, or functional desire. Instead, their
existence grounds the very possibility of rationality at those more
conventional levels.

This role, with its possibilities for self-justification or bootstrapping, carries risks. In the next two chapters I shall look at some of the
pathological excesses to which such bootstrapping is prone.

Chapter 8
Desire and Time

Truly, though our element is time,
We are not suited to the long perspectives
Open at every instant of our lives.
They link us to our losses: worse,
They show us what we have as it once was
Blindingly undiminished, just as though
By acting differently we could have kept it so.
Philip Larkin

There are two tragedies in life. One is not to get your heart's desire. The other is to get it.
G. B. Shaw

Summary

The axiological hypothesis is now tested against two classes of examples involving the temporality of emotional desire.

The first class of examples arise from two facts about the way desires envisage their objects in time. One is that desire can be either time-indexed (focused on a specific moment in time) or immediate (experienced as just being for gratification "right away"). The other is that desire envisages its satisfaction under various temporal aspects: continuous, punctual, perfect, or frequentative.

Both features result in intrinsic constraints on the possible objects of desire. First, not all different aspects are open to both immediate and time-indexed desires. For example, one cannot immediately desire anything in the frequentative aspect, because immediate desire is not able to represent the repetition at specific future times of some practice or habit. Second, and more important, the types of situations or events that can be desired can also be divided according to the mode of their unfolding in time. The classification here (which goes back to Aristotle) is between states and activities, which are spread out in time, and achievements, which involve punctual completion.

The hypothesis to be defended is that there is a relation of correspondence between desire and its object, analogous to the notion of truth for belief. Some types of events or situations are not suitable to be desired in certain aspectual modes. When the aspect of a desire does not match the type of its object, something like "false desire" results. This is especially likely to occur when we confuse "consummatory" and "ludic" desires, and it explains some instances of the "dust and ashes" phenomenon—the disappointment that sometimes attends the nominal satisfaction of our desires. Examples adduced involve tourism, sex, vice, and chocolate.

The second class of examples concerns the rationality of transferring, or on the contrary discounting, the force of desire across different times. Prima facie, our attitude to our past or future desires may seem entirely a matter of choice; these questions about transference of desire might therefore seem to offer counterexamples to the claim that there are objective constraints on emotions. But I argue that the counterexamples are only apparent.

These questions concern only time-indexed desires; they arise, in slightly different forms, in relation to all three of the types distinguished in chapter 7: subjective, self-related, and objective desires.

For subjective desires, a typical question might be whether it is rational to go swimming when you don't feel like it because next week you'll wish you had (transfer of motivation from the future). To do so seems to involve something like the "Concorde fallacy": going swimming now can neither literally satisfy the future desire, nor even modify it.

The policy involved can be exonerated, however, if the desire is actually a self-related one. But in that case it becomes subject to some constraints of consistency: the very fact that we are dealing with time-indexed desires opens up the possibility of irrationality.

In the case of objective desires, the objection to the claim of objectivity may claim support from the temporal discounting, or perspectival relativity, to which emotions and desires are subject. If mere position changes our emotions, how can they be objective? The answer lies in the perceptual analogy, which suggests that discounting and perspectival relativity are just what we should expect if real objects are apprehended by emotion and desire.

In short, the first set of considerations about time vindicate the axiological hypothesis, and the second are at least compatible with it.

All our emotions are about the past, among other things. This follows from the role of paradigm scenarios in defining their formal objects and therefore their identity. In addition, most emotions are directed at targets or propositional objects that are either past or future. Fear, regret, remorse, and guilt are obvious cases, but it is also true of love and hate. Much of what matters to us emotionally does so because it recalls or repeats some past experience (though generally we like our repetitions spiced with difference). In any case, neither excitement nor boredom makes sense except against a background of salient memories and expectations.

These platitudes raise vast questions. In this chapter I nibble at the edge of those questions to see how the axiological perspective sheds light on the temporality of our attitudes. As we shall see, the temporal dimensions of emotion affect happiness and the meaning of life. Once again, however, I shall proceed by first narrowing my focus from emotions in general to desire. My excuse, as before, is that desire itself has an emotional aspect, a phenomenological face separable from its functional link to action. Such is the wish component in regret; but the fact that regret is for the past is not crucial: some hopes or wishes for the future are equally detached from any possibility of action.

The two problems addressed in this chapter are fairly specific, although they have important implications for the scope and the limits of our freedom to decide what to value and enjoy. First, I show how we can make sense of the idea of emotional correctness, at least in relation to a relatively narrow band in quality space. I call this band of properties temporal *aspect,* by analogy with the grammatical sense of that term. Second, I consider some questions about the rationality of either *transferring* or *discounting* the force of desire across time. I shall ask, in particular, whether the common experience of caring less intensely about future emotions and desires—the perspectival relativity of emotion—undermines the possibility of emotional objectivity. I argue that it does not.

Desire and Temporal Aspect

The Paradox of Contingent Satisfaction
That one can want something, and then not enjoy it when one gets it, is just a piece of melancholy common sense. Nevertheless, it is sometimes paradoxical. It is not simply that satisfaction of your desire may not make you happy. To be sure, having any one thing that you wanted may leave you dissatisfied, if only because you lack other things. Moreover, the desired event may have repellent features you had never dreamed of. What is surprising is that even when the desire and its object are considered in isolation from their context, and

when nothing in the description of the outcome would have repelled desire, still the event can betray anticipation, leaving only the proverbial dust and ashes. The meal I so wanted to repeat may taste exactly as I remembered it, yet I find this time that I get little pleasure from it. Let us say there can be *technical satisfaction* (the truth of p) of a desire that p, without *phenomenological satisfaction* (actual enjoyment of p).

That fact makes a mystery of the connection between the object posited by a desire and what will actually satisfy it. Is it purely accidental? Bertrand Russell once proposed the extreme empiricist view that since a desire and its condition of satisfaction are separate, contingently related states, the best way to gratify any particular desire can only be discovered by experience (Russell 1921, 72). That view has a certain mad charm. Even if it is right, however, it presupposes that there is some real and regular correspondence for experience to discover. The connection between the desire that p and its satisfaction by the truth that p may be logically contingent, but it is not just accidental. And that is just as well, because if it were just accidental, then acting to secure the object of our desires would seem a hopeless gamble.

But if there is a relation of contingent correspondence between desire and object, what does this relation consist in? This question in effect resuscitates a concept first introduced—to enduring scandal—in Plato's *Philebus:* the concept of *false desires,* or more precisely *false pleasures of anticipation* (see Plato, *Philebus,* 39). So far, I have merely argued that there might be such a correspondence relation. It is time for a specific example, which will account for the paradox of contingent satisfaction.

The hypothesis I shall put forward is that at least one source of fit or lack of fit between desire and object relates to the way that the desire represents certain temporal features of the object. Some events have an intrinsic organization in time; if desire represents them as having another, there will be a mismatch between the desire and the event. To explain the type of organization involved, I first need to introduce the notion of *temporal aspect.*

Temporal Aspect
Traditional notions of grammar, especially of Greek, distinguish between tense and "aspect." (The term 'aspect' in this usage has of course nothing to do with the motivating aspect of an emotion as defined in chapter 5.) Aspectual distinctions are not concerned with whether the event is past, present, or to come. Instead, they concern how events are envisaged in time: as continuous, punctual, perfect

(or completed), or frequentative. I illustrate all four possibilities with reference to a time past, though all can apply equally to the present or future.

1. An event may be viewed as enduring through a stretch of time. In terms of an accurate current barbarism, it is viewed as *ongoing*. This is the *continuous* aspect. The imperfect tense in Indo-European languages usually expresses continuous aspect as well as past tense. Example: 'She was rich, but she was honest.'

2. An event can also be viewed as occupying a definite point in time. This is the *punctual* aspect. The Greek aorist and the French *passé simple*, although usually called past tenses, actually express punctual aspect. Example: 'On the third day she won the jackpot'.

In English the distinction between imperfect and aorist has no clear morphological markers, but it is readily expressed: it is the difference between 'She laughed (when I brought up the aorist)' and 'She was laughing (while I spoke of the imperfect).'

3. The *perfect* is also commonly but mistakenly thought of as a tense. The perfect "tense" indicates that an event is considered as fully achieved or finished. The "perfect" event, past, present, or future, can in addition be presented from the point of view of the imperfect, indicating that the perfect was appropriate over a lasting period of time, or from the point of view of the punctual, that is, of an instant in time. As examples I propose, respectively: 'By the time of adolescence, I had already learned many a trick', and 'At noon, he had gone'. The time referred to in the perfect aspect can be present, as in 'I have done it', or past, as in 'I had (already) done it (when you inquired)'.

4. Finally, the *frequentative* aspect views an event or action as taking place repeatedly or habitually in some period of time under consideration. Example: 'On Sundays I play golf'.

In reference to the present, locutions such as 'I am doing it' are used for the continuous, which can be stressed with the phrase 'I am in the process of. . . .' The punctual present is almost impossible to express, perhaps because it is difficult to think of the present as anything but the "ongoing" specious present. One might expect the "simple" present—'I do it'—to express the punctual aspect. In fact, however, the only context in which it does so is where it functions as the "historic present," and then it usually refers to the past. The historic present is a narrative "tense," with both colloquial and literary uses, suggesting that events are being viewed as points strung serially on the string of time: "So he walks in. 'Where have you been?' she goes. 'Nowhere special,' he goes." In all other contexts the simple present has lost its punctual nuance, if it ever had one, and is used almost exclusively as a frequentative. 'I play tennis' means something like "I am in the habit of playing tennis."

In relation to the future, the morphological system of English shows even less interest in the nuances of time and aspect. But it is possible by circumlocution to indicate in what aspect one is envisaging a future event: 'I'll be doing it all through next week' (continuous); 'I'll do it next week' (punctual); 'Next week it'll be done' (perfect); or 'I'll keep doing it next week' (frequentative).

The Aspect of Desire

I shall presently argue that desires have important aspectual features. To clarify this idea, let me first set aside a related but different distinction with which the aspectual might be confused. That other distinction is the familiar one between *standing* and *occurrent* desires. Occurrent desires, it might be suggested, are desires viewed in the punctual aspect. They are dated events occurring at a particular point in time, with causes and effects, if any, that could also be dated ('I feel like going to the movies tomorrow'). Standing desires, by contrast, are viewed either from the continuous or from the frequentative aspect. They are supposed to be dispositions giving rise to occurrent desires when activated by the right triggering occasion ('I want to be president someday'). (But see chapter 2, "Behaviorism.")

In this chapter I shall confine myself to the occurrent sense. But in any case the occurrent-dispositional distinction is not the distinction I have in mind. I am interested rather in the way the desire itself envisages its object and how that fits with the character of its object itself. More technically, my concern is with the temporal aspects of the *focus* of desire and the *focal property* of its object, and with the correspondence between them: the focus of desire—a property of the desire itself—may be viewed aspectually, and the actual focal properties to which the focus corresponds are of different kinds, to which different aspects may be variously appropriate.

Corresponding to the two sides of the equation—desire and focus on one side, target and focal property on the other—I now make two further sets of distinctions.

Time-Indexed and Immediate Desires

First, on the side of the desire itself, a preliminary distinction sets apart those desires that focus on a specific point in the future ('I want to come and see you Sunday') from those that do not ('She's just dying to see you'). I shall call them, respectively, *T-desires*, for "time-indexed" desires, and *I-desires*, for "immediate" desires.

As a first approach to this distinction, note that T-desires are typically specified in terms of propositional objects ('Sam desired that Steve come'), whereas immediate ones typically have direct objects ('Sam desired Steve'). This test gives some of the flavor of the distinction, but it is superficial and unreliable. A better test is that I-desires, but not T-desires, are unproblematically attributed to animals. This is related to a third criterion, which is that T-desires may involve reference to particular temporal locations. T-desires are possible only for beings capable of framing a reference to some particular time:

> One can imagine an animal angry, frightened, unhappy, happy, startled. But hopeful? And why not? A dog believes his master is at the door. But can he also believe his master will come the day after tomorrow? . . . Can only those hope who can talk? Only those who have mastered the use of a language. That is to say, the phenomena of hope are modes of this complicated form of life. (Wittgenstein 1951, 174)

It seems to me plausible, though I don't know how to prove it, that the necessary capacity coincides with the capacity for singular reference described in chapter 4.

A corollary is that T-desires, but not I-desires, are closely bound up with the possibility of planning. They are the sort of desires that we can *intend* to realize: that is to say, they are the sort of desires for the realization of which it makes sense to establish a timetable. Annette Baier once presented the case of Corlissa, who orders flowers on Friday to be delivered Sunday, in apology for the insult of which she has rightly predicted that she will be guilty on Saturday night. On Friday, though, she neither intends nor desires it. "What feature of intention is lacking [in the expectation of insult]? I suggest that what is lacking is precisely what is present in Corlissa's Friday intention to apologize, namely an implementation-plan, a *timetable* linking the present with the intended future" (Baier 1976, 15). I-desires come without any such time index; we might say they are always, phenomenologically, desires for something *right away*. But even that is misleading, because it seems to imply just what I am denying: that in I-desires the subject is conscious of some point in time (namely, *right away*) to which the desire applies. But 'right away' names no specific time.

I shall take for granted without discussion that the propositional object of desire is necessarily referred to the future in either case. This is a requirement of intelligible description, not of the phenomenology of desire itself. The third-person description of Sarah's desire must refer, *de re*, to some vague region of time later than the onset of the desire. But the I-desire's own representation (or our description of it *de dicto*) contains no time reference at all. I-desire is in this respect more "primitive," without, however, lacking the essential structure of desire. I-desire, like T-desire, explains action in the context of a desire-belief pair, from which the action's claim to rationality or irrationality is inherited. But that structure is minimal. I-desire can figure out immediate means, but it cannot make elaborate plans involving future means.[1]

So much for the distinction between T-desires and I-desires. We shall see in a moment how it relates to the fourfold distinction between temporal aspects. Together these two sets of distinctions take care of one side of the correspondence between desires and their objects. To see how that correspondence can break down, by analogy with the breakdown in correspondence we call *falsity* in the case of beliefs, let us now move to the other side—the side of the potentially satisfying event.

States, Activities, Achievements

The distinction to be made here is one that Aristotle first drew and rightly thought crucial to his analyses of virtue, pleasure, and happiness. It is the threefold distinction among *states, activities,* and *achievements*. States (being tall or generous) are passive, whereas activities (walking, contemplation) are actively engaged in, but both states and activities endure indefinitely through time. Neither needs any specific completion. They contrast in this with achievements (winning a race), which have a natural end. Achievements may take time from their beginning to their completion, but they do not exist as achievements until the moment of their completion. 'Winning a race' thus contrasts with 'walking about', as Aristotle put it, in that it can be truly said that you *have been walking about* as soon as you have started, whereas merely beginning to run a race, even if you are "in the process" of winning it, does not make it true that you have won it yet.[2]

The following remarks, then, relate three categories, or parameters: (1) whether the desire is *time-indexed* or *immediate*; (2) the *temporal aspect* under which it is desired: continuous, punctual, perfect, or frequentative; and (3) the category of the *actual object* of desire: here the alternatives are state, activity, and achievement. The hypothesis I offer can now be made explicit:

> (AP) *Aspectual correspondence*. For each *aspectual type* of object there is a natural or *privileged aspect* of desire.

That the temporal aspect of desire should match the aspectual category of its object is a requirement of rationality. In chapter 7 I noted that the constraints on emotional rationality are difficult to pin down because of the multiplicity of formal objects. In the present case we are dealing with only desire. At some risk of oversimplification, let us assume that we have only a single formal object (something like "the pleasant"). This will allow me to be more precise. In accordance with the principle of minimal rationality (R2), these constraints are bordered by constraints on what can be *consistently ascribed*. Here are some details of the constraints involved.

First, only T-desire can view the desired object in the frequentative mode. This follows from my assumption that there is no representation of temporal location available to I-desire. When we envisage the desires of other animals, we must assume that all their desires are immediate. Because we do not know how to attribute to them any references to future time, we cannot make a difference between their desiring something "right away" and their desiring it to be repeated indefinitely in the future.

Second, we can desire to feel excited or kindly, as well as to walk or play. But since these are states or activities enduring through time, the suitable aspects of I-desires for them are only the continuous and perhaps the perfect. To envisage a state or activity as object of I-desire under a punctual aspect, we must either think of it as lasting only a negligible amount of time or have in mind the onset, rather than the state or the activity itself. It may be possible to envisage a state or activity punctually in the context of a T-desire, since we can treat a period of time in the future as a point ('Tomorrow at 10, I want to go for a walk'); though this is more naturally construed as an achievement. But a punctual I-desire for an activity makes no sense: to tell *wanting to walk* from *wanting to take a walk*, one must envisage the latter as having a definite beginning and end.

Third, achievements, such as *winning*, can be desired (in the mode of I-desire) only in the punctual, the perfect, or the frequentative aspects. Aristotle points out that a *kinesis* or process "moves toward a goal, and becomes complete only when what it aims at has been produced" (*Nicomachean Ethics*, X.4). So the continuous aspect can make sense only in relation to some activity or state that is conducive to the achievement, and not in relation to the achievement itself. This is because the moment of completion cannot be decomposed into parts (though sometimes the part of the process that led up to it can).

Fourth, it might seem that anything can be desired in the perfect aspect. Although achievements, for example, are most naturally desired punctually (as in 'Calvin desires to win the race'), does it not seem equally natural to desire *to have won*? It does indeed. But that is an entirely different desire, and this fact will turn out to have important consequences.

States and activities, on the other hand, may be the objects of continuous I-desires, but only their onset can be desired punctually. And if they are desired in the perfect aspect, this amounts to the desire *that they cease to exist.* For consider what it can mean for me to desire *to have felt excited.* If we are talking about the mode of T-desire, it might mean that I wish to have had the experience, at some time or other in my life. In the mode of I-desire, on the other hand, the presumption is that I can only want to have experienced something if I am now experiencing it. This means in effect that an I-desire in the perfect aspect is a desire *for the experience to stop.* And that seems very different from a mere aspect under which the experience is desired. The importance of this too will become clear in a moment.

We can represent these facts compendiously in a three-dimensional table (table 8.1) corresponding to the three categories of facts distinguished above.

The interest of the facts summarized in this table lies in this: much of the criticism of the ways of desire by philosophical or religious moralists can be construed as claiming that some categories of desire are inferior in virtue of their intrinsic aspectual properties or in virtue of the aspectual category to which their typical object belongs. This applies to the attacks on pleasure and desire as a hopeless attempt to fill a leaky sieve, or as necessarily involving pain, or simply as worthless because ephemeral. Such attacks are familiar from Plato, from the Stoics, and from Buddhists. Most intriguing are those cases where the category to which a given pleasure belongs is disputable. Many of the moral disadvantages under which sexual desire has seemed to labor might be traced to its end having been mistaken for an achievement when in truth it should be viewed, like Aristotelian contemplation, as activity. Leaving aside (until chapter 12) the moral side of these strictures, I shall now argue that they rest on a sound semantic point.

Consummatory Desires and Ludic Desires

Recall the distinction made in chapter 7 between "objective" and "subjective" desires. This distinction can often be made in practice from a strategic standpoint, that is, in terms of the second-order desires associated with a given first-order desire (though I also argued that we cannot use this feature as an ultimate test). Chief among the I-desires that come with a negative second-order desire are what I shall call *consummatory desires.* The mark of a consummatory desire is that *its end is its end.* To put it slightly more perspicuously, the goal or

Table 8.1
Three-dimensional table of aspects, object categories, and desire types

	Continuous	Punctual	Perfect	Frequentative
State	I want to be feeling excited	*I want to feel excited (at some precise moment in the future)	I want to have felt excited ($=$ have experienced excitement?)	I want to (get into the habit of) feeling excited
ID?	Yes	No (onset only)	No (but compare: *want it to stop)	None possible
Activity	I want to be walking	*I want to go for a walk (an achievement)	I want to have had my walk	I want to (make a habit of walking after dinner)
ID?	Yes: I want to walk	No (onset only)	No (completion only)	None possible
Achievement	Nonpossible (but compare: *I want to be winning, which refers to the process leading up to the win)	I want to win (at some specific time t)	I want to have won (at time t)	I want to be a winner (that is, make a habit of winning)
ID?	No (but compare: *I want the feeling of having won: a perfect)	I want to win	I want to have won	None possible

Note: The columns represent aspectual properties of desires; main rows correspond to relevant types, and below each the row labeled 'ID' records whether, in the relevant aspect, desire can be felt for events of that specific type. Asterisks mark dubious or impossible items.

(teleological) end of a consummatory desire may be identified with its termination or (temporal) end.

Obvious paradigms of consummatory desires include hunger and a certain sort of sexual desire—specifically, the desire for male orgasm, which typically represents the cessation of desire (leading for that very reason, perhaps, to the proverbial postcoital *tristitia*). And the negative second-order desires associated with these, as well as any regret that follows their satisfaction, may be taken as an indication of their repudiation as sources of objective value. This may partly explain the bad press that bodily pleasures and desires have received from certain moralists.

Paradigms sometimes fail to have the very property they are used to illustrate. So it might be with some bodily desires: perhaps it is wrong to assimilate them to the pure cases of consummatory desires—ones that aspire to their own annihilation. Desiring the pain to stop may be such a pure case if anything is, but even then, as we shall see, there may spring up a kind of derivative but separate desire for the pleasure of relief.

Consummatory desires contrast with those that come with an implicit desire for indefinite continuation, without regard to any consummation or satisfaction. Let us call these *ludic desires:* for the paradigm of nonconsummatory pleasure and desire is *play,* and especially the undirected and nonteleological play of a child. It is that "pottering about" the intellectual form of which Aristotle dignified with the title of *contemplation.* It is also the psychological ancestor of those pleasures that Plato called *pure* pleasures.[3]

We cannot assume that only I-desires are, properly speaking, consummatory, for one can presumably look forward to some particular point in future time at which relief will come. But if an occurrent desire is purely consummatory, then it is difficult to see why immediate satisfaction would not always be preferable, *other things being equal,* to the more remote.

The following putative counterexample illustrates the need for the italicized condition. As a child I admired a certain girl as a hero of hedonism because for the sake of greater pleasure she would, for as long as she could stand it, postpone micturation. Is this a counterexample? No. She did turn an immediate desire into a time-indexed one by virtue of a hedonic calculation. But other things were not equal, for she presumably thought the increase in pleasure worth the

---

*Note that in the case of Augustine, which might also seem to offer a counterexample (see chapter 7), what he wished for was not the satisfaction of a consummatory desire but the end of a certain class of such desires—or at least the strength to ignore them.

wait.* It will do no harm to proceed, then, as if we were speaking only of I-desires.

Even a pure consummatory desire is not merely a desire *for* its own termination, for some terminations are preferable to others. Which is which depends on your ideology: Plato will prefer the itch just to cease, the sybarite will prefer to scratch. So these desires are not merely *for their own termination:* Freud was mistaken when he proposed as a general characterization of satisfaction the mere cessation of stimulation.[4] The real question is this. If consummatory desires are not literally *for* their own annihilation, do they necessarily come with a second-order desire for that end? Stephen Schiffer has argued that the desire (say) for a drink, the desire for relief of thirst, and the desire for the first desire's own termination must all be one and the same desire. His argument, as I understand it, is this.[5] There would exist no pleasure, if it were not for the first-order (reason-providing) desire. So without the latter, the second-order object would have no target. The conditions of existence for first- and second-order desires are therefore identical, and so the desires themselves must be one and the same.

If Schiffer were right, this might provide an explanation for the paradox of contingent satisfaction, at least for the limited class of consummatory pleasures: we are disappointed because we thought there were two desires (first- and second-order) up for satisfaction, but really there was only one. Consummatory pleasures would systematically keep only half their promise.

But Schiffer's view cannot be right. For if all those different formulations refer to the same desire, then even if we concede that a single desire does not have to be describable in terms of a single propositional object, still there must be a single measure of the *intensity* of that single desire. Schiffer rightly points out that we sometimes have "the frustrating but not unheard of experience of an intense desire for chocolate, or whatever, the satisfaction of which brings and was expected to bring only a little pleasure" (Schiffer 1976, 202). But this case is fatal to his view. For if the pleasure desired and the relief from desire are objects of the same desire, then the measure of relief should be a measure of the pleasure. And in turn the relief, and the pleasure, should be proportional to the intensity of the desire. This is precisely what does not hold in the case described. Quite the contrary: one could even envisage a sort of hedonic calculus based on the distinction between the "relief pleasure" and the simple pleasure. I might sometimes say, "I desire this passionately, though I am aware that the pleasure it will afford is likely to disappoint me. I prefer the relief of this painful desire *with* the disappointment, if the price of avoiding disappointment is this continuing torture." Or, on the contrary, if I am equally passionate but given to resentment, I might prefer to suffer the desire rather than be disappointed.

I conclude that a second-order desire for satisfaction of the first-order desire rides piggyback on the latter but is not identical to it. We must look for another way to understand the contingency of satisfaction.

Vice, Tourism, Sex, and the Platonic Theory of Advertising
The key, I suggest, lies in applying the axiological model to the aspectual features of desire. Desire can envisage its object in various temporal aspects, but not anything can be desired in just any aspect. An "achievement," for example, cannot be desired in the continuous aspect because it necessarily involves an undecomposable instant of time at which the achievement is consummated. This limitation, which may be rooted in our biological dispositions, introduces an element of objective correctness or incorrectness into the conception of a desired event implicit in the aspectual character of the desire. In the case of the chocolate craving, for example, the discrepancy arises because of a mistake in the desire as to the character of its own object. Eating chocolate appears to be an activity. It seems to be the sort of thing that one might enjoy doing and therefore desire in the durational aspect. But in the case of a mere craving *all that is actually desired is the consummation itself.*

That is why the pleasure of it is so disappointing: such consumption of chocolate is, indeed, a *vice.* The nature of vice is frequently misunderstood, because (like weakness of the will) it is assumed to be a moral concept, whereas in fact it is primarily a psychological one. The proper psychological definition of a vice is *something that one craves to do even though it brings no pleasure.* In terms of the notions introduced above, a vicious desire is a *punctual or perfect* desire for what is in fact a *state or activity.* That state or activity is not enjoyable—in a sense, it was not even desired, for what was desired was a mere consummation. And we now have an explanation of how that can come about, in terms of the notion of *naturally suitable aspects* for certain categories of objects of desire. We need not grant Schiffer's implausible thesis that a desire for chocolate can be the very same desire as a self-referential second-order desire for itself to end.

The difference between consummatory and ludic pleasures and their corresponding desires looms large in many fundamental disputes about satisfaction, happiness, and human nature. If the apparatus I have sketched is sound, there should be many other sorts of cases, based on different kinds of mistaken assessments of the temporal aspect of desire most appropriate to a given target. One that is the converse of the last is the Case of the Harried Tourist.

The discomfort of the harried tourist comes from the fact that in actuality the viewing of memorable sites and works of art is, if pleasurable at all, pleasurable as an activity. But the harried tourist makes the mistake of desiring to tour only in the perfect, or perhaps sometimes in the punctual, aspect. She wants not to see, but to have seen.* ("Have you done the Uffizi?" "Not yet, but we have done the Duomo.") The trouble is that it is in the nature of sightseeing to take time, and the sightseer who is only interested in having done it will get little profit for a lot of work.

Much sexual activity is no doubt construed as the harried tourist construes sightseeing. Witness the dismal view of "Lust in action" as "Th' expense of spirit in a waste of shame" so powerfully expressed in Shakespeare's famous sonnet:

> Past reason hunted and no sooner had,
> Past reason hated . . .

This can now be seen for what it is: the result of an aspectual mistake about the nature of sexuality. If the real nature of sex demands that it be treated as an activity, there will be an inevitable discrepancy between it and a desire for it that is aspectually perfect rather than continuous. It amounts to taking sex for an achievement instead of an activity. Such a mistake is likely to prove disappointing unless one overtly views sexual activity as a task engaged in for the sake of something else—money, glory, or self-esteem. For otherwise it construes play, which is valuable activity (that is, done for its own sake), as work, which is useful (that is, done for the sake of some end outside itself). Some things can be both valuable and useful, but only what is useless can be purely valuable.† There is nothing especially pleasant about the end of play. So if play is desired in the aspect appropriate to work, it will always seem more work than its ending is worth.

Here is one more way to see how the axiological perspective, together with the possibility that both focus and corresponding focal property can admit of temporal aspect, solves the paradox of contingent satisfaction. It lies in seeing how Plato's theory of Forms holds

---

*In the course of explaining the difference between the two categories of activity and achievement or process, Aristotle gives *seeing* as an example of an activity and remarks that "When you see, you have seen" (*Nicomachean Ethics*, X.4). The harried tourist's mistake is to reverse the formula.

†This, rather than the usual disingenuous mumblings about careers in law, is the proper retort to students who question the usefulness of philosophy.

the key to modern advertising. Plato thought you could never be satisfied by the ordinary targets of your ostensible desires, because those were not their real targets. The pursuit of the wrong objects could only exacerbate desire. That is precisely the principle behind contemporary advertising: you must be made to think you want (say) a Cadillac, when what you really want is some far more primal comfort. Thanks to this carefully cultivated mistake, there will be no end to your desire, and you will gratify the advertiser by coming back endlessly for more Cadillacs.

Temporal Transference and Temporal Discounting

The argument just deployed assumes that there is some objective fact of the matter about the nature of certain pleasures and activities. I have followed Aristotle, for example, in saying that seeing is by nature an activity, whereas the satisfaction of a craving is by nature an achievement. But how seriously can we take this idea? In the concluding section of this chapter I shall tentatively sketch a sanguine position. But, it might be objected, this flies in the face of the fact that in the vast majority of cases our desires simply construe their own objects as they please: *thinking (or desiring) makes it so.* One area in which we would seem especially free from rational constraints is in our attitudes to different moments of time. In the remainder of this chapter I shall be looking at cases of temporal transference of desire, with a view to meeting this objection. In contrast with the problems of aspect just discussed, which focused on I-desires, the problems of transference primarily concern T-desires. The issues raised by these cases are ones on which intuitions are likely to clash, and I do not promise to settle them. I do propose to show that they can be construed in such a way that the axiological perspective survives unscathed.

Here is why transference is a prima facie counterexample. To the question, To what extent are your present desires fixed by your past or future, and to what extent ought they to be so fixed?—the answer might seem to be, As much as you like: it just depends on how much you care about your future or your past. In what follows I try to make this answer seem less obviously reasonable.

The word 'transference' has a Freudian ring. And indeed, Freudian transference is a special form of the problem: is there true love for any but the primal mother? Can that original emotion be transferred to new objects in such a way that the new are authentically desired for themselves? I shall return to the Freudian problem in chapter 9. For now I shall be concerned not with whether emotional transfer from one object to another is rational but with the rationality of feeling desires or emotions on the basis of emotions experienced at other times.

Transfer of Motivation from the Future
Transfer from the future to the present works like this. Suppose I know somehow that next week I shall experience a certain desire, from which at the moment I am quite free. Now suppose further that I also know that next week I shall not be in a position to satisfy this desire, but that I could do so now—if I had it. Does this foreknowledge give me any present reason whatever for desiring now what would satisfy that future desire?

Let us think first in terms of a subjective desire. I have been at the seaside for a few weeks; I have been there long enough, in fact, to have become rather tired of going to the beach and swimming. Nevertheless, I am aware of the fact that I will not get another chance for a whole year or more. And so, wearily, I drag myself to the beach, feeling rather like a dutiful drudge, and conscientiously I sun and bathe. Is this irrational?

I am here assuming that if *one has a reason for doing x, then it would not be irrational for one to have the desire to do x.* This does not impugn my earlier insistence that the existence of a(n emotional) desire is not entailed by the presence of a functional want. The latter thesis is a psychological one; the former is a principle of rationality.

But the relevant criteria of rationality are far from clear. A first reaction may go against the dutiful bather. For am I not committing a sort of future-oriented version of the common but notoriously bad argument sometimes known as the *Concorde fallacy?* This fallacy got its name from the repeated decision by the French and British governments, in the 1960s and 1970s, to continue to develop and then use the Concorde supersonic jet, though every accounting confirmed that it would keep losing money. The reasoning offered was this: *Since we've invested so much in it already, we can't afford to stop now.* That is a fallacy because of the asymmetry of time: when we face a decision between two alternatives, factors common to both could not rationally affect the decision. But the past is held in common between all possible futures. Past investment, therefore, could not possibly be relevant to the present decision. Applying this reasoning, we might decide the question of the rationality of transferred desire thus: if my going swimming now will leave my future desire unaffected (as in the Concorde case the past is necessarily left unaffected by the present), then it is irrational to take that future desire into consideration.

In the case of the dutiful bather the desire is in the future, so we cannot guarantee that it *will* be unaffected. Suppose that for some reason it is likely that *if* I go swimming today, however disagreeable it seems, *then* I shall not experience the desire next week. Is this sufficient to justify saying that I have now "satisfied" the future desire? If it is, it would not be irrational puritanically to pursue now what would at some other time be a pleasure, and the Concorde fallacy does not apply.

Of the reasons for thinking that my present behavior might relieve my future desire, some are more interesting than others. One interesting class of cases derives from a self-related desire that our lives have a certain overall shape, that certain things be true of it globally. In such cases the transference of desire becomes a reason because of a second-order desire for life to have an overall pattern. (I discuss this more in chapter 9.) But that might not count strictly as satisfying the future desire.

Full-fledged desire, as opposed to wish, is necessarily oriented to the future. If it were not so, then the following advice should seem sensible:

> To cheer up if things are getting worse, just remember Heracleitus: *The way up and the way down are one and the same.* Or, translated into temporal terms, a trend for the worse is really just a trend for the better that faces the past. *So rejoice: things were once better!*

The point is that the order of time is the order of causation—whether by logic or by natural necessity—and one can fully desire only what conceivably might be caused to come about (see below). Desire is a directional marker of the arrow of time.* So there may seem to be something inherently absurd about the suggestion that I might now satisfy next week's desire. But let us ignore that problem. More important is the fact that not every method of securing the cessation of desire should count as satisfaction. Death shouldn't, for one. Less drastically, I might submit to aversion therapy, or simply remember, next week, how positively unpleasant it was to have to trudge to the beach in the hot sun and once again submit to the double assault of scorching sand and freezing ocean. But that doesn't

---

*To this it is often objected that if the order of causation coincides with the order of time, then retrocausality should be inconceivable; yet clearly, given the popularity of discussions of tachyons and time travel, it is not. Still, to follow through on the idea of time travel and retrocausality requires that we distinguish between the time line of the individual time traveler (whether human or tachyonic) and the time line of the external world (Lewis 1976). This suggests that the future is still defined, for the individual time traveler, in terms of the order of causation in that individual's life events.

seem to be the right sort of way to elude the future desire. It's too much like what might be termed "the vulgar-Buddhist recipe" for dealing with desire: *Don't satisfy, eradicate.* The more interesting version of the original case takes it for granted that there *will* be this desire next week, whether or not I "satisfy" it now. Only then—only if the vulgar-Buddhist recipe is inapplicable—could we speak meaningfully of satisfying the future desire in advance.

Transfer of Motivation from the Past
There is, in fact, a knock-down reason for rejecting the interpretation of present behavior "for the sake of" future desire in terms of the vulgar-Buddhist recipe—as aiming at the eradication rather than the satisfaction of such desire. To see this, consider Proust's character Swann. One night, tormented with doubt about Odette's relations with another man, Swann vows that in that future time when he no longer cares, he will find out the truth. But, as he also realizes, when that time comes, he will no longer care to know.

Consider now the situation of the later Swann. The existence of his now past desire is not within his power to affect. He is looking back in time now, thinking of the burning desire he used to have for something that only now has become accessible. Swann's problem will now be, *Does the fact that I once had a burning desire to discover the truth about this in the future constitute adequate reason for me now to find out— even though now I couldn't care less?* The question is at least intelligible, and since it is now too late to eradicate the desire (which is past), we are here completely free of the distracting possibility of endorsing the Buddhist course. Is the case then analogous to the Concorde fallacy after all?

Yes, in a way. The past desire, unsatisfied, is held in common between a future in which it is resuscitated to be satisfied, and one in which it is not. So why resuscitate it?

Well, why not? There is a way to rationalize the Concorde fallacy that can work here as well. All one has to do is adopt the motto of Ken Kesey's protagonists in *Sometimes a Great Notion:* "Never Give a Inch." In other words, generate a self-related desire for being the sort of person who pursues projects to the end regardless of cost. By creating an additional value, this changes the equation.

Time-Indexed Desire Can Be More Irrational
In this way, it seems we can construe attitude to past or future desires as rational, merely by adopting the right second-order attitude. But that does not mean that just anything goes. The demands of rationality act as constraints, not as guides (this was principle (R5) in chap-

ter 6). Here the constraint means that without a readjustment of values by means of second-order desires, the Concorde justification and its ilk really are irrational.

Cases like Swann's bristle with higher-order desires, which must be T-desires. That is not to say that every second-order desire has to aim for a particular point in time; but the conceptual tools must be available to distinguish between the desire for the satisfaction of the original desire and the desire for its nonexistence. Since, at least in the case of consummatory desires, satisfaction represents also the termination of the desire, that distinction can only be made if the subject has the conceptual tools required to represent first-order desires, to whatever extent is necessary for making them objects of second-order ones. And that level of linguistic, or quasi-linguistic, sophistication will plausibly be found wherever there is also the capacity for the representation of time.

Such a capacity immediately opens up more sophisticated modes of rationality—and makes irrationality possible as well. New levels of rationality are possible, because we can balance the present against identifiable losses and gains in the future and judge the difference that it makes whether the future under consideration is close or distant. (How such differences should be evaluated is a question I shall come to shortly.) But irrationality becomes possible, in a way not previously accessible, by virtue of the mistakes that it is now possible to make in the manipulation of those second-order representations. This exemplifies the principle that categorial rationality presupposes intentionality (see (R3), chapter 6).

Self-related desires are neither clear cases of high-level rationality nor clear cases of irrationality. They are, instead, intrinsically problematic, because they raise the question of the *limits of bootstrapping*—the extent to which, in the axiological realm, *feeling makes it so.* I shall say more about the limits of bootstrapping in chapter 9. For the moment I turn to a different aspect of the problem of transference: the problem of *temporal discounting*. This, in contrast to the previous questions about transference, applies neither to subjective nor to self-related desires but particularly to objective desires.

The Perspectival Relativity of Desire

It follows from the presumption of objectivity of values that if you change your mind about the value of something you desired, you should now ignore the previous desire altogether. The view that your desires at one time provide equally good reason for any other time—what Derek Parfit (1984, sec. 66) calls full *temporal neutrality*—makes sense only if one views all of one's desires as equally subjective. Compare belief again: you don't normally adjust your present beliefs in the light of past or future ones. If we assume that moral beliefs are true or false, for example, then at any particular time we are committed to the best set of beliefs we can muster at that time (see Parfit 1984, 154).*

Better, one can appeal once again to the perceptual analogy. If we think of (objective) desires as something like perceptions of value, then we might expect effects of perspectival relativity. Perspectival relativity is not the same as perspective, which is the core of irreducible subjectivity. Perspectival relativity does not literally affect beliefs, since beliefs are not susceptible to systematic change with point of view. The metaphor of points of view for beliefs is too weak for there to be even a metaphorical space in which point of view might covary with appearance.

Arguments from the existence of perspectival relativity to the absence of objectivity are fallacious; for it is precisely where there is an objective fact of the matter that one would expect to find perspectival relativity. Can we apply this to desire?

Desires and emotions change, to be sure; and in some cases we are inclined to deplore this as indicating a deficient sensibility to what is objectively desirable. But there might be an alternative interpretation. Just as a change of perspective can occur either because the scenery passes or because the observer moves, so we might take a change in felt emotion to reflect a change in our position relative to an objective target.

This may not apply to I-desires. I-desires tend to be more intense and represent the future as specious present: sometimes they can effectively obliterate other desires. They are rather like extremely myopic sight: beyond a short distance everything is an equal blur. For I-desires, the question of perspectival relativity does not arise. The intensity of T-desires, on the other hand, seems to follow some kind of inverse-proportional rule. Other things being equal, the more distant the object—in space as well as time—the less we care.

This is sometimes seen as a moral problem. It may seem to support the Kantian view that motivation by desire is irrelevant to the moral

---

*An exception is the case where I "can't remember what I believe about that" and have to look it up in my notes, perhaps. But then I don't actually believe the contrary now. Bas van Fraassen (1984) has shown that one can construct a kind of diachronic equivalent of a Dutch book against anyone willing to take odds on future changes in their own probability ratings. A Dutch book is a set of simultaneous bets guaranteed to lose in the aggregate. Being open to a Dutch book is the criterion of irrationality in subjective probability assignments.

will. For how could mere location affect the absolute worth of an act?*
Rationality, it seems, requires absolutes. (Values, like facts but unlike
things or events, are timeless.) So the temporal relativity that affects
desires must so thoroughly exclude them from any claim to evaluative rationality as to render them immune from categorial rationality
as well—from any assessment, that is, as rational *or* irrational.

Arguments against Discounting the Future
The view that it is never reasonable to discount the future has more
recently been supported by Ross Harrison (1982). There are factors
that justify discounting, he argues, but they are wrongly conflated
with the mere passage of time. In fact, they are only contingently and
unreliably correlated with time. Such factors include progress, infla-
tion, the increasing uncertainty of our knowledge about the future,
and (most important) our fading control over the more distant future.
The independent importance of control can also account for the fact
that we do not care about our past desires and emotions as much as
we should if time were indeed neutral.

These factors, it is true, are not entailed by the mere passage of
time. But they all tend to be roughly correlated with the length of
perspective. From the evolutionary point of view, it would likely have
been adaptive for the intensity of our T-desires to diminish as distance in time increases. Indeed, the analogy of perception suggests a
reductio of Harrison's argument:

> Consider the only *literal* case of true perspective: vision. Distance
> affects two things in the appearances of things: luminosity and
> size.† Both are simple consequences of the geometrical relativity
> of *angular size*. But angular size is *only contingently and unreliably*
> correlated with distance. For as things get farther away we are
> more likely to look at them through binoculars. And when they
> are too close, we might find it convenient to look at them
> through a wide-angle lens. . . .

---

*The view that emotions are morally irrelevant may also be fostered by a confusion
between perspective and perspectival relativity. Attitudes are necessarily perspectival,
as I argued in chapter 6; if perspective is confused with perspectival relativity, and the
latter is deemed incompatible with (categorial) rationality, then attitudes will be rated
arational.
†Strictly speaking, from the geometrical point of view, luminosity is affected only
where the light source is nondirectional. A perfectly concentrated laser beam of one
candle in intensity, I am told, would be visible from the moon. At least on a clear day.
Moreover, for the purposes of my analogy, only clear days need be considered: obstacles to sight, such as pollution, affect the aspect of things in ways that are not predictable from the positional facts alone.

Obviously, what is wrong with this is that it is quite irrelevant to the question whether there is a biologically rooted association between angular size and estimation of distance.

Draw concentric circles around a point of view. It is obvious that the angle subtended by an object of a given size at the inner circumference will be larger, by a factor proportional to the ratio of the radii, than the angle subtended by the same object at the outer circumference. This is the relativity of angular size. Similarly, if there is no obstacle, the quantity of light emitted by a point source will thin out in a widening circle. This kind of relativity then represents no more than the geometrical consequence of the reality of light source and point of view.

The relativity of desire may follow a similar pattern. Instead of distance in space, we are speaking of distance in time (though space too affects the intensity of desire). As we get farther away in the temporal dimension, the space of possibilities grows larger. What I desire for the immediate future is set in a field of possibilities defined by the present situation and the variations on it possible in virtue of various indeterminate factors. But in a short interval things can change only so much. Admittedly, these possibilities of change are not linear: so the situation is not here as clear-cut as it is in the case of perspective. But it does suggest that *grosso modo* it is not irrational to feel more intense desire for what is immediate, or close in time in terms of T-desires, than for what is far in the future.

We can go further. I argued in chapter 7 that emotions mimic the encapsulation of perception; in this way they contain the potential excesses of our private information explosions and support the viability of our conventional tools of rationality. Temporal discounting is just one application—probably a hard-wired feature—of this biological function. If I am to care effectively about those close to me, I may not weep as much for Hecuba.

But an objection must be faced, prompted by an obvious disanalogy with perception. Desire, I have said, is essentially for a future object. On a common view of the relation between causality and time, what is future is by (logical or physical) necessity within the range of possible effects but not of possible causes (see van Fraassen 1970). But perception standardly involves a causal chain from the target of perception to the perception state. So this makes it logically impossible that desire should literally be a form of perception.

One possible reply is that there is perception in desire, but that its object is not the envisaged event but its value, or desirability. And that is not future, but timeless. But this move comes dangerously close to reproducing the Socratic paradox, for it suggests that the object of desires is always the good, which confuses target and formal object. Anyway, it doesn't help. If value is timeless, then no question about variable temporal distance from the object of desire can arise in the first place. So, if anything is to remain of the perception analogy, we must go back to viewing the object of T-desires as being a future event.

The help we need is available, thanks to the distinction between a *target* and a *motivating aspect*. The target is a time or event referred to in the specification of the desire; it could even be a situation referred to by an irreducibly propositional object (see chapter 5, theses (I)–(III), (X), and (XI)). The motivating aspect, on the other hand, is the focal property for the sake of which the target is desired. The target-with-its-value is what desire apprehends, and the motivating aspect, which instantiates the formal object, is a property of the target. This allows us to deal with the problem of causation in the same way a causal theory of knowledge deals with knowledge of the future: the relevant causal conditions are to be specified not only in terms of direct causal chains from the event to the subject but also in terms of the existence of common causal chains leading both to the subject's desire and belief and to the target event (see Goldman 1967). On this view, we may be willing to reject the dogma that no future event can be perceived. "I can see it coming," we colloquially say. And the extension of the term to the future can be understood literally, if we think of perception as tapping into the relevant causal chain—not necessarily just at the end of it.

This is satisfying in two respects. First, our knowledge of causal chains generally grows vaguer with distance in time. So perspectival effects are just what we should expect. Second, we can see why the effect might come into play even when—because of the special features of some particular causal chain involving particularly reliable correlations—it is not actually advantageous in the given situation. Remember that evolution is a rule-utilitarian process: from the point of view of biological "design," it would make sense for us to be programmed to discount the future automatically, regardless of the reliability of particular predictions. Evolution can be expected to assign priority to the most pressing problems, and to desire distant prospects as intensely as closer ones would in most cases violate that order of priority. Placement in our temporal map is surely a generally reliable index of probability, and it is sound Bayesian rationality to weight desirabilities with probabilities.

Probabilities, however, are not the only things affected by temporal distance. The "wisdom of the body" programmed by evolution into our biology is also sensitive to the sheer practical availability of a future prospect. Roughly, this refers to what, if anything, we can relevantly do about something at present. But only roughly, because sometimes there is nothing we can do about the prospect anyway: we can want even what we cannot intend. And the same goes, of course, for what we would prevent: "Suppose we are in prison, and will be tortured later today. In such cases when we believe our future suffering is inevitable, we would not think: 'Since the torture is inevitable, that is equivalent to its being already in the past'" (Parfit 1984, 168). The starkest example is the fear of death. There has been a good deal of argument in the history of philosophy over whether it is rational to fear death. Whatever the answer to that question, it is clearly a fact that fear of death—which presumably involves a desire not to die—is subject to temporal discount. Obviously, this is not because the probabilities change: as Philip Larkin wrote, "Some things may never happen: this one will" ("Aubade"). But what changes with the probable proximity of death is the feeling we have for its "reality," including, at least sometimes, the intensification of fear (which sometimes, as on Ivan Ilyich, has vivifying effects).[6] Here is a point to abet the philosophical manic-depressive of chapter 1. Even if it is not the case that the world is more correctly seen when gloomy than when happy, it remains true that the nearness of death "wonderfully concentrates the mind" (see chapter 12). Again there seems to be some sort of biological mechanism here that allows us to be indifferent to the thought of our own death when it remains probably distant and "brings it home to us," as we so quaintly say, when it seems closer in time.

Emotional Distance
It is time to admit that temporal discounting is itself only a special case of a larger class of dimensions to which the metaphor of distance applies. Instead of literal time, for example, we could think of distance in terms of the number of conventional steps that separate us from a possible event. There is an example of this from some work in experimental psychology, which illustrates both resemblances and differences between fear and desire. John Dollard and Neal Miller (1950) were interested in the sudden regression sometimes encountered in the course of therapy for sexual impotence. They assumed a simple model according to which both the desire and the fear of sex increased with proximity to the goal. This is equivalent, of course, to positing temporal discounting of both fear or "avoidance" and desire or "approach." Accordingly, they proposed the following ingenious explanation, *more geometrico*, for the puzzling relapses observed (see figure 8.1). At the beginning of therapy the absolute quantity of fear

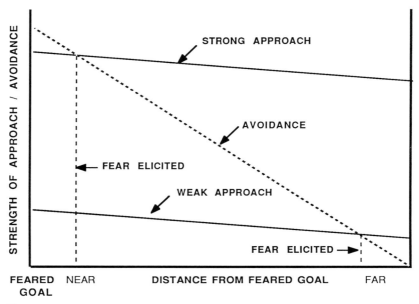

Figure 8.1
According to Dollard and Miller, the gradient of fear or "avoidance" is steeper than the gradient of desire or "approach." By strengthening approach in relation to avoidance, the patient can come closer to the goal; but if the avoidance curve still catches up before the goal is reached, the quantity of fear elicited is now greater. (Figure redrawn from Dollard and Miller 1950.)

is greater than the quantity of desire as soon as the goal seems available. Therapy effectively increases the absolute quantity of desire in relation to fear. But it turns out that the respective *rates* of discount for fear and desire are different: the "gradient of avoidance" is steeper than the "gradient of approach." When the fear is weaker in relation to desire, the patient can get closer to the goal. But for a while the fear curve can still catch up with the approach curve. And when it does so, its absolute value is much higher, which gives the appearance of a serious relapse.

Here the approach is defined not so much in terms of time as in terms of the ritual steps of courtship. When the patient takes his date to dinner, his anxiety and desire are both present, but the anxiety is manageable: there is many a conventional step twixt drinks and bed. At the beginning of therapy he is already terrified at the thought of inviting her home for coffee. After some progress has been made, he is able to get as far as some light flirting. But suddenly the anxiety becomes overwhelming, as only a few discrete steps now separate him from sexual performance.

In that example we remain rather close to the dimension of time, since the ritual steps involved are clearly correlated with time. Other metaphorical extensions of the notion of temporal distance are more problematic. One such dimension that might be interesting to explore is a sui generis concept of *emotional distance*. Emotional distance is not obviously reducible to other dimensions of distance, and it is also a dimension that can hardly be expected to be well behaved. Luckily, however, I do not have to explicate it here. For my claim is not that there are no other factors that might rationally be allowed to interfere with the purity of absolute value but only that we can give a plausible rationale for counting temporal distance among them.

I conclude that the existence of temporal perspectives affecting desire is no argument against the existence of objective desires. On the contrary: the existence of genuine perspectives is to be expected in any analogue of perception. Where a real object is accessible from various (metaphorical or literal) points of view, such relativity gives us no prima facie reason to discredit the intuition that some of our desires represent an apprehension of value. This negative result dovetails into the argument of the first part of this chapter. There I showed that we could make sense of a specific discrepancy between the temporal aspect of the focus and the corresponding aspect of the focal property. These results are admittedly limited to the context of certain temporal properties. Taken together, however, they buttress the claim that we should posit a level of objective axiological properties.

Time and Rationality

I have spoken of a distinction between objective and subjective desires, and I have speculated that we have biologically determined inclinations to view certain sorts of events in some aspect rather than others. This suggests that there might be a biological basis for some of the mechanisms that govern the temporality of desire. In the case of aspectual fit, biological factors are obviously supplemented by paradigm scenarios. In the case of the perspectival relativity of desire, we have a particularly spectacular illustration of the hypothesis offered in chapter 7 about the central biological role of emotions in the organization of rational life. Were it not for discounting, both in time and in space, we would be not careworn but literally care-buried. The emotional demands on us would as surely kill us as the surfeit of information would paralyze us, were it not for the fact that our organism allows only some of it to be salient at any one time.

The findings of this chapter are too special to support any claims about the scope of the objectivity of axiological apprehension. But they are consonant with the hypotheses advanced in previous chapters. Nevertheless, I should enter two qualifications.

First, like any claim about what is natural, a thesis about the naturally correct aspect in which to think of some sort of action or experience will be inherently controversial. In some ways my position is similar to (what should be) that of sociobiologists: I feel very confident about having established that there are some rational constraints on emotions and desires, partly traceable to biological origins. But I feel much less confident about the validity of the particular constraints I claim to have discovered. The claims made about sexual pleasure, for example, are admittedly tinged with a particular ideology. On the other hand, that ideology can be argued for: one argument in its favor is its very power to explain some of the strictures of traditional moralists against sensual pleasure.

My second qualification is that even if it is granted that there are relevant biological facts, these may not determine the psychological facts in any simple way. This is, of course, a commonplace. (It also follows fairly directly from the relative irreducibility of the psychological level of explanation, for which I argued in chapter 4.) But the way that it applies in the present context is worth noting. It is, in brief, that *biological consummations and psychological consummations need not coincide*, so that a simple inference from the former to the latter will not in general be valid. It is one manifestation of this that some desires can be, so to speak, *biologically centripetal but psychologically centrifugal*—and vice versa. By this I mean simply that from the point of view of our experience, a certain pursuit may be motivated by the desire to avoid a painful situation; bodily needs such as the avoidance of extreme temperatures or of hunger may be of this sort, where biologically speaking some definite positive goal is being pursued. At a deeper level of analysis the opposite may be the case. Since there is no real teleology in nature, what is experienced as a centripetal pull to a certain fulfillment may, biologically speaking, be driven by a purely causal mechanism.

Consider the question of whether there is a naturally correct category of sexual pleasure and desire. The vulgar sociobiological account of the sexual instinct may well be basically correct: male orgasm is a consummatory activity both in the ethological sense in which Nikko Tinbergen (1969) uses the phrase and in the sense of "H-instinct," driven by motivation, which I discussed in chapter 4. There is reason to think that, biologically speaking, male orgasm is advantageously effected as often and as quickly as possible. Nevertheless, Freud (1905d) may also be right, from the psychological point of view, in speaking of the fusing of a number of very different "component instincts" into the "mature" sexual instinct. These other "instincts," which include looking, touching, and so on, may be fused together by the experience of paradigm scenarios that link sensual joy with play. Once fused in this way, sexuality may participate more in the nature of playful activity than in that of achievement. This may explain the fact that we have the capacity to experience sexual activity as play, even though from the point of view of its strict and immediate biological goal it should be a consummation.

Much the same holds for the processes that Plato took as the paradigms of bodily pleasure, namely, those associated with the restoration of some sort of homeostatic balance. These include some forms of nutritional replenishment and some forms of the elimination of waste. They are also from the biological point of view consummations, or achievements. And they are associated with pleasure just exactly insofar as we can exercise voluntary control over behavior that can bring them about. Hence, just as we would expect, pleasure and desire are associated with elimination through micturation and defecation but not with elimination through sweating. Not that one can't enjoy sweating, or even desire it. But "I want a pee" and "I want a sweat" seem to express wants that bear different relations to their corresponding needs. Sweating isn't usually *experienced* as a mode of excretion.

All this does not mean that we must view these bodily functions, and experience our desires for them, strictly in terms of punctual or perfect consummations. And it is a further question whether, for the sake of maximizing pleasure, or for the sake of happiness, or morality, we *ought* to view them in one way or another. Nevertheless, the cases of vice, tourism, sex, and the Platonic theory of advertising have illustrated that our desires' construal of their own objects is not always compatible with satisfaction. In those cases it is at least a hypothesis worth considering that there are limits to our capacity to construe things as we please. These limits are determined by whatever determines the natural, social, and individual normality the existence of which I was driven to acknowledge in chapter 7. In chapter 9 I shall explore some of those limits: I look, in particular, at some of the ways in which bootstrapping tips into self-deception.

Chapter 9

Pathologies of Bootstrapping:

Self and Others

—*I can call spirits from the vasty deep.*
—*Why, so can I, or so can any man.*
But will they come when you do call for them?
William Shakespeare

—*But lest you are my enemy*
  I must inquire!
—*No matter, so there is but fire*
  In you, in me.
W. B. Yeats

Summary

Bootstrapping has perils. These are first illustrated by two cases of cognitive bootstrapping that fall respectively just within and just beyond the bounds of rationality. But my real quarry here are analogous cases in the domain of axiology: that is, cases where emotion does not so much contribute to irrationality as fall victim to its own devices.

The potential to mislead us both about others and about ourselves lies in the mechanisms that enable the emotions to fulfil their function in shaping and framing our cognitive and decision-making rationality.

More precisely, three central features of emotions developed so far are responsible for some pathology: the Jamesian connection of the experience of emotion to its bodily expression; the intimate connection of emotions with attention and salience; and the crucial role of paradigm scenarios in the setting up of our emotional repertoires. These are discussed in turn, with illustrative cases.

James's theory, slightly revised in accordance with the discussion in chapter 3, provides one mechanism by which emotions can fool themselves. This is "self-feigning," in which an expression of emotion designed to be deceptive is read back to the subject through bodily feeling and misleadingly induces the very emotion it was intended to counterfeit.

More scope for pathology is afforded by the crucial role of emotion in attentional salience: the redirection of attention, insofar as it is within our power, can turn out to sabotage the very aims for which it was invoked.

But the richest source of problems lies in the crucial role of paradigm scenarios in the genesis of our emotional repertoires. If, for example, I have learned my emotions in the context of an original, infantile relationship, what hope is there for an authentic relationship with a radically new object? Or, for that matter, what hope of developing a constant, nonfungible relation after an original whose very essence requires that it be given up?

The ambiguity of sublimation and perversion moves this problem to the realm of social approval and disapproval, suggesting a strong thesis of the social or contextual definition of the very nature of our emotions. Although the view defended here has strong affinities with that contextualist theory, my verdict is that emotions are not social creations in the same sense as chess moves or even language. A discrepancy between the socially prescribed scenarios and those that evoke an individual's feelings is not necessarily settled in favor of the public dialect. Once again, we confront the need to recognize a notion of individual normality. And the relation between individual and social norms is partly a political one.

The differences between emotional "idiolects" that follow from the diversity of our paradigm scenarios result in a striking peculiarity of arguments designed to induce emotions: they mostly fail, though their proponents invariably find them convincing. This turns out to follow naturally from the dramatic structure of our emotions, rooted in paradigm scenarios.

When raised once more from the interpersonal level to the social, the potential for systematic misunderstanding yields a new source of distorted or self-deceptive emotions: namely, those in which we are taken in by some emotional ideology. Consciousness raising is the answer, if there is one. But the path of emotional change is an arduous one, and simply "going with one's feelings" is not the royal road to authenticity.

How Much Can a Bootstrap Hoist?

The two conundrums examined in chapter 8 illustrated some of the power and some of the limits of bootstrapping.

The power of bootstrapping was manifested in the fact that sometimes we bestow real value on some prospect, just by choosing it. In the example of the dutiful bather we saw how placing a subjective desire under the aegis of a self-related one can make sense of a temporal transference that otherwise might seem irrational. If I find it important now to act in accordance with past or future desires, I have ipso facto made that into an object of present desire, and that need not be irrational. Self-related desires are only demonstrably irrational if they violate purely formal requirements of consistency (though the applicable constraints are hard to specify). In the case of objective desires, as opposed to subjective or self-regarding ones, not only the conjuring trick of bootstrapping but also discounting for distance in time might seem irrational. But I argued that a certain perspectival relativity of objective emotion is inevitable, and fits in with the central biological function of emotion in rational thought and action.

On the other hand, the paradox of contingent satisfaction showed that the bootstrapping power of our desires is limited. That was illustrated by the aspectual contraints on ludic and consummatory desires. Such limits on the bootstrapping power of even nonobjective desires are what we should expect, if, as I have argued, there exists a legitimate axiological level of rationality.

Sometimes bootstrapping shades into emotional self-deception. That, together with the fact that emotions have roots in variant paradigm scenarios, places obstacles in the way of both mutual and self-understanding. Those obstacles are the topic of the present chapter.

As self-deception is usually understood, it refers to false or at least cognitive irrational beliefs held for the sake of some noncognitive goal—for the sake of comfort or self-esteem, for example. In such ordinary cases of self-deception the role of the emotions is notorious. We have seen how they must play a crucial role in akrasia. And akrasia can itself be construed as involving a kind of self-deception, in which we convince ourselves that a bad reason is a good one. Or, since the cognitive perspective and the strategic perspective can respectively swallow each other up, we can alternatively construe self-deception as a species of akratic belief (see Rorty 1983a). But this confines emotions to a causal or motivational role in episodes of self-deception focusing on belief.[1] My interest here is in exploring the extent to which we may be subject to specifically axiological self-deception—affecting not just beliefs motivated by emotions, but emotions themselves.

Insofar as emotions involve beliefs, they might be said to be derivatively subject to self-deception. But I shall argue that we can also make sense of an emotion's being directly self-deceptive. One type of case shades into another. There are intermediate cases in which we are self-deceived *about* our own emotions. Sometimes the choice of description between self-deceived beliefs and self-deceived emotion may be rather arbitrary. Guy Burgess, the spy and defector, may provide an example. Some accounts of his character lead one to surmise that he extended his mastery of deception to himself. Disgruntled by his failure to be admitted into the highest coterie at Eton school, he dedicates himself to undermining the social order that Eton symbolizes. He joins British intelligence and becomes a spy for the Soviets. (See the fictionalized account by Julian Mitchell, *Another Country.*) But should we say he held a self-deceptive *belief* that the Soviets had a more just social system? Or should we describe him as indulging a self-deceptive belief *about* his emotions—mistaking for love-of-socialism, perhaps, his hatred-of-Eton? Or perhaps the latter emotion had actually become self-deceptively converted into the former, yielding a case of intrinsically self-deceived emotion. Clearly, not every instance of self-deception will fall squarely into one category or the other.

The cases I shall sample might collectively be described as exhibiting the pathology attending our capacity to induce emotions in each other and ourselves. All are based on one or more of the following characteristics of emotions: (1) the Jamesian connection of the experience of emotion to its bodily expression; (2) the intimate connection of emotions with attention and salience; and (3) the crucial role of paradigm scenarios in the setting up of our emotional repertoires. In addition, some types will lead to further discussion of several topics already broached in this book: our tendency to mold our self-ascriptions of emotions to our implicit theories about rational emotion; the role of the social dimension in determining our ideology of emotions; and the importance of our capacity for singular reference in allowing the development of the more sophisticated human capacities for nonfungible emotions. The unavoidable role of a concept of normality will also be brought into bolder relief. Such a concept of normality, defined at the triple levels of biology, social context, and individual temperament and experience, is indispensable if we are to arrive at a balanced answer to the *Euthyphro* question.

Cognitive Bootstrapping

In order to clarify the notion of bootstrapping in more general terms, I begin with two problematic cases not directly related to emotions. One, I shall argue, is indeed irrational, involving a clear violation of a certain kind of consistency. The other is a legitimate if somewhat bizarre use of the bootstrap principle.

Here then are two stories. The first, borrowed from Jon Elster, is about Niels Bohr:

> Niels Bohr at one time is said to have had a horseshoe over his door. Upon being asked whether he really believed that horseshoes bring luck, he answered, "No, but I am told that they bring luck even to those who do not believe in them." (Elster 1983, 5)

The second story is about me:

> I take vitamin C to ward off colds. What I have read about it has convinced me that, pace Linus Pauling, vitamin C is a placebo. But I believe in placebos. That belief is a rational one, because I have read in *Scientific American* that placebos are surprisingly effective.

The stories have a superficial similarity. Both exemplify bootstrapping. Are their protagonists rational? As Elster points out, Niels Bohr can be shown to be irrational by Jaakko Hintikka's principles of *doxastic rationality*:

> If your beliefs are to be consistent, it must also be possible for all your beliefs to turn out to be true without forcing you to give up any of them. (Hintikka 1962, 24)

The principle of doxastic consistency appealed to is the rationality constraint violated by Moore's paradox ("p is true, but I don't believe it"). Doxastically consistent belief requires not only that what one believes be consistent but also that it be consistent with one's believing it. Niels Bohr is doxastically inconsistent. He is explicitly committed to the following:

(1) NB believes that horseshoes will not bring luck; and

(2) Horseshoes bring luck (even) to those who believe that horseshoes will not bring luck.

(1) and (2) could both be true. But doxastic consistency requires in addition that it be possible for all of Niels Bohr's beliefs to be true *while also believed by him*. In that sense, Niels Bohr is also (doxastically) committed to (3):

(3) NB believes (1) and (2).

And the conjunction of (1)–(3) describes a straightforwardly inconsistent set of beliefs: that is to say, if (3) is true, then *something that NB believes is bound to be false*.

But consider now my own case. I am explicitly committed to the following:

(1') RdS believes that vitamin C is chemically inert; and

(2') Chemically inert substances sometimes cure colds for those who believe they will do so, and

(2'a) Vitamin C will cure my cold.

(2') is the proposition learned from *Scientific American*. So phrased, (1'), (2'),and (2'a) do not give rise to inconsistency if we suppose me to believe all of them: if we add (3'):

(3') RdS believes (1'), (2'), and (2'a),

we do not get a straightforwardly inconsistent belief set. (1')–(2'a) do not, therefore, brand me as doxastically inconsistent.

Still, don't they show me to be weird? Am I not irrational in some other way? The feeling that this is so rests on the fact that (2'a), the belief that vitamin C will be effective (even though it is chemically inert), is itself irrational.

To which I answer, Yes, it's irrational, if by that you mean that it is *groundless*. I have no good reason to believe (2'a). Certainly (2') by itself does not support it, nor is it even enough to cause the belief (2'a). So much is evidenced by the fact that I do not believe that just *any* chemically inert substance will cure my colds. My confidence must be powered by some independent prejudice in favor of vitamin C. And that prejudice, given the truth of (1'), is quite irrational.

Note, however, three points in defense of my sanity: (1) groundless beliefs are sometimes true; (2) not all my beliefs can be grounded, and there may well be some that are intrinsically rational (in the sense of chapter 7) though they are not arrived at by argument; and (3) in this case I actually have scientific evidence that it may well be true, even though it's groundless. Isn't that ground enough?

If my defense is sound, we have here a case of successful bootstrapping, where a belief (or "feeling" in the broad sense) is rationally founded on a nonrational base.*

Many cases of self-deception involve something like bootstrapping. In the case of the dutiful bather the question was this: should we consider having done something in the past, or doing it in the future, to be satisfaction of a present desire? Intuitions may differ, but there are considerations on both sides.

Here is one consideration sometimes adduced in favor of granting

---

*Jon Elster's case of sour grapes is a social kin to the placebo paradox:

> For the utilitarian, there would be no welfare loss if the fox were excluded from consumption of the grapes, since he thought them sour anyway. But of course the cause of his holding them to be sour was his conviction that he would be excluded from consuming them, and then it is difficult to justify the allocation by invoking his preferences. (Elster 1983, 109)

the seal of rationality to both the deliberate placebo-taker and the dutiful bather: As human beings and manipulators of symbols, we are inevitably and very properly the creators of our own values. And so it is quite right that for any given desire we should be allowed essentially to define the conditions of its satisfaction.

But this doctrine is not very plausible if it is used to credit individuals with the emergence of human values. It is somewhat more credible if the human value-creators in question are social groups (see below on "The Social Dimension of Emotions"). In either case we must allow some reality to the possibility of self-deception. And merely to decree that a desire ostensibly having a certain object (to go swimming today, for example) can be magically satisfied by something quite different (to have gone swimming a week ago) is surely a case of self-deception.

To grant that something is a case of self-deception may not ipso facto condemn it as altogether irrational. Self-deception is sometimes strategically rational. One possibility is that the dubious bootstrapping cases involve strategic rationality built on the foundation of cognitive irrationality: my belief in vitamin C is arrived at in ways unlikely to guarantee its truth, yet it may result in my feeling better. Since axiological rationality shares features of both cognitive and strategic rationality, however, this case provides no clear model for demarcating irrational uses of bootstrapping in emotional cases. So let us now look directly at cases involving emotions.

Self-Feigning

Erving Goffman has pointed out that a rough distinction may be made among forms of deception. One kind consists in the deliberate distortion of information that one (explicitly and intentionally) "gives": this is lying or "deceit." The other consists in information that is "given off." This class comprises a "wide range of actions that others can treat as symptomatic of the actor, the expectation being that the action was performed for reasons other than the information conveyed in this way" (Goffman 1970, 2). Deliberate misinformation by means of this type of communication is pretending or "feigning." Sometimes it trades on the fact that people tend to treat expressive behavior as a "natural sign" in Ruth Millikan's sense of the term: for expressions of emotion are typically treated as "given off." So it may fruitful to look for a kind of self-deception that bears the same relation to feigning as self-deceived belief bears to deceit. In this kind of self-deception, the self-deceiver is taken in not by her own lie but by her own pretense. This approach would lead to nothing very novel, however, if pretending to oneself resulted merely in having false beliefs. Its significance in the present context derives from the independence of axiology. If that doctrine is sound, then emotions can admit of error without reducing to mistaken beliefs. That, as we shall see, is precisely the description that cases of self-feigning call for.

An essential outcome of emotional learning is the potential for nonverbal communication. Indeed, as Carroll Izard has suggested, this may be another important biological function of emotion, which I have not yet stresed. We unreflectively assume that our capacity to feel emotions precedes both our need and our capacity to express them. But the naturalness of some expressive behavior suggests that, on the contrary, emotions might have evolved for their communication value (Izard 1977, 7). Our expressive repertoire, like any other device of communication, can be used deceptively. This can happen at a teleological or "quasi-intentional" level even before the repertoire of signals involved can be intentionally manipulated. A well-known example is the "injury feigning" of those birds that "pretend" to be wounded, dragging a wing along the ground, to distract an enemy from their brood (see Wilson 1975, 122). There is but a short step from here to the possibility of self-deception as being fooled by one's own pretense, or "self-feigning." A slight revision of James's theory of emotions will take us across that step.

One of the chief arguments against that theory was that identical physicochemical stimuli produce divergent emotions depending on the situational and epistemic context. But I argued that if we reinterpret the bodily changes involved to include those that amount to, or normally determine, the *expressive* motor events associated with the emotion, then it is no longer obvious that we cannot *feel the expressive set* of our body. This may not be all that we feel, nor does it imply that this feeling is all there is to emotion. For that would leave out the semantic aspect: an emotion *means* a formal object, that is, a property characteristic of a paradigm scenario, and *ascribes* it to a target. But this reinterpreted Jamesian theory does imply, with common sense and against the standard objections, that we can commonly *identify* our emotions *by* what we feel.

Now in cases where the expressive set is deceptive and where the deception is not consciously acted out, it is not hard to see how one could take one's own expressive state for the corresponding emotion.[2] This is what is being imputed when someone is accused of histrionics. ("Don't look so tragic: you'll only work yourself up into a state.") On this account, we can see how self-feigning is not merely a matter of acquiring false beliefs about one's own emotions. Rather, it *induces* an emotion, which is itself erroneous in its ascription of a characteristic property to an object. We have, then, in our very capacity for emotional expression, including its potential for deception, a possible mechanism for emotional self-deception of the pure type advertised above.

Attention and Will

Emotions provide a framework for our beliefs, bringing some into the spotlight and relegating others to the shade. When I am irritated at your neatness, I may continue to believe that you are generous and kind, but that will seem a very minor part of your fussy and demanding personality. At other times, though, I shall weigh these things differently. Emotions are, in part, patterns of attention. Therefore, one might expect a change in patterns of attention to entail a change in emotion. I can't be very angry any more, if I notice none of your misdeeds, nor even infer to any when there is a doubt to be resolved.

This suggests a further range of possibilities for bootstrapping, just insofar as attention can be brought under our own control. To some degree, attention is in our power. But it is a lot easier to attend at will than to withdraw one's attention at will. I can clearly keep in mind a target to be avoided: but if the avoidance sought is inattention, my efforts will be self-defeating. This is the starting point of some of the standard puzzles of self-deception. It seemed to Sartre, for example, that self-deception as commonly conceived must be self-contradictory, since it must entail careful attention to just exactly what one is sincerely unaware of (Sartre 1956, 87). So we may expect great difficulty in trying to get rid of an unwanted emotion, but more success in working ourselves into one. These are familiar facts. It does me no good to tell myself how foolish I am to miss her: for the thought is an enemy agent, calculated to fix my thoughts on just what I should forget. I should forget her smile, her eyes, her perfect nose job. . . . The best course is to fall in love with someone else: "It'll take my mind off her." Or failing that, to hate her: directing my attention onto her betrayal, her levity, her heartlessness. . . . And the same goes for self-love: "Il est facile de se haïr," said Bernanos, "le difficile est de s'oublier."

Even when it can be effected, the redirection of attention is not without its dangers. If salience is indeed of the essence, then to hold someone or something for any length of time at the center of one's attention for one purpose may profoundly change the nature of one's relation to it—sabotaging the original end. Such a change is illustrated in Thomas Middleton's *The Changeling*. Beatrice finds herself enthralled by the loathsome De Flores, whom she had hired to kill the man who stood in the way of her marrying Alsemero. T. S. Eliot's description of this process is worth quoting:

> And in the end Beatrice, having been so long the enforced conspirator of De Flores, becomes (and this is permanently true to human nature) more *his* partner, *his* mate, than the mate and partner of the man for the love of whom she consented to the crime. Her lover disappears not only from the scene but from her own imagination. . . . The tragedy of Beatrice is not that she has lost Alsemero, for whose possession she played; it is that she has won De Flores. (Eliot 1960, 143).

Freudian Transference

The relation of attention to emotion is a mutual one; a shift of attention can divert the "feel" of a situation from one paradigm scenario to another; or the evocation of a paradigm scenario may cause shifts in attention. Sometimes a situation or target evokes an expressive response that is not appropriate to it as a whole but is merely triggered by some partial aspect. The response has been associated with a paradigm scenario, defining an emotion that reads back the paradigm scenario into the present situation. This is what psychoanalysts call *transference*. The classic case of transference takes place in the analytic situation, where the patient characteristically "falls in love" with the doctor regardless of the latter's lovableness. According to Freud, "the patient does not remember anything of what he has forgotten and repressed, but acts it out . . . and in the end we understand that this is his way of remembering."[3] In other words, transference is not merely mechanical repetition triggered by a stimulus but has a semantic structure of its own, akin to that of memory. Its defining feature is that it lacks *detachability* from the paradigm scenario.

Detachability
The use of a predicate can be said to be *detachable* from its learning context in this sense. Suppose I learn a color word from a chart. I may at first associate the word 'red' with that particular patch on the chart. But that is not yet to have learned the meaning of 'red'. Once learned, the word is cut loose from its associations with the color chart. It now simply refers to the color, or to whatever instantiates it. The learning situation does not remain encrusted in the meaning of 'red', though for some time it may be more or less vividly remembered and affect the connotations of the word.
    This contrasts with the semantic structure characteristic of sym-

bols, typified by religious rites and the objects used in them. The worship evoked in the faithful *by* the bread and wine are directed *at* the body and blood of Christ. The sense of the ritual depends on an essential reference to the original ceremony: the real target is not the host but the body of Christ. For the more thorough sects, indeed, the bond of symbolization is strengthened into identity by transsubstantiation: the host *is* the body. So for the patient: (unconsciously) the doctor *is* the parent. The difference is that the average neurotic cannot endorse the identification once its role is brought to full consciousness and seeks to be cured of rather than sustained in that identification. The reason for the difference is not necessarily, as one might think, that the patient is only neurotic whereas the Christian is effectively psychotic. Unfortunately, an epistemology that entailed that verdict would be simplistic: almost any delusion is compatible with efficient mental functioning if enough people share it. It makes all the difference that the Christian's belief and corresponding emotion are *socially endorsed*. We shall see later some of the broader implications of the social-contextual determinants of emotions.

Detachability seems to emerge as a norm for the semantics of emotion, an ideal often thwarted by our tendency to symbolic interpretation. Insofar as transference turns the present target into a symbol, rather than a real target, it seems to be an undesirable affection of emotions. But the neurotic and the religious do not have a monopoly on transference. As Freud put it, transference "consists of new editions of old traits and . . . repeats infantile reactions. But this is the essential character of every state of being in love" (Freud 1915a, 168).

The origin of emotions in paradigm scenarios implies the possibility of extending that observation to emotions other than love. Two questions can then be raised: first, whether transference emotions are authentic—whether they are the emotions they advertise themselves to be—and second, whether their real targets (and motivating aspects) are their ostensible ones.

It is tempting, for the sake of simplicity, to take a hard line on both questions: emotions are always what they seem, and their objects are always the ostensible ones. And if this means that some emotions are inappropriate, then things are just as we know them. There might seem to be another theoretical option: to say that the original paradigm situation is always the real object of every subsequent emotion of the same type. But that would be rather like saying that 'red' really refers to the patch on the color chart, or the toy truck, or whatever first exemplified that color for each one of us. That seems unrealistic.

Better to go at least part way with the former option and take the target at face value; so long as we remember that in some cases the content of the emotion must be interpreted in terms of a reference to an object or target other than the ostensible one. It will follow that in order to apply the principle of minimal rationality, we may need to treat the situation *as if* it involved an inappropriate identification. To see this, consider this case description by Ralph Greenson:

> A young woman patient reacts to my keeping her waiting for two or three minutes by becoming tearful and angry, fantasying that I must be giving extra time to my favorite woman patient. . . . [H]er associations lead to a past situation where this set of feelings and fantasies fit. She recalls her reactions as a child of five waiting for her father to come to her room to kiss her good night. She always had to wait a few minutes because he made it a rule to kiss her younger sister good night first. Then she reacted by tears, anger, and jealousy fantasies—precisely what she is now experiencing with me. Her reactions are appropriate for a five-year-old girl, but obviously not fitting for a thirty-five-year-old woman. (Greenson 1967, 153)

The emotional reaction is understood as minimally rational on the basis of an identification of the analyst with the father and of the woman patient with the child that she was. On that basis the content of the emotion of anger and jealousy can be understood as fitting an original paradigm scenario, though it is inappropriate to the present situation.

This approach allows for judgments of degree with respect to the relative role of the present and the past in shaping present content: even paranoiacs, as is often remarked, are sometimes more or less persecuted. There are degrees of pathology (as there are degrees of the "self-feigning" just described), in which trouble with the semantical relation to the target is reassigned to the content or character of the emotion.

To sum up: when an emotion seems irrational or inappropriate, the principle of minimal rationality tells us that we can only make that judgment stick if we can find some minimal context in which the emotion is rational, as well as a more comprehensive one in which the irrationality is manifest. Prima facie, there are two ways in which we might effect the necessary reinterpretation. One is by switching targets: "Your anger and jealousy are not really directed at me, the analyst, but at your father thirty years ago." (Note that this may not quite work by itself: in Greenson's case we must reinterpret not only the target but also the subject, as a little girl.) But a more flexible route is to look at the character or content of the emotion itself: "This is not the kind of emotion that constitutes a normal response to your analyst making you wait a few minutes; it has the character appropriate to that of a little girl made to wait for her good-night kiss." Focusing on the content allows more nuances in the comparison of features of the present situation to the paradigm scenario.

In the special case of transference love, it is an interesting question to what extent the character of the emotion differs from its character in the original paradigm scenario. Freud himself seems to be of two minds. "We have no right to dispute," he says, that transference love "has the character of 'genuine' love." But his reason is perplexing: "Lacking to a high degree . . . a regard for reality, . . . [being] less sensible, less concerned about consequences and more blind in its valuations . . . constitute precisely what is essential about being in love" (Freud 1915a, 168–169). But "less" than what? Freud seems to change thought in midsentence: he starts out to say that one would expect normal love to be more sensible than neurotic love but switches to thinking all love equally crazy. If this is so, then the "genuineness" even of normal emotions is bought at the price of their wholesale and systematic inappropriateness—an unwelcome implausibility. Besides, Freud also thinks that emotions, like actions, can be reinterpreted as something other than they seem: transference love is itself sometimes a disguise for resistance, since it can function to distract the patient from the analytic task (Freud 1912b, 101). Nor is there any guarantee that here we have reached a rock bottom of interpretation. Resistance can itself be a form of transference—if, for example, rejection of his authority was how the patient reacted to Daddy.

What criteria should guide reinterpretation? The origin of emotions in paradigm scenarios implies that each person's emotional "dialect" will be subtly different. The content of emotions for which two people have the same name will depend on their individual temperaments and the specific details of their learning experience. We shall see presently what trouble this can cause for our penchant for attempting to argue people into emotions. When we interpret one another's emotions, we have a Whorfian problem of translation: our "idiolects" determine different experiences. So when can we place credence in interpretation?

The problem is solved in much the same way by psychoanalysis and by common sense. But the solution leads to further problems. Freud's direct answer is confusing, as we have seen. But we can construct an answer on his behalf, by looking at his strategy in a related domain. He thought of the "plasticity of instinct" as an essential and pervasive characteristic of the human psyche, manifested in normal development. The plasticity of instinct is involved in *sublimation* and also in *perversions*. What is the difference between them? On the surface the criterion seems to be that sublimations involve a greater discrepancy between the original and the substitute domains of satisfaction pursued: perversions still involve "organ pleasure" of some sort, whereas sublimations are "mental." But this is a dubious difference. The exercise of power involved in certain perversions cannot obviously be assigned to one or the other domain. Ultimately sublimations are sorted out from perversions on evaluative grounds: sublimations have redeeming social value, perversions are antisocial or by consensus found aesthetically repellent.[4] So the structural account needs to be supplemented with normative criteria. That strategy goes back to Aristotle's treatment of akrasia, in which he observed that if an act is noble, we do not call it akrasia even though it might strictly involve the same psychological mechanism. For by definition "akrasia . . . deserves blame" (*Nicomachean Ethics,* VII.5). But we should not expect to decide between these as exclusive alternatives in any particular case. For, as Freud was fond of pointing out, a characteristic mark of our deepest emotions is their ambivalence, particularly when they are generated by a conflict between self and society (Freud 1930a). There is probably no art without repression, and no sainthood without obsessive compulsion.

Commonsense judgments of authenticity and appropriateness are also seldom unequivocal. We are often content to infer what emotion someone *must* be having from our knowledge of the situation in which she finds herself. Far from granting any privileged access to the subject, we seldom hesitate to overrule her declarations if we think we see her situation clearly enough. Allowances are made for variations in individual temperament, reactivity, style, upbringing, and so forth; but once all those individual differences have been taken into account, the barrier between the neurotic, intrinsically erroneous emotion and the normal one is drawn along conventional lines. And this is—with important qualifications to which I come in a moment—as it should be. For intuitively the difference between mere transference and authentic emotion is in whether the ostensible object is actually, in its present relation to the subject, fitting for the emotion that it occasions. Otherwise, it is merely acting as a trigger for something to which it is only accidentally connected. Nevertheless, the conventional source of assessments of emotion gives rise to further questions and is itself the source of an important category of emotional self-deception.

The Social Dimension of Emotions

My account so far has implied that in some sense, and to some extent, emotions are socially determined. But that doctrine is hard to pin down clearly. It can be understood in several ways—so much so that one might be forgiven for suspecting that it derives its plausibility from one interpretation and its interest from quite another. In the simplest sense, it might simply mean that we would not *notice* emotional phenomena unless they had a public name. In this sense, we sometimes say that something "is not real unless it is recognized as a publicly acknowledged phenomenon." How we classify it when we do recognize it may then differ from culture to culture. There is something here of the bootstrap effect. Recall La Rochefoucauld's epigram that people fall in love only because they've read about it. This kind of social dependency of emotions has something to do with people's tendency to imitate and follow fashions, to "be conventional" in the sense in which being conventional contrasts with being eccentric.

Some people have claimed that because emotions are conventional in this sense, they must be *culturally relative:* that their expression, their significance, and presumably even their subjective feel differ from one culture to another. James Averill has formulated this stronger thesis: "The fact of the matter is that most standard emotional reactions are socially constructed or institutionalized patterns of response" (Averill 1976, 47). But in this form the thesis is still not unambiguous: do these conventions in fact define these emotions, or do they interpret them in some way that might allow for correctness or incorrectness?

There is a spectrum of possible views on this issue. Here is an example of the less radical view. We saw in chapter 5 that our own beliefs about the proper structure of emotions may cause us to rationalize it when it does not meet those criteria. And those criteria may themselves be socially sanctioned ones. Remember the case of Bernie, who discovers that the ground for his admiration of Wendy was a false belief. He may still feel a kind of residual admiration; but since he knows that admiration needs a motivating aspect, he may just invent one. Perhaps he does this to protect his own self-image as a discerning person who does not squander admiration. Aided by the phenomenon of the perseverance of inferred beliefs, he may then just think of Wendy vaguely as someone extraordinarily accomplished in the arts, without recalling the source of that belief. From being a case of an emotion lacking a focus, the implicit second-order theory about how emotions ought to be justified will turn it into a case of an emotion with illusory focus. And insofar as that second-order theory is socially approved, Bernie resembles the recipient of a posthypnotic suggestion. On following the suggestion, he confabulates a pretext so as to be able to interpret his own action as rational according to accepted standards. But in the case of posthypnotic suggestion we are not inclined to think that because the mistake is generated by a desire to conform to social norms, it is not a mistake at all. Self-deceptive emotions should fare no differently. Misinformation is a risk entailed by the opportunities of information that social intercourse affords: that is just a special case of the general rule that the more we are (categorially) rational, the greater our potential for (evaluative) irrationality. If we have a sophisticated view of how emotions can be assessed for rationality, that entails more possibilities of irrationality.*

The most radical interpretation of the social determination of emotions would be one that assimilates emotions to moves in a game, which have literally no existence at all outside the conventions that define the game (see Scheman 1983). A move in chess is not some previously unnoticed slice of the world. If the convention is lost, the move does not merely fail to be named and noticed: it fails to *exist*. The conventions involved here are constitutive ones, not rules of etiquette.

Robert Kraut has offered the most carefully worked out formulation so far of the thesis that (some) emotions may be socially constructed. His method is to adapt a well-known argument by Tyler Burge (1979) for the claim that, insofar as the determination of linguistic meaning is a matter of convention, what I mean is not supervenient on what is "in my head." A level of description L_1 is said to supervene on a level of description L_2, if there could be no change in L_1 without some change in L_2. (This formulation follows Haugeland 1982 in eschewing reference to any individuals at either level, thereby avoiding the question of interlevel identity.) Applied to the present case, the claim is that a full description of neural and other nonrelational states of me might be consistent with either of two different ascriptions of meaning to what I say, depending on social facts about language use in my community. Kraut points out that the claim does not rest essentially on assumptions about the conventionality of language as such but instead rests on a more general notion of *"deference*—an agent's willingness to conform to communal norms upheld

---

*This is not to say that children cannot be surprisingly sophisticated about the normal structure of emotions and their function in mediating between the social and the autonomous self. Witness Hannah, at four years, whose mother had asked, "Do you ever get mad at yourself?" "No, why should I? You do that for me."

by others" (Kraut, unpub., 19). He constructs a case in which two agents belonging to different cultures, Karl and Twin-Karl, have identical inner constitutions (and perhaps even identical individual histories), while actually experiencing different emotions.

Kraut sets the case up like this. Suppose Karl is someone who tends to get inappropriately indignant—that is, in situations that are objectively related to paradigm scenarios for what we would call mere frustration, he feels as the rest of us feel when some legitimate expectation has been violated. Now consider Twin-Karl, a member of a different community, whose brain happens to resemble Karl's right down to the last dendrite and vesicle. The difference between them is that in Twin-Karl's community "scenarios . . . which involve breaches of legitimate expectation and those that don't . . . are regarded as importantly similar vis-à-vis the emotional reactions they warrant" (p. 20). In other words, Karl is deviant but Twin-Karl is normal in relation to their respective social contexts. Under these conditions, Kraut claims, Twin-Karl is not indignant: because the social standards that define the particular emotion of indignation are lacking in his culture, that emotion simply is not available to him. Karl's emotion is inappropriate indignation, but Twin-Karl's is not indignation at all.

Kraut's position seems to lie somewhere between La Rochefoucauld's and the chess model, though closer to the latter. According to him, it is not merely the label and the "idea" of the emotion that come from society. Rather, it is the existence of the emotion itself, viewed as a "practice" in which the individual might take part.

But such practices are not, as in chess, conjured up from the rules alone. If I am roughly right in my description of the origins of paradigm scenarios, the practice is constituted in part out of natural responses, although those responses acquire cohesion and a name in the context of the relevant social situation.

Kraut's notion of *deference* suggests a way of resisting his interpretation of the case he presents. The ground for resistance can be expressed as a simple challenge: *What if I don't want to be deferent?* The analogous challenge cannot be put quite so starkly where language is concerned. For in the case of language, with the exception of stipulative definitions that it is up to me to make up, I can have no power to decide on the meaning of my own utterances: if they are English sentences, their meaning must be common coin. If we subtract that commonality, nothing is left. That is the reason that Protagoras lost his fight with Socrates by winning it: if Protagoras refused to play the game of agreement and disagreement, there was no game of language left to play.

In the case of emotions there is more room to maneuver. We need to allow for the idea that the clash of scenarios—a certain degree of self-assertion by rebellion—is essential to ego development. And I suspect the biological factors I have bundled under the name of 'temperament' may be responsible for a great many differences between individual natures in respect of the style, strength, and direction of the rebellion.

Individualistic rebellion admits of degrees, of course. Taking an unexpected or inappropriate role in a given scenario is the simplest form of rebellion: for a daughter to feel condescending toward her father, for example, reverses the standard cast in a familiar scenario. But it is also possible to rebel against the scenario itself: rising not only above principle (as I suggested in chapter 8 that a genuine emotional response must sometimes do) but also above certain emotions and their founding paradigm scenarios themselves. The example of Huck Finn and Jim works at both levels (see chapter 7). Huck's own rebellion is first-order: it conforms to a standard paradigm scenario, dictating something like compassion, but is deviant in including Jim among possible recipients of sympathy. So a definite modification is brought to the original scenario, but only, as it were, in terms of casting. Mark Twain's own consciousness, however, represents a rebellion of a higher logical order: by writing the story itself, Mark Twain consciously sets up a clash between two ways of interpreting the notion of compassion. He urges the substitution of a new scenario for the accepted double standard, according to which people come precast in roles that depend on their race. In doing this, he must of course avail himself of an already existing paradigm scenario—perhaps one deriving from Christian egalitarianism.

One more example will give some idea of the intricate way in which "first-level" and "second-level" resistance can merge. In his fascinating analysis of anorexic saints, Rudolph Bell exhibits a typical pattern in which a girl asserts absolute independence from the patriarchal hierarchy by adopting the very standards of holiness taught by that hierarchy itself. Her rebellion consists in listening only to God. Any penance imposed to curb her willfulness is then interpreted as just another way to serve God—that is, to preserve her complete autonomy (Bell 1985, 36). In this case it is not so much a matter of redistributing the roles as of manipulating the scenario in order to invert its meaning. That is bootstrapping indeed: rhetoric successfully used to manipulate oneself.

In the rest of this chapter I look more closely at the consequences of the social dimension of emotions for self-deception and mutual misunderstanding. I begin with the potential clash between the rhetorical powers of constrasting scenarios, in what I shall call *lovers' arguments*. That expression is intended as a synecdoche: I use it to refer to any attempt to move someone by *argument* to *feel* a certain way. After that I shall return to the potential clash between the individual definition of emotion and the social one. I shall explain how this sometimes gives rise to a kind of emotional self-deception consisting in the phony adoption (or, for that matter, the phony rejection) of some ideology of emotions.

Lovers' Arguments

Though love is reputed beyond reason, lovers often produce what look like arguments. Those arguments are intended to convince. They even sound convincing—to the propounder, sometimes. But they seldom succeed, even when the lovers gain their end.

What then is it that distinguishes this class of arguments that are so convincing to the proponent and so unconvincing to the hearer? Before attempting to answer this question, let me forestall misunderstanding by making my use of the expression 'lovers' arguments' more precise.

To begin with, I am not speaking of quarrels. Those may result from the systematic misunderstandings that arise from lovers' arguments in my sense, but they are not the same. But whatever is the right account of lovers' arguments, it will need to allow for a plausible explanation of the fact that so many lovers' arguments do degenerate into quarrels. Part of the reason is that a failure to convince is liable to lead to escalation. But it is the very failure to convince that needs to be explained.

Nor am I referring to arguments in the sense of the sort of "games" studied by Eric Berne's "transactional analysis." But those are better candidates, involving as they do little scenarios that define a category of manipulative games such as "See What You Made Me Do," "Furthermore," "Sweetheart," and so forth (see Berne 1978). Lovers' arguments resemble Berne's "games" in having a pragmatic intent, but they are not typically manipulative.

To manipulate someone is roughly to influence her in ways that she cannot recognize and would resist if she did. To be sure, an element of manipulation cannot be excluded from any exchange, including the most disinterested. ("I can never know whether you are really taking pleasure in our lovemaking. For I know that you love me, and therefore want to please me. So is your desire actually the product of some *ulterior motive?* Only if you didn't love me could I be sure that the pleasure you seem to take in making love is intrinsic pleasure stemming from authentic desire, and not taken merely in the thought that you are giving me pleasure. And in *that*, I would take much less pleasure.") But lovers' arguments need not be uniquely or necessarily manipulative in that sense. They are arguments that make use of devices associated with genuine *linguistic meaning*.

One crucial feature of linguistic devices is that they are in a sense "aboveboard": when I straightforwardly give you information, my intention to convey that information is not hidden:

> In speaking, the speaker intends to produce a certain effect by getting the hearer to recognize his intention to produce that effect; and furthermore . . . he intends this recognition to be achieved in virtue of the fact that the rules for using the expressions he utters associate the expression with the production of that effect. (Searle 1969, 45; paraphrasing Grice 1957)

In applying this idea, we should take account of the further distinction made by John Austin (1962) between *illocutionary acts* (strictly linguistic acts performed in speaking) and *perlocutionary acts* (more remote effects of linguistic utterances, which might be otherwise obtained). Where the intended effect is to induce an emotion or even a belief, that is a perlocutionary act. The formula just quoted from Searle applies to illocutionary acts, not to perlocutionary acts. But we can accommodate this point by adding that in the cases under consideration the chief illocutionary act is indeed to *argue* for something and that the intended effect of the argument, the perlocutionary act, is the inducing of an emotion. The intention to persuade is also "out in the open," unlike cases of manipulation, so that the hearer can tell what it is that the speaker intends her to come to believe.

In the sense just explained, then, lovers' arguments are not necessarily manipulative. They are genuine arguments, albeit of a special kind. Their defining characteristics may be summed up as follows:

> They involve a bona fide illocutionary act of *arguing*, in which premises are adduced in support of a conclusion.

> They conclude with an exhortation to some specific emotion, just as cognitive arguments conclude with a recommendation to a belief, and practical arguments to a proposed action.

> Their perlocutionary goal is therefore to *seduce*, that is, to induce a specific emotion.

To seduce, in my sense, does not always mean to induce feelings of love or sexual desire. Nor does it imply persuasion to any act. In the present extended sense, all is seduction that aims to provoke a certain emotional state.

I remarked that the most notable feature of emotional or lovers' arguments is that they almost invariably fail of their purpose. But unlike attempts to induce belief, where the arguer who fails can usually see why her argument is poor, the propounder of a failed emotional argument frequently continues to think the argument perfectly convincing. This accounts for the frustrating quality of lovers' arguments—as well as for much of their comic effect.

The wonderful section of Milan Kundera's *Unbearable Lightness of Being* entitled "Dictionary of Misunderstandings" is a culling from the possibilities generated by the fact that emotionally charged words, like 'fidelity', 'family', 'country', 'love', are the names not simply of feelings but of extended scenarios. When two people associate widely divergent scenarios with the words in question, the preconditions for communication may be missing, and the prognosis for understanding is poor. Each will continue to think of herself as a paragon of reasonableness, and of the other as a paradigm of irrationality.

This much is an individual phenomenon: it relates to arguments that people have with each other about emotional matters. But the mechanism involved can also be observed on the large screen of social ideology, where social sanctions take the place of individual self-image in motivating self-deception; from that point of view, we can no longer be entirely sure what counts as an emotion of *mine* and what is dictated by a vaster play in which I have been cast.

Consider, for example, the case of jealousy. An interesting fact about jealousy is that although some form of sexual jealousy seems institutionalized in most cultures, the actual form it takes is determined entirely by the prevalent sexual mores. Although jealousy is experienced as a private emotion, it is also a part already laid out by certain social conventions, which the individual has merely to play out.

You might think that if an emotion is highly dependent on social factors, it is the more sophisticated. But precisely because an emotion is primitive in the sense that it is beyond the reach of conscious control, it may need to be channeled and controlled by social forces. So it would be a mistake to oppose 'biologically primitive' and 'socially determined'. What is most biologically primitive may be most rigidly molded by social forces. This is surely one source of the ambivalence of our emotional life: in some sense, emotions are experienced as vital to our autonomy; yet on another level they are the very instrument of social control. As Kathryn Morgan has shown, this can generate a paradox for educators aiming to promote autonomy. For the more we discourage "repressing" children out of respect for their autonomy, the more rigidly we may be socializing them, by enlisting their passions into the service of conformity (see Morgan 1974).

To return, then, to jealousy. What is most notable about jealousy is its *infantilism*. Of all our adult emotions it is among those whose infantile roots are most apparent. Aggressive rage would be another, except that, unlike jealousy, it is something from which (in my subculture) social permission is withheld. Jealousy, by contrast, has the place it does because the social contract seems to give permission—particularly to men—for the expression of envious aggression in response to the loss of attention.

The crucial role of social permission again points to the importance of emotional *expression*. Which emotions we feel is partly conditioned by which emotions we express. And that, in turn, is largely a matter of which emotions are sanctioned. Sex therapists are well aware of this; one of their principal functions is to grant their clients permission for sexual expression. But the widespread need for sex therapy itself makes sense only in the context of a culture that by and large withholds its permission from many forms of sexual expression.

The trouble is that the principles on which social permission is granted in matters of emotion are not especially coherent. Hence the paradoxes embodied in our conceptions of love and jealousy. One example: *Love* in itself is not exclusive; nothing prevents concern for the other, sympathy, and selflessness from being beamed to several targets at once. And *sexual desire* is notoriously fungible. But just put them together, and on the prevalent ideology of love their combination takes on what neither had alone: a requirement of exclusiveness—and a recipe for jealousy. No wonder, then, that jealousy is a fecund breeder of earnestly bad arguments.

Lovers' Arguments and the Aesthetic
But what, in this area, counts as a good or bad argument? As I have defined them, emotional or lovers' arguments constitute a mode of argument distinct from both the practical and the purely epistemic. How might the goal of such an argument be achieved? The most plausible answer I can suggest rests on a parallel with *aesthetic* arguments. What is peculiar about aesthetic arguments is that they are conducted without reliable major premises. If we construe aesthetic arguments on the model of the cognitive, then a major premise of an argument for an aesthetic conclusion might be of the form, "Whenever such and such nonaesthetic properties are present, then we

should expect such and such aesthetic properties to result." But we seldom if ever know such a thing to be true. When a critic gives a reason for an aesthetic assessment, we do not hold her to such standards. The crucial differentia, as Arnold Isenberg has shown, is that the point of reasons in aesthetic arguments is not to lead to an inference but to lead to a perception.[5] Similarly, a writer, actor, or filmmaker who wants an audience to share a certain emotion will have to show the situation and the characters "in a certain light," to make the audience share a certain perspective. The technique is what Plato both practiced as "dialectic" and condemned as "rhetoric."

Emotional or lovers' arguments, like aesthetic ones, are a form of rhetoric. They involve *leading to experience* rather than *deriving a conclusion*. But though critics are also sometimes unconvincing, that parallel is not enough to explain the extraordinarily low batting average of emotional arguments. One possible explanation is that the latter do not succeed because their premises not only are difficult to establish but in fact are sometimes sheer nonsense. Take a couple of examples that do not literally involve lovers: When Camus tells us that we must strive heroically because life is absurd, or when Pascal tells us that we must live in the present, the implicit majors of those enthymemes are no doubt devoid of any clear and arguable content.* But that does not account for the fact that such arguments are convincing to whoever is propounding them at the time.

For an adequate explanation, we must resort to the notion of emotions as frames for perception and belief, and we must invoke the role of paradigm scenarios.

I have argued, in effect, that emotions are among Nature's ways of dealing with the philosophers' frame problem. They determine the salience of things noticed and of live inferential options, and so control the parameters of rationality. At the same time they are themselves subject to rational appraisal. If this is right, then an emotional argument will have as its aim the apprehension by the hearer of a certain axiological property—the *feeling* of a certain formal object. To produce this feeling in the hearer, the speaker must evoke the appropriate paradigm scenario. There lies the major difference between aesthetic arguments and lovers' arguments, with their characteristic perlocutionary failure. In aesthetic argument one may need to have prepared the ground for the perception that one wants to facilitate: I cannot easily draw attention to a feature that you lack the experience

---

*"It's true, we don't live in the present. What stops us? Some kind of universal character defect? (Suspect all allegations of universal defects!) Or is the present strictly speaking uninhabitable?" (Frayn 1974, sec. 125)

to recognize. But the background you need to interpret what you perceive is simple compared to the background involved in experiencing an emotion. For the latter involves an indefinitely complex paradigm scenario. This results in differences, subtle or not so subtle, between the emotional "idiolects" of any two individuals.

The consequence for the mutual understanding of propounder and hearer of a lovers' argument is this: the propounder sees the situation in a certain light—the light of a total scenario. For her, merely alluding to part of that scenario is sufficient for a vivid evocation of its power. For the hearer, by contrast, a different scenario may fit best, and in that case all the resources of rhetoric will be unequal to the task of seduction. The rhetoric will remain ineffective, though it seems completely convincing to its author.

In short, then, when I propound an argument intended—in my broad sense—to seduce, I very likely face a gulf between the force it seems to me to have and the force it actually has on those to whom it is directed. The reason it seems so convincing to me is that I am already in it: your role is to allow yourself to be cast. But since, as far as I am concerned, the role is there, I naturally imagine that my drawing attention to features I find salient should be sufficient for you to pick up your cue. From outside that scenario, on the other hand, there is little reason why that should work. Quite the contrary: from the outside the demand often appears literally meaningless, even mad.

That is why the real seducer, the successful emotional persuader, will not simply be content with pointing to features of her own scenario that seem salient to her. Instead, she will point to features that have already captured the imagination of the "mark." The vulgar lovers' argument says, "Come into my play: let me audition you for this part." But the real seducer says, "I come to you from your own play. Look: here is your part."

The Ideology of Emotions: Two Examples from the Natural History of Sexism

An idiolect common to many is a dialect. We have seen how different paradigm scenarios can generate subtly different emotional repertoires, or "idiolects." In some cases this is systematized by the process of socialization to differentiate whole social groups. Gender socialization, the principal mechanism for the perpetuation of a deep level of sexism, provides an example whose importance transcends philosophical illustration. Let us see, for instance, how gender socialization affects *anger* and *jealousy.*

The paradigm scenarios for anger differ between men and women with respect both to its expression and to its criteria of appropriateness (see Scheman 1980). An angry man is a "manly man," but an angry woman is a "fury" or a "bitch." Or, worse, she is called "hysterical," which denies her "real" anger altogether. This is necessarily reflected in the quality of the emotion itself. A man will experience an episode of anger characteristically as indignation. A woman will feel it as something less moralistic—guilt-laden frustration, perhaps, or sadness. Insofar as the conception of gender stereotypes that underlies these differences is purely conventional mystification, the emotions that embody them are paradigms of self-deceptive ones induced by social "deference." They illustrate the fact that in what I have been calling self-deceived emotions the self mostly connives rather than originates. We are responsible only to the extent that we are generally motivated to conform to the social and gender roles assigned to us and to the extent that we allow ourselves to be taken in by the self-feigning that results.

The case of jealousy is more complicated but exemplifies the same points.[6] A man's jealousy is traditionally an assertion of his property rights, and something of that survives in the emotional tone of jealousy as felt by many contemporary men. A woman's jealousy, on the other hand, "is regarded as nearly equivalent to shrewishness, fishwifery" (Farber 1976, 182). It is not taken as seriously (there is no feminine of 'cuckold'). Underlying the surface ideology, according to Dorothy Dinnerstein's persuasive speculations, is the fact that "the symbolic shock value of the other's physical infidelity is far less absolute for her than for him" (Dinnerstein 1976, 42). In the original scenarios in which mother-raised men and mother-raised women have learned both their sense of self and the emotions provoked when it is threatened, girls are able to identify with their mothers more than boys. Consequently, a woman is likely to feel "that she carries within herself a source of the magic early parental richness." By contrast, the man's attitude stems "from the mother-raised boy's sense that the original, most primitive source of life will always lie outside himself, that to be sure of reliable access to it he must have exclusive access to a woman" (p. 43).

Sometimes it may be tempting to appeal to a radically different paradigm scenario. Simone de Beauvoir (1952) drew a picture of women in sexist society finding their very identity defined in terms of their relations to men.[7] That suggested a prediction opposite to Dinnerstein's: that women will be far more deeply wounded by the loss of a man than men for whom love is only "the relaxation of the warrior." The difficulty of parceling out the claims of these two competing scenarios illustrates the problems posed by the attempt to apply the principle of emotional continence (PEC) in practice.

In either case the very experience of jealousy for men and women will be significantly different. Consequently, the attempt to eliminate jealousy will also be fraught with divergent meanings. For a man, to overcome jealousy is to overcome possessiveness. For a woman, there may be a twist: "I must not be possessive of my lover" may express the goal of effort in both men and women, but that effort in a woman may simply play into the possessiveness of the male and reinforce the sexist mystification. ("The reason I may not possess him is that I belong to him.") This discrepancy adds yet another level of self-deception, resulting from the assumption that the task of achieving greater rationality of emotions does not vary between the sexes—or, for that matter, from one individual to another. But if jealousy means something different to each person or to persons of each sex, that assumption is mistaken. Hence, the complex emotions that may be tied to an expectation of reciprocity in the elimination of jealousy may once again be axiologically incorrect.

The cases of anger and of jealousy and the partially gendered conventions to which they are subject provide good test cases for the "contextual" versus the "individualist" view of emotions. On the contextualist view advocated by Robert Kraut (unpub.), it is literally impossible for a male to experience female anger or female jealousy, or vice versa, even if his internal states, including the quality of his experience, could somehow be shown to be the same as a jealous or angry woman's. (Your philosophical prejudices will determine how paradoxical that seems.) On a more individualist view, this is not a definitional issue but a political one. It represents a struggle between the individual's self-definition and the society's. In a sense, we might say it represents a higher-order version of the struggle delineated by Freud (1930a). In Freud's version, the individual struggles for instinctual autonomy against the impositions of society's rules. In the "higher-order" version, the individual struggles for an autonomy of definition—for the right to interpret her own emotions in terms of individual norms, related to the unique combinations of personal experience, temperament, and social practice that have created her own particular paradigm scenario for an emotion.

Of course, someone might say, "We just don't call that 'jealousy' around here." But the dispute is not a verbal one: the answer would be, "I don't care what you call it." The rebel will not be in Protagoras's position. For Protagoras, the very meaning of words and the possibility of communication vanish the moment his autonomy is asserted. But the rebel can still describe the paradigm situations involved and give an ad hoc definition of her emotion in those terms. The fight is not about correct vocabulary but about ideology.

The Dialectic of Fungibility

I have suggested that both fungibility and its transcendence could be seen as developmental achievements (on the evolutionary as well as the ontogenetic scale). The acquisition of a conceptual scheme requires a capacity for general representation, at varying levels of specificity. But general representation allows only quasi intentionality. Full intentionality implies a capacity for singular reference. The psychological correlate of these semantical facts is that we are prepared, by certain qualities of infantile attachment to specific pleasures and comforts, for the acquisition of nonfungible attachments.

It is obviously a crucially important fact about early psychosexual development, in need of explanation, that general desires for fungible satisfactions become focused on a particular person or persons. There is then a further developmental question about how it is possible to transfer (or replace) this affection, whose target is a parent, onto a new and equally nonfungible target. That the new target— ideally the Spouse—be nonfungible is part of the ideology of love in our culture. This is not, as Morton Hunt points out, a cultural universal:

> Dr. Aubrey Richards, an anthropologist who lived among the Bemba of Northern Rhodesia in the 1930's, once related to a group of them an English folk tale about a young prince who climbed glass mountains, crossed chasms, and fought dragons, all to obtain the hand of a maiden he loved. The Bemba were plainly bewildered, but remained silent. Finally an old chief spoke up, voicing the feelings of all present in the simplest of questions: "Why not take another girl?" he asked. (Hunt 1959, 10)

Somehow, however, children growing up in our culture are supposed to learn fidelity by abandoning their first and greatest love. The ideology of love requires a synthesis of "detachment," in the semantical sense explained above, and of emotional attachment. For, although the properties on which human attachment is based are qualitative, their target is determined historically.

All this generates two further sorts of self-deceptive possibilities. One is that a desire for fungible sexual satisfaction, because it advertises itself as "love," should be *experienced* as nonfungible ("I *feel* that I love you forever"). The other is its converse: an ideology constructed out of the desire to avoid the dangers of the former ideology, which denies the need for nonfungible attachments, or even their possibility. But if psychoanalysts are right about the connection between the capacity for attachment and other aspects of human fulfillment, then the zipless fuck[8] may also be delusive as an alternative ideology of love—and delusive in the very same ideologically conditioned way.

In both cases the struggle for emotional authenticity may be fostered by *consciousness raising*. The idea is that you take stock of the paradigm scenarios in which your own feelings are rooted, and also of those that are conventionally thought of as "standard." With a little bit of luck this will enable you to assess the relative claims of different scenarios, and therefore the legitimacy of different emotions, in the situation at hand.

The Paradox of the Phony

I have spoken as if consciousness raising provided an avenue of escape from emotional self-deception. Yet in my account both appropriate emotions and self-deceptive ones have their origin in paradigm scenarios. If an ideology has the same source whether it is constructive or distorting, then self-deception seems to lodge in the very semantic structure of emotion. How can I leave conceptual room for the distinction between normal, authentic emotions and hypocritical, self-feigning, or ideologically self-deceived emotions? A theory of emotions that finds them to be learned as social roles must still find a place for those that we denigrate as mere role playing. When, in short, is an emotion *phony*?

Once again, the axiological level of reality required to make sense of emotional self-deception cannot be pried apart from the question of *human nature*. And at the core of that notion there is the ambivalence generated by the fact of bootstrapping: we make some things valuable by caring about them. But we should not care about at least some of these things, if we thought there was nothing "out there" objectively worth caring about. What is authentic and what is phony has much to do with individual autonomy in something like the sense of Jon Elster; but the cult of individual autonomy can itself be phony, if it takes no account of the constraints and possibilities of human nature. A good instance of this is in a novel by Gide (1922) about a man in pursuit of the *acte gratuit*. Gide's character, not wanting to be a slave to any determinism of passion or reason, decides to commit a completely unmotivated crime. The story demonstrates, of course, the self-defeating nature of the project; but in its attempt to escape from human nature itself the aspiration would be pointless even if it were coherent. To say this is not to repudiate the difference I formerly stressed between the Attainable and the Worthy. It amounts rather to rejecting the project of Gide's hero as unworthy.

I conclude this chapter with some remarks about the prospects for escape from various forms of emotional self-deception—including that form of self-deception which derives from the assumption that our emotional life can never change because it is rooted in our paradigm scenarios.

The access we have to our emotions, in the crucial aspects that have concerned us here, is often more difficult than access to either will or belief. Of course, a change of belief can radically alter an emotion. But this touches only the cognitive aspect, not the distinctively axiologic level that constitutes the idiosyncratic core of emotions as apprehensions of reality. We have no more direct access to the content of our emotions than we have voluntary control over the past situations in which we learned them. So one form of the phony is just this: the pretense of complete control, which can be made at various levels of awareness.

We do have some indirect control, however: we can regestalt even those early paradigms. Sometimes we do it willy-nilly, forced by fresh vision to change our emotional attitudes to our past, now seeing what seemed domineering as protective, what seemed weak as gentle, what seemed principled as priggish.

In coaxing or badgering ourselves into such regestalting, we should once again remind ourselves of the crucial role and example of the aesthetic emotions. Although our original aesthetic tastes are undoubtedly formed by early experiences, the aesthetic emotions may be an exception to the general rule that paradigm scenarios go back to infancy. I am inclined to think that they constitute emergent emotional structures, which bear witness to our capacity for fresh emotional experience, built on, but not out of, preexisting emotional repertoires. Emotions more or less mechanically constructed in the latter way, out of ready-made atoms, are also phony. Fresh emotions are not necessarily unreflective: on the contrary, the emotions of the unreflective are threatened with cliché.

Verbal argument is not useless in this process of examination. Consciousness raising—that paradigm of philosophy—largely consists in propositional description and redescription. But we must carefully note its limitations. At the level of the immediate content of emotions it doesn't help much to repeat, like incantations, "This isn't really frightening" or "There is really no reason to be angry/jealous/depressed/envious/sad." It helps a bit more to draw out the similarities with other paradigm scenarios, redescribing not the emotion but the situation: "He's being intimidating only because he's shy." But the level at which the effort of rational redescription is most useful is where I have argued much of the harm is done: at the metalevel of ideology. It is at least in part in searching out assumptions *about* emotions—about their mythical peremptoriness, naturalness, or transparency to the subject; about their identity and the "biologically determined" differences between males and females—that we are most likely to transform and reform their experienced content and emerge from self-deception. In this sort of life examination, philosophical analysis merges with psychological analysis, each strengthening the other's promise of therapeutic virtue. But both require supplementation from a yet-to-be-constructed theory of individual human nature. In the realm of the emotions, simply going with one's feelings is not the royal road to authenticity: once past the threshold of categorical rationality, our emotional innocence is lost. From then on, it is the simple life that is most likely to be phony.

Chapter 10

Interlude

Difference in sameness
is the root of all delight.
Sameness in difference
is the root of all despair.
Pseudo-Heracleitus

True Love: A Meta–Lovers' Argument

(The protagonists are Panerastes, an advocate of emotional and sexual exclusivity, and Polyphila, who favors an inclusive ideology of love and sex.)

Pan   But don't you ever feel jealous?

Poly   What's that?

Pan   When you think of him making love to his other lovers, do you feel awful and murderous?

Poly   No, why should I?

Pan   Well, then, you see it's not *love* that you feel. At best, at most, it's a different *species* of love. Brotherly love, perhaps. Mere affection. Or just friendship. But it couldn't be *real* love. Real love makes you feel jealous: that's the criterion. And without a criterion of real love, how would you ever know it?

Poly   Well, for that matter, what's the criterion of jealousy? I know various things that it isn't—grief, anger, envy—but I don't really know what it is.

Pan   Don't worry, you'll know it when you feel it!

Poly   But then why can't I know love when I feel it in the first place? That would short-circuit the jealousy test.

Pan   No such luck. Everybody knows love is painful. You'll know it all right when you find the Real Thing.

Poly   Why would I want to know it? If the Real Thing is so painful, I might do better to stay with the fake.

Pan   These protestations are quite unconvincing. The fact of the matter is that jealousy is just *inevitable*. That's just human nature. The quest for explanations, rationalization . . . it's all just so much academic prattle. Emotions are just what they are: you'll never abolish jealousy, or reform love.

Poly   But surely if there's no sensible way of arriving at a rational assessment of such feelings, then you might as well "live and let live." So why are you telling me how I *ought* to be feeling?

Pan   I'm not telling you how you ought to be feeling. I only want you to admit that feelings are powerful and autonomous forces. They have nothing to do with ideology, or rationality.

Poly   But that's just another ideology! It's one that commits *you* to the principle of emotional *laisser faire*. But I don't have to buy that. My principle is different, and rather simple. If a love affair condemns you to useless pain—pain without redeeming value—then that love affair is inferior.

Pan   Isn't that timidity verging on the pusillanimous?

Poly   I'm willing to accept the risk of pain—but only for real loss.

Pan   But the way to avoid unnecessary pain is precisely to confine yourself to an exclusive relation! That way, the worst of sexual pain and jealousy is simply avoided.

Poly   Ah, so you are the timid one. You want to avoid risk. But you can't, you know, life isn't like that.

Pan   It isn't a question of avoiding risk. It's matter of fostering the conditions under which love can thrive. Anxiety, jealousy, insecurity—they don't allow room for intimacy to flourish.

Poly   So you think the natural life of love is nasty, brutish, and short, and you want a sort of Hobbesian contract: you agree to give up your sexual liberty in exchange for a similar sacrifice in your lover. And the goal of this mutual sacrifice is the security of a quiet life, free from the pain of jealousy.

Pan   Well, it leaves you a lot freer to live your life in peace.

Poly   Only by dint of self-deception. You see, the desire for adventure on one side, and the insecurity that made you want to enter into the contract in the first place—why assume you can so easily contain them? They have their roots in biology and the unreachable paradigm scenarios of your childhood. How do you hope to conquer that?

Pan   But that's exactly why we must protect ourselves! The regulation of sex is just like the regulation of other impulses by law and custom. Aggression, for example. Obviously we're wired in such a way that our aggression is always there to be triggered—if you hit the right hypothalamic button. But that doesn't make it silly to pass laws against assault.

Poly   You mean you favor laws to regulate love and sex?

Pan   Certainly not: that doesn't follow at all! But let's just say there's a prudential point behind the old moral prescriptions. Of course they seem hopelessly idealistic sometimes, but they do help to keep the peace!

Poly   Idealistic? If your rules are meant to protect you from the bothersome aspects of love, sex, and jealousy—that sounds more like the pursuit of bourgeois comfort.

Pan   On the contrary. Actually mine is the more adventurous course: what could be more romantic, more difficult, than to attempt to integrate into one relationship all the pleasures of love, sex, and play? I'm playing for *utopia!*

Poly   Difficult, you say? But I thought your little Hobbesian contract was meant to save you pain and trouble?

Pan   You're the one who just announced as a principle that pain be avoided at all cost!

Poly   Not all pain, just useless pain: pain with no redeeming value, pain generated by conventional arrangements and impossible expectations.

Pan   I'm not swallowing all that! I don't agree that the pain of love and jealousy is "without redeeming value." On the contrary: the suffering involved lifts the lover up above the mundane and sordid conventions of Open Marriage. Jealousy is the price we pay for the ecstasies of true love. And well worth it. Just listen to the poet:

> Alas! 'tis Sacred Jealousie
>   Love rais'd to an Extream;

> The only Proof 'twixt her and me,
>   We love, and do not dream.

> Fantastick Fancies fondly move,
>   And in frail Joys believe,
> Taking false Pleasure for true Love;
>   But Pain can ne're deceive.
> (John Wilmot, Earl of Rochester, "The Mistress")

Poly   Sounds like masochism to me . . .

Pan   Well, if it sounds like that to you, that just shows that you're emotionally tone-deaf. Or rather, it's as if you could hear music only in disconnected moments. You hear no harmonies, no melodies, no phrases . . . That's why you can't tolerate dissonance.

Poly   On the contrary, I'm the one who wants the whole symphony of life and love, the diversity and richness which can come only from being emotionally available!

Pan   How you do miss the point. Pain and pleasure aren't the issue—at least not in that simple-minded way. Of course we pursue pleasure, avoid pain—but in themselves both are just first-level experience, ultimately boring unless they signify something beyond themselves.

Poly   Getting metaphysical, are we?

Pan   Remember what Captain Shotover says in Shaw's *Heartbreak House?* "Courage will not save you, but it will show that your souls are still alive . . ." Well, that's how it is with jealousy: jealousy will not save you, but it will show that your love is still alive. And since you want me to get metaphysical, I'll finish the Rochester poem I was just quoting from:

> Kind Jealous Doubts, tormenting Fears
>   And anxious Cares, when past,
> Prove our Hearts Treasure fixt and dear,
>   And make us blest at last.

Jealousy, you see, is what gives meaning to love.

Poly   You know, what you so grandly call *meaning* is just what normal people call perversion.

Pan   Perversion?

Poly   Yes, perversion, or vice: the state of mind of those who no longer enjoy the pleasures they still crave. They have to bring in props and construct scenery to keep things interesting. It smacks of what the French call "looking for noon at two o'clock."

Pan   Looking for noon at two o'clock only sounds dumb if you know which is which. How are you so sure that you know which is which?

Poly   Well, actually, I don't have to: I only need to know whether I'm enjoying myself or not. And as for you, a moment ago you were claiming that feelings are just feelings; that one can't go around wrapping them in ideology, reforming love, and so on. And now you insist that feelings are nothing without *meanings!*

Pan   Of course, if it's human it must be meaningful—it must have something to do with our past, our conception of our future—that's why I said I was playing for utopia. But we can't just make it up as we go along: even utopia must respect human nature!

Poly   Well, I see no sign of that in you. There's plenty of reason to think that sexual exclusiveness is indeed utopian from the point of view of that human nature you claim to respect. And by utopian I mean not desirable, but crazy . . . The fact of the matter is that the promiscuity of sexual attraction is just *inevitable.* That's just human nature. The quest for explanations and rationalization is just so much academic prattle. Emotions are just what they are . . .

Pan   All right, I get the point. I suppose we are up against the same corner when we're backed against the ropes . . . Let's see what else is common ground between us. One thing it seems we both agree on is that feelings *can* be evaluated.

Poly   Agreed. And maybe we agree on this too: pleasure is to be sought and pain avoided *ceteris paribus.*

Pan   The catch is, the *cetera* are seldom *paria.* And we are often put in the position of comparing incomparable dimensions of value. In any case, some aspects of value are best described without reference to the more obvious types of pleasure and pain.

Poly   Which isn't to say they won't turn out in the end to be forms of pleasure and pain.

Pan   Forms of pleasure and pain, but not necessarily commensurable forms. Anyway, that's a risk I think worth running. But what I don't understand is what *you* expect to gain by your "inclusive" policy? You self-professed libertines cut a pitiful figure, scratching wherever it itches, pursuing consummatory pleasures which can never bring lasting satisfaction. Remember Madame Bovary, who soon found in adultery "nothing but the old platitudes of marriage."

Poly   Ah, but there are different levels of play. In any game there are minor goals; if you're just rallying at tennis, you're still trying to get the ball over the net. That doesn't make tennis—let alone rallying without counting points—a consummatory activity. In its larger structure it's still ludic.

Pan   But if your goal is ludic, then you might as well stay with the same partner. Why have to learn new style, new rules, have to tell the same stories all over again . . .

Poly   Precisely: life renewed, over and over.

Pan   Not renewed: only rehearsed. There's too much unfathomable mystery to each person to be explored so fast. You never get past the preliminaries, and they're always the same . . .

Poly   I guess it all depends what you mean by "new." We each have just so many stories to tell. Same stories, new listener—that can be as good as trying to make up new stories, or hoping to hear new ones.

Pan   And the risk, the pain associated with potential loss: that's renewed over and over, too. It all depends if you prefer to play by Maximin or Maximax!

Poly   You mean it's just a matter of arbitrary choice?

Pan   In a way, maybe. But in another way, I daresay you can't do much about your own options, trapped as you are by neurotic fears of attachment that have their roots in biology and the unreachable paradigm scenarios of your childhood. How do you hope to conquer that?

Poly   I don't have to conquer it, if only I can find my own truth— what, given all that, is normal for my own individual nature! To want what it is normal for just me to want: that's emotional success.

Pan   But your subjective report about your own emotional success isn't infallible. Maybe there is such a thing as my truth, but I may not be the best expert on it.

Poly   Who if not you?

Pan   No one, perhaps. There's nothing wrong with making room in your philosophy for truths that no one might ever discover. The important point is that I might be wrong, whether or not anyone else can prove it.

Poly   Indeed, we agree on that too. Notoriously, people deceive themselves, and the most strident declarations of happiness only too frequently turn out to be a last croak of defiance before the moan of misery.

Pan   If we agree on all that, then I can make my case. I claim there is something *objectively* good about the kind of intimacy that naturally comes with sexual exclusiveness. It has a quality that must remain forever unknown to those who don't have it. No doubt it's not their fault if they don't have it, but it's a deficiency nonetheless. That's obvious from the value set upon sexual exclusiveness by the vast majority of human beings. And therefore it's something to be cultivated if you can. If you can't, you're only to be pitied.

Poly   You're mixing up two different points. One is the alleged general agreement on the value of sexual exclusiveness. I think this is a common exaggeration: often trotted out, seldom supported. But let's ignore anthropology . . .

Pan   Why ignore it? What can tell more about human nature?

Poly   I didn't mean ignore it because it's irrelevant—rather, because anthropology always needs to be *interpreted* before we can learn its lessons. Anyway, the other issue is more interesting: it's the issue of objective value. So let me ask you in your turn: what is the *substantive* value to be had from monogamy?

Pan   Well, surely that is obvious. The substance of the value involved has to do with the *attention* which lovers give to each other. That clearly necessitates sexual exclusiveness. It's a matter of both quantity and quality. Attention is just not the sort of thing that can ever be bestowed on more than one person at a time without its quality being radically changed. And as to quantity, the crass and simple fact is that time and energy are limited. We must perforce take away from one whatever we give to another.

Poly   The point about quantity is well taken. There are indeed limits to how thinly one can spread one's attention. Intimacy demands time and energy. But—if you'll allow me just one ad hominem—the cult of intimacy is not one that men of your school of thought assiduously follow. For many men think it quite possible to devote most of their waking hours to a career, while their lover waits for them. (When she's not waiting on them, that is.) Now in these cases at least, if his other commitments leave time enough to love, then *she* would have plenty of time for loving others—up to the limits of the time available while he is out on business.

Pan   You're so simplistic! You're so reductionist!

Poly   Let me finish! I'm getting to your point about quality. Not that one can be too definite about it. Maybe 'quality' is just another word for dogma. As with all matters phenomenological, one man's self-evident truth is another woman's twaddle.

Pan   Oh yes? And what happened to human nature?

Poly   I'm not denying that you might be right—I only doubt whether you can find out. In any case, I like your point about quality. I can use it to support my erotic program for the underemployed. Consider that a capacity for intimacy is not innate. It is a skill, to be acquired and perfected. It follows naturally, therefore, that one might be made better at it by practice. And surely, then, the one with more free time might usefully practice with others?

Pan   That's ludicrous! How could you practice intimacy with one person to benefit another?

Poly   Why not? That just begs the question we're arguing about. But let me leave the point as moot. There is another consideration . . .

Pan   But wait, I haven't finished with that one: even if you could, imagine what would happen if one of the two were to get all the practice! Wouldn't it lead to a terrible asymmetry between the two partners in the job of intimacy? Especially if the one practicing is the woman: for there is probably much truth in the common belief that, by and large, women are better at intimacy than men.

Poly   Well, then, perhaps we have here a brand new justification for the old double standard: poor men, they must be allowed to have affairs, because they need the practice. Women, on the other hand, being already better on the average, must not improve their game too much, for fear of gaining an unfair advantage . . .

Pan   What a disgraceful analogy. Surely you can't mean that seriously?

Poly   Maybe not. In any case, I was going to make a second point, and you've just made it for me. You seem to grant that intimacy can be learned and practiced. If so, then people must vary considerably in natural talent for it: everywhere in biology, variability is the rule.

If that's true, then some of us *should* practice more than others. But more important, it suggests that even if we can't do much to change our capacity for intimacy, our different gifts should make it easy for some to bestow as much intimacy on several persons as others bestow on just one.

Pan   How callous! That's just adding insult to the injury of infidelity! As if to say, You're not enough for me, so I must supplement you.

Poly   Well, in other contexts that never gives offense. If I'm better at fashion design, or tennis, or stock analysis, surely it's a normal thing for me to seek out others with whom I share interests and talents; no one complains about that. (Or, more exactly, when someone does complain we call that *dependency, pathological jealousy,* and we urge the sufferer to seek out psychiatric help.)

Pan   But *of course* these contexts are different. That's what's special about sex: it's a connection that intrinsically demands uniqueness in the way that partnership in tennis or a common interest in the stock market doesn't.

Poly   There you go again, begging the question. I thought you undertook to explain and justify that thesis, not merely to reiterate it. After all, we agreed not to rest any argument on the inscrutability of feelings.

Pan   Quite the contrary, it's you who are begging the question. I never agreed to treat feelings lightly. Feelings are all-important in this area. After all, what else is there for us to talk about? All I agreed to was that the mere existence of a feeling didn't amount to its immunity from criticism. I just think that where sexual love is concerned . . .

Poly   You know, I suspect your real problem is that you can't tell love from sex. It's an ancient, Christian disease, which has led to much confusion among the faithful over the centuries, and which even today often confuses the faithless . . .

Pan   Don't be pompous. That's nothing to do with me. I am neither puritan nor antisexual: I never said you *shouldn't* be promiscuous, nor did I ever deny that sex could be fun at various degrees of acquaintance short of a love affair. I merely claim that where there *is* a love affair, exclusiveness is a sine qua non. And the reason is that the gift of sexual exclusivity is a valuable one in itself, not independently of but *because* of its connection with the feelings of the persons involved.

Poly   But wait: do you value sexual exclusiveness because it brings the beloved a unique gift, or do you experience it as bringing a unique gift to the beloved because you value it?

Pan   Ah—you're trying to saddle me with the *Euthyphro* problem. A false dilemma! Human reality and human value aren't *independent* of what people believe and desire: in part, at least, that's precisely what defines reality and value.

Poly   Perhaps, but surely we all aspire to value things *because* they have objective worth. Only the most ideologically heroic of existentialists could fail to be worried about the worth of what we value being nothing but projection. If what you value is a mere projection, then why not choose the most comfortable attitude if you can?

Pan   But the thing is, that even what is or isn't comfortable isn't just *up to me*. The fact of the matter is that jealousy is just *inevitable*. That's just human nature. The quest for explanations, rationalization . . . it's all just so much academic prattle. Emotions are just what they are: you'll never abolish jealousy, or reform love.

Poly   But surely if there is no sensible way of arriving at a rational assessment of such feelings, then you might as well "live and let live." So why are you telling me how I *ought* to be feeling?

(Two or three cycles looped, they spiraled on late into the night.)

Chapter 11

When Is It Wrong to Laugh?

I laughed in all cathedrals, knowing they were mine.
Ellen Estabrook Taylor

Summary

To prepare the way for a general discussion of the bearing of emotions on the ethical life, I make a case study of laughter, or rather of mirth, the emotion that laughter typically expresses. Could there be an ethic that dictates when, if ever, it is wrong to find something funny?

Reasons might be adduced for rejecting the very idea of an ethic of mirth—that mirth is involuntary; that it is too trivial; and that whatever strictures it might be subject to are merely aesthetic. But these objections can be met, and we can think of the ethics of mirth as a "special ethic" on the model of the ethics of belief or of professional ethics.

The general strategy for showing that mirth is sometimes wrong consists in showing that it is incompatible with some objective value. One form of this idea is the claim that there is a prima facie incompatibility between its formal object and the formal object of some other appropriate attitude. This is the traditional opposition between the comic and the tragic. Unfortunately, this doctrine proves impossible to establish. The only evidence we have about whether mirth and tragic feeling are indeed incompatible in themselves is phenomenological, and verdicts disagree: some people would say that what makes, say, a Richard Pryor funny is the very same thing that makes him tragic.

A variant of this objection to mirth is the view that laughter is intrinsically incompatible with emotion as such, that it requires an "anaesthesis of the heart" (Henri Bergson). But that view confuses two different contrasts: between emotional engagement and cold detachment on the one hand, and between identification and alienation on the other. You might feel passionately alienated from me, or identify with me coldly and without emotion.

A certain kind of mirth, which I call phthonic *from a Greek word meaning "malicious envy," allows scope for wrongness in at least two different ways. Phthonic mirth need have no component of wit; instead, it expresses characteristic attitudes. Emotional attitudes are unlike beliefs in that they cannot be hypothetically adopted. (Even when we do not share the relevant attitudes, we can usually recognize them as making the joke funny to those who find it funny.) Insofar as the attitudes endorsed in phthonic mirth are evil, so is the laughter itself.*

The anhypothetical character of attitudes underlying laughter is related to their partially social origin: sometimes, actually endorsing a certain attitude seems to be convertible with being a member of the relevant community. This provides for a second way that laughter might be ethically unacceptable: where it involves a movement of alienation resulting from a self-deceptive denial of identification.

These two ways in which mirth can be assessed as wrong converge, in that in both cases they seem to stem from an axiologically mistaken attitude—in the first case, to some human predicament; in the second, to the subject's own ambivalent identification.

This leaves two other ways in which we might interpret the idea that mirth, even not phthonic, is incompatible with something objectively valuable. One, also suggested by Bergson, derives from the idea that comedy simplifies and therefore distorts. But that view itself arises from a misunderstanding. It stems from Bergson's mistaken view of how perception works, and of the role of science in yielding knowledge. Finally, mirth might be wrong simply because it takes us away from something else. That raises the difficult question of how to decide whether it is better to be frivolous or solemn. This question suggests the possibility of Saints of Frivolity, like Oscar Wilde. But that very supposition seems to undermine itself; for a saint of frivolity would be culpably solemn.

If there be validity in the axiological perspective, it must have consequences for the ethical conduct of life. I shall sketch that question in general in chapter 12; but first I turn to a more specific application. I propose to ask whether we can make sense of the idea that we can arrive at an ethical assessment of the emotion that we express in laughter. In some ways it is not a typical case, and indeed it is sometimes explicitly denied the title of emotion. Yet it fits in and will add some detail to the picture I have drawn.

Before I proceed, a word about what I take the relevant phenomenon to include. Laughter is no mere class of sounds, not even if one of the defining conditions of the class is that they be produced by humans. Hysterical laughter is not laughter, nor are the happy noises and cries of infants, nor is "laughing with pleasure." Moroever, for reasons that will emerge, my focus will not be on wit. But laughter as I am concerned with it is still not a single species but a class of responses of which some formal objects are the funny, the comical, and the ridiculous. Although these are all somewhat different, I shall lump the corresponding emotions together as *mirth*. I shall be mostly interested in mirth rather than in laughing behavior. Yet, as I hinted in chapters 3 and 9, the expression of an emotion may be of constitutive importance in defining the emotion itself, both as social reality and as subjective experience. So I shall not avoid speaking sometimes of actual laughter.

The gift of mirth is often described as central to human nature. Rabelais, who had a stake in thinking well of laughter, said it defined the human essence: "Rire est le propre de l'homme." Of the many differentiae suggested for our species, this has proved among the hardiest. Human cachinnophiles will grant other species a sense of fun, a taste for play, and even a capacity for mischief. But without repudiating the continuity of animal life, they will insist that if other animals turn out to laugh, this marks just one more way in which their intelligence and sociality are closer to ours than we thought.

I shall not attempt to explain this fact, nor to provide a comprehensive account of mirth or laughter. Instead, I shall ask how we can apply to it my contention that emotions can be rationally evaluated. Or rather, since we obviously do sometimes think it is irrational or even morally wrong to laugh, I shall ask whether we can rationalize the principles behind such assessments to construct an *ethics of mirth.*

The fruits to be expected of this inquiry are these. First, it will form a good introduction to a more general discussion of the role of emotions in the moral life as a whole. Second, it will provide an occasion to explore a little further the idea that rationality constrains what emotions can coexist in relation to the same object (see priciple (R5)). Third, it will support the view that attitudes form a domain apart, subject to an axiological mode of appraisal that differs from both the strategic and the cognitive modes. Finally, it will add to our understanding of the ambivalence so prevalent in our emotional life. I noted in chapter 1 that our vocabulary for the main emotions often comes in pairs of almost identical emotions, differing only in their sign—love and dependence, admiration and envy, indignation and resentment. We know that one is good and one is bad, but we're not quite sure how to tell them apart. And that's how it is with laughter: "You're laughing at me!"—"No, I'm not laughing *at* you, I'm laughing *with* you." That there is a distinction seems clear; but it is not always obvious how to make it in practice.

If indeed mirth and our capacity to experience it are central to human nature, that ambivalence is not surprising. For human nature has always been regarded, especially in our tradition, as both angelic and demonic. In an essay on laughter, Baudelaire wrote, "Laughter is satanic, and therefore profoundly human" (Baudelaire 1954, 716). And Milan Kundera adds this twist to the theme of ambivalence: the laughter of the angels is fanatical joy, that of the devils, skeptical mockery (Kundera 1981). So there are two forms of laughter, perfectly antagonistic—both of which can seem, in their own way, detestable.

Most of us are not single-mindedly on one side or the other. We think of laughter as a domestic though occasionally risky pleasure, like sex, which is a good thing in itself, at least when done in the right way and kept in its place. Like monarchs, we sometimes license fools to tell us truths that our friends will be too well brought up to speak. And, excepting such licensed fools, the commonsense ethics of laughter goes something like this: Laugh when it's funny, grow up and stop snickering at dirty jokes, don't laugh at cripples (unless you are one yourself), and show respect. To show respect means not to laugh, snicker, titter, chortle, giggle, or even chuckle when something is too sad, when it would be unkind, when it would offend a sacred memory, and when it might be taken to insult a mother, a country, or a religion. But a few precepts may not add up to an ethics. Can anything, indeed, properly be called the "ethics of mirth"?

Three Arguments against Taking the Subject Seriously

Against the very idea of an ethics of mirth, it might be objected that mirth is *involuntary*, that its consequences are *trivial*, and that its demands are at best *merely aesthetic*.

Laughter Is Involuntary

The first argument stems from the familiar doctrine of the emotions as passions, therefore passive. It urges that nothing that is not voluntary could be the subject of moral constraint. For, it is often repeated, 'ought' implies 'can'. But the sense in which morally significant actions must be in our power is not, as Aristotle pointed out, one that requires each one of our actions to be directly chosen among psychologically available alternatives. It is sometimes enough that we are responsible for being the kind of person who no longer has a choice in this situation. That's why drunken drivers are the more culpable for the fact that they were less able to avoid an accident. So it is no surprise to hear that someone "ought to know better" than to find a certain sexist or racist joke funny.

Besides, actual laughter (as opposed to mirth or the inclination to laugh) may generally be inhibited. And, as Aristotle again sagaciously remarked with regard to a certain Adeimantus, who is known to history only for having once burst out laughing, we don't blame someone for laughing if she's tried hard not to.[1]

Triviality
Still, it might be said that even if laughter betrays character, and even if we ought on occasion to contain it, this is merely a minor social duty, like the duty not to fart or burp. Failures of restraint can inconvenience others, perhaps embarrass or even offend them; but surely this is a matter of etiquette, not of ethics. Rules of etiquette are typically relative to a particular group: "It's all right to use such language when you're at camp with your buddies; but it just won't do at your sister's wedding." The suggestion that there are categorical Laws of Etiquette is a familiar device of the comical—either ingenuous, as in the injunction to "Never Give a Lady a Restive Horse" (Hill 1967), or ingenious, like Oscar Wilde's rule: "The only way to make up for being occasionally a little overdressed is to be always immensely overeducated" (Wilde 1894).

For two reasons, this won't do as a characterization of the difference between ethics and social convention. For one thing, it is one of the anthropologist's tasks to find underlying universal structures beneath the surface of particular social conventions. And on the other hand, a case might be made that some genuinely moral rules are relative to conventional social structures. But surely it is a necessary condition of moral significance that an act and its consequence not be trivial. Can mirth pass this test?

The association of mirth with the frivolous may encourage us to assume that it cannot be serious. Yet laughter is at least an important revealer of character; we readily make inferences about people from the nature of the focal property that occasions their laughter. We can react positively, as to revealed affinity, or negatively, with shock and revulsion, to the fact that someone finds a certain sort of joke or situation funny. In this way laughter is a powerful sorter. This is not to claim that it is always easy to pick out the relevant focal property. To say what someone is laughing at, in the sense of the target or scenario that provokes laughter, is not always to specify *what's funny about it—* the motivating aspect. Moreover, a sincere answer to that question is not always a true one. A partial guide to the nature of the true object is the character of the laughter itself, its actual sound, considered in isolation from its occasion. (Sometimes the sort of occasion it is can be easily inferred from the sound: a laugh can be cheerful, chilling, giddy, sinister, or threatening.) Imagine a man whose habitual sound of laughter is a cackle or a giggle: would you like your daughter to marry him? Even more interesting is the second-order thought experiment implicit in this example. To be imaginatively convincing, the example had to be gender-specific. Our gender stereotypes dictate that it is not feminine to guffaw, nor manly to giggle. There are assumptions buried in these reactions to the sound of laughter that cut much deeper than etiquette, as can be seen from Mary Daly's call to a feminist mirth-rebellion:

> Self-loathing ladies titter; Hags and Harpies roar. Fembots titter at themselves when Daddy turns the switch. They totter when he pulls the string. . . . Daddy's little Titterers try to intimidate women struggling for greatness. This is what they are made for and paid for. There is only one taboo for titterers: they must never laugh seriously at Father—only at his jokes. (Daly 1978, 17)

"Merely Aesthetic"?
The categories of expressiveness I have just described are coarse, as they must be to be even roughly describable. But our ears are sensitive to much finer nuances. We can be attracted or repelled by the sound of a laugh even more surely than by that of a speaking voice, without quite knowing why. "Tell me what you laugh at and I will tell you who you are," but "Let me hear you laugh and I will know if I like you." When I find a personality disagreeable, it is a normal effect of moderate vanity to hope it is because there's something wrong with the person it belongs to, not with me. It is always satisfying to find the accident of subjective distaste taking root in the objectivity of sound motives for moral disapproval. Is this possible here? Or are the preferences evoked by the expressiveness of laughter just aesthetic ones? This question is different from the one concerning the triviality of laughter; for even aesthetic questions that cut very deep may still not be held to be moral. That we are dealing with aesthetic preferences, moreover, is suggested by the variety of our reactions and by the difficulty of articulating them in terms of general principles. If this is so, the affinities or differences they reveal may not have moral significance.

In chapter 12 I shall argue that the multiple dimensions defined by the formal objects of the various emotions, including the aesthetic, will demand to be admitted into an expanded ethical domain. But for the purposes of the argument in this chapter I shall continue to assume the traditional contrast between the aesthetic and the ethical.

Even on that assumption there are good reasons for thinking that some censure of mirth is not "merely aesthetic" but properly moral.

Origins and Consequences

Central to most moral systems is an interest in consequences, actual, probable, or merely possible. This contrasts with aesthetic interest, which characteristically focuses on some object in itself. Laughter, it may be conceded, does not have very significant consequences. Henri Bergson (1940, 15–16) calls it a kind of "punishment" but stresses that it is only a social gesture: "Society cannot here intervene with any material repression, since it is not hurt materially" by what laughter is intended to punish. It is a quaint optimism that supposes that society will punish only symbolically what harms it only symbolically. But leaving that aside, we can retain from his remark the idea that the material consequences of laughter are attributable only to the meaning of laughter: in this way laughter is essentially an intentional manifestation, a sign the effect of which is based in part on convention. Yet—and this is the other side of the variety manifested by the sounds and object of laughter—laughter itself is natural to humans. It is universal, not just as a sound but as a mode of communication. As we shall see, at least one important variety of this mode presupposes sociality in that it requires a recipient or butt: someone to whom the laughter is liable, and perhaps intended, to give offense.

Not every action that gives offense is thereby *morally* offensive. Its evaluation requires that we ask why it is found offensive. Mixed marriages frequently give offense to racists, but that does not warrant moral regard. Explicitly sexual literature can be offensive to the "common decency" of "community standards." Such offenses are liable to draw upon themselves social and legal sanctions, but whether they warrant moral condemnation is quite another question. Social conventions create moral obligations only insofar as they express or embody human values that depend on sociality itself: the existence of some particular social arrangement, or mere public opinion, is not enough.

Moreover, what gives offense usually does so by virtue of its motivational origins. An observer acquainted with Gilles de la Tourette's syndrome, for example, will not be offended by the verbal products of the illness (known as *coprolalia*, the euphonious Greek for 'shit-talk'), which spring directly from a neurological disorder and not from any intent (even unconscious) to utter offensive words. Similarly, hebephrenic laughter does not express mirth: it is not, for our purposes, laughter at all. The sound of laughter is significant as laughter only if produced in the right way (see chapter 5 on "Aim"). It might therefore make sense to speak of an "ethics" of some class of acts that is concerned not primarily with their consequences but with their origins.

The notion of origins loomed large in my own discussion of rationality in chapter 6 (see especially principle (R4)). But origins can be relevant in two different ways. In one classic sense, of course, ethical assessments of particular acts are not assessments of actual consequences but of origin in the sense of "motive." For the Kantian, this appraisal of the goodness of the Will is the only truly ethical evaluation. But this is not the sense in which I speak of evaluating laughter in terms of its origin. For although we can sometimes burst out laughing on purpose, specifically with the intention of wounding someone—or omit to restrain our laughter—this is not the usual case. Nor is it very problematical. More interesting is the criticism of mirth that arises from treating it as a *symptom.* There are cases in which we say, "If you can laugh at something like that, you must be insensitive, boorish, cruel. . . ." Such strictures are related to the Kantian criticism of motives, but they are not the same. The Kantian looks at the origin of the act only in the sense of looking at the maxim or principle in accord with which the intention is formulated. The "spontaneity" of mirth, as of other emotions, makes it inappropriate for that kind of criticism. If we can answer the question, "What did you *intend* by laughing?" then it was not genuine laughter.

The notion we are looking for relates to axiological assessment, and once again we can learn from the parallel with the assessment of cognitive rationality—the "ethics of belief." Belief, like laughter, is not typically voluntary. On the contrary, if it aims at some result—apart from the attainment of its formal object—its claim to be genuine belief is undermined. The evaluation of belief is in terms of the correctness of the procedures in which it originated. It might be strategically rational to believe something in the face of the evidence because the consequences of believing it would be good. But it is always cognitively irrational—a violation of the ethics of belief.

Such a violation might be required by overriding considerations. Sometimes, perhaps, we should persuade ourselves of some comforting falsehood in order to preserve the moral strength to continue a worthwhile struggle. In some of those cases, as in my own fondness for placebos, the bootstrapping principle may be operative, so that the belief seems almost to create its own justification. And maybe it is even sometimes our duty to propagate a Noble Lie for the benefit of humankind. But these are cases where the intrinsic, universalizable ethics of belief are overriden, not cases where they appeal to consequentialist criteria for the sake of their own formal object.

Much the same can be said of "professional ethics": medical, business, or legal. All of these, more obviously than the ethics of belief, may ultimately rest on consequentialist moral considerations, but they are rules about origins—about the best *procedures* in the transactions charcteristic of each of these domains. And although they admit of exceptions, they need not violate the principle of universalizability. For exceptions to principles of professional ethics are due to articulable features of the circumstances, not to the vagaries of individual preference.

Might not the objection then be raised that all these "ethics" are so called merely by courtesy, by convenience, or by analogy? A simple argument shows that this objection would be wrong. It is always an unequivocally ethical question whether in some particular case we should allow ethical considerations *simpliciter* to outweigh or override principles of the special ethics. If these "special ethics" had no genuine ethical import, this would not be so. For suppose they merely had the status, say, of etiquette: then on most ethical principles, although hurt feelings in the protocol-minded might provide indirect moral reasons, they would be of no ethical weight in the face of genuinely moral objections.

I conclude that there are genuine examples of ethics in which the considerations are ones of appropriateness in relation to origins, not of consequences either aimed at or achieved. That, in any case, is the sense in which I shall be speaking of the ethics of mirth.

The Comic and the Tragic

When I was a boy, I went to see a matinee performance of Beckett's *Waiting for Godot*. During the intermission I struck up a conversation with an elderly woman in the next seat. She had laughed not at all, and she spoke earnestly about how gloomy the play was: as she could no doubt see that I was only thirteen years old, she was anxious that I not be misled into thinking it a comedy. The theater darkened again, and there came one of the play's moments of sheer clowning. The philosophical disquisitions of the two tramps are punctuated by the rapid tossing of a bowler hat, with machine-like precision and irrelevance. There is nothing funny in the telling of it: it was not a joke but pure slapstick, an excellently executed visual gag, and it brought the house down. Under cover of the loud laughter, the lady bent down toward me and gravely hissed, "But it isn't *meant* to be funny!"

On the contrary: these actors had worked very hard to be that funny. For as David Garrick is said to have warned a young actor: "You can fool the town with Tragedy, but Comedy's a serious business." The lady was right, I daresay, about the overall vision of the play; but what intrigued me was the presupposition of her reproof: *If something is tragic, then it can't be funny.*

This doctrine, if true, would be of great interest for the present argument. For it would provide us with one of those elusive principles laying down constraints on the coexistence of emotions. As I have pointed out, a logic of the emotions ought to provide such constraints, though often it cannot. The incompatibility of the comic and the tragic is a doctrine that has in most ages passed for common sense, or at least for an indubitable principle of aesthetics. There have been some exceptions: in the *Symposium* Plato reports that Socrates, at the end of that long night of talking and drinking, "forced his companions to acknowledge that the genius of comedy was the same as that of tragedy." But he implies that they agreed mainly because "they were drowsy and didn't quite follow the argument" (*Symposium*, 223). By and large the Greeks separated tragedy from comedy. So did their classical French followers, who, like most of the English eighteenth century, thought Shakespeare vulgar for ignoring the distinction. Yet even Shakespeare usually separated comic scenes from tragic ones. Some authors regard laughter as a substitute for tears: "Man alone," said Nietzsche (1896) "suffers so excruciatingly in the world that he was compelled to invent laughter." But even he appears to assume the two are incompatible.

What could be the nature of such incompatibility? Let us begin by distinguishing two sources, or types, of incompatibility. Two emotions might be incompatible *in the subject* or *in relation to their objects.*

The first type applies characteristically to moods. If one cannot feel elated and depressed at the same time, this cannot be because of any incompatibility between the objects of these moods—for moods have no object. Depression and elation seem to be real contraries, not merely "opposites" in some vaguer sense. If, in the traditional figure of the tragic clown, we are inclined to see someone who is both gloomy and merry, we can evade contradiction only by appealing to some sort of split-level theory. Split levels, like Plato's parts of the soul, allow each level to be pure even while explaining the possibility of inner conflict. Plato's method is explicitly designed to split faculties two by two, and we saw that it has trouble generating more than two parts of the soul. There is also a problem about how, if it succeeds in that task, it avoids succeeding too well and producing an indefinite proliferation of parts (see Penner 1971). Plato's use of this method is fallacious; but the basic principle is just a version of Leibniz's law: if two properties are incompatible, then no one thing can have them both at the same time. And if we grant that there can be more than one level, why not several?

If we adopt Plato's strategy, we implicitly construe the incompatibility on the model of the impossibility of an object being simultaneously and homogeneously red all over and green. But this cannot be the correct account of the incompatibility between laughter and alternative reactions. For although we do occasionally get into a "laughing mood," under the influence of cannabis, for example, or following relief from great tension, laughter is not objectless, as moods are. To get a better idea of what is involved in inconsistency with regard to objects, let's return to the case of inconsistent propositional objects of belief. It is not inconsistent to describe a subject as believing both that p and that not-p. But it does constitute an *ascription* of inconsistency. What's wrong with inconsistency? What's wrong with it is that it guarantees *at least one false belief*. This goes against the categorical imperative of the ethics of belief: *Believe (all and only?) what is true*. The criterion for that violation lies in the logical relations between the propositions believed—between the contents of the beliefs. As a first approximation, we might suppose the emotional analogues to propositional content to be constrained by the following principle of emotional consistency:

(PC) *Principle of emotional consistency.* If two emotional contents are incompatible, then that will guarantee that at least one emotion is *axiologically inappropriate*.

Unfortunately, examples are hard to pin down. For the objects of emotions have no criteria of identity even as dubiously clear as those of propositions. How then can we tell whether someone's emotional contents are so structured as to guarantee that at least one of them is inappropriate? We must resort, it seems, to some unexplained notion of phenomenological incompatibility. Whether the comic and the tragic are phenomenologically incompatible seems a hopeless question: both are too complicated. Let us at least narrow the case down to the *funny* and the *bitter*. As practiced by a certain kind of comedian (Lenny Bruce, Richard Pryor), it seems as though the funniness is in the very bitterness itself. Some might find this unintelligible; but any disagreement is likely to get bogged down in denials of each other's phenomenological reports. Let us then grant, at least, that some people sincerely report experiencing both responses at once. Should this report be disbelieved, or construed as self-deceptive?

Let us redescribe the situation a bit more fully in terms of the typology of objects in chapter 5. The case involves a single target: say, a Richard Pryor schtick. Call the two formal objects involved the *funny* and the *bitter*. The question is whether there are two distinct motivating aspects, and if so, what their relations are to the funny and the bitter as formal objects. The claim of incompatibility must be refined to distinguish the impossibility of joint *satisfaction* (incompatibility) from the impossibility of joint *success* (inconsistency). Recall that success was defined as the possession by a motivating aspect of the property that defines the formal object. In the case of a want, for example, the property for which I want something must actually be a good-making one. Satisfaction is the actual possession by the target of the motivating property attributed to it by the intentional state. For a want, this means that the proposition wanted is actually true. Now consider two possibilities:

1. Suppose first that there are two motivating aspects, both present in the performance: the tone of Pryor's voice, perhaps, which is apprehended as funny, and the content of his words, apprehended as bitter. Then, since the formal objects (and the corresponding emotional responses) are being attributed to those different aspects, no argument could show them to be inconsistent. That would be like claiming that it is inconsistent to say of two different propositions that one is true and the other is false.

2. The second possibility is that there is really only one motivating aspect. It is not only the same performance, but the very same aspect of it, that arouses both emotions. Here true inconsistency is a possibility: perhaps the two formal objects are inconsistent as criteria of success.

An analogy with belief will help to make this clear. No single proposition could be both true and false, not because every proposition has some property that prevents it, but because that is part of the meaning of the opposition between truth and falsity. So might it be with comic and tragic: maybe they are by their very natures related as logical contraries.

Unlike true and false, however, they are not contradictories, since the number of formal objects of emotions is large, whereas there is only one formal object of belief. This disanalogy makes axiological correctness more difficult to understand than truth. Good is already more complicated than True, in that it is subject to the "Monkey's Paw phenomenon": something good can turn out bad because of what it is conjoined with (see de Sousa 1974b); by contrast, nothing true can turn out false because of what it is conjoined with. That complication certainly applies to the axiological level as well. But the multiplicity of formal objects may be responsible for yet a further complication to axiology, which might be traced to the possibility of *higher-order moti-vating aspects*. Even if it is the quality of Pryor's voice that is the rele-vant motivating aspect, yet perhaps there are two aspects of that quality, or two aspects of some aspect of that quality, that evoke the different responses. By this reasoning every situation of type (2) might ultimately be reconstrued as one of type (1).

The trouble with the suppositions in the last paragraph is that al-though they are coherent, I cannot think of a way to establish their truth. This seems to be a place where nothing but phenomenology will give us any answer. But even if the deliverances of phenomenol-ogy were clear, they would not indicate the source of incompatibility. The incompatibility in question is not a logical matter. Rather, it is of the sort that makes it possible for us to do some pairs of things at once but not others (see chapter 3 on "Moderate Modularity"). And if indeed some people report having both types of response in regard to a single aspect, I find no argument to support the view that the two formal objects must be inconsistent.

But there remains to be explored another form of the charge of incompatibility, which proceeds with a quite different strategy.

Feeling and Thinking: The Walberg View

On this new version, the claim is not that comic and tragic are incon-sistent emotions, but that the comic is incompatible with emotion as such. I shall refer to this as the *Walberg view,* in honor of Horace Wal-pole and Henri Bergson. Walpole's quip is often quoted: "This world is a comedy to those who think, a tragedy to those who feel." In Bergson's view, "Laughter has no greater enemy than emotion. . . . The comical demands . . . something like a momentary anaesthesis of the heart. It speaks to pure intelligence." (Bergson 1940, 3–4). In naming it the Walberg view, I wish to honor its authors without car-ing too much about how accurately the version of it that they inspired conforms to their own. John Morreall has more recently argued, much like Bergson, that humor and emotion are incompatible and indeed that it is precisely in this incompatibility that its evolutionary function resides:

> In [the] development of reason, emotions would have been not a boon but an encumbrance. . . . Amusement by contrast, like artistic activities and science, would be helpful in the develop-ment of reason because it involves a breaking out of a practical and self-concerned frame of mind. . . . The capacity of humor to block emotions would also have facilitated the development of

> rationality, for emotions would often get in the way of rational thinking. . . . (Morreall 1983a, 302–303)

These points are unexceptionable in connection with wit or the laughter of incongruity, with which both Bergson and Morreall are chiefly concerned. But I shall presently introduce a different species of mirth to which they are not so clearly applicable.

The Walberg view is radical, not only because it is so sweeping, but also for its claim that laughter itself does not stem from emotion at all but rather contrasts with it. Against it I see two arguments. One is too simple. The other perhaps will seem too complicated. (Such is the Philosophical Life.)

The simple argument is that to compete with emotion, laughter needs to be in the same game. The Walberg view presupposes some sort of philosophical psychology, in which something like faculties can enter into competition. There might be models of this kind that philosophers traditionally haven't thought of; but, the argument runs, all the familiar models are basically variants of either the Aristotelian, the Cartesian, or the Platonic model. On both the Aristotelian and the Cartesian models, Intelligence (or Understanding) is viewed as a separate function or faculty from Emotion (or Will). On the Platonic, they are more like the parts of the soul of the *Republic:* each one is in some sense dominated by a particular faculty and primarily identified with it, but every faculty is represented in each homunculus. (See chapter 2.)

Consider first the Aristotelian/Cartesian picture. It allows no competition between the faculties, for they perform quite different tasks. Their organs can of course compete for resources; but the functions themselves can no more conflict than the volume control of a radio can interfere with its tuning.

But the Platonic picture fares no better. It accounts for individual differences in terms of the dominance of one part of the soul over another. In this it agrees well enough with the popular notion that some individuals are primarily analytical and others primarily empathic: on the Walberg view, such differences might account for a contrast between a dominant disposition to laugh or to feel. But the Platonic model gives us no particular reason to see those dispositions as incompatible. And that is just what the Walberg view must defend.

The correct diagnosis demands a more complicated route. The distinction so far sketched confounds two different contrasts. One is between *evaluative engagement* and neutrality or *cold detachment.** The

---

*There are nuances here that I ignore. 'Detachment' is a word sometimes used for a difficult achievement of impartiality; it can also refer to a refusal to become inappro-

other is between *identification* and *alienation*. We tend to associate cold detachment with alienation, and identification with empathy and therefore with evaluative engagement. But these are no more than associations. The two dimensions are independent. One can be evaluatively engaged with what is alien—in burning hostility or in puzzled envy—and one can be cold even while identifying with another person. ("I know exactly how she feels, but I don't care.") I can regard myself coldly and without emotion, for that matter, though not ceasing to be or feel myself. This distinction is particularly important with regard to mirth; for mirth can be dispassionate, as when it is evoked by mere wit, or emotionally involving, whether we are laughing "with" someone (involvement with identification) or "at" someone (involvement with alienation). It is no accident that real cases are seldom purely of one sort alone. One source of the ambivalence of mirth, as I shall argue in a moment, is that mirth often involves a dialectic of identification and alienation.

The evaluative involvement characteristic of laughter has traditionally—and, as I shall argue, at least sometimes correctly—been taken to involve some apprehension of evil. My hunch is that in an important class of cases there is an interaction between this element of evil and the dialectic of identification and alienation. This class of cases defines a kind of mirth, which I call *phthonic laughter,* that is particularly susceptible to moral condemnation. If this is right, then the Walberg view must be rejected: it rests on a confusion between intellectualizing detachment and emotionally involved alienation.

Phthonos, Wit and Anhypothetical Humor

Let us exorcise the evil element in laughter by giving it a name, which will distinguish it from wit and from mere amusement. I borrow from Plato the word *phthonos,* which means something like "malicious envy" (*Philebus,* 47e). It connotes both the involvement of something evil and the ambiguity between identification and alienation that characterizes jealousy. Plato applies it to the kind of laughter typically experienced at some ridiculous spectacle. Malicious ridicule, in Plato's book, is properly directed against our enemies; but it is a pleasure mixed with pain when directed at our friends. Of the many philosophers who have emphasized this element of evil, Hobbes saw especially clearly that the phthonic element is distinguishable from wit:

---

priately involved in the affairs of another person. In neither of those cases does the word connote "coldness." I use 'cold detachment' to refer to a lack of emotional involvement of any kind.

"That laughter consisteth in wit, or as they call it, in jest, experience confuteth, for man laughs at mischances and indecencies wherein lieth no wit nor jest at all" (Hobbes 1650, IX).[2] But how is the distinction between phthonos and wit to be drawn? In reaching for a hypothesis, I need a joke of undiluted nastiness; one that is as devoid of wit as possible. A rape joke will do:

> M. visits the hockey team. When she emerges she complains that she has been gang-raped. Wishful thinking.

I once had occasion to discuss this joke with a student editor who rather proudly claimed to be its author (an exaggeration, since all rape jokes are variants of the same basic joke). I pointed out to the "author" that the joke seems to imply certain beliefs. One is the belief that all women secretly want to be raped. But the "author" insisted that I had entirely missed the point: what the joke was really about, he ingenuously explained, was the "well-known fact" that M. was *promiscuous.*

In tendering this transparent reply, the young man was furthering my quest. That M. is promiscuous is indeed a hypothetical assumption of the joke. And embedded in the very use of the word 'promiscuous' in this context are something like the following propositions: that rape is just a variant form of sexual intercourse; that women's sexual desires are indiscriminate; and that there is something intrinsically objectionable or evil about a woman who wants or gets a lot of sex. These are sexist assumptions. But *merely to know this doesn't make the joke funny.* What's more, to laugh at the joke *marks you as sexist.* It is not a convincing defense to say, "I was merely going along with the assumptions required to get the point of the joke."

In every joke that is based on a story—as opposed to arising from some life situation—some assumptions, some background setting, need to be understood and accepted. "An Englishman," we begin, "a Scotsman, and an Irishman . . ." So how are the sexist beliefs just mentioned unlike the ordinary presuppositions that every joke requires?

The difference is that to find the joke funny, the listener must *actually share* those sexist attitudes. In contrast to the element of wit, the phthonic element in a joke requires endorsement. It does not allow of hypothetical laughter. The phthonic makes us laugh only insofar as the assumptions on which it is based are attitudes actually shared. Suspension of disbelief in the situation can and must be achieved for the purposes of the joke; suspension of attitudes cannot be.

Although we cannot come to find something funny by merely imagining that we share its phthonic assumptions, we intuitively know that sharing these assumptions is what would enable us to find it funny. This point is crucial. For without the possibility of this sort of second-order kowledge about the relation of attitudes to laughter there could be no criticism of other people's laughter. Indeed, there probably could be no phthonic jokes at all. In the standard case a phthonic joke requires a butt or victim, and the butt of a joke is someone who typically does not laugh but knows only too well what's funny to those who do (see Legman 1968, 9).

But perhaps someone remains unconvinced, because he does find the joke funny and disclaims the allegedly necessary attitudes. For such a man, no knock-down argument can be forthcoming, but a simple thought experiment might help. Just imagine either of two variants. In the first, some nonsexual form of assault is substituted for rape. Apart from some tenuous connection with masochism by which one might try to restore the original point, it will undoubtedly cease to be funny to anyone. In the second variant, substitute some man who (1) is not assumed to be homosexual and (2) is not the object of any particularly hostile attitude. Again, the joke loses its point. And this cannot be remedied by my saying, "For the purposes of the joke, just ignore the sexist double standard, and pretend that you think that there is something evil or contemptible about a man who fucks a lot."

My last sentence embodied a second thought experiment. If you snickered at my language, it's because you consider it naughty. That is an attitude. If you didn't, I'm unlikely to get a chuckle out of you by asking you, just for present purposes, hypothetically to think my language naughty. Though there is apparently a possible exception here: but it is only apparent and therefore "proves the rule." The supposition just made may raise a chuckle after all, but only because you agree with me and therefore find it funny to suppose otherwise. So the chuckle would really only be raised by the meta–thought experiment, and instead of a counterexample it would be merely an instance of the following principle: *It can be funny to suppose that something that is not at all funny might be funny, but only if you actually think it isn't actually funny.* (One might call this the *Python principle,* since a number of Monty Python's jokes exploit it.) This confirms my hypothesis, as well as carrying the additional empirical implication that thinking something intrinsically funny (or unfunny) is itself an attitude and not a mere belief. The present case therefore fills out the thesis sketched in chapter 6, that attitudes are beliefs that one cannot hypothetically adopt.* In turn, this anhypothetical feature of emotional attitudes provides further evidence for the independence of the axiological level from the straightforwardly cognitive.

The Social Factor

The anhypothetical nature of attitudes is related to a factor that was discussed in chapter 9: the *social* nature of emotions. One aspect of this is the social relativity of jokes. This forms the subject of one of Bergson's "fundamental observations on the Comical":

> A man was asked why he wasn't crying during a sermon which had everyone else in tears. "I'm not from the parish," he answered. What this man thought about tears is even more true of laughter. However frank it may seem, laughter always conceals a subconscious thought of community, one might almost say of complicity, with laughing companions real or imaginary. (Bergson 1940, 5)

Since the community of laughers is allowed to be imaginary, it would be hard to refute Bergson's claim. But when we actually laugh alone, what subsists of this imaginary community? At least this: when I laugh, I endorse certain attitudes, and anyone else endorsing them would probably be laughing too.

The notion of community is of independent importance because it sometimes seems to be convertible with the endorsement of an attitude. In some circumstances the question of whether one belongs to

---

*I am tempted to suggest a practical application. Most of us are not perturbed by the common charge that philosophy and humor are both useless, because we realize that only the intrinsically worthless can be purely useful. Nevertheless, we might be cheered by a concrete suggestion about how humor, at least, might be of use to philosophy. I am thinking of the task of selecting suitable apprentices to the philosophical profession. This is a tedious process, and the usual methods of selection are unsatisfactory, because they concentrate more on such relatively irrelevant facts as talent, intelligence, knowledge, and so forth. In fact, the only important factor is that the candidate should display an appropriately philosophical *attitude*. The best aptitude test is an attitude test. If what I have argued here is right, I can now justify an old dream: philosophical aptitude tests consisting entirely of jokes. The applicants' laughter would be carefully graded; and since, as I have argued, attitudes cannot be adopted at will in order to find some joke funny, we need have no qualms of conscience about settling their destiny entirely on the basis of their responses. The main practical obstacle to such a scheme is that the entire scale would have to be calibrated to a given person in a given mood; and the mood induced by the testing conditions would most likely leave all amusement below the threshold of differentiated observable response. But this is merely a technical difficulty—if indeed it is a difficulty at all. For should we really encourage those people to be philosophers who lose their sense of humor under stress?

a certain community, or shares in certain assumptions made in that community, admits of no ready answer. After long enough among the natives, the anthropologist might feel a sufficient sense of community to laugh at their jokes, even though in sober conscience she does not share their attitudes. She may not really endorse, for example, the view that chickens are dirty and pigeons are pure, even if she laughs at local jokes based on those attitudes. A feeling of community can substitute for, as well as engender, the genuine adoption of an attitude; conversely, the adoption of certain attitudes can be both a criterion of membership and a sufficient ground for being adopted as a member.

The convertibility of emotional attitudes and community involvement is what we should expect if the theory I have been defending is even roughly right. According to that "dramatic" theory, participation in a given scenario defines an emotion even as it generates the experience of a characteristic phenomenal quality or feel.

An interesting corollary is that we have here a concrete example of the possibility of changes in emotional dispositions. The convertibility of attitudes and community ensures that in at least some cases new paradigm scenarios can continue to enlarge and refine our repertoire of emotions. But what exactly does this sort of community involvement amount to? To understand how to answer this, we need to look a little more into the relations between the dramatis personae of paradigm scenarios.

Identification and Alienation: Inside and Outside

We have seen that the notion of community is related both to the endorsement of common phthonic premises and to the contrast between identification and alienation. It is time now to look more closely at the distinction between "inside" and "outside."

There are two characteristic manifestations of this distinction. First, we claim a right to laugh, by virtue of shared experience or community, at some things but not others. Second, we distinguish between laughing *at* and laughing *with* someone. These are different distinctions, but they are related in the following way: I cannot really laugh with you, unless I have the right to laugh; and I only have a right to laugh *at* you if there is a clear possibility of identification *with* you. Although Cyrano de Bergerac makes fun of his own nose, he threatens with death anyone else who makes fun of it. There is often a note of embarrassed reticence in the laughter of white people at the jokes of blacks about themselves. Yet the whites would, perhaps, readily laugh at the blacks, if the blacks weren't laughing at themselves.

What causes the unease in the one case is the thought that *they* (who laugh) *have no right to laugh;* what lifts it in the other is the thought that *they* (the others) *won't find out.* The same dynamics can be observed even more commonly nowadays in the jokes of men about women. What is wrong with laughing at people behind their backs, when the same joke would be acceptable face to face? The answer is that if you were face to face, the balance of ambivalence would tip: the alienation expressed by the joke itself would be offset by the reality of community signaled by the sharing of it.

An extreme example was related to me by someone who had been brought up among the miners of the Congo. Among these men, to laugh at cripples was not condemned as especially rude or callous. Part of what the laughter expressed in those circumstances, in which the men were exposed to great danger, is that it could happen to anyone: it had happened to you and it could have been me that it happened to, but you are not me and it wasn't. The two movements, identification and alienation, are both present here; I speculate that each is an essential element, linked with the evocation of some frightening evil, of true phthonic laughter.

The element of identification is less obvious than the alienation, but it is also necessary. G. Legman writes, "War veterans seem to be a particular target of this type of callous humor, the implication being: 'I'm glad it was him and not me!'" (Legman 1975, 540). He also speculates that if the Nazis responsible for the death chambers did not laugh, as people sometimes do at the news of a death, it was perhaps because "they didn't identify strongly enough with the subhuman Jews, and Poles, and Gipsies, of whom they were thus 'cleansing . . . the racial blood'" (p. 10).

I can now add one more layer of understanding to my previous analysis of what is wrong with laughing at a rape joke. It is not merely that it evinces its origins in sexist attitudes. It also involves the presence of a characteristic mix of phthonic fear, identification, and alienation. This combination makes it wrong to laugh, because it in effect involves another important variety of emotional self-deception. The identification is hidden by a false front of alienation, or the layer of alienation is hidden—usually all too thinly—by a second false front of identification or sympathy. For in the laughter of put-down or ridicule, the identification is part and parcel of the motivating conditions; but the aim of the joke is alienation, and it therefore constitutes a kind of denial of axiological reality. Since laughter is also generally pleasant, its wrongness in these cases characteristically adds another level of ambivalence: what is axiologically inappropriate may, from a psychological point of view, play a role in protecting the self and thus be strategically rational.

An Axiological Perspective on Laughter

So far I have argued that the Walberg view could not be giving us the right account of phthonic mirth (though it might be right for wit). For such mirth, far from abandoning emotion, presupposes a very definite emotional engagement. One way for mirth to be wrong is for that engagement to be morally wrong. I also speculated that certain forms of laughter may be wrong in a more purely axiological sense because they represent an act of harmful alienation, founded on a distortion or denial of an underlying identification. These two conclusions converge: the "unethical" in both cases involves a wrong *assessment of reality*. This brings confirmation of the parallels I have been urging between the appropriateness conditions of emotions and the truth of beliefs. The ethics of belief form not merely a remote parallel but an actual *congeneric* of the ethics of laughter. Like belief, laughter is wrong when it is grounded in the deception of self or others. This is what is entailed by viewing mirth as coming within the axiological domain. It allows us to amplify the title question of this chapter: *When is laughter good or bad for the adequacy of our attitudes to the objective world?*

On the question so formulated, Bergson suggested a third line of attack. He defined the difference between comedy and tragedy in terms of tragedy's commitment to the *particular* in contrast to comedy's interest in general *types*. According to him, comedy is "the only one of the arts that aims at the general" (1940, 114). But "the highest ambition of art is to reveal to us 'nature itself'" (p. 119), which is incompatible with the aims of practical living, because "to live is to accept from objects only those impressions that are *useful*, so that we can respond in appropriate ways" (p. 115). In sum, then, comedy is midway between the utilitarian perception of everyday life and the essential perception of the world in itself—which only higher art can claim to give us. In these terms, the cognitive defect of laughter again lies in the distortion and obfuscation of the world it purports to reveal. But Bergson's special reason for this now is that mirth necessarily invokes generalities and stereotypes. The thesis has some plausibility even from the point of view of consequentialist ethics: for if others are screened from our attention by generalities, we are less likely to treat them in ways that are adequate to what I have called their *individual nature*. More generally, insofar as it is a cognitive virtue to apprehend the world as clearly as possible, mirth must impede us in the exercise of that virtue.

Bergson's view would add plausibility to my contention in chapter 4, that the capacity for singular reference and attachment to particulars is a mark of the higher human difference. (Strictly speaking, though, Bergson fails to mark the distinction between the *specific* and the *particular*. He claims that the art of tragedy reveals the particular, but there is no argument to show that it would be any different if it were merely specific.) His thesis is also consonant with the idea that the norms applicable to an individual may stem not merely from social convention but from the individual's own particular nature. For Bergson is urging us here to pay attention to the particularity of those we encounter, as well as of the situations of life. And it would seem churlish to turn away from particular individuals to pay attention only to stereotypes.

But tempting as it is, Bergson's proposal must be rejected. It rests on two unwarranted assumptions. One is that by eliminating stereotypes and simplifications, we can have direct access to a correct vision of reality and its singular contents. The second is that simplification acts by cutting out or concealing parts of reality. The idea is that true reality—as opposed to utilitarian representations of reality—is captured by a direct intuition. If this is to involve art, it must make no use of categories and stereotypes.

This view is not credible. To be sure, the significant patterns that we find in reality often owe their significance to practical concerns. But the idea of a reality devoid of salient patterns, perceived through art, is a delusion. Simplification can be effective in drawing our attention to a pattern without, for all that, concealing or obscuring the background. But now we see it *as* background, and we therefore see the whole as differently organized. Insofar as the general types of comedy do this for us, they take us closer to reality, not farther away.

Moreover, simplification can be a means to knowledge even when it does proceed by exclusion of some elements of reality. That, as I have argued, is precisely what is true of perception, which in any given mode is only sensible of a more or less fixed range of properties. This informational encapsulation of perception, I have suggested, is temporarily emulated by emotion. It is also the normal procedure of science, which standardly considers certain features in isolation in order to understand them better.[3] If Bergson is right about the comic, then there is a good parallel between the manner in which laughter reveals axiological reality and the manner in which perception and science reveal truth. Both proceed by first isolating patterns, sometimes exaggerating detail; both shift attention away from the background to bring something else into salience. To be sure, elements isolated by science need to be reintegrated into their context for the resulting pattern to prove adequate to reality. And it is just the same with laughter: a partial view may be required for certain patterns to become salient, but a partial view becomes a distortion when we rest content with it.

So laughter can never be wrong merely because it simplifies. It would only be wrong—in the sense of untrue to reality—if one were to remain content to laugh at a single joke forever. Luckily, insofar as there is truth in the traditional theory of laughter as a response to incongruity (see Morreall 1983a), human laughter seems naturally protected against that potential sin. For incongruity requires both familiarity and surprise. As an avenue to knowledge, laughter therefore has the advantage of always seeking fresh perspectives. One can be frozen in pomposity, but only angels can be frozen in laughter.

Frivolity and Utopia

One final line on the question of the incompatibility of mirth with other emotions must be considered. Given our limited capacity for attention, humor may distract us from more serious things. The charge of frivolity is often leveled against those who laugh too much, who have too much fun to attend to the important business of life. But the problem here is one of authority: whom shall we trust to decree the criteria according to which some things (the serious ones) are more important than others (the frivolous ones)? To the enemies of frivolity, it seems more important to spend time in useful pursuits. A champion of the aesthetic will take a different stand. She may say, like Baudelaire, that "To be a useful man has always seemed to me a truly hideous thing" (Baudelaire 1954, 1209) or deplore with Oscar Wilde the "many young men who start out with a beautiful profile, and end up adopting a useful profession" (Wilde 1894, 419). Both, however, too quickly accept the equation of the serious with the useful. If we place mirth in competition with the other things to which it is more appropriately compared—serious but useless things like love, art, philosophy, or religious meditation—who is to say that laughing is not intrinsically more important? Certainly, if we are to believe Norman Cousin's account of his successful therapeutic program of laughter, it's better for one's health (Cousins 1979). But this should not count as relevant, since we have agreed that the axiological model of the ethics of laughter is inhospitable to considerations of consequences. The issue is rather about how one ought to live—about the relative place of laughter in an ideal human life. Like any valuable state or activity, frivolity can become a vice, and some people do seem to use mirth less for its virtues of revelation than for its power to distract and conceal.

The general issue of the place of emotions in human life will be taken up in earnest in chapter 12. But the claim of frivolity as both virtue and vice, in competition with other virtues and vices, highlights some of the difficulties of the topic. Take Oscar Wilde, for example, as an ideal type—a kind of Saint of Frivolity. There is a clear sense in which the world would be impoverished but for his existence. Like happiness itself, such a man is to be prized, which, as Aristotle pointed out, places him above praise (*Nicomachean Ethics*, I.12). Yet just as obviously his way of life is not universalizable, in the sense that we could not sensibly wish everyone to be like him. Like any other form of sainthood, the sainthood of frivolity comes only at the price of immense sacrifices of other prized and valuable human virtues (see Wolf 1982). Here, it seems, axiological reality mirrors the fundamental fact of biological diversity: nothing would be more abnormal, in nature, than for every member of some class to conform to the average norm. In another, strictly logical sense, though, we might indeed universalize Oscar Wilde as a type, if there is reason to think that his character expresses his *individual* normality. Although no one will be found to be quite like him, if there were another just like him in history and genetics, then he too should embody the sainthood of frivolity.

To envisage this possibility is not to pretend that we have any access to what that individual normality might consist in. We have no way of constructing that, except by a kind of extrapolation: from the reality of a man who says he put his talent into his work and his genius into his life, to the character whose role he played in playing himself. Of that character, it is difficult to imagine that he might slip out of character—since the character is precisely what he and we have constructed. But what does this mean? Does it preclude the possibility that if you took him aside and said, "Come, Oscar, let's be serious now," you could have a serious talk with him? Could he, in what brief intervals of leisure the job of dandy left him, write up mathematical and logical discoveries like Lewis Carroll? Or could we imagine him changing, not into the somewhat sentimental seriousness of *De Profundis*, but, say, into another Gerard Manley Hopkins?

My own intuitions dictate a negative answer to these questions. The ground of this intuition is that any total commitment to a definite character precludes other human possibilities. On the other hand, the absence of a commitment to a specific character also precludes other possibilities. This dilemma, which I explore further in chapter

12, is related to a social analogue involving the notion of *utopia*. Utopian types are nothing if not wholehearted: in both individual and social forms, that is their virtue and their vice. Once we have accepted Wilde's own assessment of himself as a character, we place him in rather the same category in relation to his individual standards of normality as a utopia places a whole social group. Perhaps utopias are actually fantasies that have been made to face forward instead of backward—fantasies reflecting, in their purity, particularly intransigent paradigm scenarios. The saint of frivolity, like any utopia, is a self-defeating notion. For the point of a utopia is that it should leave nothing to be desired. And that, like the fixity of angelic laughter, is a consummation devoutly to be shunned.

Chapter 12

Emotion and the Conduct of Life

He who binds to himself a joy
Does the winged life destroy.
He who kisses a joy as it flies
Lives in Eternity's sunrise.
William Blake

Death is the mother of beauty . . .
Wallace Stevens

Summary

The doctrine that emotions apprehend an axiological level of reality suggests that they should be taken seriously in ethical contexts. But their role will be as far removed from that prescribed for them by emotivism as it is from that to which they are relegated by the Kantian traducement.

Some recent rehabilitations of emotions follow Hume in parceling out a privileged class of ethically relevant emotions—altruistic emotions, directed specifically at the morally relevant traits of their targets—from changeable moods or impulses and "personal feelings" aimed at supposedly nonmoral traits.

But the principles traditionally used to enforce the dichotomy actually support a policy of more inclusive admission into the class of morally relevant emotions. One principle of distinction is based on whether an emotion can generate morally approved motives. Here I argue that self-related emotions and desires have as great a claim as objective altruistic ones to be included in the privileged class. Universalizability has also been used to keep certain ranges of emotions out of the moral preserve. But its use is really only diagnostic, as a test of commitment to minimal consistency. It keeps out moods and purely projective emotions but easily lets in both objective emotions and self-related ones.

Another consideration in favor of a more inclusive policy stems from the fact that many of our paradigm scenarios set the stage for interpersonal relations based on trust. These, in turn, are the basis of many morally significant human relations, beyond the reputedly "natural" sentiment of benevolence.

Even subjective emotions might have indirect moral relevance, as experiences, though they can make no claim to apprehend axiological properties. If a class distinction is to be made among emotions, it could only be grounded in the contrast between objective and projective emotions.

These considerations support an expansion of the ethical sphere beyond the domain of obligation, duty, and the dichotomy of right and wrong. But the ethical sphere does not englobe absolutely everything: some emotions that, like prejudices of race, class, or sex, fail to recognize themselves as projective seem to be unredeemably nasty by-products of evolution and development.

Unlike deontological moralities, an expanded ethical sphere based on the axiological perspective allows for a plurality of values. But that perspective does not claim that emotions simply apprehend the world as they find it. A crucial role must be granted to bootstrapping—the invention and creation of value.

To define the limits on that freedom to create value calls for a concept of "authenticity"—which is difficult to pin down. Some conditions for it can be given in terms of an emotion's origins: the aim of an authentic emotion must not be an "ulterior purpose"; nor can its expression be a mere ritual. Given the social origins of emotions, however, not all taint of ritual can be excluded. For paradigm scenarios are, in a sense, the defining rituals of emotion.

For that and other reasons our emotional life is pervaded with ambivalence, at various levels. When it is due to intrinsic conflicts of value, that ambivalence can be dispelled neither by alternation within a life nor by a redistribution of values over many lives. At the deepest level, ambivalence has its roots in some basic tragedies of life. These are ontological structures inherent in the human condition, in which a necessary condition for the possibility of certain goods—meaningful experience, individual freedom, and the objective apprehension of value—undermines those goods themselves. The clearest paradigm is death, which deprives us of a life that would be meaningless but for the prospect of death.

It is time to ask more generally how the possibility of rational and objective emotions bears on the ethical conduct of life. I can do little more, in the span of this concluding chapter, than to wave in the direction of some lines of inquiry. I make no attempt to produce a systematic treatment of ethics: I want only to note some consequences of the argument I have advanced in this book.

Let me put these consequences baldly before elaborating on them. This will also serve as a recapituation of some important themes.

1. I have pushed the analogy between the more "objective" emotions and perception. Emotions, I have claimed, apprehend the axiological level of reality. If that is right, then emotions can claim a crucial role in ethics; but that role will be radically opposed to that in which they are cast by the metaethical theory known as *emotivism*.

2. The way that emotions are important to ethics results in an *enlargement of the ethical sphere:* a more inclusive line around moral concerns. A much larger range of emotions is directly relevant to ethics than has been previously assumed.

3. I have argued that emotions are rooted in paradigm scenarios resulting from complex individual and social factors and that axiological correctness must be defined in terms of those paradigm scenarios. Therefore, the canons of normality according to which we must assess the rationality of emotions are ultimately *individual.* In part, moreover, our individual natures are made by judicious bootstrapping as well as formed by nature and environment. This doctrine must not be interpreted in the existentialist manner, as placing the origins of value wholly in authentic individual choice. But we do need a concept of *authenticity*—something not unrelated to Elster's concept of autonomy.

4. Rightly understood, that concept will undermine both the objectivist and the subjectivist answers to the *Euthyphro* question. The reason for this is that the *Euthyphro* question actually points to a deep conflict at the heart of any reflective ethics. It is one example of the fact that the axiological world that our emotions reveal is an objectively ambivalent one.

Ethics and the Avoidance of Emotion

Even in Utopia there must be desire. Perhaps that is why most utopias in literature are really anti-utopias: since the utopia is perfect, anything left to be desired represents a deviation from perfection, and any such deviation must bring loss. With philosophical utopias things are not very different. Philosophical utopias are called *morality,* and for the many centuries since moralities began to be invented they have sought to shelter themselves against the dual threat of relativism and contingency.* In the Kingdom of Ends, as in aristocratic Boston, there is no room for aspiration. ("Why travel? I'm already here.")

---

*Is it absurd to suppose that moralities were invented? In my sense, it is not. Any culture, or course, must embody a way of life, including sanctioned prohibitions and injunctions. But a morality is a philosophy; a way of life is not.

The emotions are not favored in this quest for absoluteness and necessity, with their contingency on the body, individual history, and social context. Yet for precisely that reason, when twentieth-century philosophers despaired of building for morality an ironclad shelter, they turned to a metaethics founded on the emotions. Emotivism in ethics is metaethical masochism: since we have no defense against subjectivity in ethics, says the emotivist, we will embrace subjectivism.

Emotivism

Emotivism began by giving up on the attempt to assign cognitive content to putative statements of morality. Moral utterances were viewed not as real assertions, linked by genuine semantics to the real world, but as actually serving only a pragmatic function. That pragmatic function varied from one version of the doctrine to another. Roughly, the options were to *express* emotion or to attempt to *induce* it (as in the "lovers' arguments" discussed in chapter 9).

Emotivism poses as a theory of the foundations of ethics: it claims that ethical judgments rest on emotions. But thoroughgoing emotivism takes neither ethics nor emotions seriously. That is its first major defect. Not to take ethics seriously, in the sense just explained, is precisely the point of the doctrine. To see why it does not take emotions seriously either, remember what was wrong with Protagorean subjectivism: since it precluded *correction* in the light of public criteria, it forfeited all claims to *correctness*. If the point of emotivism is indeed to acknowledge defeat in the search for objective ethical criteria, it must assume that there are no such criteria of correctness for emotions themselves. That, in the light of the arguments I have put forward in this book, is not to take emotions seriously. It means rejecting a whole range of discourse about the emotions, discourse in which they are assessed, not strategically as more or less pleasant states of consciousness, but axiologically as apprehensions of reality. Emotivism must reject that range of discourse, lest emotions cease to be foundational; otherwise, emotions will themselves be open to criticism from points of view the moral relevance of which cannot be excluded a priori. On pain of losing its point, emotivism must view emotions as raw facts, impervious to evaluation.

Yet on my own view, it might be objected, emotions form the basis of a system of evaluation in terms of which they can themselves be criticized. For they are axiological assessments, and if they are in turn assessed axiologically, then is there not here a vicious circularity? Not unless emotions are charged with providing the *only* ground for justification of the values in terms of which they will later be judged.

That circle would be too small for comfort. But that does not have to be the case. Emotions can take other emotions as their targets: on this much my view and emotivism agree. The difference is that for emotivism, the existence of a given set of emotions is all that is needed (even when their target is another emotion) and all there could be to settle an ethical question. On my view, it is only the beginning of an indefinite quest.

The second defect of emotivism stems from the distinguishing feature of attitudes that proved crucial to the evaluation of phthonic laughter. Since one can hypothetically adopt a belief but cannot hypothetically adopt an attitude or emotion, it follows that we cannot *conditionalize* our emotions as we conditionalize moral statements. We can utter a conditional statement having an ethical proposition as its antecedent, without being committed to that proposition: "*If* it is morally wrong to invest in South Africa, *then* it should be forbidden by law." But expressions of emotion cannot function this way, as we can see if we attempt to replace the antecedent in that conditional with an expression of emotion. We could try this: "If *Damn South African investments!* then they should be forbidden." But what is the import of that? Either the emotion is expressed in the antecedent, or it is not. If not, then the meaning of the putative moral judgment cannot, after all, consist in expression of emotion. But if it is, then, since the conditional endorses its own antecedent, the consequent simply follows without more ado. There is no conditional here at all (see Williams 1973a, and chapter 6). In sum, the second fatal defect of emotivism is that it would make nonsense of the conditionalization of ethical statements.

Are Some Emotions More Moral Than Others?

So emotivism cannot be the right metaethical theory. Nevertheless, although the power of the Kantian tradition has obscured this fact, the emotions do play a crucial role in the ethical conduct of life.[1] This was obvious to Aristotle, for whom moral education consisted essentially in the education of the emotions (see *Nicomachean Ethics*, II.2, X.9). Some emotions also play a crucial role in Hume's conception of morality, where they are valued for three reasons: because they are intrinsically agreeable; because emotions like sympathy and benevolence are useful in motivating members of a society to treat each other well; and because those emotions serve to inspire relevant moral judgments in observers.[2] But for Hume, unlike Aristotle, the genial advocacy of pleasant and useful sentiment grows out of a deep epistemological pessimism. The role played by emotion in ethics is comparable to that played by our natural propensity to belief in epistemic contexts: given the impossibility of justifying any rational opinion, we should simply allow ourselves to be swept up by our native instincts (see Winters 1981). We must be content with that, since we can hope for nothing better; but this holds out little hope for clear standards of rationality.

In any case, it is not every emotion that receives Hume's approval, but only those in a privileged class of *moral sentiments*. It is easy to see why the motives induced by emotions in general should be thought morally suspect. The actions they induce are likely to lack impartiality and to place morally irrelevant considerations over morally important ones. Notably, the classic vices or deadly sins of the Christian tradition typically involve emotions standing in the way of the exercise of virtue. Lust, and perhaps Envy, disregard others as ends in themselves and treat them as means; Pride, Avarice, Anger, and Gluttony all tend to make us neglect the impartial demands of justice; Sloth and Despair dissuade us altogether from taking ethical questions seriously. Conversely, Prudence, Fortitude, and Temperance— three of the four cardinal virtues—enjoin not so much the performance of any particular class of acts as resistance to certain emotions (see Wallace 1978). Only emotions that can be identified with virtues—sympathy, generosity, compassion—are to be ranked in the privileged class.

But if indeed there is a dichotomy between good and bad emotions, how is the cut to be made? Four principles of distinction suggest themselves.

The first is *motivational*. Some emotions seem likely to motivate moral behavior, and some do not. On the Kantian view, the former class is empty: the range of potentially motivating moral emotions shrinks to literally nothing, since a pure motive of duty must be above any suspicion of having been determined by inclination. A less stringent application of the principle, to be examined shortly, has been defended by Larry Blum. It is based on a contrast between "altruistic" emotions and other emotional phenomena such as changeable moods and "personal feelings" (Blum 1980).

The second principle is a *logical* one, which also draws inspiration from Kant. Here the picture is something like this: in order for a state to be morally significant, it must be universalizable. But that means it must be made of the right logical stuff. Emotions lack the logical backbone required for the rigors of universalization, much as a mollusk cannot be expected to run. That claim too could be weakened to embrace only some emotions, as we shall see in a moment.

The principle of universalizability applies strictly to maxims of behavior ("Could I will the maxim of my act to become a universal law of nature?") and derivatively to states, viewed as motives for some type of act ("Could I will the motive under which I act to affect anyone in my situation?"). A third principle of distinction, though closely related to universalizability, focuses instead on different *types of ethical requirements*. The effectiveness of different emotions in ensuring that those requirements are met can then be used to sort moral from nonmoral emotions. Here are three examples of traditional distinctions in this vein: between justice and benevolence; between strict duty and supererogation; and between conventional morality and natural inclinations. Because the emotions are commonly assumed to be natural, they are thought to belong with the second members of these pairs, having little to contribute to the more conventional side of morality.

Fourth, one does not have to be a dogmatic utilitarian, nor wish to reduce all value to desire, to insist that much of life's worth derives from the quality of experience—including emotions. Viewed as *experiences*, emotions might be classified according to whether they are sufficiently important to be accounted morally significant. But by what measure of importance?

The Motivational Principle: Three Kinds of Emotion
For emotions to be taken seriously in an ethical context, their power to motivate behavior must be grounded in reality. But on traditional views of ethics, which draw a sharp line between moral value and other kinds of value, being grounded in reality is only one necessary condition. A second necessary condition is that the reality in which they are grounded be of a suitable kind. Larry Blum has argued that *altruistic emotions* form a privileged subclass that satisfies both of these conditions. Altruistic emotions contrast with two other categories of emotion: *moods* and *personal feelings*.

The contrast with moods brings out the fact that altruistic emotions are objective, as opposed to projective. If I am moved to react to something merely by a subjective mood, that impulse can claim roots in no reality outside myself: "Altruistic feelings and emotions . . . involve an appreciation of another person's situation. . . . By contrast . . . moods . . . do not . . ." (Blum 1980, 16). Moods and impulses fail the first condition.

The second contrast is intended to show that altruistic emotions fulfil the second necessary condition, focusing on a privileged class of motivating aspects: "Altruistic feelings are directed towards other people in light of or in regard to their weal and woe; whereas personal feelings are directed towards others in light of their personal features" (p. 24). Personal features include qualities that are prized without being specifically moral, such as "sense of humor, vitality, integrity," which we value rather as we value aesthetic qualities. They also include qualities of attachment generated by the accidents of a common history. Both can have the same target in some particular friend, but they differ in their motivating aspect and their aim.

To mark the contrast between altruistic and other emotions in terms of "weal and woe" implies that we already know the difference between morally relevant values and other kinds of value. And the sample list of those other values should give us pause. "Wit" is standardly suspected of being frivolous; so it is not surprising to find it excluded from the privileged class of ethically relevant focal properties. But this, as I argued in chapter 11, begs the question of whether wit is among the intrinsically valuable ends of life. If it is, then wit, together with other "personal features," far from being excluded from ethical value, must be counted among its foundations. Even more obviously, why is "integrity" not an ethical value? Perhaps because it has to do only with the personal virtue of a single subject, not necessarily with her relations to others. But one should not take for granted that morality concerns only relations with others.

Blum's distinctions seem to fit the threefold distinction drawn in chapter 7: moods are subjective, altruistic feelings are objective, and personal feelings belong to an intermediate class of self-related emotions. I can agree that subjective emotions must be excluded from the privileged class. For the following reasons, however, the case against the self-related ones is not so clear.

Outside of a particular moral theory, there is no single core idea that captures what is meant by the ethical. There are at least two competing core ideas: one is the idea of what we *ought* to do; the other is the idea of human *thriving*. Each idea, of course, quickly subsumes the other.* At the very coarse level of grain, it is probably fair to say that Christian and Kantian ethics are based on the former idea, whereas Aristotelian and utilitarian ethics are based on the latter. My own plea for an expansion of the ethical belongs in the second camp.

---

*There is a certain formal similarity between the symmetrical claims of obligation and of thriving as core ideas of morality, and the symmetrical claims of objectivity and rationality as core ideas of epistemology. Each member of the pair claims to give a plausible account of the other in its own terms; no compelling argument exists for the supremacy of one perspective over the other; no plausible superordinate point of view holds out promise for such an argument; and, as a consequence, allegiance to one or the other of the contrasting views gives rise to the deepest divisions in philosophy— those we might call "temperamental" ones. Arguments between the partisans of opposing core ideas are philosophy's own lovers' arguments.

And the intuition that underlies this plea is that without some content to the notion of what it is for a human being to thrive, there is no point in working out how to distribute fairly any benefit but the minimal ones necessary for survival. If we do accept thriving as central to ethics, we must give pride of place to self-related as well as to objective desires.[3]

A second reason for admitting self-related desires into the privileged class relates to their role in our most important relations with others: our relations of love and friendship (see Badhwar 1986). As we have seen, love is apt to follow its target through changes, though not through just any changes. Love takes a singular target, though it may arise as a response to specific focal properties that the target may lose. As Amélie Rorty has argued, the historicity of those attitudes involves "dynamic permeability": as your projects change, and as you come to prize different aspects of your life, so what I prize in you will change—at least up to a point, which can vary with the degree of my disinterestedness (and the flakiness of your self-definition). In turn, the changes in each of our individual self-related desires—the changing face of those passions that give meaning to our lives—may well be influenced by the connection between us (Rorty 1986). This is a two-person version of something that arises for a single subject as well: the value of what I prize partly relates to my projects, my individual life and character, and my unique history of experience and opportunity (see Wolff 1976). These things then derive a kind of indirect objective value from the fact that my individual pursuits are among the factors that shape the individual nature in terms of which my thriving must be understood. And although it is always risky to venture opinions about what someone's individual nature requires, some things about it are sometimes beyond doubt. Most of us know people of whom it is obvious that the course of their lives, which might have been satisfying to another person or at another time, has deeply frustrated their individual temperament.

Universalizability
One ground on which the claims of personal relations, as well as self-related desires, have been ruled to be nonmoral by Kantian morality is that they lack the required impartiality. The claim is that emotions are intrinsically beyond the pale of rationality because they lack the right structure to be universalizable.

At one level this charge relates to the alleged inconstancy of emotion. Emotions are intrinsically changeable and therefore unreliable. (Note how reminiscent this is of Plato's reason for rejecting the senses' claim to yield knowledge. This is not a good augury for the present objection to the parallel claim of emotions.) On this, Larry Blum comments as follows:

> . . . changeableness and capriciousness are not so much a characteristic of all altruistic emotions as they are of weak, superficial or otherwise inadequate instances of them. . . . The form of moral assessment and criticism in all of these cases presupposes that there are appropriate emotion-based responses, which the agents in question [whose emotional responses are inconstant or weak] fail to give. (Blum 1980, 38)

This is surely right, but why limit it to the altruistic emotions? Much the same might be said of all emotions admitting formal objects, including self-related ones, or merely personal feelings—though not of moods, which lack objects of any kind. If constancy is felt to be a moral requirement on personal feelings—and in our prevalent ideology of love it notoriously has been—then it is as much a failing in a personal feeling as in an altruistic one to be capricious and unstable, and as little to be held against the category of personal feelings as such.

We do place on personal feelings requirements that they seldom meet. And to some extent this may be the result as well as the cause of a psychological misunderstanding. "But you promised to love me forever!" is the refrain of lovers' arguments about love, and it is emblematic of the poignant combination of irrationality and subjective plausibility that such arguments exhibit. But the demands we place on personal feelings might spring from more respectable sources. One is the possibility of legitimate bootstrapping. Here as elsewhere, the delusions that we cultivate may to some extent foster their own success. Sometimes we may indeed feel or continue to feel something because in the face of the sheer power of social expectation it has never occurred to us to doubt it. (Religious faith, many marriages, and some drug experiences are sometimes like that.)

Talk of constancy, however, misses the main point of universalizability. Universalizability is a *logical* requirement of which constancy, merely contingent duration, can at best be only a symptom. From this point of view, the way to make sense of universalizability as a criterion of moral relevance might be something like this:

Altruistic emotions are preeminently responses to facts about the needs and states of others. They are rooted in the reality of other people's experiences—their "weal and woe"—in a way that mere moods and impulses are not. So, naturally, they are subject to requirements of consistency and repeatability that are borrowed from truth. Although talk of "many truths" is often a useful metaphor, it is no more than that: because there is only one *real* world, no conjunction of beliefs can possibly be correct unless all its members might be true together. But because there can be many *possible* worlds, there can be many correct desires, not all of which might be realized together.

In this perspective, the requirement of universalizability looks less contentious, but also rather less interesting. Instead of being concerned with the constancy (or the inconstancy) of emotions, it can be reduced to a mere requirement of logic. And logical requirements have, in a sense, no content, although they are not trivial. They tell us how the world might be by constraining our descriptions. Here the logical requirement of universalizability works as a sort of automatic diagnostic tool, to sort our emotions into those that profess to be objective axiological responses, on the one hand, and merely subjective ones, like moods, on the other. Emotions of the latter class make no claim to objectivity, though sometimes they can actually create value, rather as losing your wallet endows the relief of finding it with disproportionately large and gratuitous value.[4]

According to this *diagnostic use of consistency,* the decisive question is not about constancy. It is whether one is committed to the second-order desire that the first-order emotion recur under relevantly similar conditions. If it does, that marks you as recognizing the possibility of "relevantly similar conditions." And that is all there is to the claim of universalizability: only those emotions are *subjective,* in addition to being *agent-relative,* which do not acknowledge the claim of consistency.* Those implicitly posit themselves as pure creators of value. As such they are committed to a strong form of subjectivity: by the diagnostic tool mentioned above, these are the only emotions that are not subject even to the trivial requirement of universalizability. Moods fit this pattern, but among emotions that have objects only infatuation does so too. In my moods and infatuations, I aspire neither to constancy nor to consistency.

What I have just said might seem open to an immediate objection. Infatuation is not objective; but what if, in my infatuation, I claim that my feelings are universalizable in at least my weak diagnostic

---

*This form of universalizability is normally equivalent to the claim of *supervenience* of the formal object of emotions on other real properties. Jerrold Levinson makes the point as follows with regard to aesthetic properties: "Two objects (e.g. artworks) that differ *aesthetically* necessarily differ non-aesthetically . . ." (Levinson 1983, 93). But in some cases, such as the "Twin-Earth" cases used by Hilary Putnam (1975) and Tyler Burge (1979) to argue against the supervenience of mental on physiological states, the first-person commitment to consistency may still hold although supervenience does not.

sense? That, surely, is an all too familiar possibility. In that case, since I accept the diagnostic test, must my infatuation not be labeled objective after all?

No. To accept a test is not necessarily to pass it. To be sure, in accepting diagnostic universalizability, I am agreeing that my emotion is supposed to apply to the real world. But that secures only categorial, not evaluative, rationality. Infatuation is irrational, almost by definition; what I have escaped by accepting diagnostic universalizability is merely the charge that my feeling belongs to that class of those that cannot be irrational. Infatuation is indeed capricious because it is projective: it covaries mainly with the subject, not with the target. In that way, although it has an ostensible target, it is more like a mood than an emotion. Its irrationality is guaranteed by the fact that it fails the test of covariance. Or, more exactly, the appropriate test would be an analogue of covariance that allows for dynamic penetrability in Rorty's sense—a kind of mutual bootstrapping. Simple covariance will not do, since it is most easily understood in terms of a single direction of matching—from world to mind—and so has no room for any element of bootstrapping.

Emotions Implicit in Personal Relations
We might caricature much moral philosophy ever since Plato as an attempt to find a selfish motive for altruistic behavior. In Hume's scheme, the chief moral sentiments are benevolence (the spontaneous inclination to promote another's good) and sympathy (imaginatively experiencing another's emotion). These are often thought of as *natural* sentiments, which incline us to virtues of supererogation rather than of duty. Sometimes they are assumed to exhaust the range of morally relevant feelings, whereas something else altogether is required to prompt us to the exercise of conventional virtues such as justice. But this leaves out the possibility that personal and social relations themselves *generate* a vast range of emotions that are more or less directly relevant to central ethical questions as traditionally conceived.

Bernard Harrison has given a good example of the sort of relation I mean. Suppose you are playing a game, which calls for the players to take turns. If the opportunity arises to cheat, someone who cares about the relationship created by the very situation of the game will be reluctant to do so, simply because entering into that relation implies as a condition that orderly turns be taken. If it is part of the game that we take turns, my repugnance to cheat (and not merely to be caught cheating) is a token of the sincerity of my continuing commitment to play. Moreover, Harrison argues, most of the self-related desires and emotions capable of giving my life interest and meaning require that I actually become engaged in relations calling for mutual trust, and therefore generating other-directed emotions and desires (Harrison 1984; see also Baier 1986). This applies both at the level "containing practices such as turn-taking or promising which lend themselves to essentially game-theoretic modes of description, and [at the] level containing a range of concepts concerned with moral relationship (*friendship, citizenship, common humanity*), which do not" (Harrison 1984, 320). Now the psychological origins of these sentiments, grounded on trust, can plausibly be traced back up a developmental path involving the gradual emergence of feelings associated with personal relation, particularly the sense of fairness, through what Lawrence Kohlberg calls the "conventional" stage of moral development.[5] This perhaps accounts for the fact that many people's actual feelings of repugnance toward cheating are limited to personal as opposed to institutional relations ("Stealing from Bloomingdale's doesn't really count as stealing!"). The reason for this lacuna in the moral sense of otherwise scrupulous people, I speculate, is simply that their upbringing has not equipped them with paradigm scenarios fostering any emotional attitudes to commercial institutions as such. (To check this out, I suggest testing the following hypothesis: those who at an early age were denizens of boarding school will feel differently about shoplifting even if they do it about as often as other adults.)

A vast array of very specific emotions concerned with personal relations may have their origins in certain kinds of social conventions and in the paradigm scenarios associated with participating in such conventions. Apart from trust and its cognates—the reluctance to cheat, the feeling of being betrayed, loyalty—we might also want to include diffidence, pride in the achievements of one's friends, and also "negative" emotions like envy, jealousy, shame, and resentment. All of these should figure in an expanded list of ethically relevant emotions.

There are two interesting corollaries of this inclusive ethical perspective. First, we should expect a certain de facto cultural relativism not just of moral *conventions* but of moral *feelings:* for some feelings have their roots in conventions. But such a measure of ethical relativism does not commit us to giving up the ethical realism that has been implicit in my claims for axiology. For that realism tells us precisely that moral feelings *will* depend crucially on the paradigm scenarios in which they are rooted. Second, such moral realism continues to be compatible with the finer grain of what I have called individual natures. Subject only to the requirements of diagnostic universalizability, the fact that a person claimed an idiosyncratic set of moral perceptions would be no argument against moral and axiological realism. Nor would it imply that either the individual or the community must be morally wrong in their perception.

Emotions as Intrinsically Valuable Experiences
So far, I have been considering whether emotions are able to play a key role in ethics from the point of view of their role in motivation, their susceptibility to universalization, and their respective roles in virtues of sociality. The intrinsic value of emotions, their fourth dimension of potential relevance, needs little comment. That (some) emotions have intrinsic value is not controversial. It follows that even moods and infatuations might have their place in the good life; but this is not to specify just what their role might be. One possibility is that even pure moods and impulses making no pretense at universalizability can contribute to life's value. Or at least they can do so just so long as they stake no claim to objectivity. As Thomas Nagel has remarked, "the more subjective the object of the desire, the more impersonal the value of its satisfaction" (Nagel 1986, 170): for nothing else enters into its evaluation than the satisfaction itself. On the other hand, when a subjective desire acknowledges the test of consistency, it offers itself up for assessment according to different criteria and may then become viciously projective.

The Expansion of the Ethical

I have been urging that we should cease to stress the issue of whether emotions are constant or reliable, or the contrast of "altruistic" versus "personal" emotions. Instead, we should ask, Which emotions are *projective* and which ones are *objective* or *perceptual?* For that excessively general question, we may substitute more specific ones:

1. What is the position of a particular emotion on the *continuum of subjectivity and objectivity?*
2. How does the dimension of *choice* apply to that emotion?
3. What does it mean for that emotion to be *authentic?*

I now consider these three questions in turn.

The Subjective-Objective Continuum
Objective, self-related, and subjective desires form a continuum. Our emotions are standardly determined by a complex of internal and external factors. If I am angry, astonished, or delighted, how much of the determining situation of those states is owed to context, to

individual physiology, and to idiosyncratic history? That this question makes good sense supports a general analogy of emotion and perception, since it can be asked as well of anything that we perceive. In the light of it our most general emotional responsibility turns out to be this: *feel things as they really are.* And that is an injunction, not to ignore the idiosyncratic determinants of our individual Weltanschauung, but on the contrary to take them into account. For our only access to the level of reality that emotions reveal is through the paradigm scenarios that have shaped our world view.

Note that if we accept the possibility of emotional criticism—both on the ground of adequacy and on the ground of consistency—then we must also accept that some particular emotion types may turn out to be ethically worthless. Racist emotions are a clear example. It is a notorious weakness of classical utilitarianism that it allows—indeed demands—that we take some account of every desirable or undesirable quality of conscious states. That appears to entail that the feelings of distress experienced by the racist at "miscegenation," for example, should be weighed against the feelings of those discriminated against. They may be given little weight, and the demands of justice may weigh against them; but if there are enough racists, then it is logically possible that, by aggregation, their feelings should come to outweigh those of their victims. Yet the decent intuition here, surely, is that the feeling of disgust experienced by the racist at the idea of miscegenation is not merely outweighed but is unworthy of any consideration whatever. Racist emotions are unequivocally nasty emotions, redeemed neither by the motives they might induce, nor by any intrinsic pleasure they bring, nor by any contribution they make to correct ethical evaluations. Envy, motiveless malice, certain forms of resentment, and despair are other examples of wholly nasty emotions. (Perhaps, though, no case is quite uncontroversial: Adam Morton once reported that a student offered as one useful function of despair that if you were about to be hanged, it would stop you from useless struggle. On the other hand, why bother to refrain from useless struggle? Presumably this would conserve your strength for later, just in case you got rescued in extremis after all.)

The axiological perspective shows how one might make sense of the idea that some emotions are unredeemably nasty. If emotions are taken simply as more or less pleasant experiences, then it is natural to throw them all onto the scales to be weighed together with everything else. But if they are judged in terms of what they can bring to our apprehension of reality, their worth should be modeled on the epistemic worth of belief: I may sometimes believe something because it is comfortable, but any weight owed to the experience of a belief as comfortable is essentially negligible insofar as I am interested in the way the world is. With some ingenuity a counterexample might be constructed from partly self-referential beliefs shared by a community. Given suitable conditions of social pressure, to feel comfortable believing that most people believe p might tend to indicate that most people do indeed believe p. But in such cases the comfort would function only as a contingent indicator of truth, not as an independent value competing with truth in its own right. Similarly, where an emotion is socially bootstrapped, feeling it may be a sign of its legitimacy, but this fact neither determines nor follows from its intrinsic value as an experience. When emotions are considered axiologically, there is nothing in the racist's discomfort that tells us anything about the objective value at stake in the situation: the racist's sentiment relates only to the racist herself.

Prejudice, by definition, is not merely a disagreeable and harmful state of mind. Unlike a mood—but like an infatuation—it does not claim merely subjective autonomy from the real world and its criteria. On the contrary, prejudice is experienced as having real objects as its targets. But it rejects the responsibility to make a response to any real and individual fact or person. Sometimes this may not seem to be the case, as when a racist evinces a benevolent paternalism toward the "inferior" race. But prejudice as such refuses to take account of the reality that underlies the putative general facts: "You are a Jew— or a woman or black—and that is all I need to know."

But why, if the nasty emotions are really that nasty, do we ever have them? In spite of my admonitions in chapter 4 against an excessively optimistic adaptationism, that question may still nag. My best answer is this: given the tinkerer's constraints on evolutionary engineering (Jacob 1977), the nasty emotions are the waste-products of paradigm scenarios indispensable to the development of more useful emotions. A capacity for emulation, for example, might be impossible to engineer in beings like us without incurring the risk that envy should develop instead.*

---

*This may be the grain of psychological truth in the Christian method of explaining away the existence of evil: perhaps, in the best of all psychologically possible worlds, there is no freedom without the ability to inflict real suffering—just as there is no emulation without the risk of envy; no enthusiasm without a fanatical bent. Though the model here is a theological one, psychology remains harder than theology—the intellectual's tennis-without-a-net. For actually there is a solution to the theological problem, though not, I shall argue, to the psychological one. Here is how to reconcile God's omnipotence, omniscience, and benevolence with the existence of evil. Free will requires that we believe our choices might be evil. God's benevolence cannot require that it be so in fact. So the right theological view must be this: neither our actions, nor

A major advantage of the axiological perspective is that it predicts the dark symbiosis of virtues and vices as a natural concomitant of the plurality of values. Even if we take seriously the qualitative properties of emotions and find a solid ground on which to sort them into good and bad, any such Manichean dichotomy is bound to remain simplistic. It may be suitable enough for dividing all possible actions into those that are obligatory and those that are not, but it is inadequate to what Bernard Williams has called the "thick" concepts of ethics in its expanded conception. Such concepts as *coward, lie, brutality, gratitude,* Williams has pointed out, are "action guiding," at the same time as "their application is guided by the world" (Williams 1985, 140). But their meaning is exhausted neither by their purely descriptive nor by any purely prescriptive content, nor can it be factored into a component of the one kind and a component of the other. That is why, as Williams elsewhere remarks, "there are few, if any, *highly general* connections between the emotions and moral language" (Williams 1973a, 208). This is no obstacle to a view that stresses only the connection of ethical terms with obligation; but then the vocabulary of obligation comprises concepts that relate to just two contrary (though not contradictory) formal objects: the forbidden and the obligatory. The axiological perspective, by contrast, predicts the facts on which Williams insists; it expands the realm of ethical relevance to encompass all emotions, with their multiplicity of specific nuances, possibly excepting the wholly nasty or the viciously projective.

To illustrate more vividly what I mean by the expansion of the ethical, compare the following two anecdotes:

> Somewhere Saint Paul urges us to live every day as if it were our last: because it might be our last, and we should at each moment be prepared to meet our Maker and answer for our sins.

This is one way that the thought of death concentrates the mind: out of fear. But there is another version:

> A great violinist once went to Pablo Casals, lamenting that he had lost his inspiration. The technique was still there, but the music no longer sang, and he was in despair. Casals' advice was like Saint Paul's, yet very different. "Whenever you take up your instrument," he urged, "play as if you were never to play again."

"acts of God" such as the Lisbon earthquake or the latest airline crash, ever actually cause *real* suffering; but we are forever precluded from finding this out. It follows that God must remain hidden. For if we actually knew that God existed, we would know that evil doesn't, and God's plan would be thwarted.

The first story represents morality in the narrow sense.[6] It threatens the unfortunate faithful with damnation, in order that by being, like Boy Scouts, ever ready for the worst, they should be more likely to obey the commandments. The second story is completely different. It is a plea for the enhancement of life that comes with the idea of its irreplaceability. And the sentiment it invites is not just fear, but joy in what is priceless. It does not say, "Since you will die, look to your obligations," but rather, "Since you will die, relish now doing what you want to be doing, for its specific character and unique place in time." The words of Paul and Casals are almost the same, but they are as different as the ant and the grasshopper: one is about *having fulfilled one's obligations*, which is work, and the other is about *joyous activity*, which is play.[7]

Let me recapitulate the discussion in this chapter so far. The use of universalizability as a diagnostic test makes it possible to draw a contrast between subjective emotions and moods and those that are committed to objectivity. On the objective side I have drawn a further contrast between two conceptions of ethics. Though both acknowledge the commitment to objectivity, one does so only along the narrow lines of the dimension of right and wrong; obligatory, permitted, and forbidden. That is morality in the narrow sense. The other is the axiological, and it carries with it an expansion of the ethical. It too is committed to minimal universalizability. It includes assessments in terms of good and bad but need not regard those as belonging to a single dimension. Its difference lies in the recognition of the multiplicity of distinct formal objects, defining incommensurable dimensions of value.

This picture of the axiological perspective, however, is not complete without taking into account the possibilities of bootstrapping—cases where "feeling makes it so"—explored in previous chapters. Those cases show that the axiological perspective cannot be insulated from the polar opposite of universalizability. At that opposite pole is the *voluntarist* view, which gives the prime role in the genesis of value to individual *choice*.

The Dimension of Choice: The Existentialist Route

Choice is a mysterious business; no less so for the fact that emotions play a crucial role in its determination. There are two loci for the potential application of choice. On the pure voluntarist view, individual emotions are simply chosen. On the alternative for which I have been arguing, emotions frame and determine the range of our possible choices without being directly willed themselves.

The first alternative, once propounded by Robert Solomon, has the exciting attraction of directly rejecting the traditional view of the emotions as passive.[8] Though attractive, however, the view is less than compelling. For the concept of choice begins with the idea that the source or cause of an action must be inside the agent; short of taking recourse to the idea of a noumenal Self, however, one is immediately forced to acknowledge that in a strict sense nothing is ever chosen.

To see this, recall Jon Elster's concept of autonomy. Autonomy was defined in terms of a contrast between "appropriate" and "inappropriate" external influences. The trouble is that the required notion of appropriateness can only be defined if we are willing to commit ourselves to a range of rationally relevant considerations. (That was perhaps the supreme advantage of the Kantian approach: if every kind of consideration is excluded except considerations of duty generated by pure practical reason, then at least we know what will and will not count as appropriate.) But from the existentialist point of view this route is useless. The core of the existentialist position is the uncoupling of choice from rationality: the existentialist wishes precisely to avoid a commitment to reason, seeking instead a notion of purely individual choice.

I have advocated using a commitment to consistency diagnostically, to single out those emotions that purport to be objective. Now the existentialist could say, "According to your diagnostic test, all my emotions are subjective. Fine! What more is there to say?"

If the argument of this book is right, that is not a viable option. I have in effect been arguing that the existentialist view, like its Platonic opposite, is just wrong. The ambiguous connection between choice and emotions should make it clear that it is the very contrast between simple projection and simple apprehension of objective properties that is mistaken. For three reasons, emotions as a class of mental states undermine the dichotomy between the active and the passive. First, the mode of their rationality is neither simply epistemic nor simply strategic. Second, our assumptions about responsibility for our emotions support neither of the simple opposing views. And third, their role as *frames* for other states gives them a determining role in choice, but also makes them too deeply rooted to be simply chosen.

Authenticity

Given that emotions are thus delicately poised between the active and the passive, the most promising concept to fill out the axiological perspective is the hybrid notion of *authenticity*. It is a notion that has often seemed the most appropriate term of ethical assessment in relation to the emotions. Where an emotional ethic holds sway, authenticity is its first injunction. But exactly what it enjoins is not easy to tell. A look at a clear case of inauthenticity may be illuminating.

Mere sincerity is to authenticity what sentimentality is to compassion. The difference seems to lie in the way that each relates to a comprehensive context, including its temporal context. Let us, then, take a closer look at *sentimentality*.

An emotion is mere sentimentality if, in the face of opportunities for action, it reveals itself to have been merely a species of contemplative *self-indulgence*. The term is revealing: for what we have against sentimentality is precisely that it is not adequately covariant with its target: it is a largely projective emotion without a clear component of objectivity of response. The self is indulged under the pretext of attending to the plight of another. In this way I have my cake and eat yours too: I get the credit due to the effort of seeing the world as it is, when in truth I am merely humoring my own projective fantasies. Moreover, as Richard Wollheim has noted, projection usually carries an element of aggression: "The great sentimentalists of fiction, the professional pitiers of Dickens and Dostoevsky, are correctly portrayed as in part the artificers of the sufferings they lament" (Wollheim 1984, 209). Inauthenticity is marked in these cases by the failure to follow the sentiment through with action, but that is merely a symptom. The underlying fault is a failure of adequate correspondence with objective reality.

To see how this is so in any given case, we need to look more closely to the origin of the emotion in its particular context. Oscar Wilde's famous definition of sentimentality—"A sentimentalist is one who desires to have the luxury of an emotion without paying for it"[9]—relates to that issue of context. What Wilde had in mind, I surmise, was the desire to have emotional experiences that are not rooted in the natural context of their normal history. Wilde's stricture, in spite of his aestheticism, contains a surprising dose of Christian masochism: one hears, vibrating not far in the background, the sound of hymns to the notion of redemption by suffering. Only a Platonic puritan could think there is *always* something wrong with desiring to experience an emotion without paying the full price of its natural context. And Plato saw the implication of this, which is to banish art (and why not carousels and water-slides as well?) for fear of promoting false emotions and desires. For at least one component of the need for art is the desire to experience the emotions called forth by death, by sexual thrall, by revenge, or by painful or ridiculous alienation, by evoking the relevant paradigm scenarios without needing to live through the actual events that are their natural causes.

Yet surely there is something insightful in Wilde's formula. The key to his insight, I submit, lies once again in appealing to a failure of axiological fit. The emotions aroused by art need not pose as applying to reality. But, outside of art, an emotion suspended from its natural context is likely to be phony precisely because it pretends to be otherwise. It is viciously projective.

Loss, for example, is the natural locus of sorrow and grief. Sometimes one may have a vicarious experience of grief in genuine sympathy, without having experienced loss directly. There need be nothing inauthentic or sentimental about that; but perhaps that is because sympathy, as Hume thought, is a natural sentiment. By contrast, to grieve for a trivial loss is sentimental, because it is divorced from its natural context of real loss.

Grief is unpleasant. Would one not then be better off without it altogether? Why condone it even when the loss is real? Perhaps we should say of it what Spinoza said of regret: that whoever feels it is "twice unhappy or twice impotent" (*Ethics*, IV.54). Laurence Thomas has suggested that the utility of "negative sentiments" (emotions like grief, guilt, resentment, and anger, which there is prima facie reason to believe we might be better off without) lies in their providing a kind of guarantee of authenticity for such dispositional sentiments as love and respect. No occurrent feelings of love and respect need be present throughout the period in which it is true that one loves or respects. One might therefore sometimes suspect, in the absence of the positive occurrent feelings, that one no longer loves. At such times, negative emotions like grief offer a kind of testimonial to the authenticity of love or respect (see Thomas 1983).*

Thomas's suggestion about the function of negative emotions sounds close to a truth, though it cannot be quite right as it stands. In his version, the value of the negative sentiments rests crucially on their being "visceral," as opposed to the nonvisceral positive senti-

---

*Note that Thomas's negative sentiments do not, with one exception, include those that I have labeled unredeemably nasty. The exception is resentment, about which there might be dispute. Thomas might claim that resentment, like grief, which he takes as his only fully worked out example, functions as a kind of testimonial to some other emotions and in this way serves Hume's third redeeming function, of encouraging sound ethical judgment in observers. Robert Kraut also favors the idea that the question to ask if you wonder whether he loves you is, How long would he mourn if he lost me? (Kraut 1986, 428). With the purely nasty emotions, however, Thomas's proposed explanation would not get very far. The ones he picks are ones I would rather describe as involving one or another grade of ambivalence.

ments of love and respect to which they bear witness. The trouble with this proposal is that the negative emotions themselves are liable to be merely dispositional. So we risk being launched into a regress: what bears witness to the authenticity of the negative emotions themselves? It seems this criterion cannot differentiate authentic from inauthentic love or respect, because it presupposes that the experience of the negative emotions cannot itself be subject to illusion. "In order to apologize," Thomas points out,

> it suffices to utter the words 'I apologize'. And these words can be produced at will; indeed, one can even order a person to apologize. However, none of this is so with feelings of sorrow and the other [negative] sentiments . . . and while there can be inappropriate displays of the sentiments, there can be no such thing as an insincere experiencing of them. . . . A person who feels guilty, though he has no reason to, is not having an insincere experiencing of guilt feelings. (Thomas 1983, 156)

It is true that sorrow cannot be summoned from as shallow a source of will as can a verbal apology. And yet it might be inauthentic without being insincere. Indeed, the claim of sincerity to be a form of authenticity is especially dubious. I am sincere if I say *what I feel now.* But that can be an evasion of a certain responsibility to convey some reliable truth about myself, my convictions, or my feelings. If you are a flake, sincerity will not redeem you. Sometimes sincerity is just a way for Wilde's sentimentalist to be dishonest on the cheap.

The notion of authenticity remains elusive. It seems, after all, that we cannot avoid looking further into the idea of *appropriate origins.* This may be unfortunate. For origins tend to be inscrutable, and criteria based on them, in epistemology and elsewhere, are notoriously doomed to yield only vague and speculative "promissory notes" for genuine explanations. I shall not claim to do more, but in a murky area this much may be better than nothing.

Authenticity and Origins

One natural requirement to place on an emotion's origins is that it should not merely be a *ritual.* For authentic emotion, almost by definition, is an individual response. It may be partly socially determined, but it must be *spontaneous* in the way that a ritual is not.

Yet that is not entirely right. For sometimes a ritual is what gives form and meaning to an emotion. This is what we should expect if the notion of paradigm scenarios is on the right track. Paradigm scenarios are the original rituals that give meaning to our present responses, however private. And where there is no adequate original scenario to fall back on, the adult ritual plays much the same function of defining and framing. This is particularly so, for example, with emotions of loss. Every culture has its mourning rituals, which, among other functions, reassure individuals that the emotion they are feeling is authentic. Mourning rituals do this, not by convincing you that your emotion is simply spontaneous, but by reassuring you that it is real *because* its expression conforms to expectations.

The notion of ritual reintroduces two further dimensions of vital importance. One is the social: an important aspect of the question of appropriate origins concerns the relation of the individual to social norms. The other is the question of the extent to which the values expressed in our attitudes to death—and other facts of life—are objectively valid or merely projective: the *Euthyphro* question again.

Death, the relation of individual to social group, and the threatening subjectivity of value are sources of radical insecurity. This is most incontrovertibly true of our own death; though the terror it inspires is a lot more obvious than why it should be feared at all. Becoming aware of the depth of our social dependency, though not usually so brutal, can also be profoundly unsettling for anyone who wonders, "Who am I?" For how can I ever answer that question without discovering—impossibly—how much of my emotion comes from me and how much is merely soaked-up social ideology? And the anxiety inherent in reflecting on the source of our values comes from realizing that to believe in the absolute validity of our socially determined values would only be self-deception.*

Authenticity and Character
As we shall see, these dilemmas admit of no solution. We can only react to them, with more or less adequate emotional response. Our responses to them, however, are by no means uniform. All are viewed by some people without anguish. Yet they are intelligible dilemmas relating to objective facts about the human condition in general. Our individual reactions to them are among the factors that shape our emotional dispositions. (The rest is not silence but chemical Grace.) And the total pattern of those dispositions, in turn, is part of what we call our character and defines our individual identity.

David Rosenthal (1984) has argued that emotions provide the most promising answer to the traditional problem of personal identity.

---

*That is why the validity of local values, like religion, is what human beings most often kill for. You don't kill people for what you really have no trouble believing. The psychoanalytic interpretation of religious and social fanaticism as a defense against doubt is too compelling to be doubted. (At any rate, *I* wouldn't kill for it.)

They account for the difference between one self and another, which the Cartesian ego cannot do since all its differentiating properties are inessential. Also, because of the complexity of the ways in which our emotions are linked to each other and to our other mental states, they account for what makes us one continuing person as opposed to a succession of person-slices. (See also Wollhéim 1984.) But our emotional dispositions themselves are subject to relations of conflict and of precedence. At what level in the layering of our being, then, does our "real" character appear? This brings us back to one of the questions posed in chapter 1: how to adjudicate jarring intuitions about whether the more spontaneous or the more reflective response best represents the authentic self. I offered no hope then of giving any general answer. Nor am I in a much better position to do so now, near the end of the present intellectual journey. The fragmentation and multiplicity of our emotional determinants shows that to ask for *the* unique certificate of origin that could warrant the authenticity of an emotion is largely futile.

In any case, the question of the *nature* of individual character cannot be entirely separated from the question of the *appraisal* of character by oneself or others. At a simple and somewhat cynical level, this is just to say that we generally try to show ourselves in the best possible light and are influenced by other people's opinions of us. But remember the therapists' dinner game of chapter 1, in which the unsuspecting were provoked to reveal their worst faults by being asked to name their finest virtues. In the light of that experiment, we might discriminate other levels of psychological reality besides self-confirming self-appraisal.

One such level comprises the possibility of *reinterpretation*. Sometimes that is a valid form of bootstrapping. If I see myself in a certain light, that just may make me so. One reason for this is that most dispositions may well be, in themselves, morally neutral. There may be some exceptions, in the form of the absolutely nasty emotions that I argued must be countenanced: if I am right about those, no prospect of reinterpretation can redeem them. From a strictly psychological point of view, however, any emotion that is willing to subject itself to diagnostic universalization, as I have defined it, can be referred to a context in which it is minimally rational. As we bathe it in increasingly capacious contexts, its moral relevance will appear, like an image under the effect of photographic developer. But flip-flops will often be possible, from a favorable to an unfavorable interpretation, as the context is enlarged or changed. That is one form of the phenomenon of ambivalence, the intricacies of which I shall explore further in these last few pages.

Layers of Ambivalence

Ambivalence comes in various grades, from common to paradoxical. The common grade includes innocent cases of opposite dispositions, which find their synthesis in some Aristotelian Golden Mean. As Leila Tov-Ruach has put it, "Most of our basic drives are paired in contraries: the drive to exploration matched with that to withdraw; the cycles of sleep and activity . . . the need for companionship and the need for solitude . . ." (Tov-Ruach 1980, 483). Such "paired contraries" are not paradoxical: they rely on each other for regulatory negative feedback. In their oscillation, they commonly admit of a moderate equilibrium, on the model of J. S. Mill's ideal mixture of "tranquillity and excitement":

> The main constituents of a satisfied life appear to be two, either of which by itself is often found sufficient for the purpose: tranquillity and excitement. . . . There is assuredly no inherent impossibility in enabling even the mass of mankind to unite both, since the two are so far from being incompatible that they are in natural alliance, the prolongation of either being a preparation to, and exciting a wish for, the other. (Mill 1863, 12)

But this reasonable hope for a Golden Mean demands a perspective in which our desires are *time-indexed* ones, so that different spans of time can be envisaged together as forming parts of a cycle or system in equilibrium. Or else, if they are *immediate,* the desires themselves, and not just their satisfaction, must come in orderly cycles. Otherwise, the phenomenology of contrary desires will entail perpetual frustration. In a mode of experience in which only the specious present exists—the infant's mode—ambivalence will be more poignant, for if you cannot bear in mind the possibilities of alternation and balance, then it will seem that the very condition that satisfies one longing absolutely precludes the satisfaction of the other. "The desire—and the terror—of the womb" is of this kind: "The danger of safety is engulfment and debility; and the danger of individual activity is exposure and judgment" (Tov-Ruach 1980, 483).

The conflict sketched in chapter 9 between individuality and social context is that infant's dilemma writ large. We need one another to give individuality to what we think and feel; but if we allow the social context to define us altogether, we lose the individuality. That is what Roberto Mangabeira Unger (1984) has called the "problem of solidarity."

The problem of solidarity might be made to look tractable, with one or the other of two sensible-sounding suggestions: either that we should look for a happy medium between crippling isolation and craven conformism, or, if that proves impossible, that we should look to *alternation* of incompatible ideals, on the model of "tranquillity and excitement."

But there is, I suspect, yet a deeper level of ambivalence, stemming not from the context-sensitivity of emotions but from the irreconcilable multiplicity of values. If so, then the search for a happy medium is idle.

Two factors have long obscured the irreconcilability of values. One is the assumption, noted at the beginning of this chapter, that we could think of morality as modeled in a "Kingdom of Ends" that is a kind of utopia: a logically possible ideal world, though one no doubt unrealizable in practice. But if utopia is a logically possible world, then all its aspects must be strictly compatible: the Good can never conflict with itself. The second factor that has obscured the disunity of value is the close link in recent philosophy between value and action. If you assume that all values must issue in principles of action, then, since you can only do one thing out of any set of incompatible options, the uniqueness of the outcome seems to be reflected back as a phony uniqueness of motivating value. But for many philosophers this view seems to be losing its charm.[10]

Still, if you can't have (or be) everything, might alternation of eating your cake and having it, integrated over a whole life, resolve the conflict?

Unless alternation merely follows a cycle of changing desires (in which each phase carries no trace of the last), alternation faces a dilemma. If, at any one time, I am aware of both desires but experience only the current phase of satisfaction, then frustration will be the only constant. For in each phase I am deprived of the valued experience of the other. On the other hand, alternation might appear to be successful from the vantage point of an integration over time, in which both contraries timelessly hold sway. But that integrating temporal perspective presupposes that we are never completely absorbed in either of the contraries. For example: some pairs of emotional temperament—hardness or softness, enthusiasm or caution, perhaps even sympathy or objectivity—represent psychologically incompatible pairs of attitudes or dispositions. Each member of each pair confronts the world in a way that is—from their respective points of view—both admirable and deplorable at the very same time. Either side of that contrast is an indispensable part of the moral universe, and the suppression of either, even for the noblest of motives, would result in impoverishment. Moreover, either side might come with a built-in proviso demanding lifetime commitment (otherwise, it would be inauthentic). In that case, as Yeats saw, the very definition of the competing ideals precludes a satisfactory alternation: "The intellect of man is forced to choose / Perfection of the life, or of the work" ("Life's Choice").

If alternation will not reconcile conflicting values, one possible solution is implied by the notion of individual natures that I have urged we should take seriously. Perhaps the reconciliation of conflicting values and ideals is not to be effected in any single individual but across several: you take the cunning, I'll take the candor; let one take the simplicity and another take the complexity; and so on.

But even this will not work. The reason is that ambivalence has yet one deeper layer. This one is not just a matter of the existence of conflicting values; instead, it lodges at the very heart of the human condition and its axiologically correct apprehension. To explain that deepest level, I first make a brief detour through the question of the rationality of the fear of death.

Is It Rational to Fear Death?
If the doctrine offered in these pages is of any use, it should have consequences for the account we should give of the most prevalent, the most puzzling, and arguably the most irrational of our fears, the fear of our own death. To sketch what these consequences are, I shall follow Amélie Rorty's recent discussion of the subject, while transposing it into my own vocabulary.

Rorty's central claims are startling and simple:

1. It is indeed irrational to fear death—in the sense of annihilation. The reason is the one Epicurus gave: Before I die, I do not experience death because I am alive. But when I am dead, no "I" is left to experience anything. So there is no such experience to be feared as death.

2. Nevertheless, the fear of death is an inevitable concomitant of the existence of dispositions to "functional fears," which are as biologically useful as pain.

3. That concomitant is not avoidable, because, for quasi-Kantian reasons,

> [a] mind capable of certain kinds of causal reasoning cannot restrict the use of such reasoning. . . . Reifying the totality of experience, illicitly treating it as if it could itself be a possible object of experience, we ask questions that are appropriate only within experience. . . . Similarly we ask these questions about the simple unified soul, the subject of experience reified as what it cannot be: an object of possible experience. These questions are both inevitable and illicit: they are built into the operations of

rational inference, and yet are improper and meaningless. (Rorty 1983b, 186–187)

4. So it is literally true that *it is both rational and irrational to fear death,* because "the two sides of the argument are not commensurable; they cannot be weighed and summarized in such a way as to allow us to determine what is, all things considered, the rational attitude towards death" (p. 188).

Is there not something intolerable about the idea that it is both irrational and not irrational to fear death? There may seem to be a way of stripping this view of its paradoxical air. We have already seen evidence that certain forms of irrationality, such as the "nasty emotions," are inevitable for biological or psychological reasons, or even for deeper sorts of reasons that Kant might have called metaphysical but that I prefer to label *engineering constraints.* We might think to dispel the paradox by suggesting that the fear of death is indeed an inevitable concomitant of necessary dispositions, but that it is not rational for all that. But this dilution of Rorty's claim would miss the point. Although her pair of claims does not form a hopeless antinomy, we can explain away the apparent paradox without artificially dispelling the mystery.

Let me first deal with the strict paradox. In the terms I have been using, we can rephrase Rorty's first thesis to say that the fear of death is *axiologically* irrational. There is no target of the fear of death; no experience about which we can ask whether it has a motivating aspect fitting the formal object of fear. Nevertheless, the upshot of the second and third theses, and what justifies the fourth, is that the fear of death is at least sometimes *strategically* rational. Given the engineering constraints of evolution, the fact that we experience such fear, like the fact that we experience pain, is something that an omniscient, omnipotent, and benevolent God would have avoided, but that—for reasons rather less deep but no less solid than Kantian necessity—evolution could not.

The mystery that does remain is that of the emotions' ambivalent core. We should expect to find that core wherever we confront the most general and universal constraints on human life. I intend the word 'confront' in a strong sense, connoting *axiological apprehension* through emotion. Those constraints are all—pace the current anthropological fashion—rooted in biology, although their apprehension, to which they owe their sting, presupposes reflective awareness. I call them *basic tragedies of life:* if they exist, they deserve a stark and pompous label. I understand the word 'tragedy' as implying a necessary conflict in which both sides are right and wrong at once, and no escape into a third alternative is possible. Each of these sources of the deepest level of ambivalence presents us with a necessary condition of a fundamental good, where that condition itself conflicts directly with the enjoyment or the perpetuation of that good.

Three Basic Tragedies of Life

The tragedy of solidarity is related to what Freud described as the unavoidable conflict between the individual and civilization (Freud 1930a). Social existence is the very condition of our individuality and in particular of the develompent of an emotional life capable of making life worth living. But individuality is in essential conflict with the social, for three reasons. The most superficial is Freud's reason: that society must curb the very instincts the regular satisfaction of which it alone makes possible. The second reason is that sociality creates the common language in which alone I can develop my individual thoughts; but if I merely repeat the sentences I have been taught, I can say nothing individual at all. The third reason is very similar, except that it concerns the repertoire of emotions rather than the resources of ordinary language. By what I feel, I can potentially distinguish myself most acutely from others. Yet my emotions perpetually risk the inauthenticity consequent on their engulfment by imitation or ideology.

The second tragedy has figured throughout this book as the *Euthyphro* question. But to label it a "question" was to mislead by suggesting that it might be answered. To encourage a shift in perspective away from that vain hope, I now rename it the *tragedy of biography*.

Why is individual biography tragic? Because, in brief, we aspire to values that would be universal, not merely in the trivial way I described as diagnostic universalizability, but substantively. Yet if our apprehension of value has its origins, as I have argued, in our individual paradigm scenarios, there is no guarantee that our values are any better than mere projections of that individual experience. Without such experience, there could be no sense of value at all. But if we are confined to it, we are imprisoned in projective subjectivity.

This has a corollary affecting our relations with others. The mystery of personality, what Yeats called "the labyrinth of another's being," fascinates us in proportion to the difference of others from ourselves. The existence of that difference is guaranteed by the origins of our emotional repertoire and therefore of our world view, in paradigm scenarios the details of which are due to the chance circumstances of individual biography. As a result, the worlds of value, of pleasure, of emotional reality with which individual temperament and history have endowed us are just accessible enough to each other for us to know that they are irreducibly different.

This seems to insult the Platonist mind (for 'Platonist' I might have said 'pre-Darwinian'), because it seems to imply that the search for an axiology as neat as truth and as universal as logic is vain. Some utopian thinkers, looking back toward a supposed past or toward distant cultures in which the individual melts happily into a communal reality, aspire to a truly coherent social order, in which the meaning of individual happiness will have all but vanished. That is a prospect as boring as eternal life: there is more to the real world than there are possible worlds dreamed up by utopians. (An important reason for this is that utopians usually forget that no utopia would be bearable without desire. An infinite regression of utopias must nest, like generations of homunculi, within the imaginations of their denizens.) The argument of this book has been that we should not give up on the view that our emotions connect us to the real world, even while they organize it for us. The diversity of our emotional sources is not a reason to despair of objectivity. Instead, it should persuade us to accept the sort of pluralism of values that the axiological perspective entails.

It is a contingent fact of history that there has generally, though not always, been enough social cohesion to stabilize a common language for our dealings with each other. I mean a common language both in the narrow sense and in the sense of a repertoire of emotions in which—between extremes of schizophrenia and depression—we can make sense of each other as well as ourselves. In the same way, it has at least occasionally been a contingent fact of history (but for how many people?) that the circumstances of life have allowed death to give to individual lives an appearance of significant form. For if life is all perfectly repetitive drudgery, or if the individual consciousness were ever truly subsumed by the communal, then even death could give it no shape. So only the lucky few have had the luxury of confronting the basic tragedies of life.

Death, relativity, and the solitude that individuality entails are evils. But they are evils that also give life meaning—providing that we are sufficiently comfortable to enjoy their contemplation in intermittent tranquillity. All three are essential sources of our emotional life, just where our emotional life is of the essence in framing the deepest standards of rationality in terms of which our projects are appraised. And from one or another of these tragedies of life many of our emotions inherit their characteristic ambivalence.

The evil of death is a particularly clear example. As Richard Wollheim has written, death is not an evil in the sense in which an experience is an evil, but because it deprives us of the expectation of continued experience:

> That death is a misfortune is not because we would be better off if we lived for ever: for immortality too would be a misfortune. . . . What it deprives us of is something more fundamental than pleasure: it deprives us of . . . phenomenology, and, having once tasted phenomenology, we develop a longing for it which we cannot give up, not even when the desire for the cessation of pain, for extinction, grows stronger. (Wollheim 1984, 269)

Experience, which conditions our capacity to care, is largely a product of the poignant exercise of choices among options framed for us by our emotional life. Immortality could make choice literally pointless: anything we might choose rather than anything else, if we had eternity, would come about sooner or later anyway. Indeed, it would, as Nietzsche envisaged, return an infinite number of times (Nietzsche 1892). God might, of course, have concealed our immortality from us, just to make us able to enjoy it. Or we might, for a while, console ourselves with the thought that in a denumerably infinite time there is room for an even bigger—"superdenumerable"— infinity of arrangements. Yet that consolation would be a treacherous one, for our finite heads could never hold more than a finite fragment of the list in memory. Besides, if that were to console us, it would be because a superdenumerable number of options cannot fit even in eternity; therefore, we would again escape from the hell of absolute satisfaction. For it is just because it seemed to promise absolute satisfaction that eternal life would deprive us of precisely that which makes life worth living.

Conclusion

I have tried, in this book, to grasp hold of a number of features of emotion that on the face of it are hard to reconcile. Emotions have deep biological roots; it is crucial to their nature and function that they are physiologically implemented in human beings. At the same time they are essentially mental—even if we grant the possibility that some of them may be unconscious. Their character as mental states involves a great complexity of informational, intentional, and causal features usually summed up as their "object-directedness." Some emotions, in particular, involve a capacity for singular reference, presupposing a metaphysics of individuals; though in practice long-lasting emotions are both aroused and sustained by the properties of their targets. The intentional complexity of emotions is what makes it possible for emotions to play a crucial role in rationality. They do this, in part, by supplementing the formal rules that we are accustomed to think of as embodying rationality. Yet they themselves are susceptible to rational assessment. We judge them by much the same principles as other states and activities that we unquestioningly appraise as more or less rational. In doing so, we need to recognize the importance of a concept of normality. But that concept must be understood neither as merely statistical nor as stemming from purely conventional rules. Instead, we must allow for the possibility of judgments of individual normality, even if we are always in an unsatisfactory epistemic position to make them with confidence. That, too, is part of the human condition: if human beings are ultimately unknowable, this is not something to be merely dispelled by methodological fiat. The necessary unknowability of even those closest to us, of the unique truth of their individual normality, has the same form as the tragedies of life I have just sketched: with it come many sources of suffering, but without it our love would lack its ultimate mystery, the acute consciousness of the impossibility of possession. Emotions are a kind of perception—perception of the axiological level of reality. And the reality they reveal is one that is tragically rich with an irreconcilable plurality of value.

Our emotional repertoires in some ways resemble our languages. Like language, emotion frames our possibilities of experience. It does so by supplementing our formal rules to make assessments of rationality possible. Far more clearly than languages, however, emotions have contents of their own. Their content, in a sense, is theater. Our emotional life is the ultimate in "method" acting: the roles we play teach us how to feel. Like language, these roles are learned in the context of human intercourse and therefore vary significantly from one culture to another. But like language they are learned on the basis of indispensable biological foundations. Like our individual idiolects, our individual emotional ranges necessarily have their deepest roots in the experiences of sociality in which they are first given form. And yet, because each idiolect is different, the possibilities for systematic misunderstandings are ever present. That is what has given emotion its undeserved reputation for irrationality. Moreover, these individual differences are not merely due to the accidents of biography, for the biological level too is rife with variations that are at once a source of richness and a source of pain.

The philosophical analysis of emotion leads to a tragic view of life. Tragedy is not single-minded gloom, but the embracing of multiplicity. The equivalent of a mystical ideal in a secular context, I suggest, is the idea of an emotional integrity that would apprehend and celebrate the fullness of what it is to be human. The ideal of emotional rationality is *adequate emotional response.* In that utopian condition we would, *per impossibile,* apprehend the rich meaning not only of our individual lives but also of the tragic dimensions intrinsic to the human condition—the barriers to complete empathy that fuel the power of love; the necessity of social bonds for individual freedom, of subjective attachment for objective value, of death for meaningful experience. To feel the human world as it is, to experience the emotional equivalent of truth, would be to feel all that, with one's whole being, all at once.

Appendix
Labeled Sentences and Principles Discussed

Chapter 5

Objects of Emotion

(I) *Target.* The *target* of an emotion is a real object, typically an actual particular, to which that emotion relates. The target is that real object, if any, *at* which the emotion is directed.

(II) *Proper target.* A target of an emotion is also its *proper target,* if and only if it would remain unchanged by the subject's possession of full relevant knowledge.

(III) *Focus, focal property, and motivating aspect.* Emotions having targets typically involve a *focus* of attention, which is the apprehension of some (real or illusory) *focal property* of the target. Under certain conditions, which define the standard case, the focal property is also the *motivating aspect* of these emotions.

(IV) *First causal condition.* A causal connection between the focal property and the occurrence of the emotion is a *necessary condition* for the former to be a motivating aspect.

(V) *Corrigibility.* There is no privilege of incorrigibility in the subject's access to motivating aspects.

(VI) *Intelligibility condition.* Motivating aspects must be *rationally related* to the emotion they cause, in the sense that they must constitute *intelligible rationalizations* for the emotion.

(VII) *Second causal condition.* For a focal property to be a motivating aspect, it must be an actual property of the target.

(VIII) *Aim.* The motivational role of emotions defines their characteristic *aims* and acts as a constraint on the character of each specific emotion.

(IX)   *Formal object.* For each emotion, there is a second-order quality that must be implicitly ascribed to the motivating aspect if the emotion is to be intelligible. This essential element in the structure of each emotion is its *formal object.*

(X)   *Relation of target to formal object.* The target of an emotion, where it exists, is a particular that has played a crucial role in the causation of the emotion in virtue of being apprehended as instantiating some motivating aspect. The motivating aspect in turn instantiates the formal object that defines that particular emotion.

(XI)   *Propositional object.* If an emotion has a purely propositional object, it consists in an attitude appropriate to some fact, proposition, event, or situation type that has a property instantiating the formal object of that emotion.

(CS)   *Conjunctive schema.* $(\exists x)$ [Commotion]x & Sx & Tx & $Ax \ldots$) (S = 'affects subject S'; T = 'has target t'; A = 'has motivating aspect a' $\ldots$)

(RS)   *Relational schema.* R(*Stfacmp*) (R is an emotion type; S is a subject; t is a target; f is a focal property; a is a motivating aspect; c is a cause; m is an aim; p is a propositional object.)

Chapter 6

Principles of Rationality

(R1)   *Success.* The formal object of a representational state defines that state's criterion of success, in terms of which the rationality of that state is assessed.

(R2)   *Minimal rationality.* It is a necessary condition of an intentional state or event's being describable as categorially rational, that under some true description it can properly (though perhaps vacuously) be said to be evaluatively rational.

(R3)   *Intentionality.* The teleology implicit in rationality applies only to intentional acts or states.

(R4)   *Origins.* The assessment of rationality of any act or belief looks both forward to consequences, logical and causal, and backward to origins.

(R5)   *Constraints.* Rationality never prescribes, but only constrains, by proscribing inconsistency and distinctions without a difference.

(R6)   *Cognitive and strategic rationality.* A representational state can be assessed in terms of the value of its probable *effects* (in the causal sense): this evaluates its *strategic* rationality, or utility. By contrast, a state is *cognitively* rational if it is arrived at in such a way as to be probably adequate to some actual state of the world that it purports to represent.

Chapter 7

(PEC)   *Principle of emotional continence.* Let your emotions be appropriate to the widest possible range of available scenarios.

(BH1)   *New Biological Hypothesis 1.* The function of emotions is to fill gaps left by (mere wanting plus) "pure reason" in the determination of action and belief, by mimicking the encapsulation of perception: it is one of Nature's ways of dealing with the philosophers' frame problem.

(BH2)   *New Biological Hypothesis 2.* Emotions are species of determinate patterns of salience among objects of attention, lines of inquiry, and inferential strategies.

Chapter 8

(AP)   *Aspectual correspondence.* For each *aspectual type* of object there is a natural or *privileged aspect* of desire.

Chapter 11

(PC)   *Principle of emotional consistency.* If two emotional contents are incompatible, then that will guarantee that at least one emotion is *axiologically inappropriate.*

Notes

Chapter 2

1. For serious treatments of the history of the philosophy of emotions, see Rorty, forthcoming. A very good account of the history of theories of mind is to be found in Flanagan 1984. For a good account of emotions in Spinoza, Hume, and Freud, see Neu 1971.
2. For a discussion of the distinction between theories and models or "schemes," see Morton 1980.
3. Plato gives varying accounts of the soul in different places. The doctrine I discuss is expounded in *Republic*, IV:435ff. The parable of the charioteer and his two steeds, which illustrates a similar view, appears in *Phaedrus*, 243ff.
4. For a couple of guides to this now vast literature, see Block 1980 and Fodor 1981.
5. See especially Alston 1967, the first chapter of Lyons 1980, and, for an admirably thorough summary of psychobiological theories, Plutchik 1980.
6. Solomon (1973) is more willing to embrace the paradoxical assimilation of the conative and cognitive theories: he argues there that judgments are chosen. For a mitigated view, questioning the dualism of the distinction between action and passion, see Solomon 1984 and Gordon 1986.

Chapter 3

1. William James's theory can be found in a number of places. One convenient source is the abridged edition of the *Psychology*, James 1892, chap. 24, pp. 373–392, to which citations in the text refer. A convenient excerpt from a different article, "What Is an Emotion?" (James 1884), is given in Calhoun and Solomon 1984, to which citations to James 1884 refer.
2. See Ekman, Levenson, and Friesen 1983. Ekman and Friesen have identified and learned to control the movements of over 100 muscles involved in a large repertoire of facial expressions. See Ekman and Friesen 1975 and Ekman 1973.
3. Pain might, however, be considered too simple to count as a genuine emotion. See Panksepp 1982 for reasons to exclude from the class of emotions affects such as surprise, disgust, pleasure, and pain.
4. The idea of circuits rather than centers controlling the manifestations of emotion is generally credited to a famous paper by James Papez (1937). Circuits involve the identification of pathways rather than "control centers," but of course the pathways must be somewhere, and so localization is also involved. In singling out these circuits, Papez was the first to assign a major functional role in the determination of emotions to the limbic system.
5. Though Panksepp gives us up-to-the minute neuroscience, all of the items on this

list, with the exception of criterion 3, can be found in Descartes 1649: see especially art. 40 and art. 74 on adaptiveness, motivation, and inertia, and art. 50 on learning.

6. For examples of the unreliability of introspection, see for example Nisbett and Wilson 1977 and the commentaries on Panksepp 1982 by Plutchik 1982 and Lutz 1982; also Pears 1984.

7. Konner 1982, 215, citing Hebb 1946 and Ursin and Kaada 1960.

8. Aristotle, *de Generatione Animalium* 1–19. For modern arguments designed to show that the meaning never does get into the mind, see Putnam 1975, Davidson 1979, Burge 1979; and see chapter 9.

9. On the matching of Parry with a real paranoiac, see especially Colby 1973, 277–278. A good description of some of the earlier versions of these models, on which I have drawn, is in Boden 1977. Other proposals for modeling psychoanalytic concepts of emotional dynamics in information-theoretic terms were also made in Peterfreund 1971 and Bowlby 1980, esp. 44–74. But as far as I know no attempt was ever made to implement a running simulation based on those ideas.

10. Two examples are parallel distributed processing or "connectionist" models, and coordinate transformation on phase spaces capable of perceptual-motor coordination. On the former, see Rumelhart, McLelland, and the PDP Research Group 1986. On the latter, see Churchland 1986.

Chapter 4

1. See Mayr 1975a. In addition, good introductions to "neo-Darwinian" evolutionary biology (the name commonly used to refer to Darwinian selectionism informed by modern genetic theory) can be found in the—often clashing—accounts in Williams 1966, Lewontin 1978, and Dawkins 1982. For an excellent anthology on evolutionary theory and its ramifications, see Sober 1984.

2. Biologists and philosophers, not to speak of theologians, have read all of these into evolution. For a few references, see de Sousa 1980.

3. This useful phrase is borrowed from Bowlby 1969. It effectively implies the point made in the present paragraph. On the relativity of adaptation, see also Lewontin 1978.

4. See, for example, Panksepp 1982, Plutchik 1980, Izard 1977, and de Rivera 1977.

5. For the classic statement of the program of sociobiology, see Wilson 1975. Versions of the fallacious argument mentioned in the text are advanced in several of the discussions collected by Ashley Montagu (1980). Other well-known assaults on sociobiology guilty of the error in question are the widely quoted one by Marshall Sahlins (1976) and the vitriolic review of Symons 1979 by Clifford Geertz (1980). For a more balanced and comprehensive (though still negative) critical appraisal, see Kitcher 1985.

6. The line is endemic in critical writings on Freud. See, for example, Barrett and Yankelovitch 1970, MacIntyre 1958, Schafer 1976, and Ricoeur 1970.

7. See Harman 1973, chap. 9, for a defense of the conception of knowledge as inference to the best explanation.

8. Many refinements are detailed in recent literature on which my broadly sketched account draws freely. See especially Taylor 1964, Woodfield 1976, Bennett 1976, chap. 2, Wright 1973, Miller, Galanter, and Pribram 1960, Lycan 1981. For some criticisms of this approach (which do not affect the use I make of it here), see Boorse 1976 and Cummins 1975. Finally, for a brilliant and original synthesis, see Millikan 1984.

9. See Hempel 1965, 245ff., and Taylor 1964, 9. I have adopted a slightly different notation.

10. Andrew Woodfield (1976, 84) traces this argument back to T. S. L. Sprigge (1971). I have modified the example slightly so as to avoid the counterobjection that the mere holding of a law is not an *event* that can be brought about by anything.

11. The diagrams in figure 4.1 are inspired by those in Goldman 1970; the example derives from Davidson 1963.

12. The existence of a relatively autonomous level of description and explanation, as a differentia of representational systems in the strong sense, has been advocated by several cognitive scientists. See, for example, Dennett 1971, 1983, Fodor 1978, and Pylyshyn 1984. For an opposing view, see Churchland 1981 and Stich 1983.

13. Notice, in (6), an engaging prefiguration of the arguments of Wilfrid Sellars (1963, 127ff.) for treating the phenomenal as a theoretical entity. This connection between Sellars and Freud is no mere coincidence. Both trace their ancestry on this point to Kant.

14. The ideas in this section derive from an important unpublished paper by Ann MacKenzie.

15. For some expressions of skepticism about the probable importance of mental concepts as we now understand them in future theories of mind, see Churchland 1981 and Stich 1983.

16. For a discussion of this issue in a strictly Freudian context, see de Sousa 1982.

Chapter 5

1. Later in this chapter I use the word 'focus' in a sense closer to one of Nissenbaum's "aspects." Her 'focus' is something like my 'target'. In several other respects her account of the so-called object-directedness of emotions, though developed independently, has close affinities with mine. Also recommended is the account of J. R. S. Wilson (1972), which is elaborated mostly in terms of the causal relations of emotion to what I call its "target."

2. In the next few pages I have adapted some ideas from Broad 1971.

3. The present use of 'target' is adapted from Wittgenstein 1951, I 476. Targets are typically referred to as direct objects of emotion verbs, or introduced with such prepositions as 'at', 'with', 'by', 'about'. But again this is a heuristic, not a criterion.

4. My usage of this term is much the same as that of William Lyons (1980) and with some variants goes back to Anthony Kenny, who says, "The formal object of ϕ-ing is the object under that description which *must* apply to it if it is to be possible to ϕ it. If only what is P can be ϕ'd, then 'thing which is P' gives the formal object of ϕ-ing" (Kenny 1963, 189). I would only change "must apply" to "must be apprehended as applying."

5. For more details on how this works out for belief and want, and the consequences for the notions of consistency appropriate to each, see de Sousa 1974b. See also chapter 6.

6. The view of logical form as presenting a theory or model of real sentences derives from Paul Ziff (1972). For an extended discussion of the notion of logical form and its uses, see Lycan 1984.

7. The lines are from W. B. Yeats, "For Anne Gregory." On the solemn research, see Dion, Berscheid, and Walster 1972.

8. For excellent discussions of the problems involved in the dialectics of change and constancy in love, see Kraut 1986 and Rorty 1986.

9. For a discussion of the related spectrum of simple to thought-dependent desires, see Hampshire 1965.

10. For arguments that "situation types are basically linguistically defrocked sentences," see Hornstein 1986, 171.

Chapter 6

1. If indeed there is an intelligible issue here. Hilary Putnam has urged that the thesis of metaphysical or "external" realism is incoherent. But Ruth Millikan has objected that *all* theories are "internal" and that Putnam's arguments against "external realism" in effect undermine themselves, because they presuppose the intelligibility of the very notion that they are supposed to show is meaningless. (Actually, Putnam has claimed only that it is incoherent, rather than meaningless. So there may be no real disagreement.) In any case, the only realism I am presupposing here is "internal." See Putnam 1976, Millikan 1984, Appendix.

2. The insufficiency of perspective-free objectivity to truth more broadly construed is a pervasive theme of Thomas Nagel's recent inquiry into subjectivity. For example: "The purely objective conception will leave something out [namely, the subjective content of 'I am TN'] which is both *true* and remarkable" (Nagel 1986, 64; my emphasis). But the various senses of subjectivity I have distinguished appear pell-mell in his book, inducing the reader to expect an argument to show that they are somehow all one. No such argument is produced; though it seems the primary sense, which Nagel argues denotes an irreducible part of reality left out by objective accounts, is perspective. Relativity and phenomenology are most prominent in connection with the relation of thought to reality, and projection figures most in discussions of value. In several places perspective merges with one of the other types. In connection with the problem of thinking of experiences that we cannot imagine (the phenomenological problem), for example, Nagel comments, "We know there's something there, something perspectival, even if we don't know what it is . . ." (p. 21). In discussing the project of stripping away layers of relativity (going from secondary to primary qualities), he writes, "This leaves us with no account of the . . . specific viewpoints which were left behind as irrelevant to physics" (p. 15). Nagel recognizes that the relativity of "agent-relative reasons" allows them to be as objective as "agent-neutral" ones (p. 153). But he seems to identify the merely "idiosyncratic" character of individual tastes with the "essentially perspectival" (p. 168). That identification is surely a mistake. For even if we all had identical tastes, the irreducibility of perspective would be untouched, though there would no longer be any worry about relativity.

3. According to Barry Stroud, this familiar claim owes more to legend than fact. See Stroud 1980.

4. See Ross, Lepper, and Hubbard 1975, Nisbett and Ross 1977, Anderson, Lepper, and Ross 1980. It is worth noting that, as the last article shows, the perseverance effect tends to be stronger if it is linked to an explanation or context provided by a scenario.

5. Williams 1973a, 211. Actually, the essential insight goes back to Frege, who pointed out that the assertion component of uttered sentences cannot be part of their meaning. If it were, then a sentence p appearing as the antecedent of a conditional would have to be asserted. But when it figures as the antecedent of a conditional, p is not asserted but merely entertained (Frege 1960, 2). The path from Frege's observation to the present point is this: if I express an emotion, on my own behalf—from my subjective perspective—then I cannot at the same time conditionalize it.

6. The approach goes back at least to Clifford 1964 and James 1897. For a modern elaboration, see Levi 1967.

Chapter 7

1. See Parfit 1984, 143ff., and Schiffer 1976. Thomas Nagel speaks in a similar vein of "subjective" and "objective" *reasons* in Nagel 1970 but adopts Parfit's terminology in Nagel 1986.
2. The description in this paragraph draws liberally from Bretherton et al. 1986, 534ff.
3. Murdoch 1970, 34. For an eloquent defense of the idea that a novel can itself be a moral achievement, see also Nussbaum 1985. There are difficult and fascinating questions about the extent to which literature can *invent* scenarios that when applied to one's own life result in "authentic" emotions.
4. In terms of Saul Kripke's theory of naming, the experience of paradigm scenarios is something like the original baptism that gives its sense to a natural kind term (Kripke 1980). In terms of Ruth Millikan's theory, where "real value" is the kind of thing an "intentional icon" "Normally" (that is, in accordance with normally established functions) maps onto, paradigm scenarios determine the class of real values to which emotions, as meaningful states, are supposed to correspond (see Millikan 1984, 112). Some important qualifications to this picture will emerge in chapter 9.
5. (PEC) is modeled on the "Principle of Continence" introduced by Donald Davidson (1970a) as the rule of rationality that is specifically broken in cases of weakness of will. It was itself modeled on a principle of statistical rationality introduced by Carl Hempel (1965).
6. Nel Noddings (1984) has begun to explore an alternative to an ethics of principle, based on adequate emotional response.
7. Patricia Greenspan has argued that it is in the nature of emotions to allow "ambivalence in persons not so irrational as to hold genuinely contrary judgments" (Greenspan 1980, 223).
8. See Jeffrey 1965. The view of emotions as disruptive of normal capacities and activities has not been confined to philosophers. For an attack on this conception in psychology, by a psychologist, see Leeper 1948.
9. According to John Haugeland (1985, 174), Yehoshua Bar-Hillel was the first (in Bar-Hillel 1960) to draw this moral from early failures to produce machine translation.
10. The example of fear of flying is discussed in unpublished work by both Michael Stocker and Patricia Greenspan.
11. For further discussion, see de Sousa 1974a.

Chapter 8

1. According to Terry Penner, such a minimally rational structure characterizes the desiderative part of Plato's soul in the tripartite scheme of the *Republic*. See Penner 1971.
2. See Aristotle (*Nicomachean Ethics*, II.5 and X.4). I follow Gilbert Ryle in using 'achievement verb' to correspond roughly to Aristotle's 'kinesis' (Ryle 1964). Zeno Vendler (1967) adds a fourth category of *accomplishments*, which includes *running a mile, drawing a circle,* and so on. Accomplishments seem designed to comprise both the winning of the race and the running that leads up to it: a phase of activity limited by some punctual completion. Aristotle means to include them among his

kineseis; I prefer to view them as composite. Nothing rides on this for my purposes here.

3. Rather puzzlingly, Plato cited smelling a rose as an example of a pure pleasure and then went on to identify pure pleasures with the intellectual ones. What smelling a rose and intellectual pleasures seem to have in common is that their anticipation is not necessarily linked with pain. They cannot therefore be afflicted with that self-destructive character that Plato thought essential to bodily desire (*Philebus*, 51e).

4. In early works (Freud 1895) this was essentially the definition of the pleasure principle. Later it came rather more appropriately to characterize the death instinct (Freud 1920g).

5. Schiffer's actual argument is rather abstruse. Since I may have misunderstood it, here are his own words:

> To act on an r-p [reason-providing] desire to φ is to φ only because one has that desire, but it is also to φ only because of one's desire for the pleasure and relief of discomfort φing affords; . . . Now there are . . . r-f [reason-following] desires to gain pleasure and to relieve discomforts . . .[but] r-p-desires are not among them. . . . [It] would be altogether a mistake to suppose that a thirst was an r-f desire to drink; for then it would have to be a desire one had because one expected drinking to be pleasurable and relieving, . . .[but] the desire to drink itself is what is discomforting and the anticipated pleasure is itself the pleasure of gratifying that desire. . . . [T]here is one and only one way of avoiding a contradiction . . . : one's desire to φ, one's desire to gain the pleasure of satisfying one's desire to φ, one's desire to relieve the discomfort of one's desire to φ—these are all one and the same desire. An r-p-desire is a self-referential desire for its own gratification. (Schiffer 1976, 198–199)

6. For some recent contributions to the debate about the rationality of fearing death, see Williams 1973b, Silverstein 1980, Rorty 1983b, Green 1982, and Nagel 1986.

Chapter 9

1. The best full-length treatment of self-deception I know to date remains that of Herbert Fingarette (1969), who takes a more comprehensive view than most. I have discussed it in de Sousa 1970.

2. A related view is defended by Kendall L. Walton (1978). Walton is discussing reactions to fiction, where suspension of disbelief is no real belief but involves real emotion. But it is not exactly the same emotion as would be generated in the presence of belief. See below on "The Ideology of Emotions."

3. See Freud 1914g. See also in the same volume Freud 1915a, 1912b. For a lucid and comprehensive modern treatment by a practicing analyst, see Greenson 1967.

4. This is greatly oversimplified. For an account of some of the complexities of Freud's actual account, see de Sousa 1982.

5. See Isenberg 1949a. A closely related thought is expressed by Frank Sibley: "People insist that aesthetic judgments should be based on, in the sense of rationally derived or derivable from, supporting reasons; but all they can sensibly insist is that the critic, having realized why the thing is or is not graceful, should be able to say so" (Sibley 1965, 147).

6. For good discussions of jealousy, see Tov-Ruach 1980, Neu 1980, and Farrell 1980. Illuminating treatments are also to be found in Farber 1976, Chodorow 1978, and especially Dinnerstein 1976.

7. In particular, de Beauvoir construes "falling in love" as an inherently self-delusive emotion, based on sexist ideology. See de Beauvoir 1952; for elaboration, see Morgan 1986.
8. The term is from Erica Jong (1973). But the concept has long been aloft.

Chapter 11

1. For Aristotle on responsibility for character, see *Nicomachean Ethics*, II. See also Blum 1980.
2. Other examples include Descartes: "Derision or mockery is a kind of joy mixed with hatred, which comes from perceiving some small evil affecting someone who seems to deserve it" (Descartes 1649, art. 148); and Spinoza: "A man hates what he laughs at" (Spinoza, *Ethics* IV).
3. Bergson thought science powerless to teach us anything about reality because of its fragmenting nature. Real understanding of reality, he thought, was only possible by some sort of direct intuition, fostered by true art, which included tragedy but not comedy. See Bergson 1903.

Chapter 12

1. Although I shall speak somewhat disparagingly of the Kantian tradition, this is not to be taken as a reflection on Kant himself. Some passages in Kant encourage the Kantian tradition's rigid rejection of emotional motivation. One well-known example is the following: ". . . there are . . . many persons so sympathetically consitituted that without any motive of vanity or selfishness they find an inner satisfaction in spreading joy, and rejoice in the contentment of others which they have made possible. But I say that, however dutiful and amiable it may be, that kind of action has no true moral worth" (Kant 1959, 14). In the *Lectures on Ethics* (Kant 1963), however, a far more flexible picture emerges.
2. Hume 1739. I have borrowed this interpretation from Blum 1980, 222, fn. 15.
3. Compare the view of Owen Flanagan, who argues, following Susan Wolf (1982), that we should "reject the thesis of the overridingness of the morally ideal because it fails to allow enough room for the development of nonmoral traits and talents" (Flanagan 1986, 54).
4. The objective-subjective distinction might be thought to coincide with the distinction between *agent-neutral* and *agent-relative* reasons in the sense of Parfit 1984. But the two are not equivalent. All agent-neutral reasons are objective in the relevant sense, but so are some agent-relative reasons.
5. For a good introduction to and discussion of Kohlberg's theory of moral development, see Flanagan 1984, chap. 5. Kohlberg's own views can be found in Kohlberg 1981. But see also, for a correction of the male bias in Kohlberg's research, Gilligan 1983 and Noddings 1984.
6. See Williams 1985, chap. 10, for the contrast between morality in a narrow sense and ethics in a more inclusive sense. Richard Wollheim (1984) takes a similar view.
7. See chapter 8. For a charming perspective on the ant and the grasshopper, see Suits 1978. And for a defense of the ant in the grasshopper's own terms, see Rives 1984.
8. See Solomon 1984. Solomon himself traces the view to Sartre. For a defense of a more traditional position on the passivity of emotion, see Peters 1962. See also Gordon 1986.

9. See Wilde 1897. The definition is quoted in Tanner 1976, 127.
10. Those who have explicitly disavowed the thought that genuine values cannot conflict include Isaiah Berlin (1969), David Wiggins (1976), Charles Taylor (1982), Stuart Hampshire (1983), Owen Flanagan (1986), and Bernard Williams (1985). In de Sousa 1974b I argued that the doctrine of the unity of the good rests on a fallacious parallel between the consistency conditions of beliefs and wants.

References

Abelson, Robert P. 1973. "The Structure of Belief Systems." In Shank and Colby 1973.

Alston, William P. 1967. "Emotion and Feeling." In *Encyclopedia of Philosophy*, ed. Paul Edwards. New York and London: Macmillan.

Anderson, Craig A., Mark R. Lepper, and Lee Ross. 1980. "Perseverance of Social Theories: The Role of Explanation in the Persistence of Discredited Information." *Journal of Personality and Social Psychology* 39:1037–1049.

Anscombe, G. E. M. 1957. *Intention*. Oxford: Basil Blackwell.

Aristotle. 1941. In *Basic Works of Aristotle*, ed. Richard P. McKeon. New York: Random House.

Arnold, Magda B. 1960. *Emotion and Personality*. 2 vols. New York: Columbia University Press.

Arnold, Magda B., ed. 1968. *The Nature of Emotion*. Harmondsworth: Penguin.

Austin, John L. 1962. *How to Do Things with Words*. Cambridge, MA: Harvard University Press.

Averill, James R. 1976. "The Sociocultural, Biological, and Psychological Determinants of the Emotions." In *Emotions and Anxiety: New Concepts, Methods, and Applications*, ed. Marvin Zuckerman and Charles Spielberger. New York: LEA-John Wiley. Reprinted in Rorty 1980, to which citations refer.

Badhwar, Neera K. 1986. *The Ethical Significance of Friendship*. Doctoral dissertation, University of Toronto.

Baier, Annette. 1976. "Mixing Memory and Desire." *American Philosophical Quarterly* 13:213–220. Reprinted in Baier 1985, to which citations refer.

Baier, Annette. 1985. *Postures of the Mind: Essays on Mind and Morals*. Minneapolis: University of Minnesota Press.

Baier, Annette. 1986. "Trust and Antitrust." *Ethics* 96:231–260.

Bar-Hillel, Yehoshua. 1960. "The Present Status of Automatic Translation of Languages." In *Advances in Computers*, vol. 1, ed. F. L. Alt. New York: Academic Press.

Barrett, William, and David Yankelovitch. 1970. *Ego and Instinct: The Psychoanalytic View of Human Nature*. Rev. ed. New York: Random House.

Barwise, Jon, and John Perry. 1983. *Situations and Attitudes*. Cambridge, MA: MIT Press. A Bradford book.

Baudelaire, Charles. 1954. *Oeuvres complètes*. Paris: Bibliothèque de la Pléiade.

Bedford, Erroll. 1957. "Emotion." *Proceedings of the Aristotelian Society* 57:281–304. Reprinted in *Essays in Philosophical Psychology*, ed. D. Gustafson. Garden City, NY: Doubleday (1964).

Bell, Rudolph M. 1985. *Holy Anorexia*. Chicago: University of Chicago Press.

Bennett, Jonathan. 1974. "The Conscience of Huckleberry Finn." *Philosophy* 49:123–134.

Bennett, Jonathan. 1976. *Linguistic Behaviour.* Cambridge and New York: Cambridge University Press.

Bergson, Henri. 1903. "Introduction à la métaphysique." *Revue de Métaphysique et de Morale* 11:1–36.

Bergson, Henri. 1940. *Le rire: Essai sur la signification du comique.* Paris: Presses Universitaires de France.

Berlin, Isaiah. 1969. "Two Concepts of Liberty." In *Four Essays on Liberty.* London: Oxford University Press.

Berne, Eric. 1978. *Games People Play.* New York: Ballantine Books.

Block, Ned, ed. 1980. *Readings in the Philosophy of Psychology.* 2 vols. Cambridge, MA: Harvard University Press.

Blum, L. A. 1980. *Friendship, Altruism, and Morality.* London: Routledge & Kegan Paul.

Boden, Margaret. 1977. *Artificial Intelligence and Natural Man.* New York: Basic Books.

Boorse, Christopher. 1976. "Wright on Functions." *Philosophical Review* 85:70–86. Reprinted in Sober 1984.

Bowlby, John. 1969. *Attachment.* Vol. 1 of *Attachment and Loss.* New York: Basic Books.

Bowlby, John. 1980. *Loss.* Vol. 3 of *Attachment and Loss.* New York: Basic Books.

Braitenberg, Valentino. 1984. *Vehicles.* Cambridge, MA: MIT Press. A Bradford book.

Bretherton, Inge, J. Fritz, C. Zahn-Waxler, and D. Ridgeway. 1986. "Learning to Talk about Emotions: A Functionalist Perspective." *Child Development* 57:529–548.

Broad, C. D. 1971. "Emotion and Sentiment." In *Critical Essays in Moral Theory.* London: Allen & Unwin.

Burge, Tyler. 1979. "Individualism and the Mental." *Midwest Studies in Philosophy* 4:73–121.

Calhoun, Cheshire, and Robert C. Solomon, eds. 1984. *What Is an Emotion? Classic Readings in Philosophical Psychology.* New York and Oxford: Oxford University Press.

Cannon, W. B. 1929. *Bodily Changes in Pain, Hunger, Fear and Rage.* 2nd ed. New York: Appleton. Excerpted in Calhoun and Solomon 1984, to which citations refer.

Chodorow, Nancy. 1978. *The Reproduction of Mothering.* Berkeley and Los Angeles: University of California Press.

Churchland, Paul M. 1979. *Scientific Realism and the Plasticity of Mind.* Cambridge: Cambridge University Press.

Churchland, Paul M. 1981. "Eliminative Materialism and the Propositional Attitudes." *The Journal of Philosophy* 78:67–90.

Churchland, Paul M. 1986. "Cognitive Neurobiology: A Computational Hypothesis for the Laminar Cortex." *Philosophy and Biology* 1:25–51.

Clifford, William. 1964. "The Ethics of Belief." In Kaufmann 1964.

Colby, Kenneth Mark. 1973. "Simulations of Belief Systems." In Shank and Colby 1973.

Cousins, Norman. 1979. *Anatomy of an Illness as Perceived by the Patient: Reflections on Healing and Regeneration.* New York: W. W. Norton.

Crick, Francis. 1979. "Thinking about the Brain." *Scientific American* 247:130–137. Issue reprinted in book form as *The Brain.* San Francisco: W. H. Freeman.

Cummins, Robert. 1975. "Functional Analysis." *The Journal of Philosophy* 72:741–760. Reprinted in Sober 1984.

Cummins, Robert. 1983. *The Nature of Psychological Explanation.* Cambridge, MA: MIT Press. A Bradford book.

Dalby, J. Thomas, Marcel Kinsbourne, James M. Swanson, and Michael P. Sobol. 1977. "Hyperactive Children's Underuse of Learning Time: Correction by Stimulant Treatment." *Child Development* 48(4):1448–1453.

Daly, Mary. 1978. *Gyn/Ecology: The Metaethics of Radical Feminism.* Boston: Beacon Press.

Danto, Arthur. 1965. "Basic Actions." *American Philosophical Quarterly* 2:141–148.

Darwin, Charles. 1896. *The Expression of the Emotions in Man and Animals*. New York: Appleton Press.

Davidson, Donald. 1963. "Actions, Reasons, and Causes." *The Journal of Philosophy* 60:685–700. Reprinted in Davidson 1980.

Davidson, Donald. 1967a. "The Logical Form of Action Sentences." In *The Logic of Decision and Action*, ed. N. Rescher. Pittsburgh: University of Pittsburgh Press. Reprinted in Davidson 1980.

Davidson, Donald. 1967b. "Causal Relations." *The Journal of Philosophy* 64:691–703. Reprinted in Davidson 1980.

Davidson, Donald. 1970a. "How Is Weakness of the Will Possible?" In *Moral Concepts*, ed. J. Feinberg. London: Oxford University Press. Reprinted in Davidson 1980.

Davidson, Donald. 1970b. "Mental Events." In *Experience and Theory*, ed. Lawrence Foster and J. W. Swanson. Amherst, MA: The University of Massachusetts Press and Duckworth. Reprinted in Davidson 1980.

Davidson, Donald. 1973. "Freedom to Act." In *Essays on Freedom and Action*, ed. Ted Honderich. Reprinted in Davidson 1980, to which citations refer.

Davidson, Donald. 1976. "Hume's Cognitive Theory of Pride." *The Journal of Philosophy* 73:744–757.

Davidson, Donald. 1979. "The Inscrutability of Reference." In *Truth and Interpretation*. Oxford: Clarendon Press (1984).

Davidson, Donald. 1980. *Essays on Actions and Events*. Oxford: Clarendon Press.

Dawkins, Richard. 1982. *The Extended Phenotype*. San Francisco: W. H. Freeman.

de Beauvoir, Simone. 1952. "The Woman in Love." In *The Second Sex*, trans. H. M. Panohley. New York: Random House, Vintage.

Delgado, J. M. R. 1969. *The Physical Control of the Mind: Toward a Psychocivilized Society*. New York: Harper & Row.

Dennett, Daniel C. 1971. "Intentional Systems." *The Journal of Philosophy* 68:87–106. Reprinted in Dennett 1978a.

Dennett, Daniel C. 1978a. *Brainstorms: Philosophical Essays on Mind and Psychology*. Cambridge, MA: MIT Press. A Bradford book.

Dennett, Daniel C. 1978b. "Why You Can't Make a Computer That Feels Pain." In Dennett 1978a.

Dennett, Daniel C. 1983. "Intentional Systems in Cognitive Ethology: The 'Panglossian Paradigm' Defended." *The Behavioral and Brain Sciences* 6:343–390.

Dennett, Daniel C. 1987. "Cognitive Wheels: The Frame Problem in AI." In Pylyshyn 1987.

de Rivera, J. 1977. *A Structural Theory of the Emotions*. New York: International Universities Press.

Descartes, René. 1649. *Treatise on the Passions of the Soul*. In *The Philosophical Works of Descartes*, trans. E. Haldane and G. R. T. Ross. Cambridge: Cambridge University Press.

de Sousa, R. 1970. Critical Notice of Fingarette 1969. *Inquiry* 13:308–321.

de Sousa, R. 1971. "How to Give a Piece of Your Mind: Or, The Logic of Belief and Assent." *Review of Metaphysics* 25:52–79.

de Sousa, R. 1974a. "Rational Homunculi." In *The Identities of Persons*, ed. A. O. Rorty. Berkeley and Los Angeles: University of California Press.

de Sousa, R. 1974b. "The Good and the True." *Mind* 83:534–551.

de Sousa, R. 1980. "Arguments from Nature." *Zygon* 15:169–191. Reprinted in *Morality, Reason and Truth*, ed. D. Copp and D. Zimmerman. New York: Rowman and Allanheld (1984).

de Sousa, R. 1982. "Norms and the Normal." In *Philosophical Essays on Freud*, ed. Richard Wollheim and James Hopkins. Cambridge and New York: Cambridge University Press.

de Sousa, R. 1984. "The Natural Shiftiness of Natural Kinds." *Canadian Journal of Philosophy* 14:561–580.

Dewdney, A. K. 1985. "Analog Gadgets That Solve a Diversity of Problems and Raise an Array of Questions." *Scientific American* 252(5):18–24.

Diderot, Denis. 1981. *Paradoxe sur le comédien, précédé des entretiens sur le fils naturel.* Paris: Flammarion.

Dinnerstein, Dorothy. 1976. *The Mermaid and the Minotaur.* New York: Harper & Row.

Dion, Karen, Ellen Berscheid, and Wendy Walster. 1972. "What Is Beautiful Is Good." *Journal of Personality and Social Psychology* 24:285–290.

Dollard, John, and Neal E. Miller. 1950. *Psychotherapy and Personality: An Analysis in Terms of Learning, Thinking, and Culture.* New York: McGraw-Hill.

Dutton, Donald G., and Arthur P. Aron. 1974. "Some Evidence for Heightened Sexual Attraction under Conditions of High Anxiety." *Journal of Personality and Social Psychology* 30:510–517.

Ekman, Paul, ed. 1973. *Darwin and Facial Expression: A Century of Research in Review.* New York: Academic Press.

Ekman, P., and W. V. Friesen. 1975. *Unmasking the Face: A Guide to Recognizing Emotions from Facial Expressions.* Englewood Cliffs, NJ: Prentice-Hall.

Ekman, P., R. W. Levenson, and W. V. Friesen. 1983. "Autonomous Nervous System Activity Distinguishes among Emotions." *Science* 221:1208–1210.

Eliot, T. S. 1960. "Thomas Middleton." In *Selected Essays.* New York: Harcourt, Brace and World.

Elster, Jon. 1983. *Sour Grapes.* Cambridge: Cambridge University Press.

Farber, Leslie. 1976. "On Jealousy." In *Lying, Despair, Jealousy, Envy, Sex, Suicide, Drugs, and the Good Life.* New York: Harper & Row.

Farrell, Daniel M. 1980. "Jealousy." *The Philosophical Review* 89:527–559.

Fingarette, Herbert. 1969. *Self-Deception.* London: Routledge & Kegan Paul.

Flanagan, Owen J., Jr. 1984. *The Science of the Mind.* Cambridge, MA: MIT Press. A Bradford book.

Flanagan, Owen. 1986. "Admirable Immorality and Admirable Imperfection." *The Journal of Philosophy* 83:41–59.

Fodor, Jerry A. 1978. "Propositional Attitudes." *The Monist* 61:501–523. Reprinted in Fodor 1981.

Fodor, Jerry A. 1981. *Representations: Philosophical Essays on the Foundations of Cognitive Science.* Cambridge, MA: MIT Press. A Bradford book.

Fodor, Jerry A. 1983. *The Modularity of Mind.* Cambridge, MA: MIT Press. A Bradford book.

Fodor, Jerry A. 1987. "Modules, Frames, Fridgeons, Sleeping Dogs and the Music of the Spheres." In Pylyshyn 1987.

Frankfurt, H. G. 1971. "Freedom of the Will and the Concept of a Person." *Journal of Philosophy* 68:5–20.

Frayn, Michael. 1974. *Constructions.* London: Wildwood House.

Frege, G. 1960. *Begriffsschrift:* chapter I. In *Translations from the Philosophical Writings of Gottlob Frege,* ed. Peter Geach and Max Black. Oxford: Basil Blackwell.

Freud, S. 1895. *Project for a Scientific Psychology.* In *The Standard Edition of the Complete Psychological Works,* ed. J. Strachey, vol. 1. London: Hogarth Press.

Freud, S. 1905d. *Three Essays on the Theory of Sexuality.* In *Standard Ed.,* vol. 7. London: Hogarth Press.

Freud, S. 1909. *Five Lectures on Psychoanalysis.* In *Standard Ed.,* vol. 11. London: Hogarth Press.

Freud, S. 1911b. "Formulations on Two Principles of Mental Functioning." In *Standard Ed.*, vol. 12. London: Hogarth Press.

Freud, S. 1912b. "The Dynamics of Transference." In *Standard Ed.*, vol. 12. London: Hogarth Press.

Freud, S. 1914g. "Remembering, Repeating and Working Through." In *Standard Ed.*, vol. 12. London: Hogarth Press.

Freud, S. 1915a. "Observations on Transference Love." In *Standard Ed.*, vol. 12. London: Hogarth Press.

Freud, S. 1915c. "Instincts and Their Vicissitudes." In *Standard Ed.*, vol. 14. London: Hogarth Press.

Freud, S. 1915e. "The Unconscious." In *Standard Ed.*, vol. 14. London: Hogarth Press.

Freud. S. 1920g. *Beyond the Pleasure Principle.* In *Standard Ed.*, vol. 18. London: Hogarth Press.

Freud. S. 1930a. *Civilization and Its Discontents.* In *Standard Ed.*, vol. 21. London: Hogarth Press.

Geertz, Clifford. 1980. Review of Symons 1979. *New York Review of Books* 26(2):2–5.

Geschwind, Norman. 1979. "Specializations of the Human Brain." *Scientific American* 247:107–117. Issue reprinted in book from as *The Brain.* San Francisco: W. H. Freeman.

Gide, André. 1922. *Les caves du Vatican.* Paris: Gallimard.

Gilligan, Carol. 1983. *In a Different Voice: Psychological Theory and Women's Development.* Cambridge, MA: Harvard University Press.

Goffman, Erving. 1970. *The Presentation of Self in Everyday Life.* Garden City, NY: Doubleday Anchor.

Goffman, Erving. 1974. *Frame Analysis: An Essay on the Organization of Experience.* New York: Harper & Row.

Goldman, Alvin. 1967. "A Causal Theory of Knowledge." *The Journal of Philosophy* 64:357–372.

Goldman, Alvin. 1970. *A Theory of Human Action.* Englewood Cliffs, NJ: Prentice-Hall.

Gordon, Robert M. 1969. "Emotions and Knowledge." *The Journal of Philosophy* 66:408–413.

Gordon, Robert M. 1986. "The Passivity of Emotions." *Philosophical Review* 95:371–392.

Gould, S. J. 1977. "The Misnamed, Mistreated, and Misunderstood Irish Elk." In *Ever Since Darwin: Reflections in Natural History.* New York: Norton.

Green, O. H. 1982. "Fear of Death." *Philosophy and Phenomenological Research* 43:99–105.

Greenson, Ralph R. 1967. *The Technique and Practice of Psychoanalysis*, vol. 1. New York: International Universities Press.

Greenspan, Patricia. 1980. "A Case of Mixed Feelings: Ambivalence and the Logic of Emotion." In Rorty 1980.

Grice, Paul. 1957. "Meaning." *Philosophical Review* 66:377–388.

Hampshire, Stuart N. 1965. *Freedom of the Individual.* New York: Harper & Row.

Hampshire, Stuart N. 1983. *Morality and Conflict.* Cambridge, MA: Harvard University Press.

Harman, Gilbert. 1973. *Thought.* Princeton, NJ: Princeton University Press.

Harrison, Bernard. 1984. Moral Judgment, Action and Emotion." *Philosophy* 59:295–321.

Harrison, Ross. 1982. "Discounting the Future." *Proceedings of the Aristotelian Society* 82 (1981–2): 45–58.

Haugeland, John, ed. 1981. *Mind Design.* Cambridge, MA: MIT Press. A Bradford book.

Haugeland, John. 1982. "Weak Supervenience." *American Philosophical Quarterly* 19:93–103.

Haugeland, John. 1985. *Artificial Intelligence: The Very Idea.* Cambridge, MA: MIT Press. A Bradford book.

Hayes, Patrick J. 1987. "What the Frame Problem Is and Isn't." In Pylyshyn 1987.

Hebb, Donald. 1946. "On the Nature of Fear." *Psychological Review* 53:259–276. (Cited in Konner 1982.)

Hempel, Carl. 1965. *Aspects of Scientific Explanation.* New York: Free Press.

Hill, Thomas E. 1967. *Never Give a Lady a Restive Horse* (selections from Hill's Manuals of Etiquette). Berkeley: Diablo Press.

Hintikka, Jaakko. 1962. *Knowledge and Belief.* Ithaca, NY: Cornell University Press.

Hobbes, Thomas. 1650. *On Human Nature.* In *English Works,* ed. W. Molesworth. 11 vols. New York: Adlers (1966).

Hofstadter, Douglas R. 1979. *Gödel, Escher, Bach: An Eternal Golden Braid.* New York: Basic Books.

Hohmann, George W. 1966. "Some Effects of Spinal Cord Lesions on Experienced Emotional Feelings." *Psychophysiology* 3:143–156.

Hornstein, Norbert. 1986. Review of Barwise and Perry 1983. *The Journal of Philosophy* 83:168–184.

Hubbard, John I. 1975. *The Biological Basis of Mental Activity.* Reading, MA: Addison-Wesley.

Hume, David. 1739. *A Treatise of Human Nature,* ed. L. A. Selby-Bigge. Oxford: Clarendon Press (1964).

Hume, David. 1777. *Enquiry Concerning the Principles of Morals.* Repr. New York: Open Court (1966).

Hume, David. 1779. *Dialogues Concerning Natural Religion,* ed. Norman K. Smith. New York: Bobbs-Merrill (1947).

Hunt, Morton M. 1959. *The Natural History of Love.* New York: Alfred A. Knopf.

Irani, K. S., and Gerald Myers, eds. 1983. *Emotion: Philosophical Studies.* New York: Haven.

Isenberg, Arnold. 1949a. "Critical Communication. *Philosophical Review* 58:330–344.

Isenberg, Arnold. 1949b. "Natural Pride and Natural Shame." *Philosophy and Phenomenological Research* 10:1–24. Reprinted in Rorty 1980, to which citations refer.

Izard, Carroll E. 1977. *Human Emotions.* New York and London: Plenum Press.

Jacob, François. 1977. "Evolution and Tinkering." *Science* 196:1161–1166.

Jaggar, Allison M. 1980. "Prostitution." In *The Philosophy of Sex,* ed. Alan Soble. Totowa, NJ: Littlefield, Adams & Co.

James, William 1884. "What Is an Emotion?" *Mind* 19:188–204. Excerpted in Calhoun and Solomon 1984, to which citations refer.

James, William. 1892. *Psychology: The Briefer Course.* New York: Harper & Row.

James, W. 1897. "The Will to Believe." In *The Will to Believe and Other Essays.* New York: Dover (1956). Reprinted in Kaufmann (1964).

Jeffrey, Richard C. 1965. *The Logic of Decision.* New York: McGraw-Hill.

Jong, Erica. 1973. *Fear of Flying.* New York: Holt, Rinehart & Winston.

Kant, Immanuel. 1959. *Foundations of the Metaphysics of Morals,* trans. Lewis White Beck. New York: Bobbs-Merrill.

Kant, Immanuel. 1963. *Lectures on Ethics,* trans. Louis Infield. New York: Harper & Row.

Kaufmann, Walter, ed. 1964. *Religion from Tolstoy to Camus.* New York: Harper Torchbooks.

Kenny, Anthony. 1963. *Action, Emotion and Will.* London: Routledge & Kegan Paul; New York: Humanities Press.

Kitcher, Philip. 1985. *Vaulting Ambition: Sociobiology and the Quest for Human Nature.* Cambridge, MA: MIT Press. A Bradford book.

Kohlberg, Lawrence. 1981. *Essays on Moral Development: The Philosophy of Moral Development*. New York: Harper & Row.

Konner, Melvin. 1982. *The Tangled Wing: Biological Constraints on the Human Spirit*. New York: Holt, Rinehart & Winston.

Kraut, Robert. 1986. "Love De Re." *Mid-West Studies in Philosophy* 10:413–430.

Kraut, Robert. Unpub. "Individualism and the Emotions." Paper delivered to the Society for Philosophy and Psychology, May 1986.

Kripke, Saul. 1980. *Naming and Necessity*. Cambridge, MA: Harvard University Press.

Kuhn, Thomas S. 1969. *The Structure of Scientific Revolutions*. 2nd ed. Chicago: Chicago University Press.

Kundera, Milan. 1981. *The Book of Laughter and Forgetting*, trans. M. H. Heim. Harmondsworth: Penguin Books.

Kundera, Milan. 1984. *The Unbearable Lightness of Being*. New York: Harper & Row.

Leeper, R. W. 1948. "A Motivational Theory of Emotion to Replace 'Emotion as Disorganized Response'." *Psychological Review* 55. Excerpted in Arnold 1968.

Legman, G. 1968. *Rationale of the Dirty Joke*. First Series. New York: Grove Press.

Legman, G. 1975. *No Laughing Matter: Rationale of the Dirty Joke*. 2nd series. New York: Bell Publishing.

Lem, Stanislaw. 1970. *Solaris*, trans. J. Kilmartin and S. Cox. New York: Walker and Co.

Levi, Isaac. 1967. *Gambling with Truth*. New York: Alfred A. Knopf.

Levinson, Jerrold. 1983. "Aesthetic Supervenience." *Southern Journal of Philosophy* supp. vol. 22:93–110.

Levy, Edwin, and Mohan Matthen. 1984. "Teleology, Error, and the Human Immune System." *The Journal of Philosophy* 81:351–372.

Lewis, David. 1972. "Psychophysical and Theoretical Identification." *Australasian Journal of Philosophy* 50:249–258. Reprinted in Block 1980, vol. 1.

Lewis, David. 1976. "The Paradoxes of Time Travel." *American Philosophical Quarterly* 13:145–152.

Lewontin, Richard C. 1978. "Adaptation." *Scientific American* 239(3):156–169.

Liberman, Alvin M., and Ignatius G. Mattingly. 1985. "The Motor Theory of Speech Perception Revisited." *Cognition* 21:1–36.

Liebowitz, Michael. 1983. *The Chemistry of Love*. New York: Little.

Lutz, Catherine. 1982. "Introspection and Cultural Knowledge Systems." *The Behavioral and Brain Sciences* 5(3):439–440.

Lycan, William G. 1981. "Form, Function, and Feel." *The Journal of Philosophy* 83:24–50.

Lycan, William G. 1984. *Logical Form in Natural Language*. Cambridge, MA: MIT Press. A Bradford book.

Lyons, William. 1980. *Emotion*. Cambridge: Cambridge University Press.

McDermott, Drew. 1987. "We've Been Framed: Or, Why AI is Innocent of the Frame Problem." In Pylyshyn 1987.

MacIntyre, Alasdair. 1958. *The Unconscious*. London: Routledge & Kegan Paul.

MacKenzie, Ann. Unpub. "The Intentionality of Desire."

MacLean, Paul D. 1960. "New Findings Relevant to the Evolution of Psychosexual Functions of the Brain." *Journal of Nervous and Mental Diseases* 135:289–301.

MacLean, Paul D. 1970. "The Triune Brain, Emotion, and Scientific Bias." In *The Neurosciences Second Study Program*, ed. F. O. Schmitt. New York: Rockefeller University Press.

MacLean, Paul D. 1975. "Sensory and Perceptive Factors in Emotional Functions of the Triune Brain." In *Emotions: Their Parameters and Measurement*, ed. L. Levi. New York: Raven Press. Reprinted in Rorty 1980, to which citations refer.

McTaggart, John. 1934. Chap. 5 of *Philosophical Studies*, ed. S. V. Keeling. London: Ayer.

Marks, Joel. 1982. "A Theory of Emotion." *Philosophical Studies* 42:227–242.

Marks, Joel, ed. 1986. *The Ways of Desire*. Chicago: Precedent Publishers.

Maynard Smith, John. 1984. "Game Theory and the Evolution of Behavior." *The Behavioral and Brain Sciences* 7:95–126.

Mayr, Ernst. 1975a. "Typological versus Population Thinking." In *Evolution and the Diversity of Life*. Cambridge, MA: Harvard University Press. Reprinted in Sober 1984.

Mayr, Ernst. 1975b. "Teleological and Teleonomic: A New Analysis." In *Evolution and the Diversity of Life*. Cambridge, MA: Harvard University Press.

Melzack, Ronald. 1973. *The Puzzle of Pain*. New York: Basic Books.

Mill, J. S. 1863. *Utilitarianism*. London: Everyman Library.

Miller, George A., Eugene Galanter, and Karl H. Pribram. 1960. *Plans and the Structure of Behavior*. New York: Holt.

Millikan, Ruth G. 1984. *Language, Thought, and Other Biological Categories: New Foundations for Realism*. Cambridge, MA: MIT Press. A Bradford book.

Mitchell, Julian. 1984. *Another Country*. New York: Limelight.

Montagu, Ashley, ed. 1980. *Sociobiology Examined*. New York: Oxford University Press.

Morgan, Kathryn P. 1974. "Socialization, Social Models and the Open Education Movement: Some Philosophical Speculations." In *The Philosophy of Open Education*, ed. David Nyberg. London: Routledge & Kegan Paul.

Morgan, Kathryn P. 1986. "Romantic Love, Altruism, and Self-Respect." *Hypatia* 1:117–148.

Morgan, Kathryn P. Unpub. "Society, Socialization, and the Impossibility of Autonomy." Paper delivered to the American Philosophical Association, (Chicago) April 1977.

Morreall, John. 1983a. "Humor and Emotion." *American Philosophical Quarterly* 20:297–305. Reprinted in Morreall 1983b.

Morreall, John. 1983b. *Taking Laughter Seriously*. New York: State University of New York Press.

Morton, Adam. 1980. *Frames of Mind*. Oxford: Oxford University Press.

Murdoch, Iris. 1970. *The Sovereignty of Good*. London: Routledge & Kegan Paul.

Nagel, Ernest. 1961. *The Structure of Science*. New York: Harcourt, Brace, and World.

Nagel, Thomas. 1970. *The Possibility of Altruism*. London and New York: Oxford University Press.

Nagel, Thomas. 1986. *The View from Nowhere*. London and New York: Oxford University Press.

Neisser, Ulric. 1976. *Cognition and Reality: Principles and Implications of Cognitive Psychology*. San Francisco: W. H. Freeman.

Neu, Jerome. 1971. *Emotion, Thought and Therapy*. Cambridge: Cambridge University Press.

Neu, Jerome. 1980. "Jealous Thoughts." In Rorty 1980.

Nietzsche, Friedrich. 1892. *Thus Spake Zarathustra*, trans. Walter Kaufmann. In *The Portable Nietzsche*, ed. Walter Kaufmann. New York: Viking (1954).

Nietzsche, Friedrich. 1896. *The Will to Power*, trans. Walter Kaufmann. In *The Portable Nietzsche*, ed. Walter Kaufmann. New York: Viking (1954).

Nisbett, R. E., and L. Ross. 1977. "Telling More Than We Can Know: Verbal Reports on Mental Processes." *Psychological Review* 84:231–259.

Nisbett, R., and T. Wilson. 1977. "Telling More Than We Can Know: Verbal Reports on Mental Processes." *Psychological Review* 84:321–359.

Nissenbaum, Helen. 1986. *Emotion and Focus*. Chicago: University of Chicago Press.

Noddings, Nel. 1984. *Caring: A Feminine Approach to Ethics and Moral Education*. Berkeley and Los Angeles: University of California Press.

Nowell-Smith, Patrick H. 1954. *Ethics.* Harmondsworth: Penguin Books.

Nussbaum, Martha. 1985. "'Finely Aware and Richly Responsible': Moral Attention and the Moral Task of Literature." *The Journal of Philosophy* 82:516–529.

Panksepp, Jaak. 1982. "Toward a General Psychobiological Theory of Emotions." *The Behavioral and Brain Sciences* 5:407–476.

Papez, James W. 1937. "A Proposed Mechanism of Emotion." *Archives of Neurology and Psychiatry* 38:725–744.

Parfit, Derek. 1984. *Reasons and Persons.* Oxford and New York: Oxford University Press.

Pears, David. 1984. *Motivated Irrationality.* Oxford and New York: Oxford University Press.

Penner, Terry. 1971. "Thought and Desire in Plato." In *Plato II: Ethics, Politics, and Philosophy of Art and Religion: A Collection of Critical Essays,* ed. Gregory Vlastos. Garden City, NY: Anchor Books.

Peterfreund, Emmanuel. 1971. *Information, Systems and Psychoanalysis: An Evolutionary Biological Approach to Psychoanalytic Theory.* New York: International Universities Press.

Peters, R. S. 1962. "Emotions and the Category of Passivity." *Proceedings of the Aristotelian Society* n.s. 62:117–134.

Plato. *The Collected Dialogues,* ed. Edith Hamilton and Huntington Cairns. Princeton, NJ: Princeton University Press (1961).

Plutchik, Robert. 1980. *Emotion: A Psychoevolutionary Synthesis.* New York: Harper & Row.

Plutchik, Robert. 1982. "Only Four Command Systems for All Emotions?" *The Behavioral and Brain Sciences* 5(3):442–443.

Putnam, Hilary. 1960. "Minds and Machines." In *Minds and Machines,* ed. Alan Anderson. Englewood Cliffs, NJ: Prentice-Hall.

Putnam, Hilary. 1975. "The Meaning of Meaning." In *Mind, Language, and Reality: Philosophical Papers.* Cambridge: Cambridge University Press.

Putnam, Hilary. 1976. "Realism and Reason" (Presidential Address to the American Philosophical Association). Reprinted in Putnam 1978.

Putnam, Hilary. 1978. *Meaning and the Moral Sciences.* London: Routledge & Kegan Paul.

Pylyshyn, Zenon W. 1984. *Computation and Cognition.* Cambridge, MA: MIT Press. A Bradford book.

Pylyshyn, Zenon, ed. 1987. *The Robot's Dilemma: The Frame Problem and Other Problems of Holism in Artificial Intelligence.* Norwood, NJ: Ablex Publishing.

Quine, W. V. 1957. "Two Dogmas of Empiricism." In *From a Logical Point of View.* Cambridge, MA: Harvard University Press.

Quine, W. V. 1960. *Word and Object.* Cambridge, MA: MIT Press.

Rey, Georges. 1980. "Functionalism and the Emotions." In Rorty 1980.

Ricoeur, Paul. 1970. *Freud and Philosophy,* trans. D. Savage. New Haven: Yale University Press.

Rives, Joel. 1984. "The Defense of the Ant—Work, Life and Utopia." *Canadian Journal of Philosophy* 14:617–629.

Rorty, Amélie O. 1978. "Explaining Emotions." *The Journal of Philosophy* 75:139–161. Reprinted in Rorty 1980.

Rorty, Amélie O., ed. 1980. *Explaining Emotions.* Berkeley and Los Angeles: University of California Press.

Rorty, Amélie O. 1982. "From Passions to Emotions and Sentiments." *Philosophy* 57:159–172.

Rorty, Amélie O. 1983a. "Akratic Believers." *American Philosophical Quarterly* 20:175–184.

Rorty, Amélie O. 1983b. "Fearing Death." *Philosophy* 58:175–188.

Rorty, Amélie O. 1986. "The Historicity of Psychological Attitudes: Love Is Not Love Which Alters Not When It Alteration Finds." *Mid-West Studies in Philosophy* 10:399–412.

Rorty, Amélie O. (forthcoming) *From Passions to Emotions.*

Rosenfield, Israel. 1985. "The New Brain." *New York Review of Books* 32(4):34–38.

Rosenthal, David M. 1983. "Emotions and the Self." In Irani and Myers 1983.

Ross, E. D. 1984. "The Right Hemisphere's Role in Language, Affective Behavior and Emotion." *Trends in Neuroscience* 7(9):342–346.

Ross, L., M. Lepper, and M. Hubbard. 1975. "Perseverance in Self-Perception and Social Perception: Biased Attributional Processes in the Debriefing Paradigm." *Journal of Personality and Social Psychology* 32:880–892.

Rumelhart, David E., James L. McLelland, and the PDP Research Group. 1986. *Parallel Distributed Processing: Explorations in the Microstructure of Cognition.* 2 vols. Cambridge, MA: MIT Press. A Bradford book.

Russell, Bertrand. 1905. "On Denoting." *Mind* 14:474–493.

Russell, Bertrand. 1921. *The Analysis of Mind.* London: George Allen & Unwin.

Ryle, Gilbert. 1949. *The Concept of Mind.* London: Hutchinson.

Ryle, Gilbert. 1964. "Perception." In *Dilemmas.* Cambridge: Cambridge University Press.

Sahlins, Marshall. 1976. *The Use and Abuse of Biology.* Ann Arbor, MI: University of Michigan Press.

Sartre, Jean-Paul. 1948. *The Emotions: Outline of a Theory.* New York: Philosophical Library.

Sartre, Jean-Paul. 1956. *Being and Nothingness,* trans. Hazel E. Barnes. New York: Philosophical Library.

Sayre, Kenneth M. 1986. "Intentionality and Information Processing: An Alternative Model for Cognitive Science." *The Behavioral and Brain Sciences* 9:121–138.

Schachter, Stanley, and Jerome E. Singer. 1962. "Cognitive, Social and Physiological Determinants of Emotional States." *Psychological Review* 69:379–399. Excerpted in Calhoun and Solomon 1984, to which citations refer.

Schafer, Roy. 1976. *A New Language for Psychoanalysis.* New Haven: Yale University Press.

Scheman, Naomi. 1980. "Anger and the Politics of Naming." In *Women and Language in Literature and Society,* ed. Sally McConnell-Ginet, Ruth Borker, and Nelly Furman. New York: Praeger.

Scheman, Naomi. 1983. "Individualism and the Objects of Psychology." In *Discovering Reality,* ed. S. Harding and M. B. Hintikka. Dordrecht: Reidel.

Schiffer, Stephen. 1976. "A Paradox of Desire." *American Philosophical Quarterly* 13:195–205.

Searle, John. 1969. *Speech Acts.* Cambridge: Cambridge University Press.

Searle, John. 1980. "Minds, Brains and Programs." *The Behavioral and Brain Sciences* 3:417–457. Reprinted in Haugeland 1981.

Searle, John. 1983. *Intentionality.* Cambridge: Cambridge University Press.

Sellars, Wilfrid. 1963. "Empiricism and the Philosophy of Mind." In *Science, Perception, and Reality.* New York: Humanities Press.

Shaffer, Jerome. 1978. "Sexual Desire." *The Journal of Philosophy* 75:175–189.

Shank, Roger C. and Kenneth Mark Colby, eds. 1973. *Computer Models of Thought and Language.* San Francisco: W. H. Freeman.

Shapiro, D. A., and D. Shapiro. 1982. "Meta-Analysis of Comparative Therapy Outcome Studies: A Replication and Refinement." *Psychological Bulletin* 92:581–604.

Sibley, Frank. 1965. "Aesthetic and Nonaesthetic." *Philosophical Review* 74:135–159.

Silverstein, Harry S. 1980. "The Evil of Death." *The Journal of Philosophy* 77:401–424.

Skinner, B. F., and J. G. Holland. 1961. *The Analysis of Behavior.* New York: McGraw-Hill.

Sloman, Aaron, and Monica Croucher. 1981. "Why Robots Will Have Emotions." In *Proceedings of the 7th International Joint Conference on AI.* Menlo Park, CA: American Association for Artificial Intelligence.

Sober, Elliott, ed. 1984. *Conceptual Issues in Evolutionary Biology: An Anthology.* Cambridge, MA: MIT Press. A Bradford book.

Solomon, Robert C. 1973. "Emotion and Choice." *Review of Metaphysics* 17:20–41. Reprinted in Rorty 1980.

Solomon, Robert C. 1976. *The Passions: The Myth and Nature of Human Emotions.* New York: Doubleday.

Solomon, Robert C. 1984. "I Can't Get It Out Of My Mind (Augustine's Problem)." *Philosophy and Phenomenological Research* 44:405–412.

Spinoza, B. *Ethics.* In *The Collected Works of Spinoza,* ed. Edwin Curley. Princeton, NJ: Princeton University Press (1985).

Sprigge, T. S. L. 1971. "Final Causes." *Proceedings of the Aristotelian Society* supp. vol. 45:149–170.

Stern, Daniel. 1977. *The First Relationship: Infant and Mother.* Cambridge, MA: Harvard University Press.

Stich, Stephen. 1983. *From Folk Psychology to Cognitive Science: The Case against Belief.* Cambridge, MA: MIT Press. A Bradford book.

Stroud, Barry. 1980. "Berkeley *v.* Locke on Primary Qualities." *Philosophy* 55:149–166.

Suits, Bernard H. 1978. *The Grasshopper: Games, Life, and Utopia.* Toronto: University of Toronto Press.

Symons, Donald. 1979. *The Evolution of Human Sexuality.* New York and Oxford: Oxford University Press.

Tanner, Michael. 1976. "Sentimentality." *Proceedings of the Aristotelian Society* n.s. 77:127–147.

Taylor, Charles. 1964. *Explanation of Behavior.* New York: Humanities Press.

Taylor, Charles. 1982. "The Diversity of Goods." In *Utilitarianism and Beyond,* ed. Amartya Sen and Bernard Williams. Cambridge: Cambridge University Press.

Tennov, Dorothy. 1979. *Love and Limerence.* New York: Stein and Day.

Thalberg, Irving. 1964. "Emotion and Thought." *American Philosophical Quarterly* 1:45–55. Reprinted in *Philosophy of Mind,* ed. S. N. Hampshire. New York: Harper & Row (1966).

Thalberg, Irving. 1977. *Perception, Emotion and Action.* New Haven, CT: Yale University Press.

Thomas, Laurence. 1983. "Morality, the Self, and Our Natural Sentiments." In Irani and Myers 1983.

Tinbergen, N. 1969. *A Study of Instinct.* London: Oxford University Press.

Tov-Ruach, Leila. 1980. "Jealousy, Attention, and Loss." In Rorty 1980.

Unger, Roberto Mangabeira. 1984. *Passion: An Essay on Human Personality.* New York: The Free Press.

Ursin, H., and B. R. Kaada. 1960. "Functional Localization with the Amygdaloid Complex in the Cat." *Electroencephalography and Clinical Neurology* 12:1–20. (Cited in Konner 1982.)

van Fraassen, Bas. 1970. *An Introduction to the Philosophy of Time and Space.* New York: Random House.

van Fraassen, Bas. 1984. "Belief and Will." *The Journal of Philosophy* 81:235–256.

Vendler, Zeno. 1967. "Verbs and Times." In *Linguistics and Philosophy.* Ithaca, NY: Cornell University Press.

Wallace, James. 1978. *Virtues and Vices.* Ithaca, NY: Cornell University Press.

Walton, Kendall. 1978. "Fearing Fictions." *The Journal of Philosophy* 75:5–27.

Wiggins, David. 1976. "Truth, Invention and the Meaning of Life." *Proceedings of the British Academy* 62:331–378.

Wilde, Oscar. 1894. "Phrases and Philosophies for the Use of the Young." In Wilde 1982.

Wilde, Oscar. 1897. *De Profundis.* In Wilde 1982.

Wilde, Oscar. 1982. *The Annotated Oscar Wilde,* ed. H. Montgomery Hyde. London: Orbis.

Williams, Bernard. 1973a. "Morality and the Emotions." In *Problems of the Self.* Cambridge: Cambridge University Press.

Williams, Bernard. 1973b. "The Macropulos Case: Reflections on the Tedium of Immortality." In *Problems of the Self.* Cambridge: Cambridge University Press.

Williams, Bernard. 1985. *Ethics and the Limits of Philosophy.* Cambridge, MA: Harvard University Press.

Williams, George C. 1966. *Adaptation and Natural Selection.* Princeton, NJ: Princeton University Press.

Williams, George C. 1975. *Sex and Evolution.* Princeton, NJ: Princeton University Press.

Wilson, E. O. 1975. *Sociobiology: The New Synthesis.* Cambridge, MA: Harvard University Press.

Wilson, J. R. S. 1972. *Emotion and Object.* Cambridge: Cambridge University Press.

Winnicott, David. 1971. *Playing and Reality.* London: Tavistock Press.

Winters, Barbara. 1981. "Hume's Argument for the Superiority of Natural Instinct." *Dialogue* 20:635–643.

Wittgenstein, Ludwig. 1951. *Philosophical Investigations.* Oxford: Basil Blackwell.

Wolf, Susan. 1982. "Moral Saints." *The Journal of Philosophy* 79:419–439.

Wolff, Robert Paul. 1976. "There's Nobody Here But Us Persons." In *Women and Philosophy: Toward a Theory of Liberation,* ed. Carol Gould and Marx Wartofsky. New York: Putnam.

Wollheim, Richard. 1984. *The Thread of Life.* Cambridge, MA: Harvard University Press.

Woodfield, Andrew. 1976. *Teleology.* Cambridge and New York: Cambridge University Press.

Wright, Larry. 1973. "Functions." *Philosophical Review* 82:139–168. Reprinted in Sober 1984.

Ziff, Paul. 1972. *Understanding Understanding.* Ithaca, NY: Cornell University Press.

Index